Author's Profile

Paul Baweja was born in Sydney, Australia. In 2007, Paul was awarded the New South Wales Higher School Certificate from LaSalle Catholic College (Sydney). In 2012, Paul earned the Bachelor of Commerce Degree from Macquarie University (Sydney). Thereafter, in 2014, Paul attained the Graduate Diploma of Chartered Accounting from the Institute of Chartered Accountants Australia (Sydney). Furthermore, Paul is the recipient of several academic awards, including the prestigious 'Golden Key International Honour Society' Award (Georgia, the United States).

In addition, Paul completed postgraduate study at the Macquarie Business School. Paul was awarded the Master of Business Administration Degree from Macquarie University (Sydney) in 2016. Paul further completed research-based postgraduate study at the Australian National University (ANU) (Canberra). Paul graduated with the Master of Diplomacy (Advanced) Degree from the ANU in 2018. Paul's Master's Degree Thesis was completed under the auspices of the ANU College of Asia and the Pacific at the Coral Bell School of Asia Pacific Affairs. Paul's research thesis was titled 'International Conflict Mediation: A Diplomatic Analysis of the U.S. Camp David Talks (1978).'

On matters of theology, in 2022, Paul completed the Certificate of Catholic Theology at the Augustine Institute (Colorado, the United States). In the same year, Paul attained the

Certificate in Biblical Studies from the Biblical Training Institute (Washington, the United States). Finally, in 2022, Paul achieved the Certificate in the Catechism of the Catholic Church from Catholic Distance University (West Virginia, the United States).

Paul is an Australian author. Paul has authored several books on Philosophy, Women's History, English Literature, English Poetry, and Theology. Over the course of nine years, Paul has written and published the epic-length 'A Philosophical Treatise of Reality,' a 500,000-word four-volume treatise released in 2021. Thereafter, Paul has authored 'The Struggle of Women' (2022), 'A Commentary on Shakespeare's Plays' (2023), 'A Critique of Milton's Paradise Lost and Regained' (2024), and 'The Providence of God' (2026). Paul's book 'The Struggle of Women' has been accepted into the Department of the Prime Minister and Cabinet Library (Brisbane).

Paul completed his graduate law degree at the University of New South Wales (UNSW) (Sydney). During Paul's tenure at UNSW Law School, he was the recipient of the 2024 Dean's List Award—Faculty of Law and Justice for first place in Law of the Sea. Paul has authored several journal articles in the 'UNSW Law Journal Student Series,' including: 'The Peaceful Settlement of Law of the Sea Disputes: Conciliation between Australia and Timor-Leste,' 'Detention in Non-International Armed Conflict is an Undeniable Reality: Demystifying the Rationale for States to Detain Members of Organised Armed Groups,' and 'The International Court of Justice: Understanding the Court's Jurisdiction.' In 2025, Paul was awarded the Doctor of Jurisprudence Degree from UNSW (Sydney).

The Providence of God

First Edition

PAUL BAWEJA

MMXXVI

First published in Melbourne,
the Commonwealth of Australia, 2026
Published by Paul Baweja
APTOR2021_enquiries@protonmail.com
Copyright © Paul Baweja, 2026
First Edition 2026 (Hardcover Book)
The moral right of the author has been asserted.
The Providence of God is written and published in accordance with
the tenets of international law. Specifically, pursuant to Article 19 of
the Universal Declaration of Human Rights (1948) which explicitly states
that: 'Everyone has the right to freedom of opinion and expression; this
right includes freedom to hold opinions without interference and to seek,
receive and impart information and ideas through any media and
regardless of frontiers.'
Scripture quotations taken from
The Holy Bible, New International Version (Anglicised edition)

A catalogue record for this
book is available from the
NATIONAL LIBRARY OF AUSTRALIA
National Library of Australia

ISBN: 978-0-6489818-7-9 (Hardcover Book)
Cover image: The Nativity of Jesus in Bethlehem
Image Credit: Pixabay
Image attribution: Nicky Pe (Austria)
Cover design by Canva
Formatted with Vellum
Printed and bound by Ingram Spark

Dedication

Paul Baweja dedicates this book to the memory of U Thant (1909-1974). U Thant was a Burmese diplomat and the third Secretary-General of the United Nations (est. 1945). U Thant was a determined figure in the tumultuous world of twentieth century international politics. U Thant was the first Asian ambassador appointed as the United Nations Secretary-General, a prestigious leadership position in which he served from 1961 to 1971. Amongst U Thant's notable achievements, the United Nation's top diplomat worked tirelessly to peacefully settle international disputes during the Cold War (1945-1991).

In the 1960s, U Thant was instrumental in facilitating the United Nations peacekeeping mission to the Congo. U Thant was indispensable in successfully resolving the 1962 Cuban Missile Crisis between the United States and the Soviet Union. U Thant was an outspoken critic of the Vietnam War (1955-1975). In addition, U Thant promoted peace in the India-Pakistan War of 1965. Beyond Africa, Asia, and the Caribbean, U Thant was deeply concerned about the hostilities in the Middle East. He was directly involved in international diplomatic efforts to bring the 1967 Arab-Israeli War to the attention of the United Nations Security Council. U Thant accomplished much to further the cause of international peace and security in the twentieth century.

Contents

Preface

The Providence of God is written for a general audience interested in Christian theology. This is not a technical book for theologians, Biblical scholars, pastors, or chaplains. Its primary purpose is to navigate through the complexity of revealed theology. *The Providence of God* endeavours to bring the believer in close connection with the Christian faith. This endeavour is achieved through acquainting the reader directly with God's word. *The Providence of God* surveys all sixty-six books within the Old and New Testament in the Holy Bible. There is a chapter dedicated to each book of the Holy Bible. These concise chapters are written to familiarise the reader with Biblical themes, concepts, doctrines, and principles.

The existential questions of life's meaning and purpose are addressed in the Holy Bible. Despite human civilisation's progress from rudimentary life in the ancient world to industrialised life in the modern world, humanity still grapples with important philosophical questions: What is the purpose of life? What is the meaning of our being in the world? The Holy Bible addresses these questions and many more, including: How to create meaningful relationships? Why is fellowship important? Why should we pray to God? How do we enhance our relationship with God? Why is mercy the path to righteousness? What to do with our freedom? Why is there evil and injustice in the world? How to responsibly manage our money? How to live the good life?

The author acquaints the reader with Biblical values, principles, and doctrines that, once effectuated into practice, shall initiate meaningful change in their life. Over the course of time, these profound changes create harmonious relationships. We are to live a meaningful and purposeful life, in fellowship with members of the community. Our heartfelt desire must include God in our life, acknowledge the importance of prayer, and cherish the opportunity to love God and humanity.

Paul Baweja
Australian Author
Sydney
Australia
January 2026

Keywords

Abraham, Adam, Ascension, Atonement, Blessing, Christ, Conscience, Courage, Covenant, Creation, Crucifixion, Curse, David, Death, Deliverance, Devil, Discipleship, Disobedience, Eternal life, Eve, Evil, Exodus, Faith, Fall of man, Fate, Favour, Fellowship, Forgiveness, Free will, Glory, God, Good, Gospel, Grace, Hope, Intercession, Jerusalem, Jesus, Job, Joseph, Justice, Justification, Kingdom, Lamb of God, Law, Love, Mercy, Messiah, Moses, Obedience, Original sin, Paul the Apostle, Peace, Prayer, Promised land, Providence, Redemption, Repentance, Resurrection, Sacrificial death, Salvation, Sanctification, Saviour, Sin, Solomon, Sovereignty, Spirit, and Wisdom.

The Providence of God

Introduction

The Holy Bible is comprised of sixty-six books. These books are central to the religious faith and practices of Christianity. The Holy Bible is the word of God. The Holy Bible is the believer's guide to the Christian faith, moral conduct, righteousness, the good life, and understanding God. In every respect, the Holy Bible is the foundational text of Christianity. We reap countless personal benefits from reading, listening, and applying the Holy Bible's principles in our life. For example, we learn how to create a meaningful relationship with God. We gain wisdom to navigate the peaks and valleys of our life. We learn how to create a purposeful and meaningful life. We secure contentment and peace with our being in the world. We perfect the art of fellowship, discipleship, and worship.

The Holy Bible consists of two components: the Old Testament and the New Testament. The Old Testament incorporates the sacred scriptures of the Jewish faith. The thirty-nine books within the Old Testament are systematically organised into several distinct sections. The first five books constitute *the Pentateuch* (i.e., Genesis, Exodus, Leviticus, Numbers, and Deuteronomy). Thereafter, *the Historical Books* (i.e., Joshua, Judges, Ruth, First and Second Samuel, First and Second Kings, First and Second Chronicles, Ezra, Nehemiah, and Esther) narrate the history of Israel from its origins through the Babylonian exile. This narrative is followed by *the Poetry Books*, which include Job, Psalms, Proverbs, Ecclesiastes, and Song of Songs. Thereafter, *the Book of the Prophets* (i.e., Isaiah, Jeremiah, Lamentations, Ezekiel, Daniel, Hosea, Joel, Amos, Obadiah, Jonah, Micah, Nahum, Habakkuk, Zephaniah, Haggai, Zechariah, and Malachi) contain the divine messages of Israel's prophets. These prophets encourage Israel to remain faithful to God's covenant. They also warn Israel of dire consequences for its disobedience to God.

The New Testament focuses on the life, ministry, and teachings of the Son of God—Jesus Christ. The New Testament encapsulates the remarkable journey of the blessed disciples, the writings of Paul the Apostle, as well as the early church's history, doctrine, and theology. The New Testament commences with *the Four Gospels* (i.e., Matthew, Mark, Luke, and John). These four gospels narrate the ministry of Jesus Christ. Followed by *the Early Church*, which contains the Book of Acts. Thereafter, *the Letters of Paul* constitute the majority of the New Testament. Pauline theology includes Romans, First and Second Corinthians, Galatians, Ephesians, Philippians, Colossians, First and Second Thessalonians, First and Second Timothy, Titus, and Philemon. Thereafter, *the Other New Testament Writings* include Hebrews, James, First and Second Peter, First, Second, and Third John, Jude, and Revelation.

The Holy Bible examines several themes that are central to the Christian faith. First, God's creation and humanity's purpose are explored. The Holy Bible commences with the Biblical story of creation, affirming the belief in God as the creator of heaven and earth. Humans are created in God's image with the transcendent purpose to live in fellowship with God. Second, original sin and redemption are explored. Major themes in the Old Testament include the fall of man, original sin, and God's vision for humanity's redemption. Throughout the Old Testament, we witness themes of fulfilment, judgement, prayer, prophecy, redemption, repentance, and worship. The Old Testament prophecies point towards the coming of the Messiah. Christians believe these prophecies are fulfilled in Jesus Christ.

The Old Testament characterises God's covenant with Israel. The New Testament affirms humanity's hope for salvation and eternal life through the Messiah—Jesus Christ. Third, the gospels in the New Testament examine the life, teachings, and ministry of Jesus Christ. The gospels incorporate themes of faith, hope, trust, love, mercy, peace, forgiveness, and grace. Fourth, a central message in the teachings of Jesus Christ is the kingdom of God is a present reality and future hope.

The Holy Bible has made a profound impact on world history, culture, law, politics, morality, philosophy, spirituality, and ethics. The Holy Bible has inspired countless works of art, music, poetry, and literature. The Holy Bible continues to influence contemporary political, economic, moral, legal, and social thought. The Holy Bible is the spiritual compass for Christians around the world. The Holy Bible is the source of spiritual transformation, ethical guidance, moral instruction, fellowship with God, and wisdom to live a blessed life.

The Holy Bible's teachings are explored in personal devotions, reading of scripture, prayer, personal reflection, Bible study, church sermons, and theological studies. Scholars also engage in critical analysis of the Holy Bible. Scholars study the Holy Bible's historical context, ancient languages, and literary form. The Holy Bible is not merely a theological text. Beyond the domain of religion, the Holy Bible influences the cultural, social, ethical, moral, and literary dimensions of human thought, behaviour, and understanding. The Holy Bible's themes, teachings, and narratives inspire and influence believers across the world. Whether the Holy Bible is perused for spiritual guidance, historical insight, or literary beauty, it remains a cornerstone of faith for Christians.

Chapter 1

The Book of Genesis

'The LORD had said to Abram,
"Go from your country, your people,
and your father's household to the land I will show you."'

Genesis 12:1
The Holy Bible (NIV)

Genesis is the first book within the Holy Bible. Genesis establishes the foundation of God's word to humanity. Genesis explores major Biblical themes, including the creation of heaven and earth, the dichotomy of good and evil, human nature, temptation, original sin, fall of man, mercy, justification by faith, and favour. In addition, Genesis provides humanity an insight into God's covenant with His chosen people.

From a theological perspective, the Book of Genesis makes it evident that God is the cause for creation of 'the heavens and the earth.'[1] God created all phenomena—humans, animals, plants, the earth, galaxies, distant stars, and the universe—from His unrivalled power. From God's act of creation, humanity bears witness to His sovereignty and power as the creator of the universe. Given that God is the creator, believers recognise His providence over human life. God's word informs our understanding of the purpose and meaning of life. In effect, without God, life has no inherent meaning or transcendent purpose. We can self-create and superimpose meaning in our life; thereby, we assume secondary purposes in the world. Nonetheless, no self-created purpose satisfies the spiritual poverty of our soul. Only God's spirit and word make our being complete in every respect.

Every person in the world is created in 'the image of God.'[2] Every person possesses inviolable dignity, value, worth, right, agency, and autonomy, simply by virtue of being human. The aforesaid proposition establishes the foundational principle of the equality of humanity, regardless of sex, race, gender, religion, creed, personal wealth, education, private property, colour, age, occupation, or any other distinguishing factor. We are commanded by God to love and respect every person, because humanity is created in God's image.

In the opening chapters of Genesis, we learn about God's plan for stewardship of creation. Adam is placed in the Garden of Eden to 'work it and take care of it.'[3] Humanity's function as stewards of the earth is established from the beginning of creation. Genesis emphasises our primary responsibility to nurture God's creation. We are commanded to be prudent stewards of earth and responsibly manage its finite natural resources. Stewardship involves the sustainable use of the earth's natural resources for our generation's benefit. In addition, we must exercise good judgement and personal responsibility to ensure resource sustainability. The present generation of humanity is entrusted with the conservation of natural resources for the benefit of successive generations.

In the epoch-making event of Adam and Eve's fall from grace, original sin enters the world. Original sin is a consequence of their disobedience to God's command. Original sin entails profound consequences for the future of humanity. Adam and Eve are 'banished from the Garden of Eden.'[4] The bliss and equanimity of Paradise is lost. Original sin results in the separation of humanity from God. Not to mention, the human experience is characterised by pain, grief, loss, trauma, sorrow, suffering, and death. Original sin affects all dimensions of the human condition. The fall of man has altered the fundamental experience of what it means to be human. The innocence of being and peace with the knowledge of good is transformed into an inferior existence which entails 'knowing good and evil.'[5]

In spite of original sin, Genesis demonstrates God's faithfulness to His covenant. For example, consider the Noahic Covenant between God and Noah after the Great Flood. In addition, God establishes covenants with Abraham, Isaac, Jacob, and Moses. In Genesis, we learn that humanity falls short in its words and deeds. Whereas, God remains faithful to His word.

God is dependable and trustworthy. God always fulfils His covenant in the fullness of time. While our journey invariably consists of peaks and valleys, we place our trust and confidence in God's providence. Through the incredible stories of Abraham, Isaac, Jacob, Moses, and Noah, we learn that God's word is infallible. The realisation of God's providence is rarely understood as it effectuates; however, its subtle effects are experienced throughout our lifetime. Therefore, God's providence is the litmus test of our faith. Do we believe, when we have not yet realised our destiny?

Abraham's journey, especially his willingness to sacrifice his legitimate son Isaac on the alter, teaches humanity the importance of unconditional obedience to God's word. Even when God's command appears incomprehensible to natural reason, we must diligently apply ourselves to honour His word. It was through Abraham's unconditional belief in God, that God 'credited it to him as righteousness.'[6] Our beliefs inform our thoughts. Consequently, our thoughts inform our actions. However, the starting point of our journey are our beliefs, values, and principles. Therefore, God 'credited' Abraham his righteousness through his belief, and not through his deeds, words, achievements, virtue, merit, or character. For Abraham's beliefs informed his thoughts and actions.

Genesis demonstrates the undeniable reality of human frailty. The greatest Biblical characters—Aaron, Abraham, Adam, David, Isaac, Jacob, Joseph, Moses, and Noah—had their imperfections, failures, errors, weaknesses, and flaws. In effect, every Biblical figure had their strengths and weaknesses. This fact highlights the universal reality of our fallen human nature. Despite our weaknesses and failures, God works with us and through us, to fulfil His providence for humanity. God's grace is evident in our imperfections. Throughout the Holy Bible, we repeatedly witness God employ remnants to fulfil His providence. No person on earth is perfect. God works in our life through belief, grace, love, mercy, peace, and faith.

Genesis demonstrates how God employs ordinary individuals to accomplish His extraordinary providence. From Jacob, the deceiver, to Joseph, the dreamer, God worked through them for the greater good of humanity. God can employ any person, regardless of their mistakes or imperfections, for the realisation of His providence. Our faith, belief, and obedience to God are the primary determinants of God's providence at work in our life.

An example of God's providence is Joseph's remarkable journey. In particular, Joseph's memorable reconciliation with his brothers who betrayed and sold him into slavery. This Biblical story highlights the importance of forgiveness. Despite Joseph's brothers' immoral conduct, he forgave them. Joseph recognises the goodness of God's providence in his life. Although Joseph's brothers' actions were intended for evil, God transformed their evil into the service of good. The scripture informs us, 'You intended to harm me, but God intended it for good.'[7] Herein we learn that God does not prevent evil from occurring in the world. Nonetheless, God permits evil to be employed in the realisation of good.

Joseph's story teaches us the unrivalled power of forgiveness. Forgiveness brings about restoration to our damaged relationships. Holding on to resentment or bitterness obstructs God's providence in our life. We must not self-sabotage our relationships from blossoming. When we constantly reflect upon the hurt and pain of traumatic events and negative experiences in our life, we self-impose an artificial limit on the realisation of our highest potential. When we choose not to forgive, we invite bitterness, envy, anger, revenge, jealousy, and distrust into our life.

Moving forward involves letting go. Letting go is a misunderstood concept. Letting go does not mean relinquishing our agency to self-determine our life trajectory. Letting go means we do not permit past events or negative experiences to obstruct our destiny. We must forge ahead with courage, confidence, and conviction.

Throughout Genesis, God's providence is evident—whether guiding Abraham, protecting Isaac, or promoting Joseph to a position of authority in ancient Egypt. God's providence unfolds perfectly, even in the midst of human failure, original sin, the fall of man, and the presence of evil. God is sovereign over all circumstances and situations. God's providence and sovereignty always prevail. Even though we do not perceive the entirety or magnitude of God's thoughts, when we trust in His providence, it brings us peace, patience, and purpose to our being.

In the final analysis, Genesis teaches humanity about God's creation. We witness the importance of faith, trust, hope, and obedience. We come to terms with the undeniable reality of original sin and its destructive consequences. We realise the importance of forgiveness in our relationships. We learn about God's covenant with His chosen people. Genesis invites us to trust in God's sovereignty and to respect the inherent dignity of human life. The sanctity of human life is unquestionable. We have a moral duty to fulfil our assignment as responsible stewards within God's creation.

[1] The Holy Bible (NIV). (2011). *The Book of Genesis*. Chapter 1, Verse 1.
[2] The Holy Bible (NIV). (2011). *The Book of Genesis*. Chapter 1, Verse 27.
[3] The Holy Bible (NIV). (2011). *The Book of Genesis*. Chapter 2, Verse 15.
[4] The Holy Bible (NIV). (2011). *The Book of Genesis*. Chapter 3, Verse 23.

[5] The Holy Bible (NIV). (2011). *The Book of Genesis.* Chapter 3, Verse 22.

[6] The Holy Bible (NIV). (2011). *The Book of Genesis.* Chapter 15, Verse 6.

[7] The Holy Bible (NIV). (2011). *The Book of Genesis.* Chapter 50, Verse 20.

Chapter 2

The Book of Exodus

'Who among the gods is like you, LORD?
Who is like you—majestic in holiness, awesome in glory, working
wonders?'

Exodus 15:11
The Holy Bible (NIV)

Exodus is a foundational book in the Holy Bible. Exodus narrates the remarkable story of the Israelites' deliverance from slavery at the hands of their Egyptian masters. Upon crossing the Red Sea on dry ground, the Israelites commence their arduous journey through the unforgiving terrain of the wilderness towards the promised land. Exodus emphasises God's faithfulness to His covenant. In Exodus, we learn the importance of obedience to God's command. Exodus details the establishment of God's covenant with His chosen people.

When God speaks to Moses through the burning bush, God declares, 'I have indeed seen the misery of my people in Egypt. I have heard them crying out because of their slave drivers, and I am concerned about their suffering.'[1] This passage of scripture demonstrates that God is compassionate and empathetic to the suffering of humanity. God expresses concern about the welfare of the Israelites. God is attentive to their pleas for compassion, justice, mercy, and redemption. We are created in God's image. We too must be compassionate towards our fellow brothers and sisters. The central theme of Exodus is God's deliverance of the Israelites from slavery in ancient Egypt.

Initially, Moses is hesitant to undertake the assignment that God has destined him to fulfil. Moses demonstrates self-doubt in his assignment. Moses does not feel adequate for the leadership assignment that God instructs him to complete. Moses reasons he will not be believed by the Israelites, nor does he envisage the Egyptian Pharaoh will listen to him. Moses does not believe that his presence commands the charisma and influence of a leader. Moses engages in negative self-talk to repudiate his God-given assignment—emancipating the Israelites from slavery in ancient Egypt. For example, consider Moses responds to God, 'I am slow of speech and tongue.'[2] In addition, Moses exclaims, 'Please send someone else.'[3] Like Moses, too often our thoughts, principles, values, and beliefs become absorbed in negative ideas. We must concentrate on the positive aspects of all that we are destined to become in the world. In being absorbed in self-limiting thoughts, Moses overlooked what God had promised him, 'I will be with you.'[4]

Eventually, Moses had a change of heart. Moses agreed to obey God's command. Thereafter, God performs miracles through Moses. God emancipates His chosen people from the unyielding chains of Egyptian oppression, slavery, and injustice. God promises the Israelites a desirable life in the promised land 'flowing with milk and honey.'[5] Exodus demonstrates that God is faithful to His covenant. God's sovereignty ensures the deliverance of the Israelites from challenging circumstances. No matter how difficult our circumstance or situation, God's sovereignty is greater than any natural or human-made force on earth.

In Exodus, we witness a grand contest between God and the Pharaoh's will. The Egyptian Pharaoh refuses the Israelites request to worship God. As a consequence, the Egyptian people are struck with several catastrophes, including the Plague of Blood, the Plague of Gnats, the Plague of Flies, the Plague on Livestock, the Plague of Boils, the Plague of Hail, the Plague of Locusts, the Plague of Darkness, and the Plague on the Firstborn. Despite these divinely ordained disasters, the Egyptian Pharaoh is adamant that the Israelites remain as slaves in ancient Egypt. Unbeknown to the Pharaoh, God was merely employing the Pharaoh as an instrument, to demonstrate God's glory, majesty, and sovereignty. This Old Testament narrative teaches humanity an insurmountable lesson—God's will prevails over humanity's will.

Following the destructive series of plagues in ancient Egypt, we witness God's formidable power with the parting of the Red Sea. The Israelites cross the Red Sea on dry ground. They secure refuge from their Egyptian masters. The burdensome shackles of servitude are destroyed. The love of liberty is realised. God's divinely orchestrated plagues and parting of the Red Sea demonstrate that He is sovereign over creation, including the elements of nature and powerful worldly rulers. God is in control of all phenomena on earth. God's power is limitless. Even when our circumstances are beyond our agency, God acts decisively to fulfil His will—God has the authoritative and final determination. God's providence does not vacillate over humanity's intentions, opinions, beliefs, or thoughts.

Throughout Moses' lifetime, he is repeatedly called to obey God's command. For example, consider Moses confronts the Egyptian Pharaoh. Moses guides the emancipated Israelites through the wilderness. Moses obeys God's instructions concerning the Tabernacle. Through Moses, the Israelites receive detailed instructions about the covenant, the law, prayer, and worship. Exodus teaches us that obedience to God's command is essential to fulfil God's providence. God's command, though sometimes difficult to comprehend by the finitude of natural reason, is for the betterment of His chosen people. Obedience to God leads to His blessing, peace, and favour.

In Exodus, we witness the holiness and glory of God revealed through His spiritual presence on Mount Sinai. At Mount Sinai, God's provides Moses with the Ten Commandments. God decrees His chosen people to be holy as He is holy. The fear of God, worship, and reverence are integral to the Israelites fellowship with God. God's holiness demands our respect and reverence. We are called to approach God with deference. We must live our life in reflection of God's holiness.

The incident with Aaron and the golden calf highlights the ever-present temptation and real danger of idolatry. When Moses was in the presence of God's spirit on Mount Sinai, the Israelites worshipped a false god. The Israelites violated their covenant with the Most High God. This tragic event emphasises the false appeal of turning to idols for our security, fulfilment, meaning, purpose, identity, or sense of belonging in the world. When the Israelites were under the leadership of Aaron, they engaged in sin. The Israelites mistakenly worshipped the golden calf; 'These are your gods, Israel, who brought you up out of Egypt.'[6] Idolatry is a serious violation of God's command. We must guard our heart and mind against positioning anything—whether material or immaterial—above our fellowship with God.

In spite of the Israelites sinful conduct with the golden calf, Moses intercedes on their behalf. Moses pleads with God for mercy. In response, God relents from His anger and reaffirms His covenant with the Israelites. Moses' sincere actions demonstrate that intercession (i.e., intercessory prayer) is a powerful and effective instrument for the forgiveness of sin. Just as Moses interceded for the Israelites, we too must pray on behalf of each other. We must beseech God to grant us mercy, forgiveness, and grace. Moses, through his honourable actions, demonstrates to humanity the importance of repentance, prayer, and compassion.

God provides for the Israelites' sustenance throughout their arduous journey in the wilderness. God ensures there is sufficient manna. God provides water from a rock. God guides the Israelites through the wilderness with the pillar of cloud by day, and the pillar of fire by night. These provisions remind the people that they must depend on God for their sustenance. God is our provider. We trust in God to satisfy our daily needs. God is faithful to provide for us, often in ways that we do not anticipate or comprehend.

The Book of Exodus informs us that Moses, though reluctant at first, has wholeheartedly embraced his vocation as a leader. In this endeavour, Moses is guided by God's providence and wisdom. Moses experiences immense challenges, from addressing the Israelites' complaints to communicating with the Egyptian

Pharaoh. Nonetheless, Moses relies upon God's grace, favour, wisdom, and blessing. We witness the strength of Moses' character. Moses demonstrates an unprecedented degree of resilience, despite the difficulties along his journey. Moses' leadership in Exodus is not characterised by prestige, pride, power, or profit, it is about the fulfilment of God's providence. Leadership is a call to serve and lead members of the community in accordance with God's will. Leadership is not about pecuniary gain, authority, fame, wealth, or social status. Effective leaders depend upon God's counsel and grace, not their inconsequential willpower.

In Exodus, God establishes the Mosaic Covenant with the Israelites. This is a conditional covenant between God and Israel. God imparts the Divine Law to the Israelites (i.e., the Ten Commandments) as a practical guide for how to live in fellowship with Him. The Mosaic Covenant and the Ten Commandments are consequential covenants between God and His chosen people. These covenants represent an agreement to obey God. Throughout the Holy Bible, the covenant with God is central to the journey of His chosen people. To live in obedience to God's laws and commands constitutes an integral part of our covenant with Him. When we apply God's word in our life, we experience His blessing, grace, and peace.

God's decrees contain detailed instructions for the construction of the Tabernacle, where His spiritual presence dwells amongst His chosen people. The Tabernacle is a sacred place to worship God. The Tabernacle symbolises God's spiritual presence in the vicinity of His chosen people. The community is commanded to be involved in building the Tabernacle. This Biblical narrative demonstrates the importance of collective worship and community participation in the realisation of God's providence. Worship, fellowship, prayer, and community are integral aspects of the believer's life. God desires to be present with His chosen people. We are called to be active participants in the realisation of God's providence.

Throughout Exodus, there are consequences for disobedience to God's command, whether it is the Egyptian Pharaoh's refusal to emancipate the Israelites, or the Israelites idolatry with the golden calf. When God's chosen people experience His mercy, there are consequences for the rejection of God's command. While God is merciful, our disobedience entails profound consequences. It is important to act in accordance with God's command. We must live in a manner that honours God's sovereignty over creation.

Exodus teaches humanity several profound lessons concerning God's providence. We learn about God's faithfulness, and the importance of obedience, holiness, and civic participation. The major themes in Exodus include God's sovereignty, mercy, love, and providence. In addition, we witness God's compassion for His chosen people. Through the Israelites, we learn about the grave dangers of idol worship. We are reminded of the significance of our covenant with God. Exodus encourages us to trust in God's providence. We must live in accordance with God's law. We must honour God's holiness in every aspect of our life. Exodus informs us that leadership is about the service of humanity and the realisation of God's providence. Exodus teaches us that God desires an intimate relationship with His chosen people. It is our obedience to God that leads to a blessed, prosperous, and fulfilled life.

[1] The Holy Bible (NIV). (2011). *The Book of Exodus*. Chapter 3, Verse 7.
[2] The Holy Bible (NIV). (2011). *The Book of Exodus*. Chapter 4, Verse 10.
[3] The Holy Bible (NIV). (2011). *The Book of Exodus*. Chapter 4, Verse 13.

[4] The Holy Bible (NIV). (2011). *The Book of Exodus*. Chapter 3, Verse 12.

[5] The Holy Bible (NIV). (2011). *The Book of Exodus*. Chapter 3, Verse 8.

[6] The Holy Bible (NIV). (2011). *The Book of Exodus*. Chapter 32, Verse 4.

Chapter 3

The Book of Leviticus

'A tithe of everything from the land,
whether grain from the soil or fruit from the trees,
belongs to the LORD; it is holy to the LORD.'

Leviticus 27:30
The Holy Bible (NIV)

T he Book of Leviticus is a complex book in the Holy
Bible. This is due to its prescriptive rules, archaic
rituals, and ancient traditions. Nevertheless, Leviticus is
a significant Old Testament Book. Leviticus contains important
lessons in relation to holiness, sacrifice, worship, and prayer. Not
to mention, Leviticus provides insight into God's covenant with
His chosen people. Leviticus emphasises how the Israelites, as
God's chosen people, are commanded to live in a manner that
honours God's holiness.

The central theme of Leviticus is God's command to
holiness. God commands the Israelites to 'be holy, because I am
holy.'[1] God's decrees and moral regulations prescribed in the
Book of Leviticus set apart the Israelites for a covenant with
Him. Holiness is not merely concerned with moral purity.
Holiness is being set apart for the fulfilment of God's providence.
God commands His chosen people to live an honourable life.
God's chosen people must honour His character in every facet of
their life.

God's spiritual presence requires moral purity. Leviticus
characterises the rituals, sacrifices, rules, decrees, and laws to be
observed to maintain purity and permit the Israelites to approach
God. The Tabernacle, where God's spiritual presence dwells, is
central to Leviticus. These detailed rituals ensure the people are
cleansed from sin, before they approach God. To be in God's
presence requires purity and holiness. We too must be cleansed
of our sin, before we approach God. God provides the means for
our repentance and atonement through sacrifices and offerings.

Leviticus consists of detailed instructions on various offerings.
These include burnt offerings, grain offerings, fellowship
offerings, sin offerings, and guilt offerings. These sacrifices are
necessary for the atonement of sin and the restoration of the

covenant between God and His chosen people. The day of atonement is an annual event of national repentance for Israel's sins. Sacrifice is a precondition for atonement and reconciliation with God. In the New Testament, Jesus Christ's crucifixion atones for humanity's sin. Christians are subject to the new covenant through Jesus Christ, in which the penalty for our sin has been satisfied. Believers in Christ do not live in condemnation or guilt of original sin. Through the Messiah, we have been redeemed and reconciled with God.

Leviticus contains specific religious laws that regulate every aspect of the Israelite's way of life, including ceremonies, rituals, and custom. Obedience to these laws is essential to the Israelite's observance of their sacred covenant with God. Disobedience, particularly in matters related to holiness, result in severe consequences, such as banishment or death. Our obedience to God's command is crucial to maintain fellowship with Him. Even though believers are subject to the new covenant through Jesus Christ, obedience to God's commandments remains an integral part in observing God's word.

Leviticus demonstrates that God cares not only about the performance of rituals or worship; however, He is also concerned about the conduct of His people. Leviticus prescribes divine laws in relation to social justice, compassion towards the less fortunate people, and the treatment of foreigners. For example, consider the following command: 'love your neighbour as yourself.'[2] We are commanded not to use 'dishonest standards'[3] in our commercial dealings with members of society. We must be considerate towards marginalised people in the community. We must appreciate that worship, morality, and ethics are inseparable in the believer's life. Holiness is reflected not only in our fellowship, prayer, and worship of God, but also in how we treat members of the community.

Leviticus details several laws that concern the welfare of the poor, widow, orphan, and foreigner. For example, consider the law of gleaning commands landowners, 'do not reap to the very edges of your field or gather the gleanings of your harvest.'[4] Landowners are instructed to leave the edges of their fields unharvested. This generosity ensures the destitute and foreigners can provide for themselves. In addition, there are specific laws that mandate honesty and fairness in business transactions, as well as equity in legal proceedings. God's heart is favourably disposed towards the less fortunate and marginalised members of society. Regardless of denomination distinctions and doctrinal differences, we must practice generosity, hospitality, fairness, and social justice in our interactions with members, particularly when it concerns the vulnerable people in society.

The Sabbath is a recurring theme throughout Leviticus. The Sabbath emphasises the importance of rest and the sanctity of time. The Sabbath is a holy day. It is a day set apart for worship and rest. It is a special gift from God to His chosen people. Similarly, the Year of Jubilee is a time when personal debts are forgiven and land is returned to its original owners. This reflects God's concern for justice and equity. Rest and recreation are important for our physical, emotional, mental, and spiritual well-being. When we engage in rest and recreation, we prioritise self-care. In addition, rest and recreation creates the opportunity to reflect on our priorities, values, ambitions, and endeavours. In order that we live a meaningful life, we must appropriate our finite time, resources, and energy on what matters most. In the final analysis, setting aside time to rest and worship God is an integral component to live a purposeful life. When we worship God, it is a reflection of our trust in His providence. Not to mention, worship is a reminder of God's sovereignty over creation.

Leviticus positions utmost importance on purity and

cleanliness, especially in relation to what is pure and impure. Leviticus contains divine laws in relation to cleanliness and conduct, while other laws are symbolic. These laws represent the requirement for our spiritual purity before the LORD. For example, consider certain animals are deemed inappropriate for human consumption. In addition, discharges of bodily fluids require purification. While physical cleanliness symbolises purity of the human body, God closely examines our heart, conscience, desires, motives, and intentions to ascertain our spiritual purity. While the specific ceremonial laws of cleanliness do not directly apply to Christians, they point to the broader principle to maintain moral and spiritual purity, so that we are set apart for God's providence.

Leviticus prescribes important duties and responsibilities assigned to priests. Priests are appointed to mediate between God and His chosen people. The high priest's function on the day of atonement is especially significant. The priest enters the Holy of Holies to offer sacrifices for the sins of the people. The high priest is an intermediary by which the people are purified from sin and become closer to God's spirit. The function of priesthood in Leviticus foreshadows the coming of Jesus Christ as the ultimate High Priest. Jesus Christ intercedes for humanity and he is the Sacrificial Lamb of God to atone for humanity's sin.

Through God's laws, decrees, and regulations, it is evident that He desires an intimate relationship with His chosen people. Not just any ordinary relationship, but one that is characterised by holiness, worship, belief, faith, confidence, and trust in Him. The detailed rituals and sacrifices are the means to empower Israel to maintain fellowship with God. The objective of these divine laws is not to prescribe rules and regulations; however, to establish a covenant between God and His chosen people. In the final analysis, God desires fellowship with His chosen people. Worship, obedience, prayer, love, praise, and holiness are the instruments by which we cultivate and maintain fellowship with God.

Leviticus concludes with a series of blessings and curses. In effect, God promises blessings for the Israelites' obedience and curses for their disobedience. The blessings include prosperity, peace, abundance, grace, favour, and God's spiritual presence. In contrast, curses are characteristic of punishment, defeat, destruction, and banishment. Our obedience to God leads to His blessings, while our disobedience leads to His curses. God's blessings are contingent upon our faithfulness to His command. Nonetheless, when we commit sin, God provides countless opportunities for our reflection, repentance, redemption, and restoration.

The Book of Leviticus teaches humanity essential lessons about holiness, sacrifice, obedience, morality, prayer, and God's covenant with His chosen people. Leviticus emphasises that God's people must be holy, as God is holy. Holiness incorporates ethical behaviour, prayer, and worship. Leviticus underscores God's concern for social justice and equity for the marginalised members of society. The Israelites are reminded of the importance of rituals, customs, and spiritual purity in being close to God. While the ceremonial laws of Leviticus are specific to ancient Israel, they point to the fulfilment of God's providence in Jesus Christ. In the New Testament, Jesus Christ is the Lamb of God. Jesus is the sinless redeemer for humanity's sin. For believers, Leviticus is a call to reflect God's holiness and justice in their life. We must approach God with reverence. Last but not least, we must demonstrate compassion in our interactions with members of the community.

[11] The Holy Bible (NIV). (2011). *The Book of Leviticus*. Chapter 11, Verse 45.

[2] The Holy Bible (NIV). (2011). *The Book of Leviticus*. Chapter 19, Verse 18.

[3] The Holy Bible (NIV). (2011). *The Book of Leviticus*. Chapter 19, Verse 35.

[4] The Holy Bible (NIV). (2011). *The Book of Leviticus*. Chapter 19, Verse 9.

Chapter 4

The Book of Numbers

'I cannot carry all these people by myself;
the burden is too heavy for me.'

Numbers 11:14
The Holy Bible (NIV)

T he Book of Numbers is the fourth book in the Holy Bible. Numbers chronicles the journey of the Israelites from Mount Sinai to the frontier of the promised land. The Book of Numbers is named after the census of the Israelites that occurred in the introductory chapters of this book. Having said that, Numbers contains a much broader theological narrative. Numbers narrates the challenges the Israelites confront in the wilderness, their disobedience, God's judgement, and His faithfulness. Despite Numbers' disheartening narrative, it contains invaluable lessons on faith, obedience, judgement, leadership, and God's provision for humanity.

One of the central themes in Numbers is the importance of our obedience to God's command. Time and time again, the Israelites complain, disobey, and fail to trust in God's providence. For example, consider when the Israelites approach the frontier of the promised land. The twelve spies report that the land is inhabited by people who are 'stronger than we are.'[1] Subsequently, the Israelites refuse to enter into the promised land in faith, for ten of the twelve spies reason, 'We seemed like grasshoppers in our own eyes, and we looked the same to them.'[2] The Israelites' failure of faith, deficit of belief, and lack of courage resulted in God's judgement—a forty-year period of wandering in the unforgiving terrain of the wilderness.

As a consequence, the generation of Israelites that were emancipated from slavery in ancient Egypt did not live to enter the promised land, because of their lack of faith. They died in the wilderness. It was the succeeding generation of Israelites, under the charismatic leadership of Joshua, which inherited the promised land. Thus, we learn the absence of faith has profound consequences, this includes being deprived of God's blessing. Our faith in God's providence is essential to move forward in life and to ensure we realise His promise. In the final analysis, disobedience to God's command results in adverse and lifelong consequences, such as missed opportunities and prolonged struggles. Our trust and obedience to God, even in the midst of difficult circumstances, is essential to fulfil His providence.

Despite the Israelites' repeated disobedience, complaints, and absence of faith, God continues to demonstrate His faithfulness towards them. For example, consider God provides manna, water, and counsel to the leaders. God honours His covenant with the Israelites. Even when the Israelites are punished, God remains committed to their future and to the fulfilment of His covenant—the Israelites inheritance of the promised land flowing with milk and honey. We learn that when there is human failure, God remains committed to His covenant. God's faithfulness is not dependent upon our performance, or lack thereof, but rather upon His compassionate nature, perfect character, and unconditional love for His chosen people.

In Numbers, we witness the importance of godly leadership. Moses, as the Israelites leader, confronts numerous challenges, including the Israelites near constant complaints. In addition, there is disagreement and rebellion amongst the Israelites. Miriam and Aaron criticise Moses' leadership; however, God reaffirms Moses as His chosen leader. When Moses' life is nearing its end, God instructs Moses to appoint Joshua as his successor to lead the Israelites into the promised land. Godly leadership is essential to guide the people. Leaders must be faithful to God's calling. Leaders must endure justified and unjustified criticism. Leaders must trust in God's providence. A righteous leader invites, inspires, influences, and illuminates believers towards the realisation of God's providence.

Even though the Israelites endure privation in the wilderness, God consistently provides for their sustenance. God ensures the provision of quail and manna to relieve the Israelites of their hunger. God provides water from a rock to satisfy the Israelites of their thirst. God protects the Israelites from the natural elements, through a 'pillar of cloud by day and fire by night.'[3] God's provisions are physical (i.e., food, water, heat, and shade) and spiritual (i.e., God's presence, counsel, grace, protection, and guidance). God provides for His chosen people, even in the midst of difficult circumstances. God satisfies the material, emotional, and spiritual needs along our journey.

When the Israelites commit sin, whether through idolatry or rebellion against Moses, God's response is often judgement. When we make mistakes, repentance is the method to restore God's favour in our life. When we go astray, we must remind ourselves that repentance is the legitimate mechanism to restore our covenant with God. Repentance recognises that we have engaged in sinful conduct. Repentance is the act by which we seek God's mercy. While divine judgement effectuates as a result of disobedience, God's mercy and grace are available to every person. We must turn to God in repentance.

In Numbers, through the enticement of Baal worship, the Israelites begin to worship the god of Moab. This immoral act results in God's wrath and judgement. The Israelites' disregard for their faith, in connection with adopting the illegitimate practices of foreign nations, results in their spiritual degradation and moral compromise. We must remain vigilant not to compromise our faith or diminish our devotion to God by observing contemporary practices, popular culture, or the secular value system of the modern world. Our allegiance to God must not be compromised.

Numbers highlights the important function of the Levites, who are set apart to serve God. The Levites are entrusted with the Tabernacle and the sacred rituals of worship. The Levites are consecrated to God to maintain holiness within their community. The Levites symbolise the importance of purity, community service, integrity, accountability, commitment, and dedication.

Believers are to live their life dedicated to God, serve humanity, and maintain a personal commitment to holiness. Just as the Levites were set apart for God, Christians must conduct themselves in a manner befitting of their 'royal priesthood.'[4]

Despite the Israelites rebellion, disobedience, doubt, and challenges, God's covenant to them regarding the promised land remained unchanged. Even Balaam, the pagan prophet who was ordered by Balak, King of Moab, to curse the Israelites conceded that he cannot do so. Instead, Balaam blessed the Israelites. For Balaam responded, 'Even if Balak gave me all the silver and gold in his palace, I could not do anything great or small to go beyond the command of the LORD my God.'[5] This Biblical narrative demonstrates, that no matter how determined a person is to oppose God's will, His providence always prevails. God's providence is unassailable. During our lifetime, opposition, loss, and failure obstruct our journey. Nonetheless, God's providence prevails in the end.

The Israelites' journey through the wilderness was subject to divine laws, commands, and decrees on how to live as a holy people. For example, consider the camp of Israel was arranged in a specific manner around the Tabernacle. Furthermore, every detail of the Israelites worship was carefully prescribed. When the Israelites obeyed God's instructions, they experienced God's presence, grace, favour, and blessing. Obedience to God's command is essential to experience God's blessing, mercy, and presence. In our life-changing decisions and routine activities, obedience to God leads to His favour.

The Israelites' journey through the wilderness was arduous. Nonetheless, God's covenant to the Israelites concerning the promised land remained unchanged. The succeeding generation of Israelites in the wilderness was given newfound hope. God reassured them that He would fulfil His covenant, despite the failures of the preceding generation of Israelites. When our journey is arduous, God's covenant provides us with joy, optimism, and hope. God's faithfulness instils us with confidence for the future, even when our present circumstances are unfavourable.

The Book of Numbers teaches humanity important lessons about obedience, trust, and God's faithfulness. Numbers reveals that while God's chosen people confront difficulties, problems, and challenges, His providence remains unchanged. God's provision is abundant, even when we factor into consideration our mistakes, flaws, and errors. Numbers underscores the importance of repentance. The Book of Numbers emphasises the dangers of humanity's unbelief and moral compromise. Numbers reiterates the importance of faithful obedience to God's command. Numbers demonstrates that God's guidance is instrumental to the success of His people. God's promise is fulfilled, despite the people's flaws. The Israelites' journey through the wilderness is an indispensable reminder of God's love, grace, mercy, and the importance of perseverance.

[1] The Holy Bible (NIV). (2011). *The Book of Numbers*. Chapter 13, Verse 31.
[2] The Holy Bible (NIV). (2011). *The Book of Numbers*. Chapter 13, Verse 33.
[3] The Holy Bible (NIV). (2011). *The Book of Numbers*. Chapter 9, Verse 15.
[4] The Holy Bible (NIV). (2011). *The Book of First Peter*. Chapter 2, Verse 9.
[5] The Holy Bible (NIV). (2011). *The Book of Numbers*. Chapter 22, Verse 18.

Chapter 5

The Book of Deuteronomy

'Love the LORD your God with all your heart
and with all your soul and with all your strength.'

Deuteronomy 6:5
The Holy Bible (NIV)

T he Book of Deuteronomy is the final book in the
Pentateuch. Deuteronomy consists of speeches by
Moses to the Israelites, before they enter into the
promised land. Deuteronomy is a reminder of the laws in the
Torah. Deuteronomy is an affirmation of God's covenant with
His chosen people. Moses encourages the Israelites to renew their
commitment to God. The Israelites are to observe God's
command faithfully. The Israelites are inspired to reside in the
promised land; the land flowing with milk and honey that God
promised to their ancestors. Deuteronomy emphasises God's love,
faithfulness, and justice. Deuteronomy underscores the
importance of obedience, covenant, and community life.

A significant theme in Deuteronomy is love. The scripture
commands us, 'love the LORD your God with all your heart, and
with all your soul, and with all your strength.'[1] This command is
the cornerstone of the faith. To love God is central to the
people's covenant with Him. Moses emphasises that to love God
is not merely an emotion, thought, idea, or feeling. Our love for
God requires action and obedience to His command.
Throughout Deuteronomy, we learn that our love for God must
be sincere and wholehearted. To love God incorporates every
dimension of our being—body, mind, heart, soul, and spirit. Our
love for God is demonstrated by our obedience and devotion to
His word.

Deuteronomy specifies the blessings that we secure from our
obedience to God's word. God promises blessings for our
faithfulness, such as prosperity, abundance, joy, peace, and favour.
On the other hand, Deuteronomy forewarns us of the curses that
result from disobedience. If the Israelites turn away from God,
then they experience adverse consequences, such as defeat in
military battles, banishment, chaos, war, and privation. In the
final analysis, our actions entail consequences. Obedience to

God's command leads us to blessings, whereas disobedience leads us to curses. We must consciously determine to obey God's command for the well-being of ourselves, our community, nation, and the world.

The covenant between God and Israel is reaffirmed in Deuteronomy. This is on the condition the Israelites remain faithful to God and His command. God promises to bless the Israelites, on the qualification they remain faithful to their covenant with Him. If the Israelites violate God's covenant, then they confront divine judgement. While God is faithful to His promise, our covenant with God requires us to remain faithful to Him. God's covenant with us is not an unconditional relationship, it involves our commitment, dedication, and integrity.

Deuteronomy affirms the Most High God is the one and only true living God. The scripture informs us, 'besides Him there is no other.'[2] At this time in world history, the declaration on monotheism was revolutionary. The ancient world was defined by polytheism and idolatry. God is the creator, sustainer, and destroyer. God is the exclusive transcendent being to whom we pray, worship, and praise. We must remain vigilant against idolatry and false prophets. We must ensure that no secular doctrine or ideology assumes the pre-eminent position of God in our life, regardless whether those doctrines or ideologies are characterised by material possessions, charismatic leaders, global institutions, or affluent corporations.

In Deuteronomy, Moses repeatedly urges the Israelites to remember God's goodness and favour. God emancipated the Israelites from slavery in ancient Egypt. God provided for the Israelites' physical, emotional, and spiritual needs in the wilderness. God guided the Israelites to the frontier of the promised land. We must acknowledge God's faithfulness in the peaks and valleys of our journey. God's faithfulness strengthens our trust and confidence in His word for the next chapter in our journey. We must demonstrate our gratitude for God's blessing and grace upon our life. Contentment assists us to remain faithful and hopeful in our confrontation with worldly challenges.

Moses emphasises the importance of introducing future generations to God's law and commandments. God's word informs us that His commandments are 'to be on your hearts;'[3] we must make them an integral part of our life. The instructions in Deuteronomy are not only about entrusting future generations with God's law; however, they are concerned with instilling a profound love for God in our heart and mind. It is imperative that succeeding generations possess the knowledge and wisdom concerning God's word. This includes not only proper instruction in the Ten Commandments and Mosaic law, but also fostering commitment and gratitude to God. Family and community perform an indispensable function in the greater scheme of humanity's well-being.

Deuteronomy cautions the Israelites not to become proud upon their possession of the promised land. The land flowing with milk and honey; the land full of abundance must not lead the Israelites to 'forget the LORD your God.'[4] Moses counsels us that prosperity leads to arrogance. We must remain vigilant against the danger of hubris. The Israelites must remember that God blessed them with the promised land. A land that provides the Israelites with prosperity, abundance, identity, and security. Our dependence, faith, and trust upon God are essential attributes to a blessed life. We must not forget that the source of our resources is God. Our success is not due to our abilities. Rather, our success is a result of God's grace.

The Book of Deuteronomy underscores the importance of God's justice in the world. Deuteronomy details how God expects the Israelites to treat vulnerable members of society and foreigners. For example, consider the law mandates fair treatment of the less fortunate people, impartiality in legal proceedings, and compassion for the foreigner—'Do not deprive the foreigner or the fatherless of justice, or take the cloak of the widow as a pledge.'[5] At the same time, God is merciful. God offers forgiveness and restoration for those who repent and turn towards Him. God is compassionate, merciful, and just. As God's chosen people, we are called to demonstrate social justice, love, and mercy in our relationships with members of the community. Justice must reflect equity; however, mercy must be extended to those who seek it. Compassion, love, and forgiveness constitute the foundation of harmonious relationships.

Moses anticipates the coming of a future prophet like himself. This is understood as a Messianic prophecy in Christian theology. This prophet will speak God's word and guide the people to redemption. In return, the people must observe his counsel. This is understood to point to Jesus Christ, who fulfils the mission of humanity's saviour. Jesus is the epitome of God's mercy, grace, love, and providence. God has granted humanity redemption through Jesus Christ. It is essential that we listen to God's messengers. For Christians, Jesus Christ is the Messiah. We are commanded to put into practice Jesus' teachings and follow his example.

Deuteronomy is a book of covenant renewal. Moses challenges the Israelites to choose between life and death, blessings and curses, and victory and defeat. The Israelites must self-determine whether to honour God's covenant, which determines their destiny; God has 'set before you today life and prosperity, death and destruction.'[6] Therefore, our actions determine our fate. The aforementioned verse of scripture informs us that God's providence respects our free will. The covenant renewal is a pivotal moment where the Israelites are given an opportunity to reaffirm their commitment to God. The Israelites are on the verge of entering the promised land.

Covenant renewal is a recurring theme in the believer's journey. We too must periodically renew our commitment to God. We must reaffirm to obey God's word. Our fellowship with God is not static, it requires our determination and perseverance to align ourselves with God's will.

Moses' leadership is closely examined in Deuteronomy. Moses is not only a religious leader of the Israelites, he is also their spiritual guide. Throughout Deuteronomy, Moses mediates God's will to the people. Moses' speeches in Deuteronomy are an authoritative reminder of God's laws. God's exhortation to Israel underscores the importance of leadership that is predicated upon faithfulness to God. Leadership is a responsibility and privilege. Leaders must lead believers by example. Leaders inspire believers to obey God's word. Leaders guide believers to be faithful to God. Believers are to be leaders in their sphere of influence. In leadership, believers must reflect God's grace, compassion, peace, mercy, justice, and love.

Moses suspects the Israelites will yield to temptation. They will be seduced by sin. Nonetheless, Deuteronomy exhibits the hope of restoration. God promises that if the Israelites repent and return to Him, with sincerity of heart, then God will gather them from exile and restore their fortunes to new heights. God promises to the Israelites, He will make them 'most prosperous in all the work of your hands.'[7] This reflects God's merciful nature, even in the midst of His chosen people's disobedience. God offers newfound hope of restoration, even after the Israelites abysmal failure. God's love, compassion, and mercy are greater than our mistakes. God is willing to restore us, when we repent and turn to Him.

Deuteronomy teaches humanity timeless lessons on love, obedience, covenant renewal, compassion, repentance, restoration, and faithfulness. Deuteronomy underscores the importance to love God with our body, mind, heart, soul, and spirit. In addition, we are commanded to educate future generations about God's word. Deuteronomy encourages our humility. We are to remember God's faithfulness. We are inspired to recommit ourselves to God's commandments. Deuteronomy emphasises God's concern for social justice. We witness God's mercy, and His covenant come to fruition. God gives us hope, even in times of distress. Ultimately, Deuteronomy encourages us to renew our commitment to God. We trust in God's provision. We are commanded to live our life as a reflection of God's holiness, justice, and mercy. The profound lessons learned from Deuteronomy are indispensable for a life of faith, both in ancient Israel and for believers today.

[1] The Holy Bible (NIV). (2011). *The Book of Deuteronomy*. Chapter 6, Verse 5.

[2] The Holy Bible (NIV). (2011). *The Book of Deuteronomy*. Chapter 4, Verse 35.

[3] The Holy Bible (NIV). (2011). *The Book of Deuteronomy*. Chapter 6, Verse 6.

[4] The Holy Bible (NIV). (2011). *The Book of Deuteronomy*. Chapter 8, Verse 11.

[5] The Holy Bible (NIV). (2011). *The Book of Deuteronomy*. Chapter 24, Verse 17.

[6] The Holy Bible (NIV). (2011). *The Book of Deuteronomy*. Chapter 30, Verse 15.

[7] The Holy Bible (NIV). (2011). *The Book of Deuteronomy*. Chapter 30, Verse 9.

Chapter 6

The Book of Joshua

'Have I not commanded you?
Be strong and courageous.
Do not be afraid; do not be discouraged,
for the LORD your God will be with you wherever you go.'

Joshua 1:9
The Holy Bible (NIV)

The Book of Joshua characterises a turning point in the Israelites' arduous journey through the wilderness towards the promised land. The Book of Joshua details the Israelites' conquest and settlement of the promised land under the leadership of Moses' successor, Joshua. The Book of Joshua is an important narrative of God's faithfulness to fulfil His covenant. We learn about the importance of obedience to God's word. Last but not least, we witness the Israelites' challenges to possess the land flowing with milk and honey that God promised to their ancestors.

A significant theme in Joshua is God's faithfulness. God honours His covenant to bequeath the promised land of Canaan to the descendants of Abraham. Despite the challenges and obstacles, God guides the Israelites into the promised land. The Israelites secure victory over their enemies. The Book of Joshua emphasises that God's covenant is certain and it is fulfilled in His timing. God is faithful to fulfil His promises. No matter how challenging our circumstances, we must position our trust and confidence in God's word. God's promises come to fruition in the fullness of time.

Joshua's leadership is characterised by his resolute commitment to God's command. In the opening chapters of this book, God specifically commands Joshua to 'Be strong and very courageous. Be careful to obey all the law my servant Moses gave you; do not turn from it to the right or to the left, that you may be successful wherever you go.'[1] The Israelites conquest of Canaan is a result of their obedience to God's command. This is confirmed in the Israelites conquest of Jericho, where their victory was a result of obedience to God's command. Obedience to God's word is crucial to our success and prosperity in life. When we obey God's counsel, even when it is inconvenient or unconventional, God leads us to victory and prosperity.

The Book of Joshua demonstrates that the Israelites' victory in battle was not due to their strength, strategy, or skill. The Israelites secured victory through God's sovereignty and providence. For example, consider the Battle of Jericho, in which God supernaturally destroyed the walls of the enemy city, 'When the trumpets sounded, the army shouted, and at the sound of the trumpet, when the men gave a loud shout, the wall collapsed; so everyone charged straight in, and they took the city.'[2] Similarly, at Joshua's request, God's intervention caused the sun to stand still during the battle against the Amorites, 'the sun stopped in the middle of the sky and delayed going down about a full day.'[3] These divine acts demonstrate how creation, and all that is within it, functions in accordance with God's providence. Our strength is finite; however, God's power is infinite. Wisdom resides in our reliance upon God's greatness, glory, goodness, grace, and guidance. We must navigate our life's major challenges in accordance with God's word.

In the midst of overwhelming odds, Joshua is repeatedly encouraged by God to 'be strong and courageous. Do not be afraid; do not be discouraged, for the LORD your God will be with you wherever you go.'[4] Joshua's courage is not based on self-righteousness, but upon his faith in God's promise, providence, protection, and presence. Joshua's assignment to lead the Israelites into Canaan was strenuous; however, God's assurance provided Joshua the strength to successfully lead the Israelites to victory. The Book of Joshua teaches us that courage, hope, faith, and strength are attained from God's spiritual presence. When we confront challenges, we remain firm in our faith. We trust that God guides us forward in accordance with His will.

Following the victory at Jericho, a member of the Israelite community undermined faithfulness, obedience, and conformity to God's command. For instance, Achan's disobedience in misappropriating devoted things from Jericho resulted in Israel's defeat at Ai. When Israel made atonement for Achan's sin, then the situation was remedied. Thereafter, the Israelites continued with their conquest of land. This Biblical event teaches humanity the importance of integrity. We learn about the collective impact of disobedience upon the community. Faithfulness and integrity matter in God's kingdom. Our actions entail consequences, both for the individual and community. Therefore, we must assume responsibility for our conduct. We must seek God's forgiveness when we make mistakes.

The Israelites' conquest of Canaan is not merely about the acquisition of territory, but the fulfilment of God's providence to establish His chosen people in the promised land as a beacon of light to the world. Joshua's leadership of the Israelites is part of a greater narrative, where God fulfils His covenant to bless all nations through Abraham's descendants. For God's word in Genesis informs us, 'Abraham will surely become a great and powerful nation, and all nations on earth will be blessed through him.'[5] The Israelites are commanded to be a holy people. They are to live in a manner that honours God. God's chosen people must live in a righteous manner that reflects God's glory and brings humanity in close proximity to God. Our actions must bear witness to God's greatness, glory, and goodness. Humanity is invited to know God and obey His word.

Joshua encourages the Israelites to renew their covenant with God. The Israelites must reaffirm their commitment to serve God. Reflection and recommitment is crucial along our journey. While the Israelites have conquered new territory, they must remain faithful to God, if they are to realise God's blessing. Joshua leads by example. He faithfully declares, 'But as for me and my household, we will serve the LORD.'[6] Spiritual maturity, personal reflection, and recommitment are recurring processes along our journey. Even though we experience God's blessing, we must periodically reaffirm our commitment to God and determine to obey His word faithfully. Our walk with God is a lifelong journey.

The Israelites conquest of Canaan is depicted as God's judgement on the Canaanite nations for their immorality. The Israelites are called to be agents of God's justice. The Israelites execute judgement against those people who have engaged in sin and idolatry. We learn that God is just. God's justice incorporates the punishment of sin. While we struggle to understand the entirety of God's justice, we trust that God is righteous in His decrees. God's judgement is impartial.

God ensures the Israelites receive respite from their enemies after they conquer the land. Joshua assumes responsibility to divide the promised land amongst the twelve Israelite tribes. This appropriation of conquered land fulfils God's covenant to provision the promised land to Abraham's descendants. The promised land represents God's blessing and the fulfilment of His covenant with Abraham. God gives His chosen people peace, power, and prosperity, when they observe His law and command. Amongst other things, the promised land represents a place of love, harmony, justice, mercy, faith, compassion, and joy.

Joshua's leadership of the Israelites is exemplary. Joshua is faithful, courageous, and obedient to God. Joshua, the leader of the Israelites, does not act out of pride, envy, or greed. Joshua consults God. Joshua carefully listens to God's counsel. Joshua involves the leaders of Israel in significant decisions that impact the community. At the end of his lifetime, Joshua holds the people accountable to their covenant with God. Joshua instructs the Israelites to renew their commitment to serve God. Good leadership involves humility, wisdom, and accountability. Honourable leaders seek God's guidance; they rely upon His strength, and lead with integrity. Leaders answer to God for their decisions and actions.

The story of Rahab, the Canaanite woman who protected the Israelite spies, is a powerful reminder that God's providence is not confined to the Israelites. Rahab, by faith, is spared from the destruction of Jericho. This demonstrates that God's grace extends beyond Israel, to all those who respond to Him in faith. Thus, we learn that God's sovereignty is universal. God is the supreme ruler over all nations. God's mercy is open to every person who responds to Him in faith. No person is beyond the purview of God's redeeming grace.

The Book of Joshua offers invaluable lessons on faith, obedience, leadership, confidence, victory, and belief. Through Joshua's journey we witness the fulfilment of God's covenant. Joshua teaches us that God is faithful and sovereign. Obedience to God's command leads us to His blessing, favour, and victory. We learn that unconventional methods constitute a part of God's providence. Joshua's leadership reminds us of the importance of courage, humility, faith, trust, and accountability. The Israelites conquest of Canaan is evidence of God's providence. Through Joshua, we learn the importance of God's chosen people remaining faithful to Him. Ultimately, Joshua encourages us to trust in God's covenant. We must seek God's guidance and remain committed to Him. God provides us with prosperity, victory, and favour, as we walk with Him.

[1] The Holy Bible (NIV). (2011). *The Book of Joshua*. Chapter 1, Verse 7.

[2] The Holy Bible (NIV). (2011). *The Book of Joshua*. Chapter 6, Verse 20.

[3] The Holy Bible (NIV). (2011). *The Book of Joshua*. Chapter 10, Verse 13.

[4] The Holy Bible (NIV). (2011). *The Book of Joshua*. Chapter 1, Verse 9.

[5] The Holy Bible (NIV). (2011). *The Book of Genesis*. Chapter 18, Verse 18.

[6] The Holy Bible (NIV). (2011). *The Book of Joshua*. Chapter 24, Verse 15.

Chapter 7

The Book of Judges

'During the night the LORD said to Gideon,
"Get up, go down against the camp,
because I am going to give it into your hands."'

Judges 7:9
The Holy Bible (NIV)

T he Book of Judges is the seventh book in the Holy
Bible. Judges chronicles Israel's history in the period
that follows Joshua's death and the establishment of the
monarchy. Judges covers a period of three hundred years. During
this time Israel experiences punishment, oppression, repentance,
and deliverance. As the title of this book suggests, the central
figures in this book are the judges. God appoints judges to
redeem the Israelites from their enemies during a time of
national crisis. Judges contains stories of victory, faith, hope,
belief, confidence, and leadership. Judges highlights the profound
moral, ethical, religious, and spiritual decline of the Israelites.
Judges offers invaluable insights on leadership, faithfulness, and
disobedience.

The recurring theme in Judges is Israel's sin. The Israelites
turn away from God and engage in idolatry. As a result, the
Israelites confront oppression, loss, and grief. The Israelites plead
to God for their deliverance. Consequently, they are redeemed by
a judge. After the judge dies, history repeats itself. The Israelites
succumb to the powerful temptation of sin. This destructive
pattern reflects the people's protracted spiritual apathy and moral
degradation. The Israelites fail to wholeheartedly embrace and
obey God's command. Spiritual apathy and neglect of God's
word results in anarchy. When we fail to remain vigilant in our
faith and devotion to God, we invite sin into our life, and its
disastrous consequences inevitably follow.

Despite Israel's rebellion, God demonstrates forbearance and
mercy. The Israelites engage in idolatry and sin. Nonetheless,
God favourably answers their appeal for deliverance, 'then the
LORD raised up judges, who saved them out of the hands of
these raiders.'[1] This demonstrates God's willingness to forgive
and restore His chosen people, even when they have wandered
astray. God is compassionate, just, and merciful. God offers

forgiveness and restoration to those who repent and turn to Him. Despite our mistakes, errors, and imperfections, God's merciful nature is omnipresent. God is willing to receive us back into His presence. God's love, forgiveness, and compassion are boundless.

Unfortunately, the Israelites engage in idolatry during the historical period of the judges. The Israelites worship false gods of foreign nations. This immoral conduct leads to their oppression, misery, and suffering. God permits the Israelites to experience the negative consequences of their actions; however, when they repent, God provides a redeemer. The Book of Judges informs us that idolatry entails serious consequences. When we position anything or anyone above God, we experience spiritual apathy and suffering. We must not compromise on our beliefs, values, principles, and ideals. Obedience to God's word secures us peace, prosperity, and freedom.

The judges are flawed individuals with personal weaknesses. Nonetheless, God employs them to bring about Israel's deliverance. Herein we witness the undeniable universality of human imperfection. Great leaders are not beyond human frailty. Nonetheless, God works with our flaws, faults, and failings to accomplish His providence. For example, consider Gideon was fearful and doubted God's calling on his life. Jephthah had a troubled past. Samson was impulsive and morally compromised. Despite their known imperfections, God worked through these characters to accomplish His providence. God employs imperfect people to fulfil His providence. Throughout the Holy Bible, God works with remnants to realise His providence. No person is beyond God's ability to redeem and utilise for the advancement of His kingdom. God works through our weaknesses to demonstrate His sovereignty, mercy, and grace.

Judges demonstrates the importance of godly leadership. When a strong, selfless, and faithful judge such as Deborah or Gideon led Israel, the kingdom experienced peace, prosperity, stability, and victory. However, when authentic leadership was absent or compromised, Israel plunged into the abysmal depths of destruction, chaos, instability, anarchy, and disorder. This leadership deficit, coupled with the absence of responsibility, demonstrates 'in those days Israel had no king; everyone did as they saw fit.'[2] Godly leadership is crucial to guide the community on the path of righteousness. Godly leadership provides peace, prosperity, and protection to the people. On the contrary, a lack of leadership leads to instability, division, and moral decadence in society. We are commanded to be leaders, whether in our family, school, church, university, workplace, community, or nation.

Several stories in Judges highlight the importance to trust in God's providence and obey His command. For example, consider Gideon is hesitant to complete his assignment; however, he trusts God. As a result, Gideon leads Israel to victory over the Midianites. In the same manner, Deborah and Barak obey God's command to wage war against their enemies. Deborah and Barak are responsible for leading Israel to its monumental victory. On the other hand, Samson's disobedience to God's command causes his downfall.

From the aforementioned historical figures, we learn that it is whom we place our trust, faith, and confidence in, that determines if we realise our destiny. It is our responsibility to realise our inherent potential—to become all that we were destined to be. Faith and obedience to God are essential for our victory and prosperity. We trust in God's providence and obey His command. This honourable approach to our conduct results in God's favour, success, joy, prosperity, and blessing. On the contrary, disobedience to God leads us to failure, loss, and defeat.

Throughout Judges, we witness the moral degradation and spiritual decline of Israel. The people repeatedly engage in sinful conduct. As a result, their fellowship with God is damaged. In the concluding chapters of Judges, Israel experiences corruption and violence. Ultimately, there is chaos and disorder in Israel. The social fabric of Israelite society begins to disintegrate. Regrettably, civil war ensues. We learn how sin manifests a corrupting influence that spreads throughout the community. The presence of sin causes division, destruction, and disaster in our life. Not only does sin damage our relationship with God; however, it also ruptures our relationship with members of the community. Sin damages the foundation of our society.

Several of the judges were unqualified by conventional standards. Nonetheless, God employed them in powerful ways. Gideon was the youngest person in his family and he originated from the weakest tribe. Notwithstanding, God employed Gideon to defeat the Midianites. Similarly, despite Samson's flaws, faults, and failings, he was employed by God to liberate Israel from the Philistines. Judges demonstrates how God employs remnants to accomplish His providence. We do not need to be powerful, competent, experienced, wealthy, knowledgeable, or qualified by conventional standards to perform an integral part in God's providence. God employs individuals who depend upon Him and are willing to run their race in faith.

Throughout Judges, we witness instances where God executes His judgement on the surrounding nations, as well as upon Israel, when they fail to honour His word. For example, consider God employs Israel's enemies to render judgement against the Israelites. God punishes the Israelites when they engage in sin. Divine judgement emphasises that God is sovereign and that sin has profound consequences, even for His chosen people. While God is merciful and offers forgiveness, we must not receive God's grace for granted. We must not assume that God condones our sinful conduct. Divine judgement is inevitable. We must repent and turn to God before it is too late.

In Judges, we witness the Israelites compromise on their

obedience to God's word. The Israelites fail to completely eliminate the Canaanites from the promised land. Consequently, this leads to negative Canaanite influence amongst the Israelites. This compromise in obedience to God's command entails long-term spiritual consequences for the Israelites. This compromise contributes to the Israelites downfall. We must obey God's word exactly as it has been decreed. Our compromise with sin, temptation, and disobedience leads us to spiritual and moral decadence. In many respects, partial obedience is disobedience, and it also entails long-term consequences. We must faithfully commit ourselves to obey God's word, without compromise, modification, or qualification.

The Book of Judges concludes with national chaos, social upheaval, and moral decadence. The scripture once again narrates, 'In those days Israel had no king; everyone did as they saw fit.'[3] This disorderly reality highlights the absence of strong and effective governance in Israel. This political and social reality points to the dire necessity for a righteous leader to guide the Israelites. Without godly leadership, anarchy and disorder prevail amongst the people. The requirement for a righteous leader is crucial to the future of Israel. This theological truth points to our saviour—Jesus Christ. Jesus is the legitimate king who brings order, harmony, social justice, redemption, and peace to humanity.

The Book of Judges offers invaluable lessons on human nature, the consequences of sin, and the importance of godly leadership. In Judges, we witness God's forbearance, compassion, justice, punishment, and mercy. Judges demonstrates that spiritual apathy, idolatry, and disobedience lead to suffering and moral decadence. On the other hand, obedience, repentance, and faithfulness bring about deliverance and peace. Judges teaches us that God works through imperfect leaders and He employs remnants. God works through humanity's weaknesses to accomplish His providence. Ultimately, Judges points to the requirement for a righteous leader. This necessity is fulfilled in the coming of King David and, finally, in Jesus Christ, the legitimate king and saviour of humankind.

[1] The Holy Bible (NIV). (2011). *The Book of Judges*. Chapter 2, Verse 16.

[2] The Holy Bible (NIV). (2011). *The Book of Judges*. Chapter 17, Verse 6.

[3] The Holy Bible (NIV). (2011). *The Book of Judges*. Chapter 21, Verse 25.

Chapter 8

The Book of Ruth

'Where you die I will die, and there I will be buried.
May the LORD deal with me, be it ever so severely,
if even death separates you and me.'

Ruth 1:17
The Holy Bible (NIV)

The Book of Ruth is a historical narrative that takes place during the period of the Judges. Ruth's life story demonstrates faith, loyalty, love, renewal, grace, redemption, and blessing. Ruth is a book on hope. Ruth personifies how God's providence unfolds through ordinary people, even in the midst of indescribable loss, grief, pain, suffering, and privation. In the Book of Ruth, we witness the realisation of God's providence in Ruth's life. This Biblical story centres on Ruth, a Moabite widow, and her mother-in-law, Naomi. The two women navigate loss, grief, and uncertainty. Despite Ruth and Naomi's challenges, God's grace, favour, provision, mercy, and faithfulness are evident.

In the Book of Ruth, we witness God's providence in the midst of difficult circumstances. The most prominent theme in the Book of Ruth is God's providence—the manner in which God works behind the scenes in our life. God orchestrates events, creates new opportunities, and guides us towards the realisation of His providence, even when we do not foresee it at the time. There is immense tragedy in Naomi's life—the death of her husband and two sons. Not to mention, Ruth has become a foreigner and widow. Nonetheless, God orchestrates events that lead to Naomi's restoration of hope and Ruth's redemption.

In the Book of Ruth, we learn that God is concerned with the finer details in our life. Even in times of unimaginable suffering, pain, trauma, grief, and loss, God's presence is with us. In fact, Naomi has become distraught at her loss; she exclaims, 'I went away full, but the LORD has brought me back empty.'[1] We do not completely understand the mystery of God's providence, but He is always at work. God's providence is for the good of humanity and His glory. In order to experience the fullness of life and testify to our faith, we need to move forward. We need to transcend our loss, grief, pain, suffering, trauma, and privation, so that we fulfil our assignment and realise our destiny.

The relationship between Ruth and Naomi is characterised by loyalty, ladyship, and love. Despite the fact that Ruth could have journeyed home after her husband died, she remained with Naomi affirming, 'Where you go I will go, and where you stay I will stay.'[2] Ruth's resolute determination to remain with Naomi in her time of grief highlights the power of loyalty in relationships, especially when the circumstances are difficult. We too must appreciate that loyalty and faithfulness, especially during challenging times, are important qualities in our relationships. Ruth's devotion to Naomi is an example of selfless commitment. Ruth demonstrates that love and friendship remain unbreakable, even during tragedy.

Ruth's integrity is demonstrated throughout this Biblical story. Ruth's perseverance and the manner in which she conducts herself is remarkable. Ruth does not avoid responsibility. Ruth works with dedication and commitment in the fields to provide for herself and Naomi. When it comes time to commence a new relationship with Boaz, Ruth acts in a manner that is respectful, honourable, and in agreement with God's word. From Ruth's conduct, we observe that integrity, discipline, loyalty, accountability, respect, and good character are crucial attributes in life. Ruth's conduct exemplifies honesty, respect, trust, faith, and honour. When we live with integrity and accountability, even during challenging situations, God's providence is at work through our actions. The manner in which Ruth conducts herself leads to God's blessing upon her life—Boaz's proposal to marry her.

Ruth, a Moabite woman, was a foreigner. Not to mention, the Moabites were historically an enemy of the Israelites. Nonetheless, God welcomed Ruth into the Israelite community. Ruth became part of the blessed lineage of David and ultimately, the genealogy of Jesus Christ. Ruth's inclusion in this great lineage reveals that God's grace and redemption extend to all people, regardless of ethnicity, wealth, power, status, property, education, sex, colour, nationality, or race. God's love and redemption are available to every person, regardless of their birth, ethnicity, sex, or heritage. Ruth's story teaches us that God's kingdom welcomes all who trust in Him. God's love, mercy, blessing, and grace equally extend to foreigners.

The theme of redemption is central in the Book of Ruth. In this story, Boaz is the guardian and redeemer of Ruth. Boaz redeems Ruth and Naomi from their destitution by marrying Ruth, and thereby, restoring their fortune and reputation. This act of redemption not only promotes physical restoration, however, it also brings emotional, spiritual, and social healing to Naomi and Ruth. Redemption is a powerful act of restoration, love, and grace. Just as Boaz redeemed Ruth and Naomi, Jesus Christ is our redeemer. Through Jesus' crucifixion, humanity secures its redemption.

The Book of Ruth highlights that miracles are possible in everyday moments. This Biblical story centres on God's provision through Ruth, Naomi, and Boaz. For example, consider Ruth's diligence in her work in the fields. Naomi's wise counsel. Boaz's compassion, hospitality, love, and generosity. These are the ways in which God's providence comes to fruition. These three characters ordinary actions demonstrate that God's providence is realised through common events, ordinary people, and the unremarkable circumstances of life.

The most important attributes we require are faith, hope, love, belief, confidence, and discipline. God provides for our needs in ordinary ways, through the people we encounter along our journey, a turnaround in our circumstances, and the environment in which we reside. We must be attentive to God's provision. Even in simple, seemingly mundane phenomena, we perceive God's providence at work. Above all, God utilises our experiences, knowledge, circumstances, and resources, to further His providence.

Ruth and Naomi perform a pivotal function in the realisation of God's providence. These two women are exemplars of courage, faith, integrity, perseverance, and wisdom. Naomi, although initially bitter with her lot in life, fulfils an important responsibility to counsel Ruth, by seeking redemption through Boaz. Ruth, a foreigner, becomes an ancestor of King David, and through the Davidic line, an ancestor of Jesus Christ. This incredible Biblical story underscores the importance of women in God's redemption of humanity. Women perform an inordinate function in the fulfilment of God's providence. The Book of Ruth highlights the importance of women in the Biblical narrative of humanity's redemption. The Book of Ruth affirms God's providence is accomplished through women.

Ruth's humility is self-evident from the commencement of this Biblical story. Ruth does not demand her rights or expect favourable treatment. Ruth humbly works in the fields to provide for Naomi and herself. Ruth's willingness to obey Naomi's instructions, while she seeks Boaz's favour demonstrates her spirit of humility, respect, and obedience. Humility is an important virtue that secures us love, favour, and honour. Ruth's humble service, forbearance, and obedience to Naomi's counsel, led to Ruth's blessing and redemption through Boaz. In our life, humility creates the opportunity to secure God's grace, blessing, mercy, and favour.

Ruth's restoration unfolds at exactly the right moment. Naomi and Ruth's return to Bethlehem coincides with the barley harvest season. This timing provides the opportunity for Ruth to meet Boaz. Boaz is a man of noble character. Boaz redeems Ruth through marriage. The timing of these events demonstrates that God's providence is never early or late, however, perfect in its timing. Therefore, we must trust in God's timing. When we do not perceive the finer details of our life coming together, we trust that God's timing in our life is perfect. God's providence unfolds at exactly the right time. We must demonstrate forbearance and confidence, as we trust God's providence to materialise in our life.

Ruth's loyalty to Naomi, her faithfulness to God, and her commitment to doing what is right, ultimately led to her blessing. Ruth's life was transformed. Ruth went from being a destitute widow in a foreign land, to marrying Boaz, a wealthy and honourable man of good character, respect, wealth, and social status. In addition, Ruth became an ancestor of King David. Naomi also experienced restoration and joy through the birth of Ruth's son, Obed, who becomes the grandfather of David. Our faithfulness, even with inconsequential matters, leads to God's blessing. Ruth's inspirational story is a testimony to God's goodness, favour, and mercy. When we remain faithful to God, even during difficult circumstances, He rewards us in the fullness of time. Faithfulness and integrity not only perfect our character, they secure God's favour.

Ruth, a Moabite woman, was not part of the covenant between God and the Israelites. Nonetheless, Ruth's decision to follow Naomi and embrace her faith, ensured Ruth became a part of King David's lineage, which is related to Jesus Christ. The inclusion of a gentile in the genealogy of Jesus Christ foreshadows God's providence of redemption for humanity. We learn that regardless of a person's ethnicity, nationality, sex, race, colour, wealth, status, private property, or education, every person constitutes part of God's providence. God's covenant extends beyond the Israelites. Ruth's story is a timely reminder that God's redeeming grace is open to every person who comes to Him in faith. God's providence incorporates all nations of the world. God is faithful to His covenant. God's mercy extends to all those who believe in Him.

The Book of Ruth offers timeless wisdom on loyalty, faith, integrity, and redemption. Ruth's journey reminds us that God is at work in the finer details of our life. God provides for us, even when we do not realise it. The Book of Ruth teaches us that faithfulness in our relationships, humility, and obedience lead us to prosperity, blessing, and fulfilment. God's grace and redemption are available to every person, regardless of circumstance, situation, wealth, age, sex, property, status, colour, education, vocation, or fortune. In the final analysis, the Book of Ruth points to the redemptive work of Jesus Christ—the redeemer of humanity. Ruth is a call to trust in God's timing and providence.

[1] The Holy Bible (NIV). (2011). *The Book of Ruth.* Chapter 1, Verse 21.
[2] The Holy Bible (NIV). (2011). *The Book of Ruth.* Chapter 1, Verse 16.

Chapter 9

The Book of First Samuel

'There is no one holy like the LORD;
there is no one besides you;
there is no Rock like our God.'

1 Samuel 2:2
The Holy Bible (NIV)

F irst Samuel narrates the transition period from the Book of Judges to the establishment of a monarchy in Israel. First Samuel recounts the lives of three instrumental characters. Samuel, the prophet and judge. Saul, Israel's first king. And David, the future king of Israel. The Book of First Samuel is full of spiritual wisdom. Throughout First Samuel we witness themes of leadership, obedience, disobedience, humility, faith, and sin.

The contrast between Samuel's obedience and Saul's disobedience is a major theme throughout the Book of First Samuel. Samuel consistently obeys God and he faithfully discharges his duties. On the other hand, Saul, despite being anointed by God, repeatedly disobeys God's command. Saul perpetuates his ruin and downfall. Saul's failure to obey God's command results in the loss of God's favour and a tragic end to his worldly reign. From Saul, we learn that obedience to God is of paramount importance. God values obedience over sacrifice. When we fail to obey God's word, or we ignore His command, we stand to lose His favour, peace, grace, and blessing. Authentic leadership is informed by obedience to God's word.

In the Book of First Samuel, we witness that God does not anoint leaders based on their appearance, status, education, wealth, power, influence, or public opinion. When King Saul did not obey God's word, God instructed Prophet Samuel to move forward in life, 'How long will you mourn for Saul, since I have rejected him as king over Israel? Fill your horn with oil and be on your way.'[1] God's word teaches us the importance to forge ahead in life, even when people, circumstances, and events do not materialise as we had envisioned.

David, the son of Jesse, is anointed as Israel's future king, not on the basis of his appearance, but for his good heart. God always 'looks at the heart,'[2] not the superficial appearance, when He appoints leaders to further His kingdom on earth. God's appointment of worldly leaders is based on their personal qualities, positive attributes, and good character, not on conventional standards of status, wealth, property, authority, education, or power. God anoints individuals who are humble and faithful, even when society overlooks them.

Saul's lack of obedience to God's word led to his demise. Saul's tragic downfall is a direct consequence of his pride and confidence in his own judgement, rather than placing his trust and faith in God. In response to Saul's disobedience, God declares, 'But now your kingdom will not endure; the LORD has sought out a man after His own heart and appointed him ruler of His people, because you have not kept the LORD's command.'[3]

In several consequential moments, Saul made decisions in which he did not seek God's counsel. For example, consider Saul performed the burnt offering himself, rather than wait for Samuel to complete this sacred offering. In addition, Saul spared King Agag's life in violation of God's command. Not to mention, Saul permitted the retention of the Amalekite's spoils of war, rather than completely obey God's command. These specific instances demonstrate Saul's pride, arrogance, and self-reliance, which resulted in God's rejection of him. We too must understand that our pride, arrogance, and self-reliance lead to disastrous consequences. When we trust in our abilities and forsake God's counsel, this approach leads to our spiritual demise. Our humility and dependence upon God are essential, to live our life characterised by faith. We must not entertain nor invite hubris into our life.

David is a prime example of God's providence functioning through unlikely individuals. David is anointed as Israel's next king, while he is still a young shepherd boy. By conventional standards, David was the least likely son of Jesse to become the next king of Israel. Despite David's youth and inexperience, he demonstrated remarkable courage, faith, confidence, and leadership. David's fine attributes were demonstrated in his decisive victory over Goliath. We learn from David's exceptional story that God can employ any person, regardless of their age, social status, power, colour, sex, wealth, property, vocation, or education. God's appointments often defy human expectations. What matters most is a heart that trusts in God and is willing to take a leap of faith, even in seemingly impossible circumstances.

The fall of Saul and the rise of David, demonstrate God's sovereignty and providence. Saul's kingship comes to an end due to his disobedience. The anointed David is prepared, in God's timing, to assume the kingship of Israel. David's journey to kingship is defined by forbearance, trust, and confidence in God. David is anointed king, long before he becomes the king of Israel. We too must place our trust in God. God is sovereign over creation. God's timing is perfect. Even when we do not understand the challenges or circumstances in our life, we trust that God effectuates His providence for us at the opportune time. Our confidence and trust in God's providence are essential to realise our destiny.

David's victory over the Philistine giant, Goliath is incredible, as it is inspiring. David, a young shepherd boy confronts Goliath, an experienced warrior, not with conventional weapons or immeasurable strength, but rather with resolute faith in God. At the onset, David boldly declares, 'the battle is the LORD's, and He will give all of you into our hands.'[4] God redeems David from this formidable enemy of the Israelites. Faith in God enables us to transcend great challenges, even when the odds are unfavourable. David's decisive victory over Goliath demonstrates, that with God's favour, we transcend obstacles, no matter how intimidating they are. Our victories, accomplishments, and successes are not due to our abilities, knowledge, skill, or talent, but due to God's grace, mercy, and blessing.

Throughout the Book of First Samuel, Samuel demonstrates the importance of prayer and intercession. As a prophet and leader, Samuel constantly prays for Israel, he seeks God's counsel and intervention. Samuel's prayers lead to Israel's victory over the Philistines. Samuel guides and assists Israel's spiritual growth and development. In contrast, King Saul's failure to seek God's counsel through prayer is one of the reasons for his tragic downfall. Prayer is a powerful instrument in the believer's life. It is through prayer that we seek God's will, intercede for members of the community, and perfect our walk with God. Prayer is essential to enhance our wisdom, resilience, and faith.

David's leadership is in stark contrast to his predecessor, King Saul. David's humility, honour, and meekness are evident. When David was anointed king of Israel, David could have taken the kingship from Saul by force, however, he did not. David demonstrated patience and good character. When Saul attempted to kill David out of jealousy, David refused to harm Saul in return. David demonstrated respect for Saul as God's anointed king. The judicious manner in which David dealt with Saul's assassination attempts on his life, demonstrate David's exemplary character. Leadership in God's kingdom is characterised by humility, servanthood, and respect for humanity. A godly leader does not seek glory, fame, power, wealth, social status, or pecuniary gain, however, they serve humanity selflessly, even when such service entails sacrifice or danger. The greatest leaders follow the example of Jesus Christ. Jesus came to serve humanity, not to be served.

Sadly, Saul's kingship ended in tragedy. Nonetheless, David's story offers a different perspective. Even though David made serious errors of judgement and mistakes, such as his affair with Bathsheba, nevertheless, David's heart remained after God. In First Samuel, we witness David's struggle with temptation, jealousy, concupiscence, and sin; however, he continually seeks to honour God's word. David's journey demonstrates that even the greatest leaders have their imperfections. Like David, we all experience failure in certain areas of our life. The good news is that God's grace offers salvation and restoration for individuals who repent and turn to God. King David's story demonstrates that God employs imperfect people to accomplish His providence. God forgives and restores those who sincerely seek His heart.

King Saul's insecurity, anger, pride, and jealousy are four factors that result in his tragic downfall. Once David's popularity increased amongst the Israelites, King Saul became envious, insecure, and fearful. Regrettably, King Saul attempted to assassinate David on multiple occasions. King Saul's insecurity caused him to make irrational decisions, which ultimately undermined his leadership, reputation, and integrity. Not to mention, King Saul's immoral actions irreparably damaged his relationship with his anointed successor, David. Through King Saul's life, we learn how jealousy, pride, anger, and insecurity damage important relationships and obstruct our spiritual transformation. Rather than be envious of the success of members in our organisation, community, society, or nation, we ought to celebrate their accomplishments. We trust that God's providence is at work in our life. Harmonious relationships are founded on humility, trust, love, and support, not on envy, fear, jealousy, insecurity, or resentment.

The Book of First Samuel teaches us many profound lessons, particularly about the nature of leadership, obedience, faith, jealousy, and the long-lasting consequences of sin. The exceptional lives of David, Samuel, and Saul illustrate that God's providence functions through the humble and faithful person. Our obedience to God is essential to secure His favour. Authentic leadership is the fruit of humility, love, community service, integrity, and a heart after God. First Samuel emphasises the importance of God's timing. We trust in God's sovereignty, and remain faithful to Him in the midst of our adversity. Through King Saul's disobedience and David's fortitude, First Samuel reminds us of the necessity to perform God's will and rely upon His grace to accomplish our assignment.

[1] The Holy Bible (NIV). (2011). *The Book of First Samuel.* Chapter 16, Verse 1.

[2] The Holy Bible (NIV). (2011). *The Book of First Samuel.* Chapter 16, Verse 7.

[3] The Holy Bible (NIV). (2011). *The Book of First Samuel.* Chapter 13, Verse 14.

[4] The Holy Bible (NIV). (2011). *The Book of First Samuel.* Chapter 17, Verse 47.

Chapter 10

The Book of Second Samuel

'It is God who arms me with strength
and keeps my way secure.'

2 Samuel 22:33
The Holy Bible (NIV)

T he Book of Second Samuel focuses on the reign
of King David. Second Samuel details David's
ascension to the throne of Israel, his epic military
victories, his failings, and the lasting consequences of his actions.
The Book of Second Samuel portrays the successes and failures
of King David. The Book of Second Samuel demonstrates how
God's covenant is fulfilled through David, despite his failures and
mistakes. Second Samuel teaches us profound lessons on
leadership, repentance, grace, justice, mercy, human frailty,
and sin.

One of the central themes in Second Samuel is God's
faithfulness to His covenant with King David. God establishes a
covenant with King David. God promises that David's
descendants shall rule Israel for ever. God decrees David's throne
will be established for eternity. God's word specifically informs us,
'Your house and your kingdom shall endure for ever before me;
your throne shall be established for ever.'[1] God's promise to
King David is fulfilled with the coming of Jesus Christ, the Son
of David. Jesus is destined to establish the promised kingdom on
earth, when an angel reveals to Mary, 'You will conceive and give
birth to a son, and you are to call him Jesus. He will be great and
will be called the Son of the Most High. The LORD God will
give him the throne of his father David, and he will reign over
Jacob's descendants for ever; his kingdom will never end.'[2] God
is faithful to His covenant, even when we are unfaithful. God
always honours His word. God's covenant is certain. God fulfils
His promise in His timing. The nativity of Jesus teaches us to
trust in God's faithfulness, even when our circumstances are
unfavourable.

King David is a remarkable and honourable leader. Despite
David's weaknesses, he is a person after God's heart. David's
leadership is characterised by reliance upon God and humility

before God. While David makes his fair share of mistakes, his willingness to repent for his sins is a positive character trait. For example, consider when David learns of King Saul and Jonathan's demise. David humbly mourns their irreplaceable loss. David also sought God's counsel in relation to his personal affairs and the good governance of the kingdom. Authentic leadership comes from a place of humility, dependence upon God, and obedience to God's will. Leaders who repent and seek God's counsel, even when they make mistakes, are those who lead with integrity, accountability, and honour.

Despite David's profound relationship with God, David's pride became evident during the later years of his reign. A notable example is when King David ordered the census of Israel. David's decision to conduct this census, was motivated by his pride to assess the military prowess of his armed forces. David exhibited hubris in ordering this national census. This was an act of self-reliance and demonstrated a lack of trust in God. This action resulted in God's judgement, and 'seventy thousand of the people from Dan to Beersheba died.'[3] In this instance, David's conduct is an example of his failure to seek God's counsel, in a matter that was not his to determine. This reckless act resulted in God's judgement. From David's mistake, we learn appointed leaders must carefully consider their decisions and seek God's counsel.

Leadership not only confers the privilege of power, however, it also entails personal responsibility. Leaders must comprehend the significance of their actions and decisions, especially when they impact the nation. Our pride and self-sufficiency are dangerous. When we trust in our strength and abilities, rather than rely upon God, we are vulnerable to sin, arrogance, pride, and temptation. Humility before God is essential to our spiritual growth and development.

Furthermore, King David's affair with Bathsheba, and his

subsequent actions to conceal this sinful conduct, results in the tragic death of Bathsheba's innocent husband, Uriah. This tragedy of David's making demonstrates the destructive consequences of temptation, concupiscence, and sin. When Prophet Nathan rebukes King David, he repents and seeks God's forgiveness. King David is forgiven for his immoral conduct. Nonetheless, there are severe and lasting consequences for David's sin. For example, consider the death of David's child born to Bathsheba. Not to mention, the ongoing strife within David's family.

We must remain mindful that sin entails profound consequences, even when we are forgiven by God. While God is merciful and willing to forgive those who repent, sin brings untold pain, suffering, grief, tragedy, destruction, misery, and despair into our life. Genuine repentance involves not only the acknowledgement of our sin, but also transformational change in our thought, speech, and conduct. Repentance is the method to bring about our restoration. When we genuinely turn away from sin and return to God, He is faithful to forgive and restore us. This is the essence of the gospel's message—Jesus Christ offers us forgiveness and reconciliation through his crucifixion. It is through Jesus Christ that we are justified before God, not because we are righteous, but because, 'Christ also suffered once for sins, the righteous for the unrighteous.'[4]

Despite David's moral transgressions, God still employs David to accomplish His providence. David's sin with Bathsheba, and the death of Uriah, could have disqualified David from kingship. Nonetheless, God continues to favour David as the king of Israel. Ultimately, God affirms David as an ancestor of the Messiah—Jesus Christ. God's redeeming grace is evident in David's life. God continues to fulfil His covenant to David, even after David's grievous sin. From David's journey, we learn that God forgives our failures and employs us to further His providence. Even when we fall short and make serious errors of judgement, God's mercy restores us. God continues to work in and through us to achieve His providence. If we turn to God in repentance, then we are never beyond the prerogative of His mercy.

The grave consequences of David's sin are witnessed in the turmoil within his own household. The most tragic example is the rape of David's daughter, Tamar by her half-brother, Amnon. This personal crisis leads to discord, disruption, and disunity in David's family, which includes the murder of Amnon by Tamar's brother, Absalom. Subsequently, Absalom leads a rebellion against King David, in which he seeks to overthrow David, the legitimate king of Israel. We learn that neglect of family relationships and our failure to address sin within the family leads to destructive consequences. King David's failure to discipline his children and manage family dynamics results in tragedy. As leaders, we must prioritise our family relationships and keep our house in order. We must ensure God's word is the guiding principle in our life.

In Second Samuel, God's justice, grace, and mercy are evident. For instance, consider King David has an affair with Bathsheba. Thereafter, David facilitates an agreement amongst his trusted comrades to have Bathsheba's husband, Uriah killed on the battlefield. Nonetheless, God's justice leads to judgement against David. God's judgement includes the death of David's child and turmoil in his family. However, God's mercy is evident. God forgives David when he repents. In addition, God administers justice against David's enemies. God also demonstrates mercy to those who are loyal to David. Therefore, God is both just and merciful. God does not condone sin; however, He offers mercy to those who earnestly repent. We must respect the attributes of God's nature. We must recognise the severity of our sin leads to God's punishment. God administers justice. We must keep our faith and trust in God's mercy.

When King David confronts rebellion from his son Absalom, his kingdom is at risk of disintegration. Not to mention, David's life is in danger. Consequently, David is forced to flee from Jerusalem. During this troublesome time, David continues to trust in God. At various moments, David demonstrates his trust in God's sovereignty. David is confident that God's providence is at work for the advancement of his greater good. Our trust in God, during a time of personal crisis is crucial. No matter how unfortunate our personal situation, God is omniscient, omnipresent, and omnipotent. We must turn to God for strength, guidance, counsel, and consolation during difficult times.

King David confronts rebellion, political intrigue, betrayal by his son, and turmoil within the kingdom. Nonetheless, the Book of Second Samuel emphasises God's sovereignty over the events of world history. Despite King David's challenges, God fulfils His promise to establish David's throne and effectuate His providence through David's lineage. Thus, God's sovereignty is evident in every situation, no matter how chaotic or disorderly it is. Even in times of personal failure, national crisis, social upheaval, economic turmoil, or political persecution, God's providence comes to realisation. No person obstructs God's providence from materialising in the world. God orchestrates events to fulfil His providence.

The Book of Second Samuel offers profound lessons on leadership, sin, repentance, divine judgement, punishment, and mercy. Second Samuel teaches us authentic leadership is based on humility and obedience to God's word. Not to mention, sin has destructive consequences. Having said that, God's mercy is available to those who genuinely repent. The Book of Second Samuel demonstrates that God is faithful to His covenant. Even when we make errors and mistakes, God restores us. God continues to work through us. Second Samuel underscores the importance of family. We must trust in God during times of personal crisis. The eternal reality that God is sovereign over creation is undeniable. In the final analysis, God's providence always comes to fruition, despite our failures, errors, mistakes, imperfections, and weaknesses.

[1] The Holy Bible (NIV). (2011). *The Book of Second Samuel.* Chapter 7, Verse 16.
[2] The Holy Bible (NIV). (2011). *The Book of Luke.* Chapter 1, Verses 31-33.
[3] The Holy Bible (NIV). (2011). *The Book of Second Samuel.* Chapter 24, Verse 15.
[4] The Holy Bible (NIV). (2011). *The Book of First Peter.* Chapter 3, Verse 18.

Chapter 11

The Book of First Kings

'God gave Solomon wisdom and very great insight,
and a breadth of understanding
as measureless as the sand on the seashore.'

1 Kings 4:29
The Holy Bible (NIV)

T he Book of First Kings chronicles ancient Israel's history. First Kings depicts the reign of King Solomon. First Kings narrates the division of the Kingdom into two distinct political entities: Israel (i.e., the northern kingdom) and Judah (i.e., the southern kingdom). First Kings chronicles the kings within these two kingdoms. First Kings not only provides a historical account; however, it details important spiritual and moral lessons, particularly in relation to leadership, wisdom, faith, idolatry, and the consequences of disobedience.

Solomon commences his reign as king of Israel. He is known for his remarkable wisdom and justice. God granted Solomon wisdom, when he earnestly requested it. King Solomon did not seek wealth, pleasure, or long life, 'so give your servant a discerning heart to govern your people and to distinguish between right and wrong.'[1] King Solomon's remarkable wisdom is evident in his decision-making. For example, consider King Solomon's astute judgement in relation to the two women who claimed to be the mother of the same baby. When the people heard that King Solomon had correctly determined the baby's birth mother, 'they saw that he had wisdom from God to administer justice.'[2]

King Solomon's reign was characterised by prosperity, peace, and the building of the Temple of the LORD in Jerusalem. The establishment of the LORD's Temple was the pinnacle of Solomon's kingship. Wisdom is the foundation of good leadership. Leaders are encouraged to seek wisdom from God. Leaders must place their trust in God's counsel, particularly when making decisions that affect members of the community. God favours individuals who prioritise wisdom, justice, and discernment over wealth, power, property, pecuniary gain, pride, and fame.

Despite King Solomon's exemplary wisdom, his later years

were defined by idolatry and compromise with foreign gods. King Solomon's several foreign wives persuaded him to worship false gods. Solomon's immoral conduct directly contradicted God's commandment and it brought judgement upon Israel. God forewarned King Solomon that because of his idolatry, the kingdom would be torn apart after his death, 'Since this is your attitude and you have not kept my covenant and my decrees, which I commanded you, I will most certainly tear the kingdom away from you.'[3]

As we witnessed with King Solomon, idolatry—the worship of false idols in the supreme place of God—has disastrous consequences. When we engage in sinful conduct, or permit negative influences that violate God's command, we relinquish God's blessing, favour, and grace. We must remain faithful to God's word and avoid spiritual compromise. This approach is crucial to maintain God's favour in our life.

The division of the kingdom of Israel after King Solomon's death demonstrates the intergenerational consequences of turning away from God's word. King Solomon's son and successor to the throne, Rehoboam, acted on the counsel of his inexperienced young advisors, instead of heeding the wisdom of the experienced elders. King Rehoboam made irrational decisions that resulted in the rebellion of the ten northern tribes in the kingdom of Israel. This division created discord within the kingdom of Israel. This national conflict resulted in the schism between the northern kingdom of Israel and the southern kingdom of Judah.

God's judgement on King Solomon's royal line of succession was affirmed when the kingdom of Israel was divided into two distinct political entities. From Rehoboam, we learn that rejection of wise counsel and turning away from God's wisdom leads to disunity, disagreement, and destruction. In particular, leaders must determine their decisions based on godly wisdom and discernment. Leaders must transcend the temptation to act out of pride, ambition, revenge, jealousy, or greed.

The reign of Ahab, one of Israel's most wicked kings, demonstrates God's judgement, justice, and mercy. King Ahab and his wife, Jezebel promoted Baal worship and persecuted God's prophets. In response, God anointed the prophet Elijah to confront King Ahab's falsehood. This led to the grand contest on Mount Carmel. As a consequence, there was divine judgement on King Ahab's house. Despite King Ahab's wickedness, God demonstrated mercy when Ahab humbled himself. King Ahab repented upon hearing Elijah's prophecy. God is just, righteous, and merciful. God judges sin; however, He also provides humanity with mercy and the opportunity for repentance. Every person secures God's forgiveness, if they truly repent and turn to God. God desires that no person perish, but that every person repents and is redeemed from sin.

Prophet Elijah prayed to God. Elijah requested fire from heaven to consume the sacrifice on Mount Carmel. This is a powerful testimony of faith, belief, hope, and prayer. Elijah boldly challenged the illegitimate prophets of the false god, Baal. Prophet Elijah trusted the Most High God to answer his prayer and prove Himself as the living God. God answered Elijah's prayer, by sending fire from heaven to consume the offering on the alter. God's answer to Elijah's prayer and acceptance of his offering demonstrated God's power, sovereignty, and supremacy over the false god, Baal. This significant event in world history reveals that there is only one true living God. Prayer is powerful. When we position our trust and confidence in God, great achievements materialise in our life. Resolute faith in God, especially in our confrontation with opposition, evil, falsehood, and doubt, leads to miraculous results. We must remain firm in our beliefs. We must earnestly pray for God's favour in our life.

Prophet Elijah's confrontation with the false prophets of Baal on Mount Carmel is a powerful example of standing firm against falsehood. Despite Prophet Elijah being outnumbered against the four hundred and fifty false prophets of Baal, Elijah boldly testified the truth about God. Elijah rejected the false god, Baal. Elijah called upon the people of Israel to make a defining choice and return to the LORD. As believers, we must remain firm in our faith. We must reject false gods and ideologies. The world presents many alternatives to God's word; however, we are called to remain faithful to the gospel and affirm its eternal truth. We must not compromise on our principles when confronted with falsehood or deception.

Israel was a divided kingdom. There were many immoral kings. Nonetheless, the Book of First Kings reminds us that God is sovereign over all nations and the fate of kings. God's word, through prophet Nathan, foretold of the division of the kingdom of Israel after King Solomon's death. This fact reveals that God is in control of world history, even during times of political crisis and social upheaval. Even when Israel's kings fail to effectuate God's will, His providence is not obstructed. God appoints new leaders and faithful prophets to fulfil His providence. God is sovereign over worldly powers. No matter how chaotic the politics within the nation, God's providence unfolds according to His will. Worldly leaders and rulers are accountable to God. God often employs flawed individuals and remnants to accomplish His providence.

The reign of King Solomon, and the subsequent division of the kingdom of Israel, highlights the importance of the legacy that leaders leave behind for the succeeding generations. King Solomon's failure to remain faithful to God in his later years necessitated a destructive impact on the kingdom of Israel. King Solomon's sin was responsible for the discord, division, and destruction in Israel under the leadership of his successor and son, Rehoboam.

King Rehoboam's pride and failure to accept wise counsel resulted in a divided kingdom. This dismal reality marked the beginning of a long period of instability and idolatry in Israel. Our actions and decisions in the present time have a profound impact on succeeding generations. As trusted leaders—whether in the family, school, workplace, church, community, university, or nation—we must be conscious of our actions. Through our leadership, we create our legacy, which we entrust to future generations. Our generation's faithfulness to God impacts the destiny of future generations.

The Book of First Kings contains profound lessons on leadership, wisdom, destructive consequences of sin, and the importance of our faithfulness to God. The Biblical stories of King Solomon's wisdom and idolatry, the division of the kingdom of Israel, and Prophet Elijah's faith to confront Baal's false prophets, demonstrate the importance of our reliance upon God. We must remain faithful to God's word. We must avoid moral compromise along our journey. God's judgement against sin and His mercy are recurring themes. We are reminded that godly leadership is indispensable to the well-being of our community.

[1] The Holy Bible (NIV). (2011). *The Book of First Kings*. Chapter 3, Verse 9.

[2] The Holy Bible (NIV). (2011). *The Book of First Kings*. Chapter 3, Verse 28.

[3] The Holy Bible (NIV). (2011). *The Book of First Kings*. Chapter 11, Verse 11.

Chapter 12

The Book of Second Kings

'As they were walking along and talking together,
suddenly a chariot of fire and horses of fire separated the two of
them, and Elijah went up to heaven in a whirlwind.'

2 Kings 2:11
The Holy Bible (NIV)

Τhe Book of Second Kings continues the narrative of Israel and Judah's history. Second Kings narrates the decline and fall of the northern kingdom of Israel and the southern kingdom of Judah. Second Kings encapsulates the reign of multiple kings, the influence of prophets, the consequences of disobedience to God, and the Israelites' exile. Through these Biblical stories, Second Kings narrates profound lessons on the consequences of idolatry, the importance of obedience to God, the assignment of prophets, and God's sovereignty over creation.

A central theme in Second Kings is Israel and Judah's suffering. This is due to their disobedience to God. A number of kings in both kingdoms follow the immoral conduct of their predecessors. These kings engage in idol worship and forsake their covenant with God. As a consequence, Israel is conquered by the Assyrians because of its idolatry and unfaithfulness to God. Similarly, Judah's immoral kings, although a select few are righteous, such as Hezekiah and Josiah, also experienced divine judgement because of their compromise with idolatry and disobedience to God's command. Obedience to God is crucial to our well-being and national prosperity. Disobedience to God's word results in consequences, both individually and collectively. Even when we do not experience immediate consequences, disobedience against God leads to our spiritual demise.

The people of Israel and Judah were misled into idolatry by their evil kings. King Ahab and his wife, Jezebel became infamous for Baal worship. Not to mention, several succeeding kings continued the illegitimate practice of idolatry. The people of Israel were repeatedly led astray by false gods. Even Judah, despite appointing some righteous kings, its people struggled with idolatry. In particular, King Manasseh of Judah was one of the most idolatrous kings. King Manasseh engaged in occult practices and sacrificed his son. This sinful conduct brought about God's judgement upon the kingdom of Judah. As a consequence, Judah capitulated to the Babylonian empire.

Idolatry—placing anything or anyone above God—embodies destructive consequences. Idolatry corrupts the heart, it results in spiritual apathy and God's judgement. Anything that assumes the pre-eminent position of God in our life—whether material possessions, political power, or desires of the flesh—becomes an idol and leads to our downfall. We must remain circumspect and vigilant against evil. The pervasive effects of sin must not define our life.

Throughout Second Kings, we witness the prophets guide the kingdom of Israel and Judah back to faithfulness in God. In Second Kings, Elijah and Elisha are the pivotal prophetic figures. Prophet Elisha performs many miracles and he continues in Prophet Elijah's legacy after the latter prophet's blessed ascent to heaven. These two prophets not only performed miracles, they courageously confronted kings and rulers, informing them to repent. Prophets perform an instrumental function to guide humanity to live according to God's word. Prophets proclaim the truth in times of moral decadence. They provide God's counsel, even when it is unpopular amongst the people. We must comprehend the truth of God's word, especially when it challenges our beliefs, thoughts, ideas, and actions. We must observe the message of God's prophets. God's word is a source of correction and guidance for humanity.

Throughout Second Kings, we witness God's sovereignty over worldly rulers. Whether the kings of Israel or Judah were righteous or immoral, God remained in control of their rise and fall. For instance, consider King Hezekiah's prayer for deliverance from the Assyrian King Sennacherib resulted in Hezekiah's miraculous victory. This historical event demonstrates God controls the destiny of individuals, leaders, and nations.

King Hezekiah was humble and repentant in his prayer before God, 'LORD, the God of Israel, enthroned between the cherubim, you alone are God over all the kingdoms of the earth. You have made heaven and earth. Give ear, LORD, and hear; open your eyes, LORD, and see; listen to the words Sennacherib has sent to ridicule the living God.'[1]

Likewise, when the people of Judah were exiled to Babylon, it was a consequence of God's judgement. Nonetheless, God demonstrated mercy. God permitted the people of Judah to return to their homeland several years later. God is sovereign over creation. No matter how chaotic the world, God's providence prevails. God is in control, even in times of uncertainty, loss, or suffering. Kings, queens, dukes, princes, empires, and nations rise and fall in accordance with God's will. In Second Kings, we learn that God employs sinful rulers to fulfil His providence on earth.

Throughout Israel and Judah's history, we witness when the people ignore God's word, they experience destructive consequences. For instance, during the reign of King Josiah, the long-lost Book of the Law is discovered in the Temple of the LORD. Upon listening to the words in this book, King Josiah tore his clothes and mourned because of his people's disobedience. King Josiah initiated reforms to ensure the kingdom of Judah obeyed God. Despite King Josiah's well-intended efforts, the people's hearts remained hardened. Ultimately, the people of Judah experienced God's judgement with their exile to Babylon. When we ignore or neglect God's word, this leads to our spiritual demise and national disaster. The Holy Bible is our guiding light in life. When we fail to read, understand, and apply its principles, we invite spiritual demise into our life. Our spiritual strength and transformation materialise, when we return to the timeless truth of God's word.

The Biblical story of King Josiah demonstrates the transformative power of repentance, prayer, worship, and obedience to God. When King Josiah discovered the Book of the Law, he realised how far Judah had diverged from God's command. Josiah immediately tore his clothes. He repented and initiated a series of national reforms, which included the destruction of idols and reinstatement of worship of God in the temple. Despite King Josiah's commendable efforts, the people's hearts remained hardened. As a result, God's judgement for Judah was not revoked. Nonetheless, King Josiah demonstrates humility, repentance, and confession in the midst of difficult times.

Humility, repentance, and confession are preconditions for our restoration, no matter how significant our spiritual demise. Spiritual growth and development commence with a change in our heart and mind. We must transform our heart and mind to concur with God's word. We must seek God's forgiveness, and initiate fundamental changes that align with God's will. However, as King Josiah demonstrates, individual repentance does not always prevent national judgement. When the people reject God's word, then His judgement is all but inevitable.

Prophet Elisha's ministry is evidence of God's provision for those who serve God faithfully. Prophet Elisha performed many miracles. For example, Prophet Elisha provided provision for the widow to repay her debts. Prophet Elisha restored the Shunammite woman's son back to life. Prophet Elisha healed the Syrian General Naaman of leprosy. Throughout Prophet Elisha's ministry, we witness God's grace towards humanity. God demonstrates His sovereignty. God reveals that He performs the impossible, when people place their trust and confidence in Him. God provides for the people who faithfully serve and trust in Him. When we trust in God, this allows us to experience His faithfulness, even in seemingly impossible circumstances. When we rely upon God, He provides in ways that exceed our expectations.

The reign of kings, both good and evil, demonstrates the profound impact of leadership upon the kingdoms of Israel and Judah. Righteous kings, such as Hezekiah and Josiah guided their people to spiritual reform and sought God's favour. In contrast, immoral kings, such as Ahab and Manasseh guided the people into idolatry and sin. The king's decrees exhibit a considerable effect on the people's relationship with God. Ultimately, these royal decrees determined the fate of both kingdoms. Leadership matters. Godly leadership is indispensable, whether it is in the family, workplace, school, church, university, community, or nation. Leaders establish the rules and set the expectations for their people. Godly leadership that seeks God's will in all things leads to prosperity, joy, and peace. On the other hand, corrupt and immoral leadership leads to moral decadence and divine judgement. We must pray and seek the appointment of godly leaders who are committed to righteousness in the community.

Following the decline of Israel and the exile of Judah, God remains faithful to His covenant. God's covenant with King David and His promises to the Israelites are not nullified by the unfaithfulness of Israel and Judah's immoral kings. Second Kings concludes on a positive note. Jehoiachin, the king of Judah is released from prison by the Babylonian king. This reveals that God's covenant to preserve a remnant of the Davidic line remains intact. God's promises do not change. God's promises are faithful, reliable, and honourable. Even when our circumstances are unfavourable, God is faithful to His covenant. God's providence is not at the behest of worldly leaders. God honours His promises, even when His chosen people are unfaithful. This is the unchanging reality of God's goodness, grace, sovereignty, and love.

Second Kings constitutes a detailed account of the consequences of idolatry, disobedience, and the rejection of God's word. Second Kings highlights the importance of obedience. We learn about the indispensable function of prophets. God's sovereignty in world history is undeniable. Humanity's repentance and reform are real possibilities. Second Kings is an important reminder to humanity, that despite God's judgement of our sin, His mercy and faithfulness remain ever-present. God provides a pathway to redemption, for those who earnestly repent before Him. Second Kings underscores the requirement for godly leadership, repentance, and a sincere heart that seeks God above all else.

[1] The Holy Bible (NIV). (2011). *The Book of Second Kings.* Chapter 19, Verses 15-16.

Chapter 13

The Book of First Chronicles

'Jabez cried out to the God of Israel,
'Oh, that you would bless me and enlarge my territory!
Let your hand be with me,
and keep me from harm so that I will be free from pain.'
And God granted his request.'

1 Chronicles 4:10
The Holy Bible (NIV)

The Book of First Chronicles contains a historical account of Israel's history. First Chronicles details the reign of King David. It narrates the establishment of Israel's monarchy. First Chronicles describes the preparatory work for the construction of the Temple of God. The scripture within First Chronicles overlaps with the Books of First and Second Samuel. First Chronicles presents a thought-provoking theological examination of Israel's history. First Chronicles emphasises God's covenant with His chosen people. We learn about the importance of worship. We are reminded of the Davidic line's significance. Last but not least, God's faithfulness is reaffirmed.

The opening chapters of First Chronicles are defined by genealogies. This theological exercise constitutes more than just a historical recollection of important figures. This genealogy establishes the faithfulness of God to His covenant with His chosen people. This genealogy traces the lineage of Israel, from the first human created by God, Adam, through to King David. This genealogy emphasises the faithfulness of God's covenant made to Abraham and his descendants. This historical record is indispensable because it demonstrates God's faithfulness to His chosen people, despite their failures, mistakes, and moral transgressions. We learn that God is faithful to His covenant with His chosen people. This genealogy reminds us that God is at work in the lives of individuals and nations throughout world history. God fulfils His promises. In the fullness of time, God brings His providence to fruition. We trust in God's faithfulness. We are reminded that God's providence is not frustrated by our infirmities.

One of the significant themes in First Chronicles is worship. A substantial part of First Chronicles focuses on King David's preparation for the construction of the temple in Jerusalem. The temple's construction is completed by his son and future King of Israel, Solomon. King David's dedication to God is evident in his organisation of the Levites and priests. King David assigns them specific duties related to the performance of music, the management of offerings and sacrifices, the administration of justice, and worship to God. During King David's tenure, worship is a pivotal attribute of the Israelites way of life. King David is a devoted leader. David ensures worship of God is institutionalised and maintained throughout the kingdom.

Worship is instrumental to the believer's life and the community of God's chosen people. Just as King David prioritises construction of the holy temple for God's spiritual presence, we too are encouraged to prioritise worship in our life. First Chronicles teaches us that worship involves consistency, dedication, integrity, and commitment. Worship must be a priority in our life. Worship is a reflection of our intimate relationship with God.

First Chronicles characterises David as an honourable king. David was not esteemed because of his values, character, virtues, appearance, personality, accomplishments, or military victories. God's word informs us that David's greatness was a result of being 'a man after my own heart.'[1] Obedience to God's word is what distinguishes David from other worldly leaders. Despite David's flaws, he is remembered as a godly leader. David sought God's guidance. David worshipped God with sincerity. Not to mention, David desired to honour God above all else. When David conceived his vision to build the LORD's Temple, he did so with a heart of devotion. However, God did not permit King David to construct the temple because he was a man of war, 'You have shed much blood and have fought many wars. You are not to build a house for my Name ... But you will have a son who will be a man of peace and rest ... His name will be Solomon ... He is the one who will build a house for my Name.'[2]

As a result of God's command, King David's untiring efforts were directed to procure valuable resources and prepare the foundation for his son and successor to the throne, Solomon, to build the temple. God values the content of our heart above our appearance, status, wealth, education, property, or achievements. King David's desire to honour God, even when he was not permitted to fulfil his vision, demonstrates that God desires a heart that is humble, obedient, and seeks to glorify Him, rather than secure fortune, wealth, pecuniary gain, status, prestige, or fame. This Biblical narrative teaches us that our motives to serve God are just as important as our actions.

In First Chronicles, King David's charismatic leadership is characterised by a vision to serve God. David fulfils his duty to the people. In addition, David guides the Israelites in prayer and worship. King David appoints leaders to assist him in the governance of the kingdom. King David appoints leaders in the military, administrative, political, legal, and religious functions of Israelite society. King David proclaims a new spiritual vision for Israel. A vision that is defined by the worship of God in Jerusalem. King David's leadership is not about the possession of power, but about the realisation of God's providence for Israel.

Leadership in God's kingdom is about service to humanity, not fame, authority, power, wealth, property, status, or territory. Leaders guide believers with humility. Leaders have a responsibility to faithfully guide believers in their walk with God. Whether in the family, school, church, university, workplace, community, or nation, leaders are responsible to guide their members in worship, obedience, and faithfulness to God's word. Godly leadership is not about the pursuit of self-interest, but about the fulfilment of God's providence.

One of the greatest accomplishments of King David's reign was uniting the tribes of Israel. Following the division of the kingdom of Israel after King Saul's death, King David worked tirelessly to unite the northern and southern tribes under one kingdom. In addition, King David made every effort to bring the Ark of the Covenant to Jerusalem, making its presence the focal point of faith and worship for Israel. Importantly, King David completed this endeavour with honour and reverence for the traditions and customs established by Moses, 'the Levites carried the Ark of God with the poles on their shoulders, as Moses had commanded in accordance with the word of the LORD.'[3] Unity and cooperation amongst God's chosen people is crucial for the fulfilment of God's providence. King David's exceptional effort to unite Israel reminds us that God desires His chosen people to be united in purpose, worship, and mission. Division weakens the congregation. Division obstructs the advancement of God's kingdom on earth. We are commanded to promote reconciliation, prioritise unity, and work harmoniously to fulfil God's providence.

The Biblical story of bringing the Ark of the Covenant to Jerusalem is a significant historical event in First Chronicles. The Ark represents God's spiritual presence amongst His chosen people. King David's joy and reverence in bringing the Ark to Jerusalem reflects the importance of God's spiritual presence in Israel. Nonetheless, King David's satisfaction was overshadowed with despair, when Uzzah handled the Ark in an indifferent manner.

Unfortunately, Uzzah's abysmal failure to treat the Ark with reverence, resulted in his untimely death, 'When they came to the threshing-floor of Kidon, Uzzah reached out his hand to steady the Ark, because the oxen stumbled. The LORD's anger burned against Uzzah, and He struck him down because he had put his hand on the Ark. So he died there before God.'[4] This Biblical narrative highlights the seriousness with which God's holiness must be treated. When we are in the presence of God, respect is of utmost importance. We cannot behave in an indifferent manner. We must treat God's spiritual presence with deference. We must recognise that worship, leadership, discipleship, and fellowship define our conduct in God's spiritual presence. God's spiritual presence is pivotal to our life. We must honour God in all that we do on earth.

King David's prayers and praise acknowledge God's sovereignty over creation. In King David's psalm of thanksgiving, after the Ark was brought to Jerusalem, David exalts God as the creator and sovereign; 'Sing to the LORD, all the earth; proclaim His salvation day after day.'[5] This psalm emphasises that all natural phenomena are subject to God's sovereignty. God's glory and majesty are recognised and honoured by His chosen people. Our acknowledgement of God's sovereignty is essential to maintain a blessed relationship with Him. When we recognise God's sovereignty and authority over creation, we trust God in every circumstance and situation. When we remember that God is in control, this theological fact informs our worship, prayer, and conscience.

King David's reign was defined by righteousness and the administration of justice in the kingdom of Israel. King David honoured God's laws. King David administered justice, and he ensured the Levites and priests were taken care of. Throughout First Chronicles, there is a recurring emphasis on the responsibility of leaders. Godly leaders must be committed to uphold righteousness. Godly leaders ensure that God's standards of justice are honoured. Leaders, whether in government, business, community, workplace, church, school, university, or family, are called to uphold righteousness and justice. Leadership is not about pecuniary gain, status, wealth, profit, private property, or power, but about the realisation of God's providence. We must ensure that God's commandments concerning justice, peace, love, equality, and righteousness are observed for the greater good of humanity.

The Book of First Chronicles teaches humanity important lessons about God's faithfulness to His covenant. We are enlightened of the importance of worship. We are reminded of the centrality of God's spiritual presence. Obedience to God and intergenerational faithfulness are essential to live our life defined by righteousness. Throughout King David's reign, we witness his heart devoted to God. David teaches us the importance of worship and how to faithfully serve and honour God. First Chronicles encourages us to recognise God's sovereignty over creation. We must praise, honour, and glorify God. Last but not least, we are to entrust the invaluable legacy of our faith for the benefit of future generations.

[1] The Holy Bible (NIV). (2011). *The Book of Acts*. Chapter 13, Verse 22.

[2] The Holy Bible (NIV). (2011). *The Book of First Chronicles*. Chapter 22, Verses 8-10.

[3] The Holy Bible (NIV). (2011). *The Book of First Chronicles*. Chapter 15, Verse 15.

[4] The Holy Bible (NIV). (2011). *The Book of First Chronicles*. Chapter 13, Verses 9-10.

[5] The Holy Bible (NIV). (2011). *The Book of First Chronicles*. Chapter 16, Verse 23.

Chapter 14

The Book of Second Chronicles

'But as for you,
be strong and do not give up,
for your work will be rewarded.'

2 Chronicles 15:7
The Holy Bible (NIV)

T he Book of Second Chronicles narrates the history of Judah, from the reign of King Solomon to the Babylonian exile. Second Chronicles presents a comprehensive account of the Davidic dynasty. Second Chronicles underscores the importance of the holy temple in Jerusalem. There is a particular emphasis on immoral kings. Second Chronicles examines the unfaithfulness of several kings towards God. Second Chronicles considers historical events that are similar to those in the Book of First and Second Kings. Nonetheless, Second Chronicles focus is on the people's faithfulness to God's covenant. We learn about the dire consequences of idolatry. We are reminded of the importance of repentance. Last but not least, God's boundless mercy is evident throughout Second Chronicles.

A central theme in Second Chronicles is our worship must be aligned with God's will. It is insufficient to worship God with the observance of rituals, customs, traditions, and cultural practices. The holy temple in Jerusalem holds a prominent and symbolic place in the believer's worship of God. Second Chronicles stresses the importance of faithful worship. King Solomon's prayer of dedication for the temple demonstrates the importance of authenticity in worship. Through worship, we honour God's holiness. Second Chronicles reinforces the faithfulness of the king and his people is interrelated with their worship and prayer to God. Not to mention, God's grace and blessing are contingent upon the people's obedience to His word and their faith.

Through learning about King Solomon's life, we understand that authentic worship comes from a heart of love and obedience to God. Worship is not merely about rituals, music, songs, festivals, and church services. Worship is about how we honour God, obey His command, and acknowledge His holiness. God desires genuine faith, love, respect, and obedience from His chosen people. God is not interested in our superficial acts of worship. Worship of God incorporates our beliefs, thoughts, and actions.

Throughout Second Chronicles, the rise and fall of various kings demonstrates how repentance before God is crucial to forgiveness. When good kings, such as Jehoshaphat and Hezekiah humble themselves before God, repent for their nation's sins, and seek God's mercy, God responds favourably. God grants these honourable kings redemption, grace, mercy, and victory. Conversely, when immoral kings were unfaithful to God's word, particularly those evil kings who led the people into idolatry, God's judgement was effectuated without delay.

Repentance is the method to our restoration. When individuals or nations turn away from sin and seek God's forgiveness, He is merciful and willing to restore them. Second Chronicles teaches humanity that humility and repentance possess the potential to change the course of world history. Through our spiritual transformation, we bring about God's mercy and redemption. Even during difficult times of divine judgement, we must keep our faith in God's goodness.

Several kings in Second Chronicles, such as Asa, Hezekiah, and Jehoshaphat place their trust and confidence in God during times of national crisis. As a result, God redeems these kings from their enemies. For example, consider when King Asa confronted a military threat. King Asa sought God's intervention through prayer. As a result, King Asa secured a miraculous victory against his enemies. Similarly, King Jehoshaphat relied upon God's counsel. As a result, he too was victorious against a formidable enemy.

When we trust in God's providence, sovereignty, mercy, and grace, it brings us victory in our endeavours. Second Chronicles teaches us that when we confront difficulties, we must trust in God and rely upon Him in prayer. This approach leads us to miraculous outcomes. Faith in God, especially in times of crisis, invites God's mercy and grace into our life. When we believe in God, a turnaround is possible in our personal affairs.

Second Chronicles emphasises the responsibility of leaders to guide their people toward faithfulness in God. Good kings, such as Asa, Hezekiah, Jehoshaphat, and Josiah faithfully governed the kingdom of Judah. As a result, God blessed their kingdom with peace, prosperity, and power. However, evil kings, such as Ahaz and Manasseh, brought about God's judgement on their kingdom because of their disobedience, corruption, and idolatry. Second Chronicles teaches us that leaders have a profound impact on the well-being of the people. The actions of a leader either bring about God's blessing or curse. Leaders have the potential to guide a nation into destruction and demise, or alternatively, towards peace and prosperity. This reality underscores the importance of good leadership that guides the people to obey God's word.

A recurring theme in Second Chronicles is the destructive consequences of idolatry on the nation. Several kings, including Manasseh, misguide the people into idol worship. Even though God gave such kings the opportunity to repent from sin, they did not redeem themselves. In the course of world history, we learn of divine consequences, when leaders abandon God's word. Despite King Manasseh's profound sin, coupled with the fact that he misguided the kingdom of Judah into idolatry, God demonstrates mercy when King Manasseh humbled himself in repentance, 'then Manasseh knew that the LORD is God.'[1]

Idolatry and disobedience to God result in profound consequences. While God is compassionate, He does not indefinitely tolerate a continual turning away from His word. Thus, our faithfulness to God is imperative. Idolatry not only dishonours God; however, it leads to personal and national ruin. Second Chronicles teaches us that God's mercy must not be taken for granted. We must not assume God's forbearance with humanity's sin is inexhaustible. We must avoid moral compromise with sin. The powerful temptation of sin cannot be satisfied, period.

The kings of Judah and Israel rise and fall in accordance with God's will. For example, consider the fall of Jerusalem is a direct consequence of Judah's disobedience to God. Nonetheless, in the midst of God's judgement, His grace and mercy are evident. The return of the exiled Israelites to their homeland, demonstrates that when God's people are punished for their misconduct, God's providence still prevails. God's providence is not obstructed by our failures, errors, mistakes, faults, imperfections, or weaknesses. God is sovereign over the destiny of empires, nations, kings, and queens. God's providence prevails, even when we determine choices that are contrary to His providence. Whether in times of judgement, mercy, or restoration, God's providence and sovereignty cannot be superseded. This divine knowledge encourages believers to trust in God's goodness and mercy during difficult circumstances.

The temple in Jerusalem is the epicentre of God's spiritual presence on earth and the focal point of Israel's worship. Second Chronicles provides details on the construction of Solomon's temple and its dedication to God. King Hezekiah's social reforms and King Josiah's revival of worship to God demonstrate how the temple was pivotal to the people of Judah. The destruction of the temple symbolises God's judgement upon the kingdom for its people's unfaithfulness.

Second Chronicles concludes with the power of hope after the Babylonian exile of the people of Judah. King Cyrus of Persia decrees the exiled Israelites return to Jerusalem and reconstruct their temple; 'The LORD, the God of Heaven, has given me all the kingdoms of the earth and He has appointed me to build a temple for Him at Jerusalem in Judah. Any of His people among you may go up and may the LORD their God be with them.'[2] This consequential event in world history characterises the beginning of Israel's restoration.

The aforementioned historical event reflects God's goodness, grace, mercy, and faithfulness. God honours His promises to redeem His chosen people from exile in Babylon, despite their sin, unfaithfulness, and disobedience. God's mercy offers humanity hope, despite His divine judgement. The return of the Israelites from exile demonstrates, that even in our darkest moments, God offers us a newfound path to freedom, peace, restoration, and prosperity. When we repent and turn to God, He restores us, just as He did with the Israelites.

Desirable attributes which defined the reign of King Hezekiah, Jehoshaphat, and Josiah include their dependence on prayer and God's counsel during their kingship. For example, consider King Jehoshaphat sought God's guidance when confronted with an army that vastly outnumbered his armed forces. God responded to King Jehoshaphat's request with deliverance. Similarly, King Hezekiah prayed when he confronted the Assyrian invasion. As a result, God miraculously redeemed the kingdom of Judah with a resounding victory.

Prayer and God's guidance are vital in every circumstance, whether in times of loss, national crisis, grief, suffering, or uncertainty. The aforementioned examples of these righteous kings demonstrate that turning to God in prayer brings us guidance, peace, protection, forgiveness, victory, and redemption. Prayer is an acknowledgement of our dependence upon God. Prayer is an invitation for God's intervention in our personal affairs.

The remarkable historical accounts of King Hezekiah and Josiah highlight the power of spiritual transformation. Both these honourable and righteous kings decreed major religious reforms to restore worship of the living God. Hezekiah and Josiah put an end to idol worship in the kingdom of Judah. They also reinstituted observance of God's commandments in the kingdom. Their royal reforms were accompanied by a return to covenant faithfulness and a renewal of the people's commitment to God. Spiritual renewal and mindfulness bring about our transformation. In the midst of sin, evil, and idolatry, leaders must turn to God. Leaders are responsible to guide members of the community on the path of righteousness. Reform commences with our repentance and commitment to obey God's word.

The Book of Second Chronicles teaches humanity important lessons about the necessity of faith, worship, the function of godly leadership, the power of repentance, and the centrality of our obedience to God. These factors collectively determine our spiritual well-being. Second Chronicles emphasises God's sovereignty, the importance of prayer, and the requirement for our spiritual reform. Second Chronicles concludes with a message of hope and restoration. Second Chronicles reveals that following divine judgement, God's boundless mercy offers us a pathway back to Him. God's redeeming grace results in a future defined by renewal, rejuvenation, and restoration. Second Chronicles encourages us to remain faithful to God. We trust in God's sovereignty. We demonstrate confidence in God's providence. Our life must be characterised by commitment, love, and obedience to God.

[1] The Holy Bible (NIV). (2011). *The Book of Second Chronicles*. Chapter 33, Verse 13.
[2] The Holy Bible (NIV). (2011). *The Book of Second Chronicles*. Chapter 36, Verse 23.

Chapter 15

The Book of Ezra

'Rise up; this matter is in your hands.
We will support you,
so take courage and do it.'

Ezra 10:4
The Holy Bible (NIV)

The Book of Ezra focuses on the exiled Israelites return from Babylon to Jerusalem. We learn about the reconstruction of the temple, and the re-establishment of the community's religious practices. The Book of Ezra is a Biblical story of restoration, revival, and renewal. In addition, Ezra is a profound narrative that underscores the importance of obedience to God's command. Through Ezra, we learn about godly leadership, spiritual transformation, and the challenges associated with being faithful in difficult circumstances.

One of the themes in the Book of Ezra is God's faithfulness to His covenant. After seventy years of captivity in Babylon, the return of the exiled Israelites to their homeland constitutes a fulfilment of God's covenant. This restoration is not due to the virtue of the Israelites, but because God is faithful to His covenant. God fulfils His covenant, even when the circumstances are unfavourable, or when His chosen people are unfaithful. God is sovereign. God's providence comes to fruition according to His will and timing. We trust God to honour His covenant with us, just as He did with the Israelites.

Ezra is a scribe and faithful teacher of the Mosaic law. Throughout the Book of Ezra, there is an emphasis that people adhere to God's word. Ezra was appointed by God to lead the Israelites to obey God's word. The reconstruction of the temple was not only a physical assignment, but also a spiritual one. The temple's reconstruction requires the people's faithfulness to God. Obedience to God's word is pivotal to our spiritual transformation. It is not sufficient to merely read or recite God's word. We must effectuate the Biblical principles we learn into practice. We attain our spiritual transformation, when we apply God's word in our life.

Ezra's commitment to study, observe, and teach the Mosaic law demonstrates the importance to apply God's command in our life. In addition, we must assist members of the community to understand and live in accordance with God's word. Throughout the scripture, we learn that Ezra 'devoted himself to the study and observance of the Law of the LORD, and to teaching its decrees and laws in Israel.'[1]

Ezra's leadership performed an instrumental function in the spiritual and religious revival of the returning Israelites. Ezra was a priest and scribe. Ezra was a spiritual leader who led the Israelites in repentance, worship, and obedience to God's command. Ezra's faith-based leadership, combined with the righteousness of King Cyrus of Persia, ensured the temple's reconstruction. Honourable leadership is imperative to guide the people in their relationship with God. Leaders who prioritise God's word, obey Him, and guide humanity to live faithfully are crucial to foster spiritual renewal across the community. Leaders must demonstrate obedience to God's command. Leaders must educate humanity in God's word. Leaders must guide believers toward repentance and holiness.

Ezra demonstrates commitment to prayer. Ezra seeks God's guidance for the Israelites. Before the Israelites return to Jerusalem, Ezra proclaims a fast. Ezra recognises the Israelites dependence upon God for their journey home, 'there, by the Ahava Canal, I proclaimed a fast, so that we might humble ourselves before our God and ask Him for a safe journey.'[2] In addition, Ezra prayed in response to the people's sins. Ezra sought God's mercy, grace, and forgiveness. Ezra's prayers were characterised by humility, confession, and appeal to God's compassionate nature. Prayer is an integral part of the believer's life. Prayer acknowledges our dependence upon God. Prayer invites God's counsel and wisdom into our life. Ezra's prayer demonstrates the importance of humility and repentance. We must recognise God's holiness and sovereignty. We must accept the reality that humanity is in dire need of God's mercy.

In times of difficulty and uncertainty, prayer is essential to secure God's favour, grace, and wisdom.

The reconstruction of the temple confronted significant opposition from the surrounding enemies, such as the Samaritans. God's word narrates that the enemies of Judah obstructed the Israelites reconstruction endeavour, they 'bribed officials to work against them and frustrate their plans during the entire reign of Cyrus king of Persia and down to the reign of Darius king of Persia.'[3] Despite the enemies' threats, opposition, and discouragement, the reconstruction of the temple continued with God's blessing and the godly leadership of Ezra and Zerubbabel. This Biblical event is an example of God's providence.

The opposition did not obstruct the Israelites reconstruction efforts. The restoration of the temple was successfully completed with God's grace, favour, and blessing. Likewise, restoration in any area of our life, whether moral, emotional, intellectual, social, psychological, financial, or spiritual, requires persistence, especially in the midst of opposition or discouragement. Just as the Israelites confronted opposition, we too confront challenges when we complete our God-given assignment. The indispensable elements to our success are trust in God's covenant and confidence in His faithfulness.

Ezra's principled leadership underscores the importance of community for the Israelites. The reconstruction of the temple and the re-establishment of worship in Jerusalem was a community effort. The Israelites worked together. They rebuilt the altar and thereafter, celebrated the Feast of Tabernacles. Ezra's proclamation of the law in the presence of the Israelites, and the subsequent covenant renewal, emphasises that God's chosen people must collectively worship and serve Him. Community is vital to our worship and service to God. Our faith is not an individual journey, but a communal one. We are to encourage, support, and promote accountability in our worship and service to God. To strengthen the body of Christ requires cooperation, mutual support, and commitment.

When Ezra discovered the Israelites sin, in particular idolatry, his response was one of remorse, reflection, and repentance. Ezra requested the Israelites to confess their sin to God. The Israelites responded with collective repentance. As a result, the Israelites experienced spiritual renewal and restoration of their covenant relationship with God. Confession and repentance lead to our restoration. The Book of Ezra demonstrates that when God's chosen people humble themselves, confess their sins, and return to God, He responds with forgiveness and restoration. We always find hope in God's mercy, no matter how far we have strayed from Him.

God employed the Persian King Cyrus to fulfil His divine promise to return the exiled Israelites to Jerusalem. Despite not being a believer of the Most High God, Cyrus the Great was an instrumental character in God's providence to restore the Israelites to the promised land. The Persian King Cyrus issued a proclamation by royal decree, to facilitate the return of the Israelites to Jerusalem. This historical event highlights that God employs believers and non-believers alike to accomplish His providence. God's providence is not limited by our expectation, belief, experience, social status, education, authority, knowledge, wealth, or power. God can employ any person, including those who may not share our faith, to accomplish His providence. This theological fact encourages us to trust in God's sovereignty. We must remember that God's providence is at work, even when we cannot perceive how the future unfolds.

The restoration of Israel was not only a physical restoration of the temple and the city's walls. This historical event also constituted the people's spiritual transformation. The Israelites not only rebuilt the physical structures of their city, temple, and homes; however, they recommenced worship of God and observance of His commandments. This renewal involved a change of heart and a commitment to obey God's word. Spiritual renewal is not merely characterised by external changes in our life and society. Spiritual renewal involves a psychological transformation of our being that aligns our values, ideas, beliefs, priorities, thoughts, and actions with God's will. Authentic restoration incorporates a transformation of the spiritual, emotional, moral, and ethical dimensions of our being. God encourages us to not only rebuild what is broken, but also to renew our heart, mind, and spirit in obedience to Him.

The Book of Ezra offers profound lessons on God's faithfulness and the importance of our obedience to God's word. The Book of Ezra underscores the importance of prayer, repentance, and community life in our spiritual transformation. The Book of Ezra demonstrates that when God's chosen people humble themselves and turn to Him, He is faithful to restore and bless them. Ezra's distinguished example of dedication to God's word, commitment to holiness, and persistence in the midst of opposition, offers guidance to believers. We too must honour God and realise His providence in our lifetime.

[1] The Holy Bible (NIV). (2011). *The Book of Ezra.* Chapter 7, Verse 10.
[2] The Holy Bible (NIV). (2011). *The Book of Ezra.* Chapter 8, Verse 21.
[3] The Holy Bible (NIV). (2011). *The Book of Ezra.* Chapter 4, Verse 5.

Chapter 16

The Book of Nehemiah

'By day you led them with a pillar of cloud,
and by night with a pillar of fire
to give them light on the way they were to take.'

Nehemiah 9:12
The Holy Bible (NIV)

T he Book of Nehemiah chronicles the reconstruction of the walls of Jerusalem. Nehemiah acquaints us with the spiritual renewal of the Israelite community after their return from exile. The Book of Nehemiah focuses on Nehemiah's charismatic and godly leadership. We learn about the challenges Nehemiah and the Israelites confront to restore Jerusalem's walls. The Israelites demonstrate commendable efforts to re-establish faithfulness and loyalty to the Most High God. Nehemiah was a cupbearer to King Artaxerxes of Persia. Nehemiah was a man of good fame and character; he served in the king's royal court. God assigned Nehemiah the mission to lead the Israelites to rebuild Jerusalem's walls.

Nehemiah's journey demonstrates that God does not always employ religious leaders or prominent figures to accomplish His providence. God can employ any person who is faithful and obedient to Him. God employs ordinary people to accomplish His extraordinary providence, regardless of their citizenship, education, social status, power, wealth, knowledge, experience, age, sex, vocation, or position. Our faithfulness and willingness to serve God are the most important factors. In a symbolic step of faith, Nehemiah's journey begins with prayer, 'When I heard these things, I sat down and wept. For some days I mourned and fasted and prayed before the God of Heaven.'[1] Before Nehemiah determined a new course of action, he sought God's counsel. Nehemiah expressed sorrow for the current state of Jerusalem. Nehemiah beseeched God to bestow him favour with the king, 'and because the gracious hand of my God was on me, the king granted my requests.'[2]

Nehemiah repeatedly turns to God in prayer before he makes important decisions or resolves significant challenges. Prayer is the foundation of our actions. In moments of uncertainty or difficulty, we must seek God's wisdom through prayer. Through

God's grace, Nehemiah possessed a purposeful vision and exhibited strong leadership for the Israelites to rebuild Jerusalem's walls. Nehemiah was strategic, well-organised, and focused on the mission at hand. In addition, Nehemiah knew how to inspire and motivate the Israelites to work effectively, despite the constant opposition they encountered. Nehemiah's godly leadership was characterised by courage, wisdom, accountability, honesty, and integrity. Effective leadership requires vision, strategy, values, organisation, and charisma to inspire members of the community. Leaders guide believers by personal example. Leaders work alongside the believers whom they inspire.

Nehemiah confronted relentless opposition from Geshem, Sanballat, and Tobiah. These three figures disparaged the Israelites. They intimidated the Israelites from completing their monumental assignment—the reconstruction of Jerusalem's walls. For example, consider the following message by Sanballat, 'What are those feeble Jews doing? Will they restore their wall? Will they offer sacrifices? Will they finish in a day? Can they bring the stones back to life from those heaps of rubble—burned as they are?'[3] Nehemiah responded with faith. Nehemiah prayed to God for strength and perseverance in the midst of intimidation. Nehemiah encouraged the Israelites to remain vigilant and focused on their mission. When we observe God's word and further His providence, opposition is inevitable. Therefore, we must confront challenges with faith, confidence, and trust in God's mercy, sovereignty, and grace. We must continue to work towards the completion of our assignment, despite the discouragement that we encounter along our journey.

The reconstruction of Jerusalem's walls was a community effort. Each group of workers was assigned a section of the wall to rebuild. This collective effort demonstrated the unquestionable power of unity and cooperation to achieve a common objective.

Unity and cooperation are essential attributes to accomplish our assignment. When we work together, we combine our unique strengths, talents, knowledge, skills, expertise, and abilities. When we work together, we transcend obstacles. The synergy of community accomplishes grand objectives for the advancement and betterment of society.

Nehemiah was committed to social justice and integrity in his leadership and assignment. Nehemiah confronted corruption amongst the leaders and people, such as the exploitation of less fortunate people, 'What you are doing is not right. Shouldn't you walk in the fear of our God to avoid the reproach of our Gentile enemies?'[4] As a matter of principle, Nehemiah refused to take advantage of his esteemed position. Nehemiah did not accept privileges that are part and parcel of a pre-eminent leadership position. Nehemiah established a good example of selflessness and accountability. Integrity and accountability are fundamental to godly leadership. Leaders must be honest, fair, and serve with commitment to benefit the community. Godly leaders position the welfare of community members above their self-interest.

Once the walls of Jerusalem were rebuilt, Nehemiah organised a spiritual transformation of the Israelites. The Israelites confessed their sins. They repented and recommitted themselves to God. This spiritual renewal was characterised by understanding and obedience to God's word. A renewed commitment to worship God, and a pledge to obey His command is indispensable to our transformation. Spiritual renewal requires our repentance. We must demonstrate our commitment to God's word. The personification of God's grace is our willingness to enact significant changes that align with God's will. Personal transformation commences with our heart and mind. Our transformation involves a renewal in our thought, speech, and conduct.

Nehemiah's extraordinary journey was not smooth sailing. Nehemiah encountered several setbacks from the enemies of Judah. These setbacks included rumours, threats, and discouragement. Nonetheless, Nehemiah remained persistent in his assignment to rebuild Jerusalem's walls. Nehemiah's ability to remain focused and keep the Israelites motivated reveals the importance of perseverance when we endeavour to fulfil God's providence. Perseverance is indispensable when we confront obstacles. Even when our circumstances are unfavourable, perseverance to perform God's will leads us to success in our endeavours. Faithfulness in our confrontation with adversity brings God's providence to fulfilment.

The proclamation of the Law by Ezra brought the people to tears. The Israelites realised how far they had strayed from God's command. Thereafter, the Israelites renewed their commitment to God's word. When we renew our commitment to God, this action has the ability to redefine our life. In addition, we must prioritise to read, learn, and apply God's word in our life. This allows us to attain a profound understanding of God's will for our life. We are responsible for the advancement of our spiritual growth and development. The greater the time and effort we dedicate to study God's word, the greater our opportunity to reflect upon it and implement its timeless principles in our life.

The reconstruction of Jerusalem's walls was completed in record time—fifty-two days! This accomplishment put Nehemiah's enemies on notice, 'all the surrounding nations were afraid and lost their self-confidence, because they realised that this work had been done with the help of our God.'[5] Thereafter, the Israelites celebrated 'joyfully the dedication with songs of thanksgiving and with the music of cymbals, harps, and lyres.'[6] They praised God for His faithfulness. This monumental community celebration, upon the completion of Nehemiah's assignment, demonstrates the importance to honour the realisation of God's providence. We must express our heartfelt thanks for God's provision, wisdom, and guidance in our life. Celebration and thanksgiving are indispensable aspects of community life. We must take the time to thank God for what He has done in our life. We must recognise that every victory is a priceless gift from God.

The Book of Nehemiah teaches humanity several important lessons in relation to prayer, leadership, unity, integrity, the collective power of community, and the importance of spiritual renewal. Nehemiah demonstrates the fulfilment of our assignment requires perseverance. We learn to confront opposition with faith. We are reminded that our commitment to God's word must be resolute. Nehemiah's fine example of leadership, accountability, and service provide an ideal model for believers today. Nehemiah's journey encourages believers to trust in God's providence. We must cooperate as a community to further God's providence. We must steadily work towards the completion of our assignment.

[1] The Holy Bible (NIV). (2011). *The Book of Nehemiah*. Chapter 1, Verse 4.

[2] The Holy Bible (NIV). (2011). *The Book of Nehemiah*. Chapter 2, Verse 8.

[3] The Holy Bible (NIV). (2011). *The Book of Nehemiah*. Chapter 4, Verse 2.

[4] The Holy Bible (NIV). (2011). *The Book of Nehemiah*. Chapter 5, Verse 9.

[5] The Holy Bible (NIV). (2011). *The Book of Nehemiah*. Chapter 6, Verse 16.

[6] The Holy Bible (NIV). (2011). *The Book of Nehemiah*. Chapter 12, Verse 27.

Chapter 17

The Book of Esther

'For if you remain silent at this time,
relief and deliverance for the Jews will arise from another place,
but you and your father's family will perish.
And who knows but that you have come to your royal position for
such a time as this?'

Esther 4:14
The Holy Bible (NIV)

T he Book of Esther is a Biblical narrative of God's providence. This book captivates our imagination. Esther demonstrates remarkable fortitude. Esther's story is a testimony to the triumph of good over evil. The events in scripture take place during the reign of Persian King Xerxes. This Biblical narrative is based on a Jewish woman named Esther, who becomes the Queen of Persia. Queen Esther performs a pivotal function to redeem the Israelites from annihilation. In the process, Esther realises her God-given destiny. Although God is not explicitly mentioned in the Book of Esther, God's providence guides Esther to rescue His chosen people.

In the Book of Esther, God's providence is a central theme. We witness God's providence in action through three perfectly timed events. First, Esther's ascension to the throne as Queen of Persia. Second, Mordecai's discovery of an evil scheme to assassinate King Xerxes. Third, the reversal of fortune in relation to Haman's evil stratagem. These three significant historical events demonstrate that God's providence and sovereignty are unassailable. God is at work behind the scenes to protect His chosen people. These monumental events unfold in such a manner that makes God's sovereignty indisputable. God is at work, even when we do not perceive it. God orchestrates worldly events in a manner that aligns with His providence. God utilises unexpected circumstances and ordinary individuals to accomplish His will. We trust in God's sovereignty, mercy, justice, and providence. God is our guiding light, especially in times of uncertainty.

One of the significant themes in the Book of Esther is courage. The moral courage to do what is right. Queen Esther demonstrates incredible bravery when she risks her life to approach King Xerxes uninvited. Through Queen Esther's reply to Mordecai, we learn that she responds to the situation at hand with wisdom and finesse, 'Go, gather together all the Jews who are in Susa, and fast for me. Do not eat or drink for three days, night or day. I and my attendants will fast as you do. When this is done, I will go to the king, even though it is against the law. And if I perish, I perish.'[1]

Queen Esther does not retreat from the challenge to confront King Xerxes about Haman's evil plot, even though this meeting could have resulted in her untimely death. Courage is necessary to stand up for what is right, especially when human life is in peril. Faithful action in the midst of danger or adversity brings about God's deliverance. The Biblical story of Esther teaches humanity that God encourages us to affirm our faith, even when the consequences of our altruistic actions are uncertain.

Esther was an ordinary woman who found herself in an extraordinary situation. Esther's rise to queenship was not of her own strength, desire, or ambition, however, it was secured by God's grace. Esther was not of noble birth; her upbringing was modest. Queen Esther did not seek power, wealth, status, property, glory, or fame. Having said that, God employed Queen Esther in a crucial moment in world history to bring about the salvation of the Jewish people. Queen Esther's remarkable story teaches us that God can employ any person—even a person who is ordinary or insignificant—to fulfil His providence. We must be receptive to God's providence. We trust that God utilises our gifts, position, abilities, skills, talent, expertise, knowledge, and circumstances, no matter how inconsequential they are, for the fulfilment of His providence.

Queen Esther requests the Jewish people to fast and pray to God for three days, before she approaches King Xerxes. Queen Esther's humility and dependence upon God demonstrates the importance of divine counsel and intervention in times of personal or national crisis. Prayer and fasting are powerful instruments to seek God's guidance, blessing, and favour. When we confront challenges or difficult decisions, it is imperative that we humble ourselves before God. We must seek God's will through prayer, fasting, and intercession.

The evil figure of Haman stands in stark contrast to Queen Esther and Mordecai's good character. Haman's pride, anger, and hatred of Mordecai lead him to plot the destruction of the Jewish people. Haman's demise is a direct result of his arrogance and unwillingness to humble himself. Pride and arrogance lead to our destruction. Haman's tragic story reveals how unchecked pride, hatred, and selfish ambition ultimately lead to one's downfall. On the other hand, the attribute of humility is honoured by God. Herein we are reminded of the Biblical principle that God opposes the proud; however, He gives grace to the humble person.

It is no coincidence that the consequential events in the Book of Esther unfold in God's perfect timing. For example, consider Esther is chosen as Persia's Queen at an opportune time. Mordecai uncovers the plot to assassinate King Xerxes at a pivotal moment in world history. King Xerxes experiences difficulty sleeping the night before Queen Esther's intervention. This leads King Xerxes to rediscover Mordecai's good deeds. Without a doubt, God's providence was at work. God's providence ensured that every moment was perfectly timed to facilitate the redemption of His chosen people. God's timing is always perfect, even when we do not understand it. There are moments in our life, when we perceive our objectives are not fulfilled, milestones are not accomplished, or desired progress is not realised. However, God's providence comes to fruition at exactly the right moment. Queen Esther's story teaches us that confidence in God's providence is important.

Queen Esther's willingness to confront evil in the form of Haman's genocide plot against the Jewish people demonstrates the importance to stand up for what is the morally right course of action. Queen Esther could have remained silent and permitted this horrific ordeal to unfold. Instead, Queen Esther utilised her royal position of influence to intervene and redeem her people from tragedy. Moral courage is necessary to stand up against injustice, even when doing so entails personal risk. Queen Esther's willingness to act, despite the personal risk involved teaches us the importance of courage. We must ensure truth and righteousness prevail, even when we confront great opposition or personal danger. We must take decisive action when impediments arise along our journey.

In the end, Haman's evil plot against Mordecai is unravelled. Haman is undone. King Xerxes orders Haman's execution, 'so they impaled Haman on the pole he had set up for Mordecai.'[2] Haman's fate is an important reminder that God's justice prevails in the end. Evil may temporarily possess the advantage; however, God's providence ultimately prevails. Those who are oppressed are liberated. Those who act with malice are punished. God's justice prevails on earth. When evil is pervasive in the world, God's sovereignty is not subject to dispute. God ensures justice is done in His timing. We secure peace in the knowledge that malevolent people do not go unpunished. We find peace in the knowledge that God vindicates oppressed people.

Queen Esther possessed influence and goodwill with King Xerxes. The scripture informs us that King Xerxes responded to Queen Esther upon her approach, 'What is it, Queen Esther? What is your request? Even up to half the kingdom, it will be given you.'[3] Notably, Queen Esther utilised her royal position wisely to rescue her people from imminent danger. Queen Esther did not act out of self-interest. Queen Esther did not remain silent or misappropriate her royal position for personal gain, but rather, she acted for the greater good of the community.

We all possess influence to varying degrees. Whether our influence is small or great, every person makes a consequential difference in the world. Queen Esther's righteous example teaches us that we must utilise our position, knowledge, resources, wealth, expertise, and influence to promote good, advocate for social justice, and advance God's providence. Our influence must be employed for the egalitarian benefit of humanity. We must not merely employ our influence to advance our self-interest, maximise pecuniary gain, or enhance our reputation.

While Queen Esther performed a pivotal function in redeeming the Jewish people, her success was not achieved alone. Queen Esther called on the Jewish community to fast and pray with her. Queen Esther demonstrates the power of collective action and solidarity in moments of national crisis. The deliverance of the Jewish people was a community effort. Mordecai and Queen Esther worked in concert to ensure their people's survival. Mordecai and Queen Esther's cooperation teaches us that community is important in the realisation of God's providence. We are not meant to navigate difficult ordeals alone. There is synergy in community action and collective prayer. The deliverance of God's chosen people in the Book of Esther is a timely reminder, that we must support and encourage one another, especially in times of adversity.

After the Jewish people were redeemed, they established the Feast of Purim to celebrate their deliverance. By God's redeeming grace, 'their sorrow was turned into joy and their mourning into a day of celebration.'[4] This feast reminds us of God's grace and the turnaround of the Israelites fortune. This celebration includes the giving of gifts to the less fortunate people and support for the underprivileged members of the community. Celebration and thanksgiving are essential to honour God's goodness. It is important that we acknowledge the ways in which God has intervened in our life. When we express thanks and demonstrate gratitude for our deliverance, this ensures that we remain within God's grace, mercy, and favour.

The Book of Esther teaches humanity consequential lessons about God's providence. We learn about the importance of courage. We are reminded of the need to act with integrity and righteousness in the midst of adversity. The Book of Esther emphasises the importance of prayer, humility, and community to transcend challenges. Queen Esther's story demonstrates that God can employ any person to accomplish His providence. We learn that justice, righteousness, and deliverance ultimately prevail. The Book of Esther encourages us to trust in God's timing. We must be courageous in our quest for righteousness and truth. We must employ our influence, power, knowledge, wealth, and resources for the benefit of humankind.

[1] The Holy Bible (NIV). (2011). *The Book of Esther.* Chapter 4, Verse 16.
[2] The Holy Bible (NIV). (2011). *The Book of Esther.* Chapter 7, Verse 10.
[3] The Holy Bible (NIV). (2011). *The Book of Esther.* Chapter 5, Verse 3.
[4] The Holy Bible (NIV). (2011). *The Book of Esther.* Chapter 9, Verse 22.

Chapter 18

The Book of Job

'I know that my redeemer lives,
and that in the end He will stand on the earth.'

Job 19:25
The Holy Bible (NIV)

The Book of Job is one of the most profound and complex books in the Old Testament. Job grapples with the existential questions of despair, identity, meaning, suffering, faith, confidence, grief, trauma, belief, and loss. We become acquainted with the divine nature of God's providence, mercy, and justice. The Book of Job's profound lessons are theological, spiritual, and philosophical in nature. The Book of Job offers insight into the relationship between God and humanity. The central theme within Job is the complexity of the human condition. This book examines the suffering of people who are deemed innocent and good. Job, a righteous man, experiences immense suffering, despite his commendable devotion to God.

Job's friends allege that his suffering is the determinative result of his sinful actions or immoral conduct. This unfounded proposition reflects a common misconception—our suffering is punishment for sin. However, Job's narrative challenges this unfounded assumption. Job demands that we reconsider our thoughts and beliefs pertaining to suffering. The Book of Job reveals that our suffering is not always a direct consequence of sinful conduct. Job's experience suggests that our suffering occurs for reasons that are beyond our understanding and agency. Throughout this theological dialogue, Job's three friends; Bildad, Eliphaz, and Zophar, grapple with the question: Why does Job suffer?

Job's well-intentioned friends attempt to explain his suffering based on logic, reason, knowledge, experience, and wisdom. Nonetheless, Job maintains that their answers do not justify his traumatic suffering. In the end, God directly speaks to Job out of a mighty whirlwind. God does not provide an explanation for Job's immense suffering. Nonetheless, God's message emphasises the profound depth of divine wisdom and the finite limit of human understanding. God reminds Job that humanity cannot adequately reason the complexities of His supernatural thoughts. Human understanding is inadequate to ascertain the causal inference of why we suffer, even when our actions are honourable, noble, righteous, and virtuous. Job's experience of suffering is a testimony to the following verse of scripture in the Gospel of Matthew, 'He causes His sun to rise on the evil and the good, and sends rain on the righteous and the unrighteous.'[1]

Nonetheless, Job's integrity is a distinguishing personal attribute in his discourse with God. Despite Job's intense suffering, and the emotional, psychological, and physical stress it imposes upon him, Job does not curse God. Job demands an explanation from God for his suffering. Job's righteousness is affirmed, even though he endures pain and suffering, 'In all this, Job did not sin in what he said.'[2] Job maintains his faith and trust in God, even when he does not understand the cause for his loss and suffering. Job's willingness to question God, and voice his pain to God, reveals that faith does not equate to passive acceptance of our fate. We may not understand why we encounter the experiences that we do in our life. Nonetheless, faith incorporates a candid and frank discourse with God about how we feel and what we experience in our life. The Book of Job invites us to respectfully share our experiences—the good and evil—with God.

One of the fundamental themes in the Book of Job is the sovereignty of God. God responds to Job's legitimate questions concerning suffering with a reminder of His authority, autonomy, and agency. In the significant speeches from the whirlwind, God points to His creation of the universe, the natural world, humans, animals, and plants. God emphasises that His wisdom and providence are far beyond the confines of human comprehension. This dialogue makes it certain that God is in control of creation, even during the distressing times that we experience loss, pain, grief, trauma, and suffering.

Job's encounter with God brings him to a place of humility, 'I am unworthy—how can I reply to you? I put my hand over my mouth.'[3] Although Job does not receive a direct answer to his question: Why did I suffer? It is the immediate experience of God's spiritual presence and the revelation of divine wisdom, which leads Job to acknowledge his all too human limitations. Job reasons, 'I know that you can do all things, and that no purpose of yours can be thwarted.'[4] Job subsequently repents that he questioned God in a manner that was presumptuous. The Book of Job teaches us, that humility before God is a precondition, to understand one's place in God's creation.

The discourse between Job and his three friends—Bildad, Eliphaz, and Zophar—represents the endless quest for knowledge, wisdom, and answers to humanity's greatest existential questions. This theological discourse between Job and his friends demonstrates their failure to console Job. Throughout this discourse, we realise that we cannot know everything about God's providence and His creation.

Instead of offering Job genuine consolation, his friends accuse him of sinful conduct. They argue that his suffering is through some fault of his making. Job's friends teach us a crucial lesson about the hidden dangers of reasoning, judgement, assumptions, and condemnation. When Job's three friends fail to offer true understanding or genuine empathy, God rebukes Job's friends, 'I am angry with you and your two friends, because you have not spoken the truth about me, as my servant Job has.'[5] Job's story reminds us that our wisdom is finite. Therefore, compassion, forgiveness, love, and empathy, rather than entertaining unfounded assumptions, which promote bias and flawed judgement, is the appropriate response in times of suffering.

In the end, God restores Job's fortunes. God blessed Job with 'twice as much as he had before,'[6] even though the rationale for Job's suffering is never comprehensively explained. This divine restoration demonstrates, that while God's thoughts are mysterious and the methods of His justice sometimes indiscernible, there is hope that God redeems us from grief, suffering, pain, trauma, loss, and tragedy. The Book of Job encourages us to trust in God's justice, even when His mercy is not immediately apparent. The Book of Job highlights the importance of tenacity. We have the ability to experience restoration after considerable loss, grief, trauma, pain, suffering, and adversity.

The Book of Job teaches us that our faith is not dependent upon understanding the mysteries of God's providence. Our faith is not contingent upon absolute answers to life's many perennial questions. Job's final words reveal that faith is to trust in God's goodness, mercy, grace, blessing, providence, justice, and sovereignty. We must trust in God, even when we do not adequately comprehend the reason for our suffering. Job responds, 'Surely I spoke of things I did not understand, things too wonderful for me to know.'[7] Thus, our lasting and profound commitment to faith is established in our covenant with God. Faith cannot be understood through intuition, knowledge, education, reason, feeling, experience, emotion, understanding, or wisdom. Ultimately, faith is based on divine revelation.

In the final analysis, the Book of Job examines several important questions that concern the nature of suffering, divine justice, mercy, the limitations of empirical knowledge, and the undeniability of evil in the world. The Book of Job encourages humanity to be humble, faithful, and acknowledge the mystery of God's providence. Job's remarkable journey is a call to affirm our faith in God, even in the midst of immense suffering. We do not possess the categorical answers to our countless existential questions. Nonetheless, we must run our race in faith, and to the best of our ability.

[1] The Holy Bible (NIV). (2011). *The Gospel of Matthew.* Chapter 5, Verse 45.

[2] The Holy Bible (NIV). (2011). *The Book of Job.* Chapter 2, Verse 10.

[3] The Holy Bible (NIV). (2011). *The Book of Job.* Chapter 40, Verse 4.

[4] The Holy Bible (NIV). (2011). *The Book of Job.* Chapter 42, Verse 2.

[5] The Holy Bible (NIV). (2011). *The Book of Job.* Chapter 42, Verse 7.

[6] The Holy Bible (NIV). (2011). *The Book of Job.* Chapter 42, Verse 10.

[7] The Holy Bible (NIV). (2011). *The Book of Job.* Chapter 42, Verse 3.

Chapter 19

The Book of Psalms

'Be still, and know that I am God;
I will be exalted among the nations,
I will be exalted in the earth.'

Psalm 46:10
The Holy Bible (NIV)

T he Book of Psalms is a diverse collection of songs, prayers, and poems. Psalms expresses the full spectrum of human emotions, thoughts, and feelings, from joy and praise, to lament and despair. Psalms is a source of peace, inspiration, consolation, hope, faith, love, and motivation for countless generations of believers. The Book of Psalms offers believers insight into how to strengthen their fellowship with God. The Psalms are filled with countless expressions of praise and worship of God. The Psalms reflect God's greatness, power, glory, perfection, majesty, and goodness.

Many of the Psalms commence and conclude with commands to praise God. Worship is characterised not merely as an unconscious and repetitive action, but rather as a conscious determination and manifestation of our will. Worship embodies our acknowledgement of God's sovereignty over creation. Praise and worship of God are an integral part of the believer's life. Worship of God is not confined to church services or special occasions, for example, consider Good Friday, Easter Sunday, or Christmas. Worship is an expression of our gratitude, love, praise, and devotion to God. We must demonstrate our appreciation to God in all that we do. We ought to recognise God's majesty and sovereignty over creation.

Throughout the Book of Psalms, God is characterised as 'our refuge and strength, an ever-present help in trouble.'[1] In times of disaster, distress, and danger, we ought to pray to God for assistance, protection, and deliverance. In moments of fear, anxiety, or uncertainty, God is our sanctuary. We are encouraged to disclose our fears, burdens, troubles, and sorrows to God. We must trust in God to secure our peace, strength, love, and protection in the world. God is our safe haven in times of tribulation.

Many of the Psalms are filled with expressions of lament—

prayers that express sorrow, confusion, pain, fear, spiritual poverty, or doubt. For example, consider the following verse, 'My God, my God, why have you forsaken me? Why are you so far from saving me, so far from my cries of anguish?'[2] Alternatively, consider this particular verse, 'My soul thirsts for God, for the living God. When can I go and meet with God?'[3] These two psalms demonstrate to us the importance of being honest with God about our emotions, feelings, and experiences.

The aforementioned psalms demonstrate that God welcomes our emotions, thoughts, feelings, and experiences, even when they are filled with trauma, pain, suffering, or frustration. It is important to be sincere with God in our prayers. God does not expect us to have our affairs in perfect order. There is no genuine purpose to portray that everything in our life is perfect, when the reality is otherwise. Lamentation and honesty in prayer allow us to process grief, trauma, pain, suffering, and loss, while we remain connected with God. We have confidence in the fact that God understands our experiences and He is ever-present with us in our pain.

A recurring theme in Psalms is the declaration of God's faithfulness and love. In fact, in Psalm one hundred and thirty-six, at the end of all twenty-six verses we are reminded, 'His love endures for ever.'[4] No matter the circumstances, the one hundred and fifty psalms repeatedly affirm that God's love does not fail. God's promises are trustworthy. God's providential care for His people is without end. God is faithful, even when we are not. God's love and promises are authoritative and eternal. When we confront challenges or feel abandoned, we trust in God's faithfulness to fulfil His word and to provide for our needs. God's love is steadfast. We always depend upon God.

The Psalms affirm that God is sovereign over creation—the universe, earth, nations, people, animals, and plants. Despite the undeniable presence of evil, injustice, pain, and suffering in the world, the Psalms affirm that God adjudicates with wisdom, mercy, love, and justice. We possess confidence in the knowledge that God's timing is perfect. We must place our trust and confidence in God's sovereignty. When we do not understand how God's providence materialises, or why things are the way they are in our life, we trust that 'in all things God works for the good of those who love Him.'[5] We keep our faith in God's timing. We believe that God's providence includes a transformative vision for our life. We hope in the strength of good to prevail over the weakness of evil.

Several Psalms emphasise the importance of reflection upon God's command, word, and promises. The first Psalm informs us, 'Blessed is the one who does not walk in step with the wicked or stand in the way that sinners take or sit in the company of mockers, but whose delight is in the law of the LORD, and who meditates on His law day and night. That person is like a tree planted by streams of water, which yields its fruit in season and whose leaf does not wither—whatever they do prospers.'[6]

The psalmist reveals that God's blessing is received by our acceptance of God's command. We are blessed when we live in accordance with God's word. Meditation on scripture is the mechanism for our spiritual growth and development. Daily reflection upon God's word strengthens our relationship with God. God's word assists us to ascertain His plan for our life. God's word provides guidance in times of adversity, pain, and suffering. When we meditate on God's word, it aligns our heart and mind with God's providence.

Some of the Psalms convey messages of confession and repentance following acts of sin. For example, consider David's prayer of repentance after he committed adultery with Bathsheba. This psalm highlights the importance that we acknowledge our mistakes before God. We must seek God's forgiveness. We must be restored in fellowship with God. King

David writes the following psalm as atonement for his sin, 'Have mercy on me, O God, according to your unfailing love; according to your great compassion blot out my transgressions.'[7] Repentance is essential for our spiritual well-being. When we sin, we must confess and turn to God. God's mercy is great. God forgives those who genuinely repent. Repentance leads to restoration and the renewal of our fellowship with God.

Many Psalms emphasise that God desires genuine worship from the believer's heart, not merely the performance of rituals and sacrifices. God values a contrite heart and broken spirit over the mere observance of religious practices and superficial prayers. King David makes this undeniable reality known to us, 'My sacrifice, O God, is a broken spirit; a broken and contrite heart you, God, will not despise.'[8] Authentic worship arises from the believer's heart. God is not interested in spurious worship that lacks sincerity. God desires us to approach Him with a humble heart. We must offer our praise and worship to God with sincerity, love, and gratitude.

Several of the Psalms contrast the righteous believer with the immoral people in the world. The Psalms reveal the righteous people are blessed by God, while the immoral people confront divine judgement. We are reminded that God's justice is inescapable, 'Do not fret because of those who are evil or be envious of those who do wrong; for like the grass they will soon wither, like green plants they will soon die away. Trust in the LORD and do good; dwell in the land and enjoy safe pasture. Take delight in the LORD, and He will give you the desires of your heart.'[9]

The Psalms unequivocally affirm that when we live in accordance with God's command, this leads us to equanimity, joy, contentment, love, and prosperity. To live a righteous life leads us to God's blessing. Although the world offers us pleasure, material possessions, gold, wealth, and property, authentic and lasting joy is secured when we live in alignment with God's will. Obedience to God's command secures us joy, peace, contentment, and fulfilment in life. On the contrary, acts of sin ensure we traverse the path of brokenness, bitterness, hate, envy, damnation, jealousy, regret, anger, and separation from God.

The Psalms emphasise that God's spirit is proximate to those who experience pain and suffering; 'The LORD is close to the broken-hearted and saves those who are crushed in spirit.'[10] God listens to the prayers of disheartened people. God offers them peace, strength, and restoration. God's spirit is always present when we are in the midst of pain. When we experience sorrow, loss, trauma, or despair, God is present with us. God is concerned for our emotional and spiritual well-being. God is prepared to heal our wounds. This important message of hope and inspiration is reaffirmed in the Book of Isaiah, where God's word informs us, He will give us 'a crown of beauty instead of ashes, the oil of joy instead of mourning, and a garment of praise instead of a spirit of despair.'[11]

The Psalms repeatedly affirm that God is an honourable judge. God punishes the immoral person and He vindicates the righteous person. Even though evil may prosper in the world, divine justice ultimately prevails in God's timing. God ensures justice is done, 'the wicked plot against the righteous and gnash their teeth at them; but the LORD laughs at the wicked, for He knows their day is coming.'[12] While we do not always witness justice in our lifetime, we trust that God judges the immoral and rewards the righteous in His timing. We must not take matters into our own hands or seek revenge. God is just. God ensures accountability for humanity's immoral actions. God's judgement is inescapable. God's judgement is final and without appeal.

Several of the psalms highlight God blesses those people who live honourably, particularly in respect to philanthropy towards the less fortunate people. We must not forget that 'good will come to those who are generous and lend freely, who conduct their affairs with justice.'[13] Those who are compassionate and generous to the marginalised people are promised God's favour, grace, mercy, and blessing. Generosity is pleasing to God and it brings us His blessing. Concern for the poor, destitute, and marginalised people is an integral part of loving humanity. When we give generously, we reflect God's heart of compassion and experience His blessing.

The Book of Psalms teaches humanity consequential lessons about worship and praise. We must be honest in our prayers. We are encouraged to confide our thoughts, emotions, feelings, and experiences with God. We must trust in God's providence. Psalms encourages us to secure peace in God during times of adversity. Psalms is a call to seek forgiveness through repentance. Psalms invites us to live in obedience to God's will. Psalms commands us to meditate on God's word. We must be authentic in our worship. We must uphold God's justice and promote peace in the world. Ultimately, Psalms encourages us to reflect on the range of emotions and feelings encapsulated within the human condition. Psalms promotes the realisation of a meaningful, genuine, and intimate relationship with God. A blessed relationship with God is characterised by trust, charity, praise, honesty, love, mercy, integrity, forgiveness, and worship.

[1] The Holy Bible (NIV). (2011). *The Book of Psalms.* Psalm 46, Verse 1.
[2] The Holy Bible (NIV). (2011). *The Book of Psalms.* Psalm 22, Verse 1.
[3] The Holy Bible (NIV). (2011). *The Book of Psalms.* Psalm 42, Verse 2.
[4] The Holy Bible (NIV). (2011). *The Book of Psalms.* Psalm 136, Verses 1-26.

[5] The Holy Bible (NIV). (2011). *The Book of Romans.* Chapter 8, Verse 28.

[6] The Holy Bible (NIV). (2011). *The Book of Psalms.* Psalm 1, Verses 1-3.

[7] The Holy Bible (NIV). (2011). *The Book of Psalms.* Psalm 51, Verse 1.

[8] The Holy Bible (NIV). (2011). *The Book of Psalms.* Psalm 51, Verse 17.

[9] The Holy Bible (NIV). (2011). *The Book of Psalms.* Psalm 37, Verses 1-4.

[10] The Holy Bible (NIV). (2011). *The Book of Psalms.* Psalm 34, Verse 18.

[11] The Holy Bible (NIV). (2011). *The Book of Isaiah.* Chapter 61, Verse 3.

[12] The Holy Bible (NIV). (2011). *The Book of Psalms.* Psalm 37, Verses 12-13.

[13] The Holy Bible (NIV). (2011). *The Book of Psalms.* Psalm 112, Verse 5.

Chapter 20

The Book of Proverbs

'Above all else, guard your heart,
for everything you do flows from it.'

Proverbs 4:23
The Holy Bible (NIV)

The Book of Proverbs is a collection of wisdom literature. Proverbs contains practical wisdom on how to live the good life. Proverbs is complete with timeless affirmations that apply to various dimensions of our life, from our relationships and career, to our finances and spiritual growth. Proverbs is about applying God's wisdom in our decision-making and judgement. One of the foundational themes of Proverbs is that wisdom begins with the 'fear of the LORD.'[1] This means that we demonstrate reverence for God. We acknowledge God's sovereignty and majesty. We live in accordance with God's will.

Practical wisdom is not merely concerned with the accumulation of empirical knowledge. Practical wisdom informs our way of life. Practical wisdom is immersed in sincere, honest, and respectful fellowship with God. Reverence for God is the foundation of all wisdom. We are encouraged to demonstrate wisdom in our decisions and choices; however, our wisdom must be grounded in fellowship with God. Understanding and applying God's word is instrumental to live judiciously.

In Proverbs, wisdom and understanding are described as 'more profitable than silver and yields better returns than gold.'[2] Wisdom is the foundation to enact sensible decisions and avoid harmful choices. Wisdom assists us to cultivate peace, prosperity, and patience. Wisdom informs our understanding to live a righteous, honourable, and good life. Therefore, we must seek wisdom above all else. The pursuit of wisdom is our greatest priority. Wisdom leads us to a prosperous and fulfilled life. Wisdom assists us to navigate life's complexities, challenges, and crises. Wisdom brings us joy, happiness, love, equanimity, contentment, and success.

Proverbs emphasises that knowledge and understanding are imperative to live the good life. Knowledge refers to facts and information, whereas understanding is the ability to apply knowledge in a productive and beneficial manner. Empirical knowledge is insufficient to live the good life. Wisdom involves understanding how to apply knowledge and determine sensible choices. We must continually grow in our knowledge and understanding in all areas of our life, especially in our fellowship with God.

Throughout Proverbs, there is the contrast between the sagacious person and the imprudent person. Imprudent people are those who reject God's counsel. They ignore God's word. They live for the pursuit of self-interest, profit, pecuniary gain, and pleasure. In contrast, 'the wise listen to advice.'[3] We must not permit our life to be defined by the desires and pleasures of the world. Imprudence leads to our downfall, whereas wisdom leads to the productive and good life. Imprudent people often make decisions based on their irrational emotions, impulse, desires, passions, feelings, or pride. They do not consult God's word, employ rational deliberation, and engage in self-reflection. God's word counsels us to choose wisdom over imprudence. The long-term consequences of imprudence lead us to ruin.

Humility is a distinguishing characteristic of judicious people. Proverbs associates humility with wisdom. Proverbs acknowledges that pride and arrogance lead to one's downfall. God's word is unequivocal, 'Pride goes before destruction, a haughty spirit before a fall.'[4] The humble person is attentive, conscientious, diligent, and recognises their dependence upon God. We must demonstrate humility. Humility empowers us to learn, grow, and determine sensible decisions. Humility creates the opportunity for God's grace and word to guide our journey. We are reminded that God 'shows favour to the humble.'[5]

Proverbs informs us of the power of words. Our words possess the ability to honour or discredit a person. The judicious person carefully selects their words. The prudent person speaks with truth, compassion, love, and encouragement. They avoid gossip, slander, and deceit in their conversations. Therefore, we must prudently consider our words before we speak. Our words have a lasting impact on members of the community. We must exercise discernment in our words, so that we strengthen members in the community, rather than diminish them. Our words have incredible power, both for good and evil; 'the words of the reckless pierce like swords, but the tongue of the wise brings healing.'[6] When we converse with wisdom and integrity, we reflect God's character in our relationships. Our speech possesses the potential to realise God's providence in our life.

Proverbs emphasises that discipline and correction are preconditions for our growth and development. Whether it is self-discipline, or counsel from fellow believers in the community, discipline refines our character. Discipline assists us to enhance our moral reasoning and strengthen our conscience. Discipline makes us mindful of our errors, flaws, mistakes, and omissions. Self-discipline and good counsel are imperative for the perfection of our character. Judicious people recognise the importance to learn from their mistakes and continually refine their character. It is our responsibility to reflect God's character in our image, for we are created in the image of God.

Proverbs reinforces the importance to develop positive relationships with members of the community. Proverbs emphasises the immeasurable value of friendship, marriage, fellowship, brotherhood, sisterhood, and community. Proverbs cautions us against the dangers of morally reprehensible relationships. We must be conscious of the negative influence of the immoral person. We must exercise discernment in our relationships. The people we surround ourselves with influence us for good or evil. It is incumbent upon us to foster relationships that promote our spiritual growth, the advancement of good, and the proliferation of righteousness in the world. We must avoid relationships that direct us away from God's presence. Our relationships determine our destiny, 'walk with the wise and become wise, for a companion of fools suffers harm.'[7]

Proverbs consistently emphasises the importance of integrity in all areas of our life, whether in business, marriage, professional relationships in the workplace, or our friendships. A person of integrity is honest, trustworthy, and consistently does what is right, 'whoever walks in integrity walks securely, but whoever takes crooked paths will be found out.'[8] We must live with integrity. Integrity is the foundation of the moral, righteous, and good life. It is imperative that we make decisions that align with God's word. Even when no one else observes our actions, we are reminded that God is omnipotent, omnipresent, and omniscient. A life of integrity enhances our reputation and fosters trust and confidence amongst members of society.

Proverbs compares the diligent worker with the indolent person. Proverbs emphasises a strong work ethic leads to God's favour, prosperity, and success. On the other hand, idleness brings about poverty and ruin. The scripture informs us that 'lazy hands make for poverty, but diligent hands bring wealth.'[9] Diligence, perseverance, and responsibility are indispensable components of the good life. We ought to apply ourselves diligently in our work. Success and prosperity are secured through consistent effort and perseverance. Therefore, we must approach our work with accountability, excellence, and integrity.

Proverbs teaches us that generosity leads to God's blessing. Those who are generous with their time, resources, knowledge, and experience secure God's favour. In the New Testament, Paul the Apostle, reinforces this message, 'whoever sows sparingly will also reap sparingly, and whoever sows generously will also reap generously.'[10] Philanthropy assists the less fortunate members of the community. Philanthropy is an instrument which reflects God's concern for humanity. We promote philanthropy through acts of compassion, charity, volunteer work, and community service. Being generous with what we have—whether that be our wealth, time, knowledge, talent, experience, or skill—brings God's blessing to members of the community and ourselves. Generosity is a reflection of God's character. Generosity is a mechanism to selflessly serve humanity.

Proverbs encourages us to trust in God's wisdom, rather than rely upon our finite understanding. While it is important to gain empirical knowledge and make judicious decisions, ultimately, the vision for our life must align with God's will. We trust that God presides sovereign over our life. We place our trust and confidence in God's providence. Practical wisdom and thoughtful action are important. Nonetheless, we recognise that God's thoughts are superior to the depth of our natural reason. Therefore, we seek God's guidance and submit to His will. Trust in God's providence and sovereignty, brings us tranquillity.

Proverbs contains several warnings against the temptation of sin, especially in relation to sexual immorality, greed, jealousy, envy, and anger. Proverbs enlightens us to avoid situations where we might succumb to temptation. We are encouraged to live our life defined by integrity, patience, righteousness, justice, and responsibility. We must turn our heart and mind away from the temptation to sin. Sin often begins with minor compromises or trivial temptations; however, it leads us to destructive consequences. It is important to avoid places, situations, and relationships that lead us towards sinful conduct. We must demonstrate self-control in our thought, speech, and action.

The Book of Proverbs provides practical and timeless wisdom for everyday life. Proverbs underscores the importance of wisdom and knowledge that is predicated upon God's word. Proverbs encourages us to act with humility, integrity, and diligence. Proverbs teaches us the immeasurable value in fostering good relationships, honest speech, and generosity. Proverbs counsels us against the dangers of imprudence, sinful conduct, and idleness. When we seek God's wisdom and apply it in our life, we live our life reflective of God's character. Such an approach to living brings God's blessing to ourselves and the people around us.

[1] The Holy Bible (NIV). (2011). *The Book of Proverbs.* Chapter 1, Verse 7.

[2] The Holy Bible (NIV). (2011). *The Book of Proverbs.* Chapter 3, Verse 14.

[3] The Holy Bible (NIV). (2011). *The Book of Proverbs.* Chapter 12, Verse 15.

[4] The Holy Bible (NIV). (2011). *The Book of Proverbs.* Chapter 16, Verse 18.

[5] The Holy Bible (NIV). (2011). *The Book of James.* Chapter 4, Verse 6.

[6] The Holy Bible (NIV). (2011). *The Book of Proverbs.* Chapter 12, Verse 18.

[7] The Holy Bible (NIV). (2011). *The Book of Proverbs.* Chapter 13, Verse 20.

[8] The Holy Bible (NIV). (2011). *The Book of Proverbs.* Chapter 10, Verse 9.

[9] The Holy Bible (NIV). (2011). *The Book of Proverbs.* Chapter 10, Verse 4.

[10] The Holy Bible (NIV). (2011). *The Book of Second Corinthians.* Chapter 9, Verse 6.

Chapter 21

The Book of Ecclesiastes

'There is a time for everything,
and a season for every activity under the heavens.'

Ecclesiastes 3:1
The Holy Bible (NIV)

The Book of Ecclesiastes is a thought-provoking and introspective book in the Old Testament. Ecclesiastes is a philosophical inquiry, in as much as it is a theological text. The Book of Ecclesiastes is admired for its insightful reflections on the meaning and purpose of life. Ecclesiastes is traditionally attributed to King Solomon and it explores the transient nature of being in the world. Ecclesiastes is complete with profound insights on life, work, and the pursuit of pleasure. We are enlightened to the limits of experience and knowledge. We learn about the mystery of God's providence. In the end, the insights we obtain from divine revelation transcend our sensory experience and empirical knowledge.

The opening chapters of Ecclesiastes convey that life is a temporary, transitory, and troublesome affair. The author refers to the world and our existence as 'utterly meaningless!'[1] The author of Ecclesiastes reflects on the brevity of life and how our well-meaning endeavours to transform the world are inconsequential. Despite our endless exertion, the world continues, and 'there is nothing new under the sun.'[2] Life is ephemeral, uncertain, and unpredictable. Therefore, we must recognise life's inherent nature.

Our being in the world is defined by impermanence. We must acknowledge the temporary nature of our life. This enlightened perspective on life allows us to focus on what truly matters. For example, consider fellowship with God, marriage, family, friendships, community service, philanthropy, generosity, love, faith, mercy, justice, and forgiveness. Ecclesiastes is a call to action. We must cherish each and every moment of our life. We must accept that the answers to many existential questions that concern life are beyond our knowledge and experience.

Throughout Ecclesiastes, the author attempts to find meaning and fulfilment from various endeavours, passions, and ambitions.

For example, consider the pursuit of profit, pleasure, wisdom, wealth, employment, pecuniary gain, entertainment, accomplishments, knowledge, and achievement. In the final analysis, the author concedes that these endeavours are unfulfilling. The author narrates their direct and immediate experience of life, they attest 'I denied myself nothing my eyes desired; I refused my heart no pleasure. My heart took delight in all my labour, and this was the reward for all my toil. Yet when I surveyed all that my hands had done and what I had toiled to achieve, everything was meaningless.'[3] While worldly pursuits are not inherently wrong, they are inadequate to provide us with everlasting satisfaction.

The fulfilment that we seek, along with our purpose, are found by service to God and humanity. We create a meaningful life by the completion of our God-given assignment. Everything else—pleasure, wisdom, success, private property, knowledge, social status, and personal wealth—is transient. The pursuit of wisdom is characterised as 'chasing after the wind.'[4] The author asserts that 'with much wisdom comes much sorrow; the more knowledge, the more grief.'[5] This demonstrates the shallow depth of our understanding. When we learn and acquire greater knowledge, experience, and wisdom, this results in our increased dissatisfaction with our condition of being in the world. The author concludes that we ought to appreciate the simple things in life. Ultimately, it is our reverence for God and trust in His providence, through which we secure our life's purpose and meaning.

Ecclesiastes acknowledges that life incorporates uncertainty, inequality, suffering, discontent, and injustice. At times we perceive the righteous suffer, whereas the wicked unjustly prosper in the world; 'there is something else meaningless that occurs on earth: the righteous who get what the wicked deserve, and the wicked who get what the righteous deserve.'[6] Not to mention, our good intentions, thoughts, ideas, or plans do not always proceed as envisaged. There is inequity in the world. Much of what occurs in the world is beyond our agency and self-determination.

Throughout Ecclesiastes, the author emphasises that God presides sovereign over creation. While we do not always understand God's providence, we trust in Him. We are commanded to trust God's providence even in the midst of life's vicissitudes. While life is disheartening and unjust at times, we are reminded that God is in control. We do not understand everything that happens in our life. Life is not a coherent narrative of events and moments. Having said that, we trust that God has an assignment for our life. Ecclesiastes is a call to trust in God's providence. We ought to relinquish our illusory control of things that we cannot change.

In the reality of life's transient nature, the author of Ecclesiastes encourages people to 'find satisfaction'[7] in the simple pleasures of life. For example, consider scenic walks in natural reserves. Watch the sunset by the harbourside. Cook a hearty meal with a loved one. Surf the waves at the beach. Tend to the garden. Consume a cup of our favourite coffee with our spouse. Engage in a thoughtful conversation with a friend. Watch a science fiction movie with the children. Listen to classical music while driving in the countryside. Read a romantic novel with many twists and turns. Spend quality time with our loved ones during the Easter vacation. While these simple pleasures are not the ultimate source of life's fulfilment, they are pleasures that ought to be appreciated with a sense of gratitude. We must value the simple joys of life. While life is transitory, there is much happiness and contentment in everyday moments. These simple pleasures are part of God's creation. These good pleasures are meaningful, when received with 'gladness of heart.'[8]

Ecclesiastes characterises wisdom as a positive attribute that benefits our life. However, the author recognises that wisdom has its limitations. Wisdom does not resolve all of our life's problems. Even the wisest person cannot fully comprehend God's providence, or understand all of life's mysteries. We are counselled, 'No one can comprehend what goes on under the sun. Despite all their efforts to search it out, no one can discover its meaning. Even if the wise claim they know, they cannot really comprehend it.'[9] In fact, wisdom brings sorrow. Wisdom makes one aware of the imperfections and impermanence of our being. Wisdom enlightens us to the injustices in the world. Wisdom is invaluable, however, it has its limits. To seek wisdom is good; however, we must acknowledge that answers to certain existential questions remain beyond our comprehension. The pursuit of wisdom is a noble endeavour. Nonetheless, we must concede that not everything in our life is capable of rational understanding or scientific explanation. Humility is a precondition to navigate life's great complexities and make peace with the human condition.

Ecclesiastes reflects a pragmatic perspective on the institution of employment. The Book of Ecclesiastes acknowledges that people labour endlessly for material possessions that are temporary and do not bring them perpetual satisfaction. In any case, we are reminded, 'what do people get for all the toil and anxious striving with which they labour under the sun? All their days their work is grief and pain; even at night their minds do not rest.'[10] Employment is an integral part of the good, productive, and meaningful life. Having said that, employment becomes meaningless when it is the exclusive enterprise of our life. Without the proper perspective on God, employment becomes stressful and wearisome.

The institution of employment possesses inherent meaning, when it aligns with God's providence for our life. While employment is a precondition to the good life, it is not the ultimate purpose of our existence. When we work to further God's will, then our work takes on a whole new meaning. When we utilise our experience, knowledge, and talent to honour God and provide for humanity, employment becomes personally rewarding and enriching. When God's word is at the centre of our life, then employment assumes a whole new dimension. Employment is a gift from God, when we understand and apply it as an instrument for the realisation of God's providence.

Ecclesiastes enlightens the reader to remember the unchanging reality of death, and the eternity that follows our temporary life on earth. The author of Ecclesiastes reflects on the inevitability of death and the uncertainty of what happens afterward. The recognition of life's temporary nature motivates us to live our life with eternity in mind. We must make decisions that reflect our faith in God. When we effectuate our conscious and free-willed actions, we must reflect on eternity, rather than merely factor into consideration our immediate and present incentives, rewards, motivations, circumstances, and desires. Given the undeniable brevity of life, and the inevitably of death, we are obliged to consider how we live and what we prioritise in our lifetime. Our thoughts, beliefs, and actions must be informed by an eternal perspective. We must demonstrate an enlightened understanding that our relationship with God and our character are of utmost importance.

Ecclesiastes concludes with a strong emphasis on the fear of God. Our obedience to God's command is the purpose of our life. We must not forget that 'God will bring every deed into judgement, including every hidden thing, whether it is good or evil.'[111] Ecclesiastes acknowledges the uncertainties and frustrations of life. Nonetheless, Ecclesiastes concludes that a life lived in reverence and obedience to God is the most honourable way to live. We must fear God and keep His commandments. Life's complexities, uncertainties, and transient nature make it difficult to create an orderly and meaningful existence.

Nonetheless, the answer according to Ecclesiastes, is to live with reverence for God and in obedience to His word. This is the foundation for an honourable life. A good life that is meaningful and fulfilling, even in a world full of concerns, cares, challenges, chaos, and crises.

Ecclesiastes encourages us to be content with our lot in life. We must be grateful for God's blessing in our life. The endless pursuit of personal gain—private property, personal wealth, pleasure, knowledge, and success—only leads us to discontent. On the other hand, contentment with our possessions and achievements, combined with gratitude, leads us to peace, joy, and happiness. Contentment combined with gratitude is the modus operandi to a meaningful life. We must be thankful for what we have, rather than constantly strive for greater personal gain. Contentment, as opposed to greed or envy, leads us to a peaceful and rewarding life.

The author emphasises that wisdom assists us to navigate life's complex challenges. While the future is unpredictable, we must determine to live wisely and make the best use of our time. The Biblical message in Ecclesiastes is evident—live wisely, even though the future is uncertain. While we cannot exercise control over many things within our environment, we must determine sensible choices that honour God. Wisdom assists us to navigate life's peaks and valleys. God's word assists us to create a future defined by faith, trust, love, peace, and hope.

The Book of Ecclesiastes teaches us that life is transient and unpredictable. Life is not always subject to self-determination. Despite this reality, the author encourages us to secure satisfaction in the simple pleasures of life. We must secure our fulfilment through God's word. In spite of the unchanging reality of death, and the timelessness of eternity, we are encouraged to live wisely. Ultimately, Ecclesiastes encourages us to live our life characterised by love, humility, contentment, and reverence for God. We must trust in God's sovereignty, grace, mercy, and providence. We must live in obedience to God's word. When we focus on what truly matters and embrace the gifts and talents that God has graced us with, we secure contentment and meaning, even in the midst of life's inevitable vicissitudes.

[1] The Holy Bible (NIV). (2011). *The Book of Ecclesiastes.* Chapter 1, Verse 2.

[2] The Holy Bible (NIV). (2011). *The Book of Ecclesiastes.* Chapter 1, Verse 9.

[3] The Holy Bible (NIV). (2011). *The Book of Ecclesiastes.* Chapter 2, Verses 10-11.

[4] The Holy Bible (NIV). (2011). *The Book of Ecclesiastes.* Chapter 1, Verse 17.

[5] The Holy Bible (NIV). (2011). *The Book of Ecclesiastes.* Chapter 1, Verse 18.

[6] The Holy Bible (NIV). (2011). *The Book of Ecclesiastes.* Chapter 8, Verse 14.

[7] The Holy Bible (NIV). (2011). *The Book of Ecclesiastes.* Chapter 5, Verse 18.

[8] The Holy Bible (NIV). (2011). *The Book of Ecclesiastes.* Chapter 5, Verse 20.

[9] The Holy Bible (NIV). (2011). *The Book of Ecclesiastes.* Chapter 8, Verse 17.

[10] The Holy Bible (NIV). (2011). *The Book of Ecclesiastes.* Chapter 2, Verses 22-23.

[11] The Holy Bible (NIV). (2011). *The Book of Ecclesiastes.* Chapter 12, Verse 14.

Chapter 22

The Book of Song of Songs

'Flowers appear on the earth;
the season of singing has come,
the cooing of doves is heard in our land.'

Song of Songs 2:12
The Holy Bible (NIV)

T he Song of Songs, also known as the Song of Solomon, is the most poetic and allegorical book in the Holy Bible. Song of Songs is characterised by lyric poetry. Song of Songs can be interpreted in several different ways. This Old Testament book contains invaluable lessons that extend far beyond the romantic or platonic context. The profound lessons within the Song of Songs are perceived through various dimensions, such as spiritual, physical, emotional, theological, and social.

The Song of Songs highlights the beauty of romantic love between a man and woman. Reading between the lines, the Song of Songs is concerned with much more than aesthetic pleasure. This book portrays an intense and profound love that is passionate, intimate, and mutual. Both the man and woman express their admiration, desire, and commitment to one another. The lovely and beautiful poetry symbolises genuine romance between the man and woman, 'his left arm is under my head, and his right arm embraces me.'[1] The Song of Songs emphasises the importance to appreciate and respect the unique qualities of our spouse. The vivid descriptions of beauty are equally corporeal and transcendent. Love incorporates not only attraction and romance; however, love is also characterised by maturity, forgiveness, understanding, friendship, equality, generosity, and commitment.

While the Song of Songs is primarily about love between a man and woman, it can also be interpreted as an allegory of God's love for His chosen people. The passionate love between the bride (i.e., the Church) and the bridegroom (i.e., Jesus Christ) reflects the profound depth of God's affection and intimacy for His chosen people. This intimate and loving relationship described in Song of Songs symbolises the union between God and the believer. Just as the bride and bridegroom delight in one another's company, God desires to have an intimate and meaningful relationship with His chosen people.

The Song of Songs celebrates the beauty of love within the context of a committed, respectful, and loving relationship. Song of Songs informs us that our ability to experience emotions, feelings, pleasure, and love are gifts from God. We are encouraged to express these positive attributes in the appropriate context—marriage between husband and wife. Song of Songs affirms the goodness, happiness, and joy that informs the expression of love. Song of Songs counters opinions within contemporary culture that discourage or inhibit the display of intimacy between married couples. Song of Songs emphasises the importance of forbearance in love. We must demonstrate patience and exercise self-control. There is a right time and place for love to flourish. The voice of the bride often urges forbearance, for example, consider the verse 'Do not arouse or awaken love until it so desires.'[2] This infers the intimacy of love must not be imposed or forced between the parties.

Song of Songs emphasises the importance to cherish, trust, and desire our spouse. The lovers express their heartfelt desire to be with one another. Their eagerness to be in each other's presence is self-evident. The act of courting—whether physical, social, or emotional—is a sign of the depth of one's love and commitment. The Song of Songs vividly demonstrates that there is no barrier in the world that keeps lovers apart for long, 'Listen! My beloved! Look! Here he comes, leaping across the mountains, bounding over the hills.'[3] The Song of Songs conveys that genuine love and heartfelt desire are not merely a reflection of beauty. Forbearance, understanding, forgiveness, respect, integrity, accountability, and commitment are the attributes of love. The anticipation and longing for one's beloved, is part and parcel of what makes the intimate experience of love mesmerising.

The Song of Songs characterises love with respect, equality, and admiration. Both the man and woman express their heartfelt desires, feelings, emotions, and thoughts in relation to one another. This mutual respect elevates their relationship beyond superficial attraction. Unlike ancient cultural norms, where women were treated unequally, the Song of Songs portrays women as an equal partner in the relationship. The woman actively participates in the expression of her desires, feelings, emotions, and thoughts to her spouse.

The equality of man and woman promotes love between the husband and wife in accordance with God's providence for humanity. This dignified and respectful manner in which the man and woman love each other reconciles with the Biblical story of the creation of Adam and Eve in the Book of Genesis. For God created 'woman from the rib he had taken out of the man.'[4] The rib is a symbolic focal point in terms of human anatomy. The fact that Eve was created from Adam's rib symbolises that Eve is side by side and equal with Adam, not beneath, or above him. Song of Songs demonstrates a flourishing and expressive relationship between the sexes, rather than one characterised by domination, possession, exploitation, or manipulation.

The Song of Songs celebrates the exclusivity and permanence of love within the bond of marriage. The two lovers express a profound desire for each other's company. There is a sense of dedication, commitment, and loyalty between the two lovers throughout this poem. The relationship between the man and woman is characterised by trust, honour, and mutual faithfulness. The jealousy that is sometimes expressed, for example, consider the bride's possessive love for her groom, is perceived as an expression of her deep affection and desire to protect their relationship, rather than an act of jealousy.

The Song of Songs exhibits a universal perspective of love

that is physical, emotional, social, and spiritual. The two lovers in this beautiful poem become one entity. The duo is united in body, mind, soul, and spirit. This highlights the interconnected nature of marriage. The emotional, physical, and spiritual dimensions of the husband and wife are united to form a singular entity in the institution of marriage. Song of Songs invites the reader to appreciate their spouse as a whole person—body, mind, soul, and spirit—as part of their marriage covenant. This is a timely reminder, that love involves an unconditional acceptance and genuine appreciation of our partner as they are.

The lovers in the Song of Songs express their profound emotional and physical intimacy for one another. There is real vulnerability in the lovers' affection for each other, as they candidly share their thoughts, feelings, emotions, and desires. This implies that love is predicated upon openness, trust, and affinity. Beyond the physical dimension of love, the emotional and relational connection between the lovers is pivotal to their relationship. For love to endure the test of time, it requires more than surface-level attraction. Love requires emotional intelligence, trust, bonding, and intimacy through shared life experiences.

The lovers in Song of Songs are described as possessing a magnetic and captivating presence. The power of attraction, not just physical, but also emotional and spiritual, is a recurring theme in this poem. Love is a transformative and magnetic force. Love is the binding force that brings a man and woman into marriage. The institution of marriage offers the husband-and-wife meaningful personal connection, new shared experiences, and the opportunity to create a family. The language employed in the Song of Songs is one of affirmation. Both lovers affirm each other's worth, dignity, value, respect, and beauty, which constitutes an archetype for how love empowers couples in their marriage.

The Song of Songs invites us to celebrate love as a source of joy and happiness in our life. The poem's tone is filled with exuberance and delight in the romance between the man and woman. This Biblical story reminds believers that being in love is a captivating and unforgettable experience. Love is special. Love is to be cherished. The richness and beauty of love is an intimate experience between husband and wife. Love is a gift from God. We are encouraged to perceive love—both human and divine— as a precious gift that must be nurtured, expressed, and protected.

In the final analysis, Song of Songs teaches humanity that love, whether between two people, or between humanity and God, is beautiful, sacred, and transformative. The purpose of our life is to know, experience, and realise the embodiment of love. We are commanded to love God and humanity. Song of Songs demonstrates that love is not merely about the heated passion of sexual intimacy, but about mutual respect, personal commitment, expression of feeling, thought, and emotion. Love is the heartfelt desire for our spouse and our spiritual connection to God. The timeless lessons of this poem equally apply to marriage and our understanding of God's love for His chosen people. Song of Songs is an eloquent poem with a profound message on the nature of love, intimacy, and faithfulness.

[1] The Holy Bible (NIV). (2011). *Song of Songs.* Chapter 2, Verse 6.
[2] The Holy Bible (NIV). (2011). *Song of Songs.* Chapter 2, Verse 7.
[3] The Holy Bible (NIV). (2011). *Song of Songs.* Chapter 2, Verse 8.
[4] The Holy Bible (NIV). (2011). *The Book of Genesis.* Chapter 2, Verse 22.

Chapter 23

The Book of Isaiah

'But those who hope in the LORD will renew their strength.
They will soar on wings like eagles;
they will run and not grow weary,
they will walk and not be faint.'

Isaiah 40:31
The Holy Bible (NIV)

I saiah is a prophetic book in the Holy Bible. Isaiah exhibits a diversity of themes, such as judgement, hope, salvation, mercy, justice, and repentance. The Book of Isaiah contains prophecies in relation to Israel, Judah, and the surrounding nations. Isaiah details profound revelations about God's nature, character, sovereignty, majesty, justice, and providence. Throughout Isaiah, God is depicted as sovereign over not only Israel, but all the nations on earth. Even when foreign nations are more powerful or wealthy than Israel, Isaiah reminds us that God is in control of world history. God administers justice in creation. Isaiah declares that the nations are like a 'drop in a bucket'[1] in comparison to God. Isaiah emphasises God is all-powerful. Isaiah teaches us that God's sovereignty extends throughout creation. No worldly power supersedes God's will.

Isaiah emphasises God's holiness, divinity, and righteousness. The famous vision in the Book of Isaiah, where Isaiah visualises God seated on His throne surrounded by seraphim declaring, 'Holy, holy, holy is the LORD Almighty,'[2] reveals God's transcendent spiritual purity. This scripture verse teaches humanity that God is devoid of sin. God's holiness is a fundamental attribute of His eternal spirit. God's holiness means that He is a just judge. Isaiah's prophecies include timely warnings of humanity's impending judgement for sinful conduct, such as idolatry, injustice, murder, and the immorality of foreign nations.

A recurring theme in the Book of Isaiah is our necessity for repentance. Isaiah instructs Israel to turn away from idolatry, injustice, evil, immorality, and sin. The Israelites are commanded to return to God. Isaiah emphasises that repentance leads to our restoration. Not only in the Book of Isaiah; however, throughout the Holy Bible, God is characterised as merciful and prepared to forgive those who sincerely seek Him. Isaiah offers us an open invitation to repent; 'Seek the LORD while He may be found; call on Him while He is near. Let the wicked forsake their ways and the unrighteous their thoughts. Let them turn to the LORD, and He will have mercy on them.'[3]

The Book of Isaiah contains powerful prophecies about the coming of the Messiah who brings redemption to Israel and the world. This proposition is evident when Isaiah refers to the Messiah with several distinguished names, such as the 'Wonderful Counsellor, Mighty God, Everlasting Father, Prince of Peace.'[4] These passages of scripture in Isaiah are central to Christian theology, as they point forward to the coming of Jesus Christ. The Book of Isaiah characterises the Messiah as the 'man of suffering.'[5] In effect, Isaiah foretells the coming of Jesus Christ who atones humanity for original sin. Christ brings about our redemption. For Christians, Isaiah's message is a prophetic description of the crucifixion of Jesus Christ.

Isaiah teaches us that God's providence for humanity's redemption is not confined to Israel; however, it is for all nations and people of the world. Isaiah declares that in the last days, 'the mountain of the LORD's Temple will be established as the highest of the mountains.'[6] People from all nations shall worship God. This scripture verse points to the establishment of a future kingdom where peace, justice, mercy, grace, and righteousness reign on earth. This blessed kingdom includes all people who seek the LORD. Isaiah speaks of a time when 'the wolf will live with the lamb.'[7] This revelation symbolises the coming of universal peace, love, and justice on earth.

A significant portion of the Book of Isaiah is devoted to warnings of judgement against the sin and idolatry of Israel, Judah, and the surrounding nations. Isaiah reveals that God's justice is administered against those people who refuse to repent and continue in rebellion against His will. Several chapters in Isaiah pronounce judgement on various nations, such as Assyria,

Babylon, Cush, and Egypt. God's judgement demonstrates that no nation is exempt from His sovereignty. All people are held accountable for their actions.

Isaiah teaches humanity that sin necessitates destructive consequences, for individuals, the community, nations, and the world. In all cases, we are assured that God's justice prevails. However, the Book of Isaiah reminds humanity that God's justice is tempered with mercy. God does not secure satisfaction in the execution of judgement. God's punishment is a means of last resort. God seeks the repentance and restoration of His chosen people.

In the midst of judgement, suffering, and national crisis, Isaiah encourages God's chosen people to trust in God's provision. For example, consider when Judah confronted the existential threat of the Assyrian invasion, King Hezekiah turned to God in prayer. In response, God redeemed the city from its enemies. The message is self-evident: when God's people trust in His mercy, power, grace, and sovereignty, they secure deliverance, peace, and security. In addition, Isaiah reminds believers that those who 'hope in the LORD will renew their strength.'[8] Isaiah teaches us that God strengthens those who position their faith in Him.

Isaiah's prophetic message counsels humanity to remain faithful and obedient to God. Isaiah answers God's call to be a prophet with the words, 'Here am I. Send me!'[9] Isaiah demonstrates the importance of obedience to God's command, even during difficult or uncomfortable circumstances. The Book of Isaiah advances the concept of a suffering servant, who assumes responsibility for the people's sinful conduct. This Biblical principle teaches us that sometimes God's servants are called to suffer on behalf of humanity. The suffering servant embodies unconditional love, service, compassion, and sacrifice for the greater good of human civilisation. Prophets demonstrate selfless love for humanity.

Notwithstanding the repeated warnings of God's judgement, Isaiah contains several prophecies of hope for the future, particularly in relation to the restoration of Israel. Isaiah speaks of God's consolation for His chosen people and the forgiveness of their sins. In addition, Isaiah characterises the future glory of Jerusalem, which shall be a light to the nations of the world. Furthermore, Isaiah foretells the creation of 'new heavens and a new earth.'[10] This is a time when God's chosen people experience peace, joy, prosperity, and happiness. This majestic vision of the future points to the fulfilment of God's providence. A reality of being in which there is no sorrow, pain, suffering, grief, misery, loss, trauma, or injustice on earth.

The Book of Isaiah contains profound insights into the divine nature of God. In Isaiah, we learn about God's justice, mercy, sovereignty, and providence. God has a majestic vision for the salvation of Israel and the world. Isaiah encourages us to repent for our transgressions. Isaiah offers hope for humanity's future. Isaiah challenges believers to trust in God's provision. Isaiah anticipates the coming of the Messiah, whose suffering and glory provides the method of redemption for humanity. The Book of Isaiah teaches humanity about the undeniable tension between God's judgement and mercy. We appreciate the need for faith and repentance in our journey. Last but not least, we are reminded that God is the source of our restoration and peace.

[1] The Holy Bible (NIV). (2011). *The Book of Isaiah.* Chapter 40, Verse 15.
[2] The Holy Bible (NIV). (2011). *The Book of Isaiah.* Chapter 6, Verse 3.
[3] The Holy Bible (NIV). (2011). *The Book of Isaiah.* Chapter 55, Verses 6-7.

[4] The Holy Bible (NIV). (2011). *The Book of Isaiah.* Chapter 9, Verse 6.

[5] The Holy Bible (NIV). (2011). *The Book of Isaiah.* Chapter 53, Verse 3.

[6] The Holy Bible (NIV). (2011). *The Book of Isaiah.* Chapter 2, Verse 2.

[7] The Holy Bible (NIV). (2011). *The Book of Isaiah.* Chapter 11, Verse 6.

[8] The Holy Bible (NIV). (2011). *The Book of Isaiah.* Chapter 40, Verse 31.

[9] The Holy Bible (NIV). (2011). *The Book of Isaiah.* Chapter 6, Verse 8.

[10] The Holy Bible (NIV). (2011). *The Book of Isaiah.* Chapter 65, Verse 17.

Chapter 24

The Book of Jeremiah

'You will seek me and find me,
when you seek me with all your heart.'

Jeremiah 29:13
The Holy Bible (NIV)

The Book of Jeremiah is a powerful and poignant account of the life and ministry of Jeremiah. Jeremiah is one of the prophets in the Old Testament. Jeremiah's prophecies span a period of turmoil and national crisis for Judah. The kingdom of Judah is confronted with the imminent destruction of Jerusalem, the exile to Babylon, and the collapse of the Davidic monarchy. Despite the Book of Jeremiah's overtones of judgement and punishment, there are important lessons on hope, redemption, faithfulness, and mercy.

One of the central themes of Jeremiah is the inevitability of God's judgement when His people persist in sin, idolatry, and disobedience. Jeremiah repeatedly warns the people of Judah concerning their unfaithfulness to God. Despite Jeremiah's warnings, the people refuse to repent. Their disobedience results in destruction. God directs the King of Babylon, Nebuchadnezzar to conquer the people of Judah. Regrettably, Judah's idolatry and its reliance upon false gods results in the kingdom's spiritual decay. Jeremiah condemns the worship of idols. He also denounces superficial religious rituals that have impeded the people from fellowship with God. While the people of Judah are subject to captivity for seventy years, we are reminded that God judges each person in accordance with 'their deeds and the work of their hands.'[1]

Despite God's impending judgement, He continually offers opportunities for repentance. Jeremiah emphasises God's willingness to forgive. Jeremiah's prophecy is predicated on the people returning to God and repenting for their sins. However, the people repeatedly reject this call. This Biblical prophecy underscores the importance of confession and turning back to God before it is too late. Jeremiah proclaims God's message to the people; If Judah repents of its sin, God shall negate His forthcoming judgement. Jeremiah's prophecy informs humanity that God's judgement is not predetermined. God's judgement is averted through our repentance. God's grace is boundless. God's mercy is open to humanity, as long as we recognise our error and repent.

The Book of Jeremiah's primary message concerns God's judgement. Nonetheless, there are also prophetic messages about God's faithfulness. Despite Israel's repeated unfaithfulness, God offers Israel a future defined by hope, love, grace, mercy, and blessing. God establishes a new covenant with His chosen people, where God shall 'put His law in their minds and write it on their hearts.'[2] Hope is not lost for humanity. In fact, Jeremiah offers one of the most well-known passages on hope in the Holy Bible: "For I know the plans I have for you,' declares the LORD, 'plans to prosper you and not to harm you, plans to give you hope and a future."[3] Although this promise was given to the Israelites in exile in Babylon, it demonstrates God's providence of redemption and restoration for humanity.

Throughout the Book of Jeremiah, God makes it evident that He is in control of all nations, not only Israel. God employs foreign powers, like Babylon to accomplish His providence. In Jeremiah, God's providence incorporates judgement and punishment. This reality affirms that no worldly power is beyond God's sovereignty. God determines world history. Jeremiah's prophecies reveal, that even in times of national crisis, God's sovereignty is not undermined. For instance, consider in the midst of the people's exile from Jerusalem to Babylon, God informs the Israelites to establish themselves in this foreign land and seek the welfare of Babylon, because 'if it prospers, you too will prosper.'[4]

The Book of Jeremiah underscores that God's justice is not arbitrary. God's justice is faithfully administered in His holiness, sovereignty, grace, and righteousness. The people of Judah reject God's command. As a consequence, God's judgement is executed against the people's immorality and corruption. God's judgement is not without a purpose or cause. God imposes His judgement to purify and restore the people. Despite God's judgement, He repeatedly demonstrates mercy. Jeremiah encourages Israel to repent with the promise of God's forgiveness. The Book of Jeremiah contains several instances where God declares His intention to restore His chosen people, even after they experience severe consequences for their sins.

Jeremiah's life and ministry demonstrate the obligations and responsibilities of being faithful to God's command. Jeremiah experienced rejection, imprisonment, and anguish. Jeremiah's ministry was characterised by sorrow, despair, and loneliness. This reality teaches us that faithfulness to God often comes with considerable pain and suffering. Jeremiah is referred to as the 'weeping prophet,' because of his deep sorrow over the fate of his people. Jeremiah's emotional and spiritual agony is an example of how God's servants suffer for the sake of humanity's welfare.

Jeremiah's experience and commitment to ministry reflects the challenges associated with remaining faithful to God's word. Obedience to God's word is arduous and it requires personal sacrifice. We witness this sobering reality affirmed in the New Testament with Paul the Apostle. For example, consider Paul endures considerable privation and injustice in his endeavour to spread the gospel. Paul experienced beatings, stoning, shipwreck, deprivation of liberty, hunger, and thirst. Nonetheless, Paul continued to dutifully fulfil his assignment until the end of his lifetime.

From the beginning of Jeremiah's life, God had an assignment for him. God instructed Jeremiah to be a prophet to the nations. Despite Jeremiah's reservations, God anointed him. This demonstrates that God empowers those whom He destines to fulfil His providence. God's providence prevails despite our weaknesses, failures, errors, mistakes, doubts, and fears. In spite of Jeremiah's initial hesitation to fulfil God's calling, God reassured Jeremiah that He will provide the requisite strength, grace, and wisdom to fulfil his destiny. This Biblical story teaches humanity that God appoints people who are unqualified. God employs remnants to fulfil His providence. God empowers His chosen people to accomplish their assignment. To realise God's providence, we must exhibit faith, belief, trust, and confidence in Him.

Similarities exist between Jeremiah and Gideon's life story narrated in the Book of Judges. Gideon had his fair share of doubts and reservations. Gideon felt inadequate to complete the assignment that God had destined for him. Gideon responded to God, "Pardon me, my LORD,' Gideon replied, 'but how can I save Israel? My clan is the weakest in Manasseh, and I am the least in my family."[5] Nonetheless, Jeremiah and Gideon demonstrated that faith overcomes doubt. Trust overcomes fear. Belief overcomes inadequacy. We too must depend upon God to fulfil our destiny.

Jeremiah condemns the people's half-hearted religious rituals that are disconnected from a genuine dialogue with God. In the Book of Jeremiah, God expresses His disapproval against the people who place their trust in customs and rituals; however, neglect justice, righteousness, integrity, and devotion. Worship, according to Jeremiah, is not concerned with customs and rituals. Worship is about the alignment of our heart with God's will. Jeremiah teaches us the importance to know and understand God, rather than boast about one's reputation, fame, vocation, social status, property, or wealth. This is the legitimate basis for our fellowship with God. Jeremiah stresses that a sincere relationship with God incorporates humility, justice, and righteousness, not merely our perfunctory performance in the world.

The people of Judah accept God's judgement for their sin. Ultimately, God's judgement brings the people back to Him. God's judgement is a means for the people's redemption. In the Book of Jeremiah, God declares, 'I will discipline you but only in due measure; I will not let you go entirely unpunished.'[6] This message teaches us that God's judgement, while difficult to endure, is not without a purpose or cause. God's judgement restores, refines, and purifies His chosen people. Even in the midst of judgement, God's compassion, forgiveness, mercy, and love for His chosen people are evident. In the Book of Jeremiah, God's affectionate love for Ephraim is evident, 'Is not Ephraim my dear son, the child in whom I delight?'[7] This demonstrates that when God punishes His chosen people, His love for them remains ever-present. God desires His people to experience restoration, joy, peace, and prosperity.

The Book of Jeremiah teaches us important lessons about God's character. We learn about the nature of sin, repentance, judgement, and restoration. Jeremiah underscores the urgency to respond to God's command to repent. We must accept the sobering reality of God's justice. It is incumbent upon us to be receptive to God's mercy. Jeremiah highlights the personal sacrifice to faithfully obey God's command. We are enlightened to the importance of heartfelt worship. Jeremiah gives us hope of our future restoration through God's covenant with humanity. Jeremiah is complete with prophetic warnings concerning God's judgement. Having said that, Jeremiah is an enduring testimony to God's faithfulness, love, and desire for the redemption of His chosen people.

[1] The Holy Bible (NIV). (2011). *The Book of Jeremiah*. Chapter 25, Verse 14.
[2] The Holy Bible (NIV). (2011). *The Book of Jeremiah*. Chapter 31, Verses 33.

[3] The Holy Bible (NIV). (2011). *The Book of Jeremiah.* Chapter 29, Verse 11.

[4] The Holy Bible (NIV). (2011). *The Book of Jeremiah.* Chapter 29, Verse 7.

[5] The Holy Bible (NIV). (2011). *The Book of Judges.* Chapter 6, Verses 11-16.

[6] The Holy Bible (NIV). (2011). *The Book of Jeremiah.* Chapter 30, Verse 11.

[7] The Holy Bible (NIV). (2011). *The Book of Jeremiah.* Chapter 31, Verse 20.

Chapter 25

The Book of Lamentations

'The LORD is good to those whose hope is in Him,
to the one who seeks Him.'

Lamentations 3:25
The Holy Bible (NIV)

T he Book of Lamentations is a collection of prayers and lamentations attributed to the prophet Jeremiah. Lamentations expresses sorrow, regret, and grief over the destruction of Jerusalem. Lamentations narrates the Jewish people's exile to Babylon. Lamentations characterises the anguish the Jewish people experience during their exile. The Jewish people confront the destructive consequences of sin, the loss of Jerusalem, and the absence of God's blessing. Despite the Jewish people's despair, the Book of Lamentations contains messages of hope, justice, and faith. In Lamentations, we become acquainted with God's mercy, love, and grace.

One of the significant Biblical lessons deduced from Lamentations is the undeniability of suffering. The Book of Lamentations is filled with expressions of misery, pain, loss, and grief. Jeremiah expresses the Jewish people's profound emotional and physical anguish. Jeremiah demonstrates it is imperative to grieve when we confront privation and loss in our life. Lamentations demonstrates it is sensible to express our sorrow, pain, suffering, loss, and frustration to God. Jeremiah candidly questions God's providence; however, this is respectfully done in the context of prayer to God. Jeremiah demonstrates that in our time of grief, we ought to convey our innermost thoughts and feelings to God.

Lamentations characterises the Jewish people's suffering as a result of their sin and rebellion against God. Jerusalem's destruction and the people's exile is the inevitable consequence of their idolatry, injustice, immorality, and disobedience to God's command. This Biblical narrative informs us that sin encompasses severe consequences that lead to suffering. Lamentations is not explicitly about repentance. Nevertheless, the overwhelming sense of grief and sorrow over sin encourages believers to reflect upon the importance of repentance and turning to God, before it is too late. The people mourn for what has been lost. There is an understanding that sin leads to destruction; however, repentance brings forth restoration.

Lamentations affirms that the people's suffering is not without a cause. The scripture informs us, 'The LORD has done what He planned; He has fulfilled His word, which He decreed long ago.'[1] Thus, the people's suffering is part of God's justice. The people's suffering is not without an explanation. God is a righteous, merciful, and equitable judge. God's providence permits the people to experience the destructive consequences of their actions. Lamentations teaches us that God's justice is not defined by cruelty or capriciousness. God's justice is a reflection of His holiness and the moral order of the universe. Lamentations demonstrates that God's punishment, although painful, is not characterised by vengeance. God's punishment functions as corrective justice. In the Book of Lamentations, the question is put to the believer: 'Why should the living complain when punished for their sins?'[2] This inquiry infers that our suffering is not without an antecedent cause. Our suffering is a means of purification from sin and correction from error. From a theological perspective, suffering encourages people to examine their relationship with God.

Even in the darkest moments of our life, when we feel overwhelmed by grief, Lamentations reminds us that God's providence is paramount. Jeremiah acknowledges the devastation of Jerusalem and the people's exile are acts constitutive of God's sovereign will, 'Who can speak and have it happen, if the LORD has not decreed it?'[3] This Biblical truth informs us that when our suffering is overwhelming, God is sovereign and nothing in creation takes effect without His authority or knowledge. Lamentations does not provide convenient answers to the complex existential questions of grief, loss, trauma, pain, tragedy, and suffering. Nonetheless, Lamentations encourages believers to trust in God's providence, even when His providence is not discernible to human reason. Jeremiah's resolute faith in God's sovereignty, despite the devastation, teaches us that God's providence is greater than human understanding. We must accept that God's providence is incomprehensible to the faculty of reason.

In the midst of sorrow, Lamentations highlights God's compassionate, merciful, and faithful nature. In Lamentations, Jeremiah declares, 'Because of the LORD's great love we are not consumed, for His compassions never fail. They are new every morning; great is your faithfulness.'[4] This is one of the many hope-filled verses in the Book of Lamentations. This passage of scripture is a reminder, that in the midst of judgement, God's love, grace, and mercy are ever-present. Despite the profound grief expressed throughout the Book of Lamentations, there is optimism that God does not abandon His chosen people. Jeremiah's proposition is in agreement with the fact, that God restores Jerusalem and His chosen people. Lamentations informs us that no matter how desperate our situation or circumstances, there is hope for restoration through God's mercy, love, and grace.

Lamentations teaches us the importance to disclose our pain, grief, suffering, and loss to God through prayer. The Book of Lamentations is a prayer of lament. Lamentations demonstrates that in our deepest sorrow, God is the one to whom we must turn to confide our sentiments. Prayer in times of suffering is a tangible expression of our faith in God. Prayer is also a method to strengthen our fellowship with God. Through prayer, we receive God's mercy, love, and grace. In Lamentations, Jeremiah cries out to God 'from the depths of the pit,'[5] he asks God to hear and answer his prayers. When we are in the midst of suffering, prayer to God is an integral part of our restoration.

Lamentations   expresses   the   undesirable   feeling   of abandonment by God. Nonetheless, Lamentations affirms that God is just, sovereign, and merciful. At times, Jeremiah struggles with God's apparent silence. The Book of Lamentations consists of prayers that remind us, even in the midst of our pain and suffering, we must turn to God for consolation, courage, and contentment. This paradoxical proposition infers that God's spirit is not always felt in our immediate presence; however, His spirit is omnipresent. God is omnipresent, even in our most painful moments and tragic experiences. Jeremiah contrasts humanity's faithlessness with God's eternal faithfulness. The Israelites have been unfaithful; however, God's covenant is not nullified by human failure, error, or incompetency. Lamentations teaches humanity that even when we fail, God remains faithful to His covenant.

The Book of Lamentations is not only concerned about our individual laments, but also laments of a communal character. The people's collective expression of grief represents the sorrow of a nation. Often times, the people mourn together. This highlights the importance of communal mourning in times of national crisis. The community assumes shared responsibility for its people's successes and failures. Lamentations informs us the fate of the community is correlated to the actions of its members. Sinful conduct by an individual brings about collective suffering to the people. The communal dimension of Lamentations encourages the church to unite people through prayer, worship, and fellowship. The church possesses an indispensable function to address the moral problem of sin in our society. The church must perform its constructive part in the restoration of people who are broken-hearted.

One of the profound lessons in Lamentations is Jeremiah's resolute determination to keep his faith in God, even in the midst of disillusionment, despair, disaster, and discontent. Despite the profound loss, there remains trust in God's goodness, peace, love, grace, and mercy. This teaches us that faith is not a fair-weather virtue, but an admirable attribute that must endure through life's peaks and valleys. Jeremiah's faith holds steadfast, not because his suffering has ceased, but because of God's faithfulness. This teaches us that faith endures, even when our circumstances dictate otherwise. God's faithfulness provides the foundation for the endurance of privation and loss.

Lamentations demonstrates the undeniable necessity for God's mercy during times of judgement. The Book of Lamentations concludes with an earnest petition for God's mercy and humanity's restoration. The people confess their sin and beseech God not to hold it against them. The people beseech God to remember and restore them. This Biblical message teaches us that when we assume responsibility for the consequences of our actions, there is the opportunity for repentance and hope in God's mercy.

The Book of Lamentations provides us with insight into the nature of suffering, God's administration of justice, and humanity's necessity for God's mercy. While Lamentations is characterised by despair, grief, loss, and mourning, it also holds onto the hope of God's unfailing compassion, love, grace, and faithfulness. Lamentations reinforces the importance of prayer in times of grief. We are enlightened to the reality of community responsibility for sin. We find certainty in God's sovereignty, mercy, and justice. Even in the midst of our privation, we must hold on to hope. In the final analysis, Lamentations encourages us to keep our faith in God's love, providence, and mercy, even in the darkest moments of our journey.

[1] The Holy Bible (NIV). (2011). *The Book of Lamentations.* Chapter 2, Verse 17.
[2] The Holy Bible (NIV). (2011). *The Book of Lamentations.* Chapter 3, Verse 39.

[3] The Holy Bible (NIV). (2011). *The Book of Lamentations.* Chapter 3, Verse 37.

[4] The Holy Bible (NIV). (2011). *The Book of Lamentations.* Chapter 3, Verses 22-23.

[5] The Holy Bible (NIV). (2011). *The Book of Lamentations.* Chapter 3, Verse 55.

Chapter 26

The Book of Ezekiel

'Then the Spirit lifted me up,
and I heard behind me a loud rumbling sound
as the glory of the LORD rose from the place where it was
standing.'

Ezekiel 3:12
The Holy Bible (NIV)

E zekiel is a complex and symbolic book within the Old Testament. Ezekiel was a prophet during the Babylonian exile. This was a time when the Kingdom of Judah was destroyed and the Israelites resided in captivity. Ezekiel contains prophecies of God's judgement, visions of God's majestic glory, and acts constitutive of God's providence. Ezekiel reveals God's promise of future restoration for His chosen people. Last but not least, Ezekiel embodies spiritual lessons for humanity.

Ezekiel affirms God's sovereignty over creation. Throughout the Book of Ezekiel, we witness God's providence. God demonstrates that He is in control of Israel and the surrounding nations destiny. Ezekiel commences with a powerful vision of God's glory. Ezekiel highlights God's infinite power and indisputable sovereignty. This majestic vision demonstrates that God is not bound by time, matter, space, energy, or human understanding. No matter how desperate our circumstances or situation, God is sovereign over creation. God's providence is realised throughout world history.

A significant portion of Ezekiel is concerned with God's judgement. God's judgement is not indifferent to the good and evil actions of humanity. Ezekiel repeatedly warns Israel and foreign nations about the consequences of their sin and idolatry. God's judgement upon Jerusalem and Judah is a consequence of the people's unfaithfulness to Him. For example, consider the people engage in acts of idolatry, injustice, and disobedience. We are reminded that sin has consequences; therefore, God shall 'judge us according to our conduct.'[1] Ezekiel warns us that rebellion against God leads to destruction; however, he also underscores that God's judgement is fair and righteous.

The fundamental moral lesson learned from Ezekiel is the

importance of responsibility. God emphasises that every person is accountable for their actions, not for the sins of their children, parents, grandparents, or ancestors. This Biblical principle challenges the mindset of the generation of Israelites, whom assumed they were judged on the sins of their predecessors. Ezekiel informs us that every individual is responsible for their conduct, both the good and evil. God holds each person accountable for their actions and their disobedience to His word.

Ezekiel proclaims God's message for the Israelites to repent for their sins. God desires for the people to be redeemed. The Israelites shall not be punished, so long as they turn away from their immoral ways. God's message is unequivocally clear— 'Repent and live!'[2] Ezekiel's prophecy on repentance demonstrates God's merciful heart. God is compassionate, even in the midst of His judgement. Repentance involves a genuine transformation of our heart and mind. It is insufficient to merely observe religious rituals, traditions, customs, and practices. God desires sincere transformation in the life of every believer. The opportunity for repentance is a blessed sign of God's grace in our life.

Ezekiel's journey as a prophet demonstrates the importance of responsibility to obey God's word. Ezekiel is called to communicate the cold hard truth to a rebellious people. God informed Ezekiel that the chosen people are hard-hearted and defiant to God's word. Nonetheless, Ezekiel is commanded to communicate God's word faithfully to them. Ezekiel's symbolic actions—such as 'lie on your left side and put the sin of the people of Israel upon yourself,'[3] and 'shave your head and your beard'[4]—demonstrate God's judgement. God's prophets often reveal uncomfortable or inconvenient messages that reflect God's will. Obedience to God's command incorporates sacrifice, rejection, and suffering. Notwithstanding, it is crucial to convey

God's word truthfully and faithfully. God strengthens and equips His messengers to fulfil their assignment.

Ezekiel emphasises the importance of holiness and the requirement for God's chosen people to live in accordance with His command. The Israelites repeatedly violate God's word through idolatry and other sinful practices. In the Book of Ezekiel, God condemns spiritual leaders that fail to observe holiness and administer justice across the nation. God's holiness requires that His chosen people reflect His character. God commands His chosen people be set apart. The Israelites must live a righteous life that honours God. Authentic worship and obedience to God requires a lifetime of commitment to His word.

The prophet Ezekiel experiences a vision of 'God's glory departing from the temple'[5] in Jerusalem due to the people's sin. This is a dramatic and heartbreaking moment. This vision symbolises God's separation from His chosen people. However, in the subsequent chapters of Ezekiel, there is a vision of 'God's glory returning to the new temple.'[6] This symbolises newfound hope and restoration for Israel. God's spiritual presence is indispensable to humanity. When the people turn away from God, they experience the invaluable loss of God's spiritual presence and blessing. Nonetheless, God promises to return and restore His chosen people, when they repent and turn away from their sinful conduct.

In the midst of God's judgement, the Book of Ezekiel contains promises of the people's future restoration. The vision of 'the valley of dry bones'[7] symbolises Israel's spiritual renewal and the people's future restoration. God promises to gather His chosen people from foreign nations, restore them to their land, and renew their heart and spirit. Despite God's judgement, He is a God of restoration and renewal. There is hope for those who repent and return to God. God's providence for His chosen people is not their downfall, but rather their restoration and spiritual renewal. Despite the people's failure, God promises to restore them.

The Book of Ezekiel foretells a bleak outlook for Israel and the surrounding nations. Foreign nations such as Ammon, Edom, Egypt, Moab, and Tyre are condemned for their pride, injustice, disobedience, and idolatry. This Biblical message demonstrates that God's judgement is not confined to His chosen people. God's judgement extends to all nations on earth. God is just. God holds all nations accountable for their conduct, especially for their treatment of His chosen people. Through this Biblical message, we learn that God's word has moral and ethical significance for humanity. People, communities, societies, and nations are responsible to live in accordance with God's commandments.

God promises to renew His chosen people's heart and spirit. The Biblical promise of spiritual transformation points to the formation of a new covenant, one that is fulfilled in Jesus Christ. This new covenant incorporates the Holy Spirit. This new covenant empowers believers to live in accordance with God's will. God desires to transform His chosen people, so they embrace a godly life. Authentic spiritual transformation is not attained from the performance of external rituals, or observance of time-tested traditions. Spiritual transformation arises from a change of heart—a heart that is renewed by God's Spirit. This points to the divine experience of being born again through the Holy Spirit.

God condemns Israel's leaders for failing in their duty concerning the stewardship of the people. God compares the Israelite leaders to unfaithful shepherds who have neglected and scattered the flock. God is the legitimate shepherd of His chosen people. God shall raise up a faithful shepherd to protect His chosen people. God cares deeply for His chosen people. God does not leave His chosen people without godly leadership. This Biblical metaphor of the shepherd reminds us that God is both the leader and protector of His chosen people. In the New Testament, within the Gospel of John, we learn that Jesus Christ assumes responsibility as 'the Good Shepherd'[8] of God's chosen people. As a result, Jesus Christ fulfils Ezekiel's prophecy.

The Book of Ezekiel teaches humanity profound lessons about God's sovereignty, holiness, justice, grace, judgement, providence, love, and mercy. Ezekiel underscores the importance of responsibility and repentance. The Book of Ezekiel highlights the importance of faithful leadership. Ezekiel points to the future hope of restoration and spiritual renewal. Despite Ezekiel's revelation of God's judgement, this book is ultimately a message of hope in the coming of the Messiah. God promises to restore His chosen people. God renews the people's heart and mind. God guides the people forward with His spiritual presence. The Book of Ezekiel invites us to live in the light of God's holiness. We are empowered to experience spiritual transformation in our life. Most importantly, we are commanded to trust in God's providence.

[1] The Holy Bible (NIV). (2011). *The Book of Ezekiel.* Chapter 7, Verse 3.

[2] The Holy Bible (NIV). (2011). *The Book of Ezekiel.* Chapter 18, Verse 32.

[3] The Holy Bible (NIV). (2011). *The Book of Ezekiel.* Chapter 4, Verse 4.

[4] The Holy Bible (NIV). (2011). *The Book of Ezekiel.* Chapter 5, Verse 1.

[5] The Holy Bible (NIV). (2011). *The Book of Ezekiel.* Chapter 10, Verse 18.

[6] The Holy Bible (NIV). (2011). *The Book of Ezekiel.* Chapter 43, Verse 5.

[7] The Holy Bible (NIV). (2011). *The Book of Ezekiel.* Chapter 37, Verse 1.

[8] The Holy Bible (NIV). (2011). *The Book of John.* Chapter 10, Verse 11.

Chapter 27

The Book of Daniel

'As for you, go your way till the end.
You will rest, and then at the end of the days you will rise
to receive your allotted inheritance.'

Daniel 12:13
The Holy Bible (NIV)

T he Book of Daniel is a captivating book in the Old Testament. The Book of Daniel is complete with dramatic visions and prophecies. The Book of Daniel chronicles the Babylonian exile during the reign of the Persian empire. The Book of Daniel narrates the Biblical story of Daniel and his three companions (i.e., Abednego, Meshach, and Shadrach). The Book of Daniel is a combination of history, theology, prophecy, and apocalyptic literature. The Book of Daniel teaches humanity profound spiritual lessons on God's sovereignty, grace, faithfulness, and providence. Through the Book of Daniel, we learn the importance of perseverance and fortitude in the midst of tests, tribulations, and trials.

The Book of Daniel emphasises God's sovereignty over the rise and fall of empires and worldly rulers. This undeniable Biblical reality is highlighted in Daniel's interpretation of King Nebuchadnezzar's initial dream and his subsequent 'dream of the four great beasts.'[1] In both these dreams, Daniel reveals that God is in control of world history. God determines the destiny of every nation on earth. No matter how powerful worldly rulers or empires, God's providence is the determinative factor in world history. Believers trust in God's providence, especially when political, economic, legal, or social conditions are uncertain or oppressive. In the final analysis, God's providence cannot be thwarted by any worldly power.

Daniel and his companions personify the importance of faithfulness to God. Even in a foreign land with pagan influence, Daniel and his companions remain loyal to God. For example, consider Daniel determines not to 'defile himself' with the king's royal food and wine.'[2] In addition, Abednego, Meshach, and Shadrach refuse to worship the golden idol established by King Nebuchadnezzar's royal decree. These young men boldly declare to the king, 'we will not serve your gods or worship the image of gold you have set up.'[3] This Biblical narrative demonstrates our faithfulness to God takes precedence over personal convenience, social status, self-interest, or public opinion. Faithfulness to God is our highest priority, even when we find ourselves in difficult circumstances. Whether we are subject to exile, experience duress, or confront persecution, believers must remain faithful to God's command. Believers must remain firm in their faith.

In the Book of Daniel, Abednego, Meshach, and Shadrach are threatened with death for their refusal to worship King Nebuchadnezzar's golden idol. Despite King Nebuchadnezzar's threats to throw them into the fiery furnace, these three young men confidently declare their unconditional trust in God. They trust in God to redeem them, but even if He does not, they shall not compromise on their faith. God honours those who courageously uphold truth, justice, and righteousness, even in the midst of exile, persecution, or death. This Biblical narrative reminds believers to remain confident in God's providence to redeem humanity. At the same time, we must accept God's will in situations where our deliverance is not guaranteed.

Daniel is portrayed as a faithful man of prayer. Daniel seeks God's wisdom, guidance, and providence through consistent and earnest prayer. Daniel's prayer for the restoration of Israel is an ideal model of repentance, humility, and confession. Prayer is imperative to maintain our fellowship with God, especially in times of personal crisis. We must humble ourself before God, confess our sins, and intercede for members of the community. These are important facets of our spiritual life. God responds to sincere prayer with wisdom, love, compassion, and mercy.

Similar to the ordeal that Abednego, Meshach, and Shadrach confronted in the fiery furnace, Daniel is thrown into the lion's den. Daniel refused to obey King Nebuchadnezzar's royal decree. In defiance, Daniel continued to pray to the living God. The Most High God sent an angel to prevent the lions from devouring

Daniel in the den. The following morning Daniel answered to King Nebuchadnezzar, that God had spared his life, 'They have not hurt me, because I was found innocent in His sight.'[4] God is faithful to redeem His chosen people in times of trial and adversity. While God does not always prevent suffering, God is omnipresent with His chosen people in the midst of it. God's grace provides humanity with protection and deliverance. This historical event enlightens believers to trust in God's providence, even during a perilous situation.

In the Book of Daniel, King Nebuchadnezzar is humbled by God after he becomes proud and fails to acknowledge God's sovereignty. Nebuchadnezzar is exiled, during this time he learns to acknowledge God's sovereign authority. In the fullness of time, Nebuchadnezzar humbles himself before the Almighty living God. Our humility before God is imperative. Arrogance and pride lead to our downfall. On the contrary, humility creates the opportunity to experience God's blessing, mercy, and grace. The Biblical story of King Nebuchadnezzar informs us that those who exalt themselves are humbled; however, those who humble themselves before God are exalted.

The Book of Daniel is characterised by prophetic visions about the future. These visions include the rise and fall of empires, the blessed coming of the Messiah, the victory of good over evil, and the establishment of God's kingdom on earth. Daniel's vision foretells the coming of a kingdom that is indestructible—a kingdom ruled by the Son of God. In effect, Daniel's vision refers to the coming of the Messiah. God's providence for humanity is realised through His beloved son— Jesus Christ.

God's providence incorporates the establishment of His kingdom on earth. In the midst of social upheaval, economic crisis, legal uncertainty, and political turmoil, the believer's hope is realised through Jesus Christ. Believers are confident that God's kingdom prevails and that Christ's eternal reign brings justice, equality, love, mercy, prosperity, and peace on earth. Scripture enlightens us to this reality—'His kingdom will be an everlasting kingdom, and all rulers will worship and obey him.'[5] This Biblical message encourages believers to live with an eternal perspective.

The prophecies in the Book of Daniel demonstrate that God's providence determines the trajectory of world history. God's providence is revealed to His chosen people. The fulfilment of these prophecies provide incontestable evidence of God's faithfulness and sovereignty over world history. Prophecies strengthen the faith of God's chosen people. Prophecies affirm God's righteousness prevails over creation. The fulfilment of God's covenant provides reassurance and encouragement to humanity. Believers are assured that God's word is authentic and reliable. Believers trust in God's blessing for their future.

The Book of Daniel affirms, that despite the rise of powerful earthly kingdoms, for example, consider the Babylonian empire, the Medo-Persian empire, and the Roman empire, God's sovereignty is eternal. God's kingdom triumphs over worldly institutions. In the Book of Daniel, the rock that strikes the statue represents God's kingdom, which cannot be destroyed, 'the God of Heaven will set up a kingdom that will never be destroyed … it will itself endure for ever.'[6] Earthly kingdoms and rulers are ephemeral; however, God's kingdom is eternal. This theological reality enlightens believers to prioritise God's kingdom above all else. We must live with the belief that God's kingdom is eternal. The Book of Daniel encourages humanity to place its hope in the victory of good over evil.

Daniel remains faithful to God throughout his life. Daniel accurately interprets dreams, visions, and revelations from God. God honours Daniel's faithfulness. God bestows favour upon Daniel. For example, consider Daniel has influence with King

Nebuchadnezzar and King Darius. In addition, God grants Daniel honour, fame, and status in Babylonian society. Indeed, Daniel is appointed to serve in the King's royal court. At one point in Daniel's life, he is promoted to the third highest ruler in the Babylonian kingdom. Through Daniel's story, we learn that God rewards those who remain faithful to Him, even when it is difficult. Daniel's life narrative demonstrates that our faithfulness secures God's favour, peace, grace, and blessing. When we faithfully obey God's word, this leads to recognition, respect, and honour.

Throughout Daniel's life in Babylon, he remained resolutely committed to his faith. Despite the pressure and undue influence of a pagan culture, that demanded conformity and obedience to worldly rulers, Daniel remained true to his faith. Daniel's refusal to compromise on his beliefs, principles, and values, even at the risk of death, is a powerful example of how to live one's faith in a secular environment. Like Daniel, we are to remain faithful to God in the midst of a modern world that is defined by secular values and material ambitions. Like Daniel, believers must remain firm in their faith. Believers trust in God's word. In a temporal world characterised by concupiscence, covetousness, pecuniary gain, greed, pride, wealth, private property, and envy, we must prioritise God above all else.

The Book of Daniel teaches humanity invaluable lessons about God's sovereignty. We learn the importance of remaining faithful to God. We receive assurances that God's providence prevails in the midst of adversity. The Book of Daniel encourages believers to remain steadfast in their faith. Believers trust in God's providence and redemption, while they anticipate God's eternal kingdom. Daniel's story is a timeless example for believers to demonstrate courage, prayer, humility, and trust in God's providence. The Book of Daniel encourages believers to live faithfully in all circumstances. We must keep an eternal perspective in mind. We must perceive far beyond the immediate challenges of our lifetime. We must look forward to the glory of God's eternal kingdom. We must ensure the realisation of God's promises in our life.

[1] The Holy Bible (NIV). (2011). *The Book of Daniel.* Chapter 7, Verses 2-3.

[2] The Holy Bible (NIV). (2011). *The Book of Daniel.* Chapter 1, Verse 8.

[3] The Holy Bible (NIV). (2011). *The Book of Daniel.* Chapter 3, Verse 18.

[4] The Holy Bible (NIV). (2011). *The Book of Daniel.* Chapter 6, Verse 22.

[5] The Holy Bible (NIV). (2011). *The Book of Daniel.* Chapter 7, Verse 27.

[6] The Holy Bible (NIV). (2011). *The Book of Daniel.* Chapter 2, Verse 44.

Chapter 28

The Book of Hosea

'But you must return to your God;
maintain love and justice,
and wait for your God always.'

Hosea 12:6
The Holy Bible (NIV)

The Book of Hosea is a prophetic book within the Old Testament. The Book of Hosea is attributed to the prophet Hosea. It contains Hosea's prophecies and writings. The Book of Hosea focuses on the themes of God's love, judgement, compassion, grace, and mercy. The Book of Hosea chronicles Hosea's journey as a symbolic representation of God's covenant with Israel. Hosea was instructed by God to marry Gomer, an unfaithful woman. Hosea's troubled marriage to Gomer is a Biblical metaphor for Israel's unfaithfulness to God. The Book of Hosea teaches humanity important lessons on love, sin, repentance, forgiveness, mercy, and compassion.

One of the salient attributes of Hosea's life is his marriage to Gomer, an unfaithful woman. God instructs Hosea to wed Gomer, even though she is adulterous. This broken marriage symbolises God's unconditional love for Israel, despite its unfaithfulness to Him. In spite of Israel's idolatry and sin, God's love for His chosen people endures. God's love is unconditional and persistent, even when His chosen people are unfaithful. God's love does not depend upon our faithfulness. God continues to pursue His chosen people. God offers them redemption, despite their failures and errors of judgement. This Biblical story teaches us that God's love for humanity is not based on our worthiness, but on God's goodness and grace. God honours His covenant, even when we fail to fulfil our commitment to Him.

The central theme in Hosea is God's steadfast love. Despite Israel's unfaithfulness, God's love endures. The Israelites worship false idols and seek their security in foreign alliances, rather than remain faithful to God. As a result, Israel confronts God's judgement. The Israelites are characterised by spiritual alienation and moral turpitude. Hosea repeatedly warns us that sin has profound consequences, these include brokenness, loss, grief, and separation from God. Sin separates us from God's love and leads us to moral decadence and spiritual demise. When people or nations reject God's command and follow their irrational desires, or worship false idols, they experience a breakdown in their fellowship with God. This creates spiritual chaos and disorder in our being. Sin results in the destruction of our life. Hosea informs humanity on the undesirable consequences of sin and the importance of faithfulness to God.

Throughout the Book of Hosea, God instructs Israel to repent and return to Him. God urges the Israelites to live in righteousness, for 'it is time to seek the LORD.'[1] God promises that He will redeem and restore the Israelites, if they turn away from idolatry and other sinful practices. God is willing to forgive and restore Israel; however, Israel must confess its sin and return to Him in humility and sincerity. God promises to the Israelites, 'I will heal their waywardness and love them freely.'[2]

Repentance is the instrument to restore fellowship with God. When we confess our sins and turn to God, He forgives and redeems us. The Book of Hosea teaches humanity that God's mercy is greater than our sin. Not to mention, when we sincerely repent to God, there is hope for our renewal and restoration. Confession empowers us to acknowledge our fallen state of being in the world. Confession is the legitimate method to overcome sin and evil. Confession enables us to secure redemption and re-establish a state of grace with God.

In the Book of Hosea, God declares, 'I desire mercy, not sacrifice.'[3] God's word reveals that He does not desire our tokenistic rituals or religious formalism. God desires our love, faithfulness, and obedience. Worship is characterised by forgiveness, redemption, and love. Worship is about the cultivation of fellowship with God. God desires a heart of love and loyalty, not the tokenistic performance of rituals. This Biblical message encourages believers to carefully examine their life. We must ensure that our worship and devotion to God is sincere.

Hosea frequently refers to the covenant between God and Israel. God and Israel enjoy fellowship based on mutual faithfulness. Israel's sin is symbolically characterised as a violation of its covenant with God. Despite Israel's unfaithfulness, God promises to restore the covenant and renew His unconditional love for His chosen people, 'I will betroth you in faithfulness, and you will acknowledge the LORD.'[4] Our relationship with God is defined by covenant; it is based on mutual faithfulness. God is committed to His chosen people; however, we are also responsible to remain faithful to God. This highlights the seriousness of relationships that are affirmed by covenant. Whether it is our relationship with God, or our spouse, there is an obligation upon us to demonstrate loyalty, faith, trust, love, respect, and commitment.

Hosea proclaims God's judgement and the consequences of Israel's sin. In addition, Hosea foretells God's grace, mercy, provision, and restoration for Israel. God expresses His profound emotional struggle between His judgement and love for His chosen people. God declares that He will not 'carry out my fierce anger,'[5] but will remember His compassion, for 'my heart is changed within me.'[6] God's judgement is equitable and righteous. Nevertheless, God's mercy and love are greater. When God judges and punishes sin, He is also compassionate. God desires to restore His chosen people. Hosea informs us that despite the unavoidable consequences of our sinful conduct, God's mercy is abundant. God's mercy is available to every person who repents and returns to Him.

The Book of Hosea reveals God's forbearance with Israel, even as it continues to engage in sinful conduct. God reflects on His love for Israel from its formative years as a nation, despite its repeated transgressions against His word. God's forbearance is evident throughout the Book of Hosea. God continues to counsel His chosen people to return to Him. God is merciful, forgiving, compassionate, and gracious. God provides the Israelites with many opportunities to repent and return to Him. However, there is a limit to God's forbearance. Eventually, God's judgement must be executed. We learn that when God's judgement is postponed, time is of the essence. There exists a finite opportunity for humanity to repent. This theological reality encourages us to respond to God's counsel with gratitude and repentance before His forbearance is exhausted. We must acknowledge that God is slow to anger; however, God is just in His judgement.

Hosea confronts Israel's injustice. Israel's leaders and its people engage in corruption and exploitation. The LORD speaks through the Prophet Hosea, 'there is no faithfulness, no love, no acknowledgement of God in the land.'[7] God is displeased not only by Israel's religious infidelity, but also its moral transgressions, this includes injustice toward the vulnerable people. God is concerned about justice, equity, morality, and righteousness in the world. It is insufficient to remember God in our prayers, when our actions do not reflect His justice, goodness, and holiness. Worship of God leads us to a life that upholds righteousness and compassion for humanity, especially for the less fortunate and marginalised people.

The Book of Hosea repeatedly demonstrates that God's love is everlasting, compassionate, and righteous. When Israel turns away from God and worships false idols, God instructs the Israelites to return to their rightful ways, with the promise of restoration, 'I will respond to the skies, and they will respond to the earth; and the earth will respond to the grain, the new wine and the olive oil.'[8] Hosea's profound love for his beloved wife, Gomer is an ideal representation of God's pursuit of His chosen people, despite their waywardness. God's love is steadfast and constant. No matter how far we stray, or how unfaithful we become, God's love encourages us to return to Him. This is a timely reminder of God's grace and His willingness to forgive and restore those who engage in sinful conduct.

Hosea foretells God's judgement. Nonetheless, the Book of Hosea concludes with a vision of hope, faith, and restoration. God promises to redeem Israel, restore its fortunes, and bless the nation once again, provided the Israelites return to Him in repentance. God promises not to judge and punish the Israelites' sin. Instead, God grants the Israelites an unmerited opportunity to secure His blessing, grace, and mercy. In the midst of God's judgement, there is hope for our restoration. God's mercy, favour, and grace are more powerful than our sin. When we return to God in repentance, He restores us, heals our brokenness, and reaffirms our covenant. The future holds the possibility of restored fellowship with God. We have the opportunity to experience a renewed sense of peace, love, forgiveness, and purpose in our lifetime. In the end, we are reminded 'the ways of the LORD are right; the righteous walk in them, but the rebellious stumble in them.'[2]

The Book of Hosea teaches humanity profound lessons about the nature of God's love, judgement, compassion, grace, and mercy. Hosea inspires believers to remain faithful to God. Believers must understand the consequences of their sinful conduct. When we make mistakes, we must repent and return to God. Hosea's journey and prophecies inform us that God does not value ceremonial worship. God desires our sincere love, faithfulness, integrity, commitment, and holiness. The Book of Hosea emphasises that while God's judgement is an undeniable reality, His love and mercy are greater. When we return to God, there is hope for our restoration and salvation.

[1] The Holy Bible (NIV). (2011). *The Book of Hosea.* Chapter 10, Verse 12.

[2] The Holy Bible (NIV). (2011). *The Book of Hosea.* Chapter 14, Verse 4.

[3] The Holy Bible (NIV). (2011). *The Book of Hosea.* Chapter 6, Verse 6.

[4] The Holy Bible (NIV). (2011). *The Book of Hosea.* Chapter 2, Verse 20.

[5] The Holy Bible (NIV). (2011). *The Book of Hosea.* Chapter 11, Verse 9.

[6] The Holy Bible (NIV). (2011). *The Book of Hosea.* Chapter 11, Verse 8.

[7] The Holy Bible (NIV). (2011). *The Book of Hosea.* Chapter 4, Verse 1.

[8] The Holy Bible (NIV). (2011). *The Book of Hosea.* Chapter 2, Verses 21-22.

[9] The Holy Bible (NIV). (2011). *The Book of Hosea.* Chapter 14, Verse 9.

Chapter 29

The Book of Joel

'The threshing-floors will be filled with grain;
the vats will overflow with new wine and oil.'

Joel 2:24
The Holy Bible (NIV)

T he Book of Joel is a concise prophetic book in the Old Testament. Nonetheless, the Book of Joel contains important lessons on repentance, divine judgement, and restoration. The Book of Joel is attributed to the prophet Joel. This book is associated with a locust plague that devastates Judah. This catastrophe represents God's judgement against the people. In spite of the loss and destruction, Joel envisages a future outpouring of God's Spirit. The Book of Joel concludes on a positive note with hope of restoration for God's chosen people.

Joel commences with a destructive locust plague that has cleared the land of its produce. There is nothing of value that remains on the land, 'the fields are ruined, the ground is dried up; the grain is destroyed, the new wine is dried up, the olive oil fails.'[1] This Biblical narrative symbolises God's judgement against the people of Judah for their sin, idolatry, and rebellion. This locust plague is a timely reminder to the people. The plague urges them to repent for their sins. We are reminded that sin brings forth destruction, individually, across the community, and the nation. Just as the locust destroys the land's produce, sin destroys lives, relationships, families, communities, and nations. Joel encourages us to examine our life and recognise the devastating consequences of turning away from God's word. God's judgement is just. God's word forewarns us of His judgement. We have the opportunity for repentance. We are prompted to repent and return to God.

In response to this national crisis, Joel encourages the people to repent, he urges them to 'rend your heart, and not your garments.'[2] As a result, the people fast, mourn, and seek God's mercy. The people of Judah acknowledge their sins and turn away from their wicked ways. Repentance is the instrument to experience God's restoration in our lifetime. Repentance involves not only confession, but also the restoration of our fellowship with God. A transformation of ourselves incorporates a change in our thought, speech, and behaviour. When we sincerely repent, God is merciful and willing to restore us. This teaches humanity that God is prepared to forgive those who genuinely seek Him.

Joel emphasises that God's nature is merciful and forgiving. God is gracious and compassionate. Despite the people's sin and rebellion, God instructs them to return to Him with the promise of restoration and deliverance, 'He sends you abundant showers, both autumn and spring rains, as before. The threshing-floors will be filled with grain; the vats will overflow with new wine and oil.'[3] God's response to our heartfelt repentance is redeeming grace, not judgement.

God's character is defined by compassion, love, justice, grace, forgiveness, and mercy. No matter how far we have fallen, God's love, favour, and grace are greater than the sum of our mistakes. God's desire is not to punish humanity; however, to heal and restore us. This theological fact encourages us to approach God with deference and confidence. We know that God is gracious. God forgives those who repent before Him. God not only forgives us, but He also restores what has been lost in our life. When we turn to God, He restores the areas of our life that have been damaged by questionable decisions, temptation, mistakes, moral compromise, or errors of judgement. The Biblical story of Joel provides humanity with hope. In the midst of our brokenness, grief, and pain, we are restored by God's redeeming grace.

The Book of Joel contains a prophecy concerning the 'outpouring of God's Spirit on all people.'[4] This prophecy is fulfilled in the New Testament in the Book of Acts on the Day of Pentecost,[5] when the Holy Spirit empowers believers for service, confession, and witness. The Holy Spirit is an invaluable gift from God. The Holy Spirit is received by any person who believes in God, regardless of their age, gender, sex, colour, race, ethnicity, marital status, education, vocation, personal wealth, private property, or social status. God empowers humanity with His Spirit. We must live a righteous life and serve God. This Biblical truth teaches us that God's kingdom is universal. God's kingdom is not confined to a select proportion of humanity, it is open to all believers.

Joel refers to the day of the LORD. This is a time when God judges the immoral and redeems His chosen people. On this day, God administers judgement upon the enemies of His chosen people. This is also a day of salvation for those who are faithful and repent. The day of the LORD is a reminder that God ensures justice is done. While it is a day of judgement for those who refuse to repent, it is also a day of hope for those who return to God. The certainty of God's judgement upon humanity's sin motivates us to live righteously. We must be prepared for the coming of Christ. The eternal truth of salvation in Christ reminds us to hold on to hope of eternal life in heaven.

The prophet Joel proclaims God's judgement on the surrounding nations, particularly those nations that caused injury to Israel. God judges all nations for their actions. Israel is restored to its rightful place in the world. God is a just judge. God administers justice to the oppressed and marginalised people. God holds every person accountable for their conduct. God's word assures believers that injustice does not go unpunished. Those people who have been wronged secure divine justice. We are encouraged to trust in God's righteousness. We must promote social justice in our community.

Before calling the people to repentance, Joel instructs them to consecrate themselves. The people must be set apart as holy before God. Repentance involves our renewed commitment to live in accordance with God's word, this includes holiness, righteousness, and faithfulness. Repentance is not only about abstinence from sinful conduct. Repentance means to consecrate our body, mind, heart, and spirit to God's will. Repentance is an open invitation for us to live a holy life. As God's chosen people, we must set ourselves apart for His providence. This Biblical message teaches us that repentance includes the commitment to live in obedience to God's word. We must live our life defined by integrity, purity, love, faith, honesty, justice, and righteousness.

In the midst of God's restoration, Joel speaks of the joy experienced by God's chosen people. The land is restored. God's blessings are bestowed upon the people and they rejoice. Through God's grace, 'in that day the mountains will drip new wine, and the hills will flow with milk.'[6] The people are called to celebrate and give thanks to God for His mercy, grace, blessing, and provision. When God restores and blesses His people, there is cause for celebration, happiness, peace, and gratitude. Repentance leads us to joy in God's spiritual presence. God's chosen people experience His goodness, mercy, and faithfulness. This Biblical message encourages us to live with a grateful heart. We must rejoice in God's blessing and providence.

God's judgement is not limited to Israel. God's judgement extends to all nations; 'I will gather all nations … I will put them on trial.'[7] The universality of God's judgement emphasises that His kingdom is not restricted to a particular community, clan, ethnic group, people, or nation. The Most High God is the God of all nations. God administers justice to all people. God's justice is impartial. God's judgement is irrevocable. God's kingdom is universal. These theological truths remind us of God's concern for humanity and the world. God delivers justice and restoration to all nations. Joel teaches us to embody a cosmopolitan perspective of God's kingdom. We must seek God's will for humanity, not only for our family, community, or nation.

The Book of Joel enlightens humanity about God's compassionate nature. We learn about God's desire for humanity's repentance. We witness God's love, grace, mercy, blessing, and peace. Joel emphasises that while our sin brings forth God's judgement, His love offers restoration and atonement to humanity. The promise of the outpouring of the Holy Spirit empowers God's people to persevere in their journey. The certainty of the day of the LORD encourages us to live in holiness and readiness to God's providence. Joel invites us to acknowledge the seriousness of our sin. We learn about the unmatched power of repentance. We secure confidence in the hope of our restoration and renewal through God's redeeming grace.

[1] The Holy Bible (NIV). (2011). *The Book of Joel.* Chapter 1, Verse 10.

[2] The Holy Bible (NIV). (2011). *The Book of Joel.* Chapter 2, Verse 13.

[3] The Holy Bible (NIV). (2011). *The Book of Joel.* Chapter 2, Verses 23-24.

[4] The Holy Bible (NIV). (2011). *The Book of Joel.* Chapter 2, Verse 28.

[5] The Holy Bible (NIV). (2011). *The Book of Acts.* Chapter 2, Verse 17.

[6] The Holy Bible (NIV). (2011). *The Book of Joel.* Chapter 3, Verse 18.

[7] The Holy Bible (NIV). (2011). *The Book of Joel.* Chapter 3, Verse 2.

Chapter 30

The Book of Amos

'But let justice roll on like a river,
righteousness like a never-failing stream!'

Amos 5:24
The Holy Bible (NIV)

The Book of Amos is a Biblical narrative written by Amos, one of the minor prophets in the Old Testament. Amos' prophetic message concerns God's judgement against Israel. Amos conveys God's message of justice, righteousness, and repentance. Amos is a shepherd from Tekoa in Judah. God appoints Amos to reveal a prophetic message to the northern kingdom of Israel during a time of moral decadence and social injustice. Often regarded as the Book of God's judgement, Amos contains invaluable lessons for humanity on social justice, worship, love, forgiveness, atonement, mercy, and righteousness.

Throughout the Book of Amos, the prophet Amos proclaims God's judgement on Israel and the surrounding nations for their sinful conduct. In the opening chapters, Amos condemns the sinful conduct of Israel's neighbours (i.e., Ammon, Damascus, Edom, Gaza, Judah, Moab, and Tyre), before he turns to Israel. This theological reality establishes the universality of God's judgement. God holds all nations accountable for their conduct, especially when they commit acts of injustice, violence, evil, and idolatry. Humanity is reminded that sinful conduct entails catastrophic consequences. While God is compassionate, merciful, and gracious, He does not permit our sinful conduct to remain unpunished. Amos reminds us that God's justice prevails. Individuals, communities, societies, nations, and the world are held accountable for their immoral actions. Therefore, we must live our life defined by integrity, good character, godly values, truth, honesty, social justice, equality, faith, and righteousness.

Amos unapologetically criticises the social injustice prevalent across Israel. The Israelites have oppressed the disadvantaged people, exploited the vulnerable people, and permitted corruption in their legal system. Amos condemns the wealthy people for living a life of luxury, while they demonstrate indifference to the suffering of the marginalised and vulnerable people in society. Amos informs us of the prevalence of injustice throughout Israelite society, 'You levy a straw tax on the poor and impose a tax on their grain. Therefore, though you have built stone mansions, you will not live in them; though you have planted lush vineyards, you will not drink their wine.'[1]

God is deeply concerned about social justice, especially concerning the unfortunate and marginalised people. Authentic worship and righteousness are inseparable from our commitment to social justice. A society that neglects the needs of its destitute people and oppresses the vulnerable people acts contrary to God's will. This Biblical narrative challenges believers to advocate for social justice, equality, fairness, peace, love, and mercy in their communities and nations.

Despite Israel's observance of religious customs and traditions, Amos condemns the Israelites for their tokenistic rituals and perfunctory ceremonies. The Israelites continue to offer sacrifices and observe religious festivals; however, their hearts and minds remain distant from God. As a result, God declares, 'I hate, I despise your religious festivals; your assemblies are a stench to me. Even though you bring me burnt offerings and grain offerings, I will not accept them,'[2] because they are not accompanied by righteousness and justice. God desires our sincerity in worship, not the mere observance of custom.

Worship is characterised by a good heart that seeks justice, righteousness, and holiness. God does not desire our perfunctory religious rituals. God desires a transformed life that reflects His character, nature, and will. Amos teaches us that our worship must be genuine. Our worship must align with God's providence. Our character is reflected in our everyday actions. Furthermore, our character is defined by how we treat each other in society, especially the most vulnerable people.

Amos repeatedly encourages the Israelites to seek God and

repent for their immoral actions. Amos prudently warns the Israelites of God's judgement. God's message is unambiguous: 'Seek me and live.'[3] While Amos foretells destruction, he holds on to hope that the people's repentance leads to God's mercy, grace, and restoration. There is always the opportunity for our repentance. God is merciful to those who return to Him. While God's judgement is inevitable for the people who refuse to repent, He desires to extend mercy, grace, and restoration to those who humble themselves and seek His forgiveness. This Biblical principle teaches us the importance of repentance. We are assured that God forgives and restores those individuals who return to Him in sincerity, honesty, love, and faith.

Throughout the Book of Amos, the prophet Amos emphasises God's sovereignty over creation. God's providence directs the fate of all nations on earth. God employs foreign powers to accomplish His providence, 'When disaster comes to a city, has not the LORD caused it?'[4] God's justice is not confined to Israel. God judges all nations for their sinful conduct. God's sovereignty extends throughout creation. God's judgement is impartial. No empire, kingdom, nation, or individual is beyond God's sovereign authority. This Biblical principle teaches us that we must recognise God's sovereignty. We must align our thoughts and actions with God's will. God's providence is unassailable. In all things, God's providence comes to fruition.

In the Book of Amos, God declares that He despises Israel's religious festivals and offerings, because they are not accompanied by justice. God affirms, 'Let justice roll on like a river, righteousness like a never-failing stream!'[5] This is a powerful declaration that God does not desire to witness the performance of tokenistic rituals. God desires to observe individuals, families, communities, societies, kingdoms, and nations practice social justice, equality, love, mercy, hospitality, generosity, brotherhood, sisterhood, and righteousness.

Worship is not characterised by the mere performance of religious duties. Worship is characterised by living honourably, morally, ethically, and righteously. God desires that His chosen people not only perform religious rituals, but they also live in accordance with His commandments, especially in relation to justice, fairness, integrity, and righteousness. Amos' prophetic message encourages believers to integrate their faith with righteous conduct. Believers must ensure their actions reflect God's heart for justice, love, goodness, compassion, peace, forgiveness, and mercy.

As Amos pronounces God's judgement, there remains an opportunity for the Israelites to repent for their sins and secure restoration. For example, consider God declares, 'Seek good, not evil, that you may live.'[6] God offers Israel the opportunity to mitigate its impending destruction through repentance. This demonstrates that God's mercy is accessible to humanity, even in the midst of His judgement. While God's judgement is just and inevitable for [unrepentant] sin, He extends grace and mercy to those who turn to Him in repentance. No person is beyond the purview of God's mercy. Even in times of judgement, God extends humanity the blessed opportunity to return to Him and secure His forgiveness. This theological assertion encourages us to respond to God's word with humility. We know that God is willing to forgive and restore humanity. Therefore, are we prepared to demonstrate repentance for our immoral conduct?

Amos speaks of the day of the LORD. This is a time when God judges Israel for its sins and He punishes the immoral people, 'Why do you long for the day of the LORD? That day will be darkness, not light.'[7] However, for those people who are faithful and seek God, the day of the LORD brings forth blessing and restoration. The day of the LORD is the predestined time of God's judgement for the unrighteous people. On the other hand, it symbolises a time of blessing for those people who remain faithful to God's word. The day of the LORD reminds us that God administers justice across kingdoms, empires, and nations. For those people who are unrepentant, it is a day of judgement. On the contrary, for the faithful believer it is a day of redemption, salvation, and restoration. This Biblical prophecy encourages us to live with readiness for the coming of Christ and the establishment of God's kingdom on earth. We must demonstrate justice, honour, integrity, truth, and righteousness in the world. We must ensure our heart and mind are aligned with God's will.

The Book of Amos is known for its categorical messages on God's judgement. Nonetheless, the Book of Amos concludes with an optimistic vision of Israel's future restoration. God promises to restore David's 'fallen shelter'[8] and return His chosen people to their homeland. God blesses His people with prosperity, peace, and power. When we factor into consideration God's judgement, His providence for His people's restoration, salvation, and sanctification is not obstructed. For Israel, this restoration points to the future fulfilment of God's covenant, the coming of the Messiah to atone humanity for original sin. For believers, the scripture assures us that no matter how difficult the present time, God's providence is characterised by restoration, compassion, salvation, and forgiveness.

The Book of Amos provides humanity with invaluable lessons about God's justice. We learn about God's concern for the welfare of the oppressed people. Amos acquaints us with the importance of worship. While Amos informs the people of God's judgement, Amos also encourages the people to repent, promote social justice, and live with integrity. The Book of Amos emphasises that God desires His chosen people to live a righteous life that reflects God's heart for justice, mercy, love, peace, and compassion. Even in the midst of God's judgement, there is hope of our restoration through repentance and returning to God.

Amos' prophetic message remains relevant in this day and age. We are commanded to live honourably, worship God with sincerity, and seek His mercy and restoration in our life.

[1] The Holy Bible (NIV). (2011). *The Book of Amos.* Chapter 5, Verse 11.

[2] The Holy Bible (NIV). (2011). *The Book of Amos.* Chapter 5, Verses 21-22.

[3] The Holy Bible (NIV). (2011). *The Book of Amos.* Chapter 5, Verse 4.

[4] The Holy Bible (NIV). (2011). *The Book of Amos.* Chapter 3, Verse 6.

[5] The Holy Bible (NIV). (2011). *The Book of Amos.* Chapter 5, Verse 24.

[6] The Holy Bible (NIV). (2011). *The Book of Amos.* Chapter 5, Verse 14.

[7] The Holy Bible (NIV). (2011). *The Book of Amos.* Chapter 5, Verse 18.

[8] The Holy Bible (NIV). (2011). *The Book of Amos.* Chapter 9, Verse 11.

Chapter 31

The Book of Obadiah

'The day of the LORD is near for all nations.
As you have done, it will be done to you;
your deeds will return upon your own head.'

Obadiah 1:15
The Holy Bible (NIV)

T he Book of Obadiah is a concise book in the Old Testament. Obadiah is a prophetic book that addresses the nation of Edom. Obadiah is one of the twelve minor prophets. The prophet Obadiah proclaims God's judgement against Edom, for its sins against Jerusalem and Judah. Obadiah's prophecy demonstrates to humanity the destructive consequences of pride, fame, wealth, and glory. The Book of Obadiah teaches humanity invaluable lessons on spirituality, morality, divinity, and ethics.

Obadiah cautions Edom about its unbridled pride, especially its arrogance that emerges from its advantageous geographical location in the mountains. Edom's strategic location provides the Edomites with a false sense of security. Consequently, the Edomites renounce their trust and confidence in God. In response, God's message to the Edomites is unequivocal, 'the pride of your heart has deceived you.'[1] God condemns the Edomites for believing that they were beyond His sovereign authority. God's judgement against Edom demonstrates that no nation circumvents His will. In effect, the Edomites pride and self-reliance deceived them, this resulted in their downfall. We learn that humility and recognition of God's sovereignty are essential to avoid our fall from grace.

Edom is condemned, not only for its pride, but also for its assistance to the Babylonians during the destruction of Jerusalem. The Edomites rejoiced in Israel's misfortune. They also participated in the looting and violence against God's chosen people, 'On the day you stood aloof while strangers carried off his wealth and foreigners entered his gates and cast lots for Jerusalem, you were like one of them.'[2] God perceives each and every act of injustice on earth. As a consequence, God holds nations and individuals accountable for their ill-treatment of humanity, especially when it comes to oppression, betrayal, injustice, exploitation, and cruelty. God is omniscient. God perceives when we are indifferent to the suffering of humanity, or we actively participate in evil acts against humanity. Our voluntary and conscious performance of sinful acts does not circumvent God's providence.

To make matters worse, there is a bond of brotherhood between Edom and Israel. The Edomites were the descendants of Esau, they were related to Israel (i.e., the descendants of Jacob). This fact makes Edom's betrayal egregious. Instead of rendering assistance to their brotherly nation in its hour of need, the Edomites acted as enemies of the Israelites. Relationships, in particular family, friendships, marriage, community, and across nations incorporate considerable moral significance. Betrayal within these trusted bonds is particularly grievous. Loyalty, solidarity, and camaraderie for one's brothers and sisters are essential to live in accordance with God's will.

Obadiah's prophecy reveals that God possesses sovereignty over all nations and kingdoms, not only Israel. God judges Edom for its actions and omissions. Not to mention, God promises Israel's future restoration. God's judgement against Edom and the eventual triumph of Israel over its enemies demonstrates that no nation is beyond God's sovereignty. God's providence defines world history. God ensures justice is administered across all nations. No nation, empire, kingdom, or person circumvents God's judgement or obstructs His sovereignty. God's providence is not obstructed by human endeavours.

Comparable to the prophetic messages of the other minor prophets in the Old Testament, Obadiah proclaims the day of the LORD. This is a future time when God administers judgement upon the nations for their sins. With respect to the unavoidability of judgement, we are reminded, 'as you have done, it will be done to you; your deeds will return upon your own head.'[3] This is a future event in which God rights all wrongs and establishes His kingdom on earth. The day of the LORD reminds us that justice is not always secured amongst the present generation. We are commanded to live with the expectation that God judges the world. In the fullness of time, God administers justice and establishes His kingdom on earth.

Through Obadiah, God proclaims judgement against Edom. God employs Obadiah to foretell a future time of Israel's restoration. This restoration is part of God's will for His chosen people. In the end, Israel triumphs over its adversaries. No matter the present situation or circumstances, God's will for His chosen people includes restoration, prosperity, and victory of good over evil. Obadiah's prophetic message provides encouragement to believers who are suffering or confront injustice. Obadiah reminds us that God is omnipotent, omnipresent, and omniscient.

God's judgement against Edom emphasises that His justice is not arbitrary. God's justice is established in His holiness. Persons or nations that act in a manner contrary to God's will—such as demonstrating prideful, evil, malevolent, or unjust conduct—are held accountable for their immoral conduct. Believers must live in accordance with God's holiness and justice. This approach to life is paramount for our prosperity. Righteousness incorporates mercy, forgiveness, peace, love, brotherhood, sisterhood, and justice. Believers are to demonstrate these distinguished attributes in their life.

The Book of Obadiah is a timely reminder to humanity of God's commitment to social justice. Obadiah assures us of God's sovereignty over all nations. Believers must act with humility and righteousness. Obadiah teaches humanity that while injustice prevails temporarily, God's kingdom ultimately triumphs on earth. We must be careful not to permit conceit, pride, or arrogance to define our character. No matter the accomplishments, victories, milestones, and successes that we attain, our life is only a transient phenomenon. Therefore, we must conduct ourselves with a mindset that perceives far beyond the here and now. We must conduct ourselves in a manner that affirms our allegiance to God. In the fullness of time, what truly matters is our character, credibility, and conscience.

[1] The Holy Bible (NIV). (2011). *The Book of Obadiah.* Chapter 1, Verse 3.
[2] The Holy Bible (NIV). (2011). *The Book of Obadiah.* Chapter 1, Verse 11.
[3] The Holy Bible (NIV). (2011). *The Book of Obadiah.* Chapter 1, Verse 15.

Chapter 32

The Book of Jonah

'To the roots of the mountains I sank down;
the earth beneath barred me in for ever.
But you, LORD my God,
brought my life up from the pit.'

Jonah 2:6
The Holy Bible (NIV)

The Book of Jonah is well-known in the Old Testament. The Book of Jonah narrates the story of Jonah, a prophet whom God commands to proceed to Nineveh. Jonah's mission is to encourage the Ninevites to repent. Initially, Jonah objects to the performance of God's will. Prophet Jonah's disobedience leads to a series of dramatic events throughout world history. The Book of Jonah offers a number of important Biblical lessons on obedience, compassion, repentance, mercy, forgiveness, and love.

The Book of Jonah commences with Jonah being commanded by God to proceed to Nineveh. Instead, Jonah 'ran away from the LORD,' [1] and he fled to Tarshish. Jonah's disobedience leads to a formidable storm at sea. Thereafter, Jonah is swallowed by a large fish at sea. Disobedience to God's calling entails serious consequences, not only for the individual concerned, however, also for humanity. In any case, God's will is not thwarted. We must trust and obey God, even when God's command is inconvenient to perform or difficult to comprehend. When we turn away from God's command, this leads us to adversity. Having said that, God's mercy is available for our repentance and restoration.

Throughout this Biblical story, God demonstrates His sovereignty over creation, including humanity and nature. For example, consider God sends a violent storm. God commands the large fish to swallow Jonah. God's providence directs Jonah to fulfil his assignment. God causes the leafy plant to grow, wither, and die. These events demonstrate that God's providence governs creation. We recognise God's sovereignty over creation. No event comes to fruition without God's authorisation. This universal reality includes natural events and our personal circumstances. When we trust in God's sovereignty, this brings us profound peace, even in times of turmoil or uncertainty.

One theological lesson that we deduce from the Book of Jonah is God's willingness to demonstrate mercy, even to those whom Jonah despises. Nineveh was a city known for its immorality. Jonah persistently resented the thought that God would forgive such immoral people. However, when the Ninevites repented, God relented from the destruction that He had envisaged, 'When God saw what they did and how they turned from their evil ways, He relented and did not bring on them the destruction He had threatened.'[2]

The scripture informs us that God's mercy is not restricted to any nation, ethnicity, social group, race, or community. God's love extends beyond Israel to all nations, even those that are distant from Him. This theological reality encourages believers to adopt a broader perspective of God's mercy. Believers must disseminate God's message of repentance, love, compassion, blessing, and mercy throughout the world, without regard to nationality, kinship, or community.

The Ninevites positively respond to Jonah's warning. The Ninevites repent, this includes the King of Nineveh, the nobility, and the common people. God witnesses the Ninevites repent. As an act of mercy, God spares the city of Nineveh from imminent destruction. Repentance, means to turn away from evil and humble oneself before God. Repentance leads to forgiveness of sin and restoration. This historical event underscores the importance of a repentant heart, not only for the Ninevites, but for humanity.

After the Ninevites repented, they were spared from destruction. This caused Jonah to become angry with God's compassion and forgiveness towards the Ninevites, 'But to Jonah this seemed very wrong, and he became angry.'[3] Jonah reasoned that the Ninevites did not deserve God's forgiveness, because of their immorality. Jonah personally struggled to comprehend God's compassion, forgiveness, and mercy towards the Ninevites.

Jonah's partial perspective of the situation reveals his self-righteousness and lack of understanding of God's heart towards humanity.

Unconsciously, we can adopt a mindset of self-righteousness. We may rationalise that certain people are unworthy of God's mercy. Jonah's story challenges believers to consciously examine their heart and mind. We must unequivocally reject any ideology, doctrine, belief, or thought, that promotes a sense of superiority or biased judgement towards any member of humanity. Every person deserves God's love, mercy, blessing, and forgiveness. We must universally share God's grace with humanity.

God informs Jonah that 'He is concerned for the great city of Nineveh.'[4] A city with over 120,000 people, and also the many animals within the city. This is a timely reminder that God's compassion incorporates every person on earth. Beyond humanity, God is concerned for the welfare of animals. God expresses His concern about the welfare of the world, this includes humanity, animals, plants, and the natural environment. Believers are called to reflect God's will and providence for creation. We must protect humanity, but also extend our care, compassion, and concern towards all other life forms within God's creation. This reflects our intergenerational duty of stewardship. We must align our heart and mind with God's compassionate nature.

Jonah's journey reveals that even prophets are imperfect people. Despite Jonah's assignment, he resented God's mercy toward the Ninevites. Jonah became angry with God, when He did not act as Jonah had envisaged or expected. However, God benevolently taught Jonah important lessons, such as the value of mercy, love, grace, forgiveness, and compassion. God is compassionate towards humanity, this includes His prophets and servants. When we struggle to comprehend God's providence, His love and mercy provide us with the opportunity to mature, learn, and align our thoughts and actions with His will. We are never too far gone to receive God's mercy and redeeming grace.

Jonah's desire for God's judgement upon Nineveh was noticeably distinct from God's providence to forgive the Ninevites. Jonah desired for the city of Nineveh to be destroyed. God's providence was for Nineveh to repent and be redeemed. When God's will prevailed, this challenged Jonah's finite understanding of God's justice, providence, love, and mercy. The prophet Isaiah's revelation about God is a timely reminder, 'For my thoughts are not your thoughts, neither are your ways my ways.'[5] God's providence does not always align with our vision, beliefs, values, or expectations. Believers must trust in God's wisdom, even when His providence does not align with their finite understanding or partial perception of the world.

In the final chapter of the Book of Jonah, prophet Jonah expresses his [unjustified] grief in relation to the withering away of the leafy plant that provided him with shade from the scorching sun. We learn that 'God provided a leafy plant'[6] and subsequently, He caused it to become withered. God utilised this leafy plant to teach Jonah a lesson on compassion. Given Jonah is concerned about this leafy plant, how much more is God concerned about the Ninevites?

God values compassion and teaches us to care deeply for humanity. In particular, we must reach out to people who are distant from God's word. In the New Testament, this theological assertion is affirmed by the Messiah in the Parable of the Wandering Sheep in the Gospel of Matthew. For the Messiah declares, 'If a man owns a hundred sheep, and one of them wanders away, will he not leave the ninety-nine on the hills and go to look for the one that wandered off?'[7] Every person is equally valuable by the virtue of human dignity. Since every person is made in the image of God, every person is of immeasurable value to God.

The Book of Jonah teaches us about God's heart for mercy, justice, grace, redemption, love, and compassion. We learn the importance of obedience to God's word. Jonah's life story challenges us to reconsider our attitudes and opinions towards humanity. We must embrace God's egalitarian vision of the world. We must not perceive the inviolable and universal principle of human dignity through a biased, prejudicial, partial, and limited perspective. Human dignity is not defined by race, colour, sex, gender, nationality, education, income, age, vocation, social status, private property, or personal wealth.

If we are to become more like God's character, and if we are to truly embody the Holy Spirit within us, then we must treat every person with compassion, love, generosity, hospitality, mercy, equality, and dignity. An egalitarian perspective of humanity refines our character. Equality enhances our conscience. Empathy enriches our lived experience. Therefore, we must employ our empirical knowledge to perform good actions. We must perfect our state of being in the world.

[1] The Holy Bible (NIV). (2011). *The Book of Jonah.* Chapter 1, Verse 3.

[2] The Holy Bible (NIV). (2011). *The Book of Jonah.* Chapter 3, Verse 10.

[3] The Holy Bible (NIV). (2011). *The Book of Jonah.* Chapter 4, Verse 1.

[4] The Holy Bible (NIV). (2011). *The Book of Jonah.* Chapter 4, Verse 11.

[5] The Holy Bible (NIV). (2011). *The Book of Isaiah.* Chapter 55, Verse 8.

[6] The Holy Bible (NIV). (2011). *The Book of Jonah.* Chapter 4, Verse 6.

[7] The Holy Bible (NIV). (2011). *The Book of Matthew.* Chapter 18, Verse 12.

Chapter 33

The Book of Micah

'Your hand will be lifted up in triumph over your enemies,
and all your foes will be destroyed.'

Micah 5:9
The Holy Bible (NIV)

T he Book of Micah is a prophetic text within the Old
Testament. Micah contains Biblical messages on
judgement, hope, and restoration. Micah was a prophet
to the northern kingdom of Israel and the southern kingdom of
Judah. Micah's profound prophecies reflect the moral decadence,
widespread injustice, and idolatry prevalent in these two
kingdoms at the time. Micah foretells the coming of a righteous
saviour—Jesus Christ.

Micah denounces the widespread injustice, corruption, and
oppression in the kingdom of Israel and Judah. Micah
unequivocally condemns the wealthy and privileged people who
exploit the less fortunate and vulnerable people across both
kingdoms, 'woe to those who plan iniquity, to those who plot
evil.'[1] In addition, Micah criticises the religious leaders who
mislead the people and the illegitimate prophets who speak
untruths, 'therefore night will come over you without visions, and
darkness, without divination. The sun will set for the prophets,
and the day will go dark for them.'[2]

Micah proclaims to the people that God is deeply concerned
with widespread injustice, particularly injustice towards the
unfortunate, oppressed, and marginalised people. Injustice,
exploitation, and corruption constitute immoral acts in God's
creation. Individuals in esteemed positions of power are held
accountable for how they treat humanity. As believers, we must
take a stand against oppression and promote social justice on
earth.

In the Book of Micah, the people inquire: What should we
offer or sacrifice to appease God? God's word is unequivocal.
God values justice, compassion, mercy, righteousness, and
humility, more than sacrifice or sin offerings. God's word informs
us, 'He has shown you, O mortal, what is good. And what does
the LORD require of you? To act justly and to love mercy and to

walk humbly with your God.'[3] Worship is not about the performance of rituals or sacrifices. Worship is to live our life genuinely reflecting God's character. Believers must act with justice, demonstrate compassion, and walk faithfully with God.

Our actions must align with our words. How we treat members of the community is a reflection of our sacred relationship with God. When we carefully examine God's word, it is unequivocal that He has prescribed ethical, moral, and spiritual instructions for humanity's conduct. To live justly means to treat people with fairness, love, mercy, compassion, dignity, equality, and integrity. To demonstrate mercy towards one another means to act with compassion, tolerance, love, and understanding. Last but not least, when we walk humbly with God, it means we live with trust and confidence in God's providence. In all that we do, we must acknowledge God's sovereignty over creation. We must walk in obedience to God's word.

Micah proclaims God's imminent judgement against Israel, Judah, and the surrounding nations. Micah warns of the destruction of Samaria (the capital of Israel) and Jerusalem (the capital of Judah) because of the people's sinful conduct. Micah foretells God's judgement against the nations that oppress God's chosen people. God judges all nations and people, this includes His chosen people. No nation or person is exempt from God's justice. Micah's prophecy is a timely reminder, that God's impending judgement constitutes a warning to humanity. If we do not repent, God's judgement is a certainty of our existential reality. We must live with an appreciation of the universal truth; God is omnipotent, omnipresent, and omniscient. God administers His righteous judgement in the fullness of time.

Micah encourages the people to repent for their sins. It is incumbent upon humanity to recognise that God forgives and restores those who return to Him. Micah emphasises that God is merciful, compassionate, and forgiving, 'Who is a God like you, who pardons sin and forgives the transgression of the remnant of his inheritance? You do not stay angry for ever but delight to show mercy.'[4] God offers forgiveness and restoration to those who truly repent. No matter how far we have fallen, the mistakes that we have made, or the errors in our judgement, God's mercy is greater than our sin. Repentance creates the opportunity to receive God's grace and secure our restoration. Ultimately, God desires to heal and restore humanity.

In one of Micah's prophecies, he proclaims the coming of a saviour who brings peace, forgiveness, and justice to humanity: 'But you, Bethlehem Ephrathah, though you are small among the clans of Judah, out of you will come for me one who will be ruler over Israel, whose origins are from of old, from ancient times.'[5] This is a direct prophecy of the blessed birth of Jesus Christ, who is born in Bethlehem. God's providence includes the coming of a righteous saviour who establishes God's kingdom of justice, peace, love, and righteousness on earth. This Biblical prophecy points to the Messiah (i.e., Jesus Christ), it reminds us that God's covenant is faithful, eternal, and true. When our circumstances or situation is difficult, we must seek encouragement and hope in the knowledge that God's providence comes to realisation.

Micah foretells judgement and destruction for Israel and Judah. Nonetheless, the prophet Micah also expresses hope for their restoration and the eventual coming of God's kingdom on earth. The faithful remnant is redeemed. God's people are comforted, healed, and restored. Even in times of divine judgement and privation, God offers humanity hope. There is always the promise of restoration for those who remain faithful to God's word. God's judgement is not His final act. God's mercy and compassion prevail in the end. This Biblical message encourages believers to hold on to hope, even when they confront difficult circumstances in their life.

Micah demonstrates that God is not concerned with the performance of religious acts, when they are not accompanied by repentance, love, faithfulness, and justice. God desires His people to embody a sincere heart that desires justice, mercy, love, and humility. To evaluate our actions, God considers our intentions, desires, motives, and conscience. While religious rituals and practices are important, they are meaningless, when they are not accompanied by our commitment to live in accordance with God's word. Worship is reflected in how we live, not merely our speech and conduct at religious ceremonies, festivals, or events.

Micah marvels at God's boundless compassion towards humanity. Micah proclaims: 'Who is a God like you, who pardons sin and forgives the transgression of the remnant of his inheritance? You do not stay angry for ever but delight to show mercy.'[6] God's compassionate nature and forgiveness are central to His character. Despite the sinfulness of His people, God is prepared to forgive those who turn to Him in repentance. God's mercy triumphs over judgement. God delights to demonstrate mercy to those who earnestly seek it.

Micah proclaims the future establishment of God's kingdom on earth. A kingdom where peace, justice, love, and righteousness prevail. The Book of Micah characterises this desirable reality using a metaphor of the mountain of the LORD; 'the highest of the mountains; it will be exalted above the hills, and peoples will stream to it.'[7] This is a vision of a future time when the nations come to Jerusalem to worship God. A time when there is no more conflict. A time when peace and prosperity prevail.

The pinnacle of God's providence is the establishment of His righteous kingdom on earth. A kingdom where social justice, love, peace, harmony, righteousness, morality, and equality prevail. This divine vision provides believers with hope for the future. God's perpetual reign brings about the restoration of all things in creation. Believers are to live in anticipation of God's kingdom. Believers are Christ's ambassadors whom further justice, love, equality, brotherhood, sisterhood, and peace on earth.

The Book of Micah teaches us about God's concern for justice, mercy, love, and humility. The prophet Micah encourages us to put God's word into practice. Micah's prophecy points to the coming of the Messiah. We are to reaffirm our hope in God's kingdom on earth. No matter the unfavourable circumstances or challenges that we confront in our lifetime, we have trust and confidence in the LORD. God's kingdom prevails on earth. Our salvation is not obtained through good deeds; however, it is secured through the Messiah. Through Jesus Christ, we are justified before God. Peace be with you.

[1] The Holy Bible (NIV). (2011). *The Book of Micah.* Chapter 2, Verse 1.

[2] The Holy Bible (NIV). (2011). *The Book of Micah.* Chapter 3, Verse 6.

[3] The Holy Bible (NIV). (2011). *The Book of Micah.* Chapter 6, Verse 8.

[4] The Holy Bible (NIV). (2011). *The Book of Micah.* Chapter 7, Verse 18.

[5] The Holy Bible (NIV). (2011). *The Book of Micah.* Chapter 5, Verse 2.

[6] The Holy Bible (NIV). (2011). *The Book of Micah.* Chapter 7, Verse 18.

[7] The Holy Bible (NIV). (2011). *The Book of Micah.* Chapter 4, Verse 1.

Chapter 34

The Book of Nahum

'The LORD is good,
a refuge in times of trouble.
He cares for those who trust in Him.'

Nahum 1:7
The Holy Bible (NIV)

The Book of Nahum is a prophetic book within the Old Testament. The Book of Nahum is concerned with God's impending judgement against Nineveh, the great capital city of the Assyrian empire. The prophet Nahum foretells the demise of Nineveh due to its immorality, violence, social injustice, corruption, moral decadence, and idolatry. Nahum's prophetic message is one of God's judgement. The Book of Nahum contains invaluable lessons for believers.

The opening verses of the Book of Nahum characterise God as 'jealous and avenging.'[1] We learn that God executes vengeance against His enemies. Nahum underscores God's justice. Nahum reveals that God does not overlook acts of sin or evil. Thus, we are reminded that God holds immoral people accountable for their actions. God is just. God does not permit evil acts to remain unpunished. God is compassionate and merciful. God is righteous. This Biblical message is a timely reminder to humanity, that justice is a fundamental attribute of God's character. Therefore, God holds humanity responsible for their actions.

Nahum emphasises God's sovereignty over creation, this includes His providence over nature and the affairs of nations. We are reminded that 'the LORD is slow to anger but great in power; the LORD will not leave the guilty unpunished.'[2] The opening chapter of Nahum employs imagery of natural disasters, such as earthquakes, storms, and fire to characterise God's power. Nahum reminds the people that no person or nation supersedes God's will, this includes the mighty Assyrian empire. God is sovereign over creation and the nations of the world. God's sovereign authority encompasses all phenomena, from the natural world to the political leaders of nations, kingdoms, principalities, dukedoms, and empires. This universal reality encourages believers to trust in God's providence. Humanity must position its trust and confidence in God's word. The future of the world is determined in accordance with God's will.

While God is merciful and compassionate, Nahum makes it known that God's forbearance is not inexhaustible. Through the prophet Jonah, Nineveh had previously experienced God's mercy. Nonetheless, the Ninevites actions, which are characterised by evil, corruption, and violence, have reached a point of no return. Therefore, God's judgement is imminent. God's forbearance is matchless; however, it is not without end. There comes a point in time, when God's judgement is unavoidable, especially for those who continually reject God's mercy and persist in the performance of immoral deeds. Nahum's prophecy is a timely reminder to humanity, there is a limit to God's forbearance. Therefore, we must repent for our sinful conduct. We must turn to God, before it is too late.

Nineveh's destruction is a consequence of its people's sinful conduct. The Assyrians were notorious for their cruelty, violence, and idolatry. Nahum makes it unambiguous, the Ninevites immoral actions are responsible for their downfall, "I am against you,' declares the LORD almighty.'[3] The city of Nineveh is described as the 'city of blood.'[4] This dismal representation demonstrates the considerable extent of Nineveh's corruption. Sin always leads to destruction and demise. While it appears to humanity that evil prospers for a short period of time, evil results in God's judgement. We must not accept any delusions in relation to evil in the world. This universal reality highlights the importance to live the good life that honours God's word. We must avoid sinful conduct. We must practice righteousness, integrity, honesty, and justice in the world.

While the Assyrians are judged, Nahum assures the people of Judah that God will protect and restore them. The Book of Nahum informs us, 'The LORD is good, a refuge in times of trouble. He cares for those who trust in Him.'[5] This is a reminder that God is a refuge for His chosen people. God provides His chosen people with protection and safety. In times of trouble and fear, God is our refuge and security. God protects those who trust in Him. Ultimately, God redeems His people from evil. Believers secure peace in the knowledge that, despite immorality in the world, God's providence is not circumvented.

Nahum's prophecy is not an empty threat. Nahum's prophecy is a declaration of God's judgement. The fall of Nineveh is described in vivid detail. Nahum assures the people that no phenomenon obstructs God's will in creation; 'It is decreed that Nineveh be exiled and carried away.'[6] The destruction of Nineveh is catastrophic and definitive, just as God had determined. God's judgement is certain and unavoidable for those who refuse to repent. Just as God declared His judgement upon Nineveh, He also administers His judgement on all those who persist in immoral actions defined by sin and evil. Nahum's prophecy encourages believers to live with an awareness of God's justice. Believers must live their life defined by integrity, morality, love, compassion, joy, peace, credibility, righteousness, mercy, and faithfulness.

Nahum's prophetic message concerns the destruction of Nineveh. Nevertheless, Nahum's message epitomises God's sovereignty and justice over creation. The destruction of Nineveh is an example of how God dethrones worldly powers that engage in evil acts. The Book of Nahum concludes with finality in relation to Nineveh's fate. This Biblical message reinforces that God's justice prevails against all worldly leaders and empires. Ultimately, God's kingdom triumphs over evil. While earthly powers and transient kingdoms rise and fall, God's kingdom endures for eternity. The glory of God's kingdom is without beginning or end. God's justice prevails. Believers must live in anticipation of God's decisive victory over evil.

Nahum condemns Nineveh for its violence, corruption, and

oppression, especially towards God's chosen people. The Assyrians were known for their brutality. Consequently, God's wrath is directed at the Assyrians for their cruelty, injustice, and exploitation of humanity. God is opposed to the oppression and exploitation of vulnerable and marginalised people. Throughout the scripture, God reveals His heart for the oppressed people. God promises judgement upon those who misappropriate their authority, power, status, wealth, or position to harm humanity. Believers are commanded to unite against oppression and promote social justice.

Nineveh, once a powerful and mighty city of the ancient Assyrian empire, immediately disintegrates under God's judgement, 'the river gates are thrown open and the palace collapses.'[7] The demise of the Assyrian empire is a sobering reminder that no person, empire, kingdom, or nation, no matter how powerful, circumvents God's judgement, if they persist in evil actions. The fall of Nineveh is a warning to all nations and individuals. No worldly power, no matter how powerful, stands against God's judgement. This Biblical lesson encourages humanity to reject evil. We must repent for our sins and engage in confession, before it is too late.

Nineveh's obliteration is not merely the effectuation of God's punishment; however, it also constitutes restoration. Through divine judgement on Nineveh, God restores order in the world, which had been disrupted by the Assyrians' wickedness. This divine restoration brings peace and justice to those who are faithful to God, 'no more will the wicked invade you; they will be completely destroyed.'[8] God's judgement is not arbitrary. God's judgement serves to restore order, peace, and justice in the world. While God's judgement is painful and difficult to witness, it leads to the restoration of peace, justice, righteousness, and order in accordance with God's will.

The Book of Nahum reminds us that while God is

compassionate, He does not tolerate evil indefinitely. The administration of God's justice is certain. God executes His judgement upon all people, nations, and empires who persist in the performance of acts defined by sin, evil, social injustice, immorality, or oppression. However, for God's chosen people, He is a refuge, sanctuary, and protector. The Book of Nahum teaches humanity that God ensures the restoration of peace, justice, and order through His righteous rule as sovereign over creation.

[1] The Holy Bible (NIV). (2011). *The Book of Nahum.* Chapter 1, Verse 2.

[2] The Holy Bible (NIV). (2011). *The Book of Nahum.* Chapter 1, Verse 3.

[3] The Holy Bible (NIV). (2011). *The Book of Nahum.* Chapter 2, Verse 13.

[4] The Holy Bible (NIV). (2011). *The Book of Nahum.* Chapter 3, Verse 1.

[5] The Holy Bible (NIV). (2011). *The Book of Nahum.* Chapter 1, Verse 7.

[6] The Holy Bible (NIV). (2011). *The Book of Nahum.* Chapter 2, Verse 7.

[7] The Holy Bible (NIV). (2011). *The Book of Nahum.* Chapter 2, Verse 6.

[8] The Holy Bible (NIV). (2011). *The Book of Nahum.* Chapter 1, Verse 15.

Chapter 35

The Book of Habakkuk

'His splendour was like the sunrise;
rays flashed from His hand,
where His power was hidden.'

Habakkuk 3:4
The Holy Bible (NIV)

The Book of Habakkuk is a concise prophetic text in the Old Testament. Habakkuk contains several invaluable messages on faith, justice, morality, and trust in God's providence. In the midst of uncertainty and suffering, Habakkuk reminds us to run our race to the best of our ability. One perspective to understand the Book of Habakkuk is that it represents a compilation of prophet Habakkuk's lamentations. The prophet Habakkuk questions God's goodness, because Habakkuk witnesses tragedy, evil, grief, corruption, immorality, and injustice in the world. In spite of evil in the world, we are reminded that God humbles the proud. God affirms the righteous people by their faith in Him. The Book of Habakkuk reaffirms that God is omnipotent, omniscient, and omnipresent.

The prophet Habakkuk inquires: Why does God permit injustice, evil, and wickedness to prevail on earth? Habakkuk presents the argument, 'the law is paralysed, and justice never prevails. The wicked hem in the righteous, so that justice is perverted.'[1] Habakkuk is deeply concerned by God's deafening silence in the midst of humanity's undeniable suffering. God responds by revealing that He is raising up the Babylonians to execute His judgement against the evildoers. Habakkuk is concerned with God's proposal to employ a wicked empire to administer divine justice. Having said that, Habakkuk is reminded that God's providence is at work, even when it does not accord with our finite understanding. When God's providence perplexes us, we must remember that God is sovereign. God's providence is beyond human comprehension. To trust in God's providence requires our complete confidence in Him.

God instructs Habakkuk to transcribe His revelation. Habakkuk is instructed to wait for God's timing to witness the effectuation of this revelation. God assures Habakkuk that 'the righteous person will live by his faithfulness.'[2] This theological concept of the righteous person living by faith is a recurring theme throughout the Old and New Testament. We witness the Biblical doctrine of the righteous person living by faith reaffirmed in the Book of Galatians, 'Clearly no one who relies on the law is justified before God, because 'the righteous will live by faith.''[3] In addition, this theological doctrine is also reaffirmed in the Book of Hebrews, 'But my righteous one will live by faith.'[4] Finally, in the Book of Romans, we witness the confirmation of righteousness once again, 'For in the gospel the righteousness of God is revealed—a righteousness that is by faith from first to last, just as it is written: 'the righteous will live by faith.''[5]

To live by faith means to trust in God's word and promises. Even when we experience difficult circumstances or opposition, we must remain loyal to God. Our faith in God is not an inconsequential belief. Faith is the enduring, eternal, and everlasting trust in God. It is through faith that believers are strengthened, even in times of considerable privation and deprivation. It is only by faith that we are justified—through the Messiah—as righteous before God. To receive and keep the faith is a blessing beyond description.

Habakkuk makes a second complaint to God. This time Habakkuk inquires: Why does God employ a wicked nation, such as Babylon to punish His chosen people? Habakkuk is troubled with the idea that God empowers an empire, that is more corrupt than Israel, to be the instrument of His judgement. God assures Habakkuk, that while He employs the Babylonian empire to execute His judgement, the Babylonians themselves do not circumvent God's judgement.

God administers justice against the Babylonians as well. This fact is confirmed by 'the five woes'[6] against the Babylonians. God pronounces a series of woes against the Babylonians. This serves to punish them for their pride, greed, evil, and immorality.

The Babylonians' inordinate reliance upon their strength and self-sufficiency leads to their downfall. The Babylonian empire's disintegration reminds us that hubris is the great enemy of human civilisation. Through the Babylonian's historical example, we learn an important Biblical principle: To position our security and trust in power, authority, social status, education, knowledge, private property, personal wealth, or to live in pride without the acknowledgement of God, leads to our fall from grace. Humility and dependence upon God are instrumental to avoid our downfall that results from unbridled pride.

In the Book of Habakkuk, God reveals 'the earth will be filled with the knowledge of the glory of the LORD as the waters cover the sea.'[7] This passage of scripture affirms the triumph of God's glory, grace, and providence to restore all things. Despite our worldly struggles, our transcendent purpose on earth is to further God's providence in the world. When believers strive for the advancement of God's glory and kingdom, this gives them hope. Believers know that God's providence is accomplished in the fullness of time. God's kingdom reigns on earth.

In the final chapter, Habakkuk prays to God. Habakkuk acknowledges God's sovereignty, even though Israel's future is bleak. Habakkuk reflects on God's mercy throughout world history. Habakkuk expresses his faith in God to redeem humanity. In the final verses of the Book of Habakkuk, despite the imminent destruction of the land, the loss of crops, and other valuable resources, Habakkuk declares that he will 'rejoice in the LORD, I will be joyful in God my saviour.'[8] Faith accepts that the human condition incorporates undeniable suffering, privation, loss, and grief. Having said that, faith affirms unconditional trust in God's goodness, sovereignty, mercy, blessing, grace, and providence. Habakkuk teaches humanity several important lessons. We must embody a mindset defined by peace, love, contentment, and joy in God. We must live our life defined by faith, no matter our circumstances or situation.

In the midst of God's judgement and the difficult circumstances that Habakkuk and Israel confront, God promises that His vision will 'certainly come'[2] to fulfilment at the appointed time. Consequently, those individuals who keep the faith are duly rewarded. To keep the faith is not an inconsequential endeavour, but rather an ongoing commitment to trust in God through our challenges, issues, concerns, and problems. Endurance in our faith, even when it is difficult, is essential to our fellowship with God.

The Book of Habakkuk teaches humanity profound theological lessons about what it means to trust in God during times of adversity. We learn about the certainty of God's justice. We appreciate the importance to live by faith. The triumph of God's kingdom on earth is indisputable. Habakkuk encourages believers to maintain hope, confidence, and trust in God's sovereignty, even when our circumstances are disadvantageous. The Book of Habakkuk invites believers to consider a profound fellowship with God. A fellowship that is predicated upon faith, worship, and trust in God's word, timing, and justice. In the end, we must embrace the presence and function of God's providence throughout creation.

[1] The Holy Bible (NIV). (2011). *The Book of Habakkuk.* Chapter 1, Verse 4.

[2] The Holy Bible (NIV). (2011). *The Book of Habakkuk.* Chapter 2, Verse 4.

[3] The Holy Bible (NIV). (2011). *The Book of Galatians.* Chapter 3, Verse 11.

[4] The Holy Bible (NIV). (2011). *The Book of Hebrews.* Chapter 10, Verse 38.

[5] The Holy Bible (NIV). (2011). *The Book of Romans.* Chapter 1, Verse 17.

[6] The Holy Bible (NIV). (2011). *The Book of Habakkuk.* Chapter 2, Verses 6-20.

[7] The Holy Bible (NIV). (2011). *The Book of Habakkuk.* Chapter 2, Verse 14.

[8] The Holy Bible (NIV). (2011). *The Book of Habakkuk.* Chapter 3, Verse 18.

[9] The Holy Bible (NIV). (2011). *The Book of Habakkuk.* Chapter 2, Verse 3.

Chapter 36

The Book of Zephaniah

'The LORD your God is with you,
the Mighty Warrior who saves.'

Zephaniah 3:17
The Holy Bible (NIV)

The Book of Zephaniah is a prophetic book that is written by Zephaniah, one of the twelve minor prophets. The prophet Zephaniah proclaims God's judgement upon the people of Judah and the surrounding nations, this includes the Ammonites, Assyrians, Cushites, Moabites, and Philistines. Nonetheless, God's mercy preserves hope for humanity's future restoration. Despite its sombre themes of judgement, punishment, and destruction, Zephaniah points to God's grace and the restoration of His chosen people. The Book of Zephaniah highlights that God's justice is inseparable from His love.

Zephaniah commences with a pronouncement of God's imminent judgement, not only on Judah, but also on the surrounding nations. God's word informs us, 'I will sweep away everything from the face of the earth.'[1] Zephaniah characterises the destruction of earth, the obliteration of idols, and the purification of God's chosen people. God's judgement is administered against the immorality of the people. The people have engaged in acts of idolatry, injustice, evil, corruption, and the exploitation of the vulnerable and marginalised people.

Beyond Judah and Jerusalem, Zephaniah proclaims God's judgement upon foreign nations—Ammon, Assyria, Cush, Moab, and Philistia—which have caused injury to God's chosen people. God's judgement is impartial and universal. No empire, nation, kingdom, or people, whether Israel or a foreign nation, circumvents the consequences of sin and disobedience against God's word. Zephaniah's prophetic message is a timely reminder of the seriousness with which God judges and punishes sin.

Zephaniah condemns Judah for its idolatry, immorality, and worship of false gods. For example, consider the people of Judah continue to engage in Baal worship. Zephaniah speaks out against those individuals who participate in traditional religious rituals and practices with a false heart. Zephaniah confirms that our actions, without genuine faith are meaningless to God. Zephaniah foretells the imminence of the 'great day of the LORD.'[2] Despite this, the city of Jerusalem is described as rebellious, defiled, and an oppressor of the destitute people. Regrettably, the people are 'still eager to act corruptly in all they did.'[3] God desires worship that reflects a heart of righteousness and obedience to Him. God is not interested in the mere performance of religious acts, customs, or rituals. Zephaniah emphasises the requirement for integrity, honesty, and purity before God.

Zephaniah pronounces misfortune upon foreign nations, this includes Ammon, Assyria, Cush, Moab, and Philistia for their pride and arrogance. Their self-sufficiency and scornful attitude towards Israel have led to their downfall. Pride and self-reliance are harmful to our being in the world. Those who exalt themselves and disregard God's sovereign authority eventually confront God's judgement. Humility before God is a precondition for us to prosper, both as an individual and community.

Zephaniah foretells of a time when God purifies the nations on earth. God will 'purify the lips of the people'[4] and restore them to righteousness. The faithful 'remnant of Israel'[5] remains, and they live in peace and righteousness. God refines and purifies His chosen people through His judgement. God offers humanity the hope of restoration. God's punishment is for the purification of His chosen people. God's providence envisions a blessed and brighter future for humanity, where the people worship God in faith.

Zephaniah urges God's chosen people to gather together. They are counselled to obey God and repent before His judgement befalls them. This prophetic message is to humble God's chosen people. They must possess a heart characterised by righteousness. To repent and seek God's mercy are preconditions to prevent His judgement. Even in times of God's punishment, there is an opportunity for people to turn to Him in humility and repentance. Believers must not relinquish the opportunity to secure God's blessing, grace, and mercy.

In the final chapter, Zephaniah proclaims an inspirational message of hope and restoration. Following God's judgement, He promises to gather His chosen people. God heals the people's wounds, and restores their fortunes. God's word imparts the following message, 'The LORD, the King of Israel, is with you; never again will you fear any harm.'[6] God's spirit is omnipresent amongst His chosen people. There is no more fear, hatred, injustice, poverty, or oppression. God reigns over His people with glory, goodness, and grandeur. God's people experience contentment with His love, and 'He will rejoice over them with singing.'[7] Although God's judgement is unavoidable and necessary, His providence is for the restoration of His chosen people. Following severe punishment, God brings about restoration and joy to His chosen people. God's love, mercy, and grace triumph over evil.

Zephaniah's prophecy reveals that God's sovereignty extends beyond Israel to the surrounding nations. God is the arbitrator of humanity. Our actions are judged in accordance with God's justice. God is not merely concerned with any one nation or people. God's sovereignty and judgement extends to the world. This theological reality affirms God's sovereignty over creation and His ability to bring about punishment and justice across people, cultures, continents, kingdoms, empires, principalities, dukedoms, and nations. God's providence is not restricted by the variations and distinctions across human civilisation.

The Book of Zephaniah concludes with the people rejoicing.

The future restoration of Israel is characterised by joy, peace, happiness, and celebration. The people sing and rejoice because of God's salvation. God receives great delight in His people's restoration. Joy is obtained from the realisation of God's presence, peace, mercy, justice, love, and favour. Despite the privation that results from God's judgement, the outcome for those who trust in God is joy and peace in His spiritual presence. God's word promises us, 'I will bring you home. I will give you honour and praise among all the people … when I restore your fortunes before your very eyes.'[8]

The Book of Zephaniah, while primarily focused on God's judgement, provides hope to those who repent and seek forgiveness. Zephaniah reminds us of God's justice. We learn about God's desire for our worship of Him. We are enlightened of God's providence to bring about restoration and joy to His chosen people. Through God's justice and punishment, there is the unrivalled opportunity for renewal, restoration, and redemption. The Book of Zephaniah reminds humanity, that any society, community, kingdom, empire, or nation established on morally corrupt practices does not stand the test of time. We must establish our life upon God's word and counsel, so that we flourish and prosper.

[1] The Holy Bible (NIV). (2011). *The Book of Zephaniah.* Chapter 1, Verse 2.

[2] The Holy Bible (NIV). (2011). *The Book of Zephaniah.* Chapter 1, Verse 14.

[3] The Holy Bible (NIV). (2011). *The Book of Zephaniah.* Chapter 3, Verse 7.

[4] The Holy Bible (NIV). (2011). *The Book of Zephaniah.* Chapter 3, Verse 9.

[5] The Holy Bible (NIV). (2011). *The Book of Zephaniah.* Chapter 3, Verse 12.

[6] The Holy Bible (NIV). (2011). *The Book of Zephaniah.* Chapter 3, Verse 15.

[7] The Holy Bible (NIV). (2011). *The Book of Zephaniah.* Chapter 3, Verse 17.

[8] The Holy Bible (NIV). (2011). *The Book of Zephaniah.* Chapter 3, Verse 20.

Chapter 37

The Book of Haggai

'Then Haggai, the LORD's messenger,
gave this message of the LORD to the people:
'I am with you,' declares the LORD.'

Haggai 1:13
The Holy Bible (NIV)

The Book of Haggai is a concise prophetic book within the Old Testament. Haggai narrates the reconstruction of God's temple in Jerusalem following the Babylonian exile of the Israelites. The Book of Haggai contains a series of prophetic messages revealed by prophet Haggai to the people of Judah in 520 BC. Haggai encourages the people of Judah to reconstruct God's temple. They are to prioritise God's providence in their life. Despite its brevity, the Book of Haggai offers profound lessons on God's sovereignty, judgement, faithfulness, and providence.

Haggai criticises the people of Judah as they prioritise the reconstruction of their own homes and the pursuit of pecuniary gain, while they neglect the reconstruction of God's temple. The prophet Haggai conveys the LORD's message to the people, 'Is it a time for you yourselves to be living in your panelled houses, while this house remains a ruin?'[1] God's temple remains in ruins since the Israelites return from exile. The people of Judah were preoccupied with their personal prosperity. As a consequence, they experienced privation and harvest failure throughout the land.

Haggai teaches humanity to prioritise God's providence in our life. It is essential that we ensure God's will is performed. When the people failed to prioritise the reconstruction of God's temple, they experienced crisis, loss, grief, misery, and privation in their life. Similarly, when we abandon our spiritual priorities, for the pursuit of worldly gain, we preclude the fullness of God's blessing, grace, love, and peace. God desires our obedience and commitment to Him above all else, 'But seek first His kingdom and His righteousness, and all these things will be given to you as well.'[2]

When the people of Judah understood Haggai's prophetic message, they responded with a symbolic step of faith. The people of Judah collectively engaged in the reconstruction of God's temple. God promises to be with the people and bless them as they begin this important assignment. God speaks through the prophet Haggai to the people. God reaffirms to the people, 'I am with you.'[3] The people's obedience to God results in a renewed sense of purpose, optimism, hope, and favour. Our obedience to God's command leads us to His blessing. When we align our actions with God's will, we secure His provision, peace, and presence in our life. Though the people of Judah were disobedient, God demonstrates His mercy and willingness to bless them, when they repent and act in accordance with His will.

When the people responded to Haggai's prophetic message to rebuild God's temple, God emboldened the spirit of the leaders and the people to take decisive action. This divine act demonstrates that when God instructs His people to obey, God empowers them to fulfil the assignment He directs them to complete. We need to commit ourselves to action, in order to complete our God-given assignment. We cannot remain idle, waiting for God to give us a sign. We must seize the initiative to effectuate God's word into practice. We must actively participate in the realisation of God's providence in the world, by the completion of our assignment. God's word empowers us to fulfil His providence; however, we must take the leap of faith ourselves.

Haggai addresses the people's discouragement. The people of Judah perceive the temple they are constructing as devoid of the majestic grandeur and opulence that was characteristic of Solomon's temple. As a result, the people are disheartened. Nonetheless, God reassures the people this new temple shall be filled with greater glory than Solomon's temple; 'the glory of this present house will be greater than the glory of the former house.'[4] This Biblical message teaches us not to be deceived by appearances and representations. It is the time, effort, and dedication to construct God's temple that is of importance, not its splendour or extravagance.

While the people were discouraged by the absence of grandeur in the new temple, God reminded them that His glory and presence made it more majestic than Solomon's temple. God's presence is far more valuable than any material phenomenon in the world. God's favour in our life outweighs worldly fortune, prosperity, wealth, personal accomplishments, and success. God's love provides humanity immeasurable peace.

In the midst of the people's discouragement in relation to the reconstruction of the holy temple, God reassures them that He is with them. God fulfils His covenant with His chosen people. God encourages the people to remain dedicated and resilient. They must work faithfully and not harbour doubt or fear. God has promised His grace and blessing upon the people. Throughout the Book of Haggai, we are reminded that God's spiritual presence remains with His chosen people through the peaks and valleys of life, 'my spirit remains among you. Do not fear.'[5] God's faithfulness to His covenant provides the foundation for our strength, persistence, and hope. Even when our circumstances are unfavourable or difficult, God is faithful to His covenant. God's presence, power, and provision are reliable. No matter our circumstance or situation, we trust in God's faithfulness.

The prophet Haggai proclaims another revelation which concerns the holiness of the people and their offerings. Haggai makes the point that merely offering sacrifices to God is insufficient, if the people do not live in accordance with God's word. God desires His chosen people to be holy. The people's actions must reflect God's wisdom. God reassures the people, that their future blessings are conditional upon their repentance and obedience to His word. Our holiness and obedience to God's command is not only about the observation of customary practices, or the performance of honourable actions. Our holiness and obedience are about our intentions, motives, beliefs, and desires. God does not bless actions that are performed with malevolence, hubris, ignorance, evil, corruption, or hatred. Our actions must align with God's will for us to secure our sanctification. At the same time, God promises us that if we align ourselves with His word, He will bless us, even if our circumstances or situation are not ideal.

In the final message of the Book of Haggai, God speaks to Zerubbabel, the governor of Judah. Through Haggai, God informs Zerubbabel that He will 'shake the heavens and the earth.'[6] God informs Haggai that He will make Zerubbabel like His 'signet ring.'[7] This verse of scripture symbolises God's sovereignty, power, and authority over creation. Haggai proclaims a prophecy that points to the fulfilment of humanity in the coming Messiah, Jesus Christ, who descends from the Davidic line (i.e., Zerubbabel's ancestor). God is sovereign over creation, this includes the rise and fall of nations, empires, kingdoms, and rulers. God's majestic vision for the future of humanity is indisputable. God fulfils His covenant, even when our circumstances are disadvantageous. God's promise to Zerubbabel, even though given in a specific historical context, points to the forthcoming kingship of Jesus Christ.

Haggai assures the people, that although the present temple is modest, God's providence and timing are perfect. The glory of the new temple surpasses the glory of Solomon's temple. The people are reminded that God's providence is not limited by human expectation, experience, skill, expertise, talent, understanding, or knowledge. God's providence functions in accordance with His will and purpose. God's timing is always perfect. When our endeavours are frustrated, or we feel uncertain about the future, we trust that God's providence effectuates in

His timing. God's promises are fulfilled, and they far exceed what we had envisaged.

The Book of Haggai is as an important reminder for humanity to participate in the realisation of God's providence. We are commanded to trust in God's faithfulness. We must honourably fulfil our duty to complete our assignment. In doing so, we must rely upon God's power, peace, and presence. When we neglect our God-given assignment, and in its place, we pursue trivial endeavours, then we relinquish God's favour. The prophet Haggai taught the people the importance of ensuring their priorities in life are correctly ordered. If we are to achieve our life's transcendent purpose—to serve God—then God must be at the centre of our life, not on its periphery.

[1] The Holy Bible (NIV). (2011). *The Book of Haggai*. Chapter 1, Verse 4.

[2] The Holy Bible (NIV). (2011). *The Book of Matthew*. Chapter 6, Verse 33.

[3] The Holy Bible (NIV). (2011). *The Book of Haggai*. Chapter 1, Verse 13.

[4] The Holy Bible (NIV). (2011). *The Book of Haggai*. Chapter 2, Verse 9.

[5] The Holy Bible (NIV). (2011). *The Book of Haggai*. Chapter 2, Verse 5.

[6] The Holy Bible (NIV). (2011). *The Book of Haggai*. Chapter 2, Verse 21.

[7] The Holy Bible (NIV). (2011). *The Book of Haggai*. Chapter 2, Verse 23.

Chapter 38

The Book of Zechariah

'The LORD will be king over the whole earth.
On that day there will be one LORD,
and His name the only name.'

Zechariah 14:9
The Holy Bible (NIV)

T he Book of Zechariah is an enthralling and prophetic book in the Old Testament. Zechariah contains a collection of divine visions, oracles, and prophetic messages that are revealed to the people of Judah upon their return from exile in Babylon. Zechariah's prophecies encourage the reconstruction of God's temple. These Biblical prophecies promote the renewal of spiritual life and the hope of future restoration. The Book of Zechariah points forward to the coming of the Messiah. The Book of Zechariah is complete with vivid imagery and symbolism. The Book of Zechariah offers profound Biblical lessons for the people of Judah and believers in the contemporary era.

The prophet Zechariah begins his ministry by encouraging the people of Judah to return to God. Zechariah explains to the people that their ancestors experienced God's judgement because of their disobedience. God is not indifferent to the situation that confronts the people of Judah. God is concerned about their repentance and restoration. God's love for His chosen people is resolute. Therefore, God instructs His chosen people to repent, not out of anger, however, out of genuine concern for their well-being and prosperity. When we deviate from God's command, His mercy provides us with the opportunity to correct our mistakes. We have the opportunity to make our crooked paths straight again. It is our responsibility to avail ourselves of God's mercy.

Zechariah's mystical visions commence with a series of horsemen who report to God about the condition of the earth. Despite the chaos and oppression, God is sovereign over all nations. God's providence brings peace to His chosen people. Zechariah's vision teaches humanity that in times of uncertainty, it is essential to remember that God is sovereign over creation. When our circumstances are beyond our control, God's providence functions behind the scenes to bring about His vision for our life. God's sovereignty extends over creation. God's providence is for the betterment of His chosen people.

One of Zechariah's immediate concerns is the reconstruction of the holy temple in Jerusalem. The people are slow to complete the temple's reconstruction work. Nonetheless, Zechariah's vision encourages the people to continue this important endeavour until its completion. Zechariah reminds the people the holy temple's reconstruction is central to the restoration of their fellowship with God. For the LORD has spoken, 'I will return to Jerusalem with mercy, and there my house will be rebuilt.'[1]

Furthermore, Zechariah witnesses another divine vision. This time of a golden lampstand and two olive trees. In this vision, the LORD imparts invaluable wisdom to humanity. God informs us, we must complete our assignment on earth, 'not by might nor by power, but by my Spirit.'[2] This Biblical revelation symbolises the eternal presence of God's Spirit to empower Zerubbabel and Joshua to complete the reconstruction of God's temple.

The reconstruction of God's temple is a symbol of God's presence and the renewal of spiritual life in Israel. The theological lesson is self-evident: Our spiritual well-being is predicated upon God's spiritual presence. In order for the people of Judah to accomplish their objective of completing God's temple, they must complete their God-given assignment. We are not alone in the completion of our assignment. The Holy Spirit empowers us to accomplish our assignment. When we spiritually renew ourselves, we must focus on God's divinity and providence, not on our desires, endeavours, and aspirations.

God informs Zerubbabel that the reconstruction of the temple is not accomplished by knowledge, merit, willpower, skill, expertise, virtue, wisdom, ability, strength, or resources, but only by God's Spirit. This Biblical message reminds the people that success in their objectives is secured through God's grace.

Discipline, motivation, perseverance, and willpower, while necessary, are insufficient to accomplish our destiny. It is only through the power of the Holy Spirit that we fulfil our God-given assignment. The Holy Spirit empowers us to experience spiritual fulfilment in our life. God provides the requisite strength, wisdom, and guidance that we require for the completion of our assignment. We must rely upon God, and not on our abilities to fulfil our assignment. Peace be with you.

Zechariah foretells the coming of a branch. This is a person who shall 'build the temple of the LORD.'[3] This blessed figure is both priest and king. They bring righteousness, goodness, love, and peace to earth. In the fullness of time, this figure is the Messiah. The Messiah unites the institutions of priesthood and kingship in the person of Jesus Christ. In addition, Zechariah proclaims prophecies about the future coming of a humble king who brings peace on earth. This humble king comes riding on a donkey, 'see, your king comes to you, righteous and victorious, lowly and riding on a donkey.'[4] Zechariah's remarkable prophecy is fulfilled in Jesus Christ. In the Gospel of Matthew, Jesus' triumphal procession into Jerusalem is on a donkey; 'see, your king comes to you, gentle and riding on a donkey.'[5]

Zechariah concludes with a final chapter that proclaims a divine revelation. According to Zechariah, 'the day of the LORD is coming.' [6] This is a blessed vision of the future day of the LORD. A day when God decisively defeats His enemies and establishes His eternal kingdom on earth. This eschatological vision points to the perpetual reign of Jesus Christ as king over all nations and worldly powers, 'the LORD will be king over the whole earth. On that day there will be one LORD, and His name the only name.'[7]

Zechariah proclaims a vision of the Messiah. Jesus Christ brings peace, justice, restoration, love, and salvation to humanity. Jesus Christ, as the fulfilment of Zechariah's prophecy, is the saviour of humanity. The Messiah is a humble servant and honourable king. The Messiah brings spiritual renewal to humanity. The Messiah establishes God's eternal kingdom on earth. Believers anticipate Jesus Christ's return in glory and his eternal reign over creation.

In another divine vision, Zechariah perceives the high priest Joshua stand before God. Joshua is dressed in soiled clothes; this symbolises Israel's sin. However, God changes Joshua's soiled clothes and dresses him in new garments. God's sovereign act signifies the purification and restoration of His chosen people. Thereafter, Zechariah speaks of a future time when a 'fountain will be opened to the house of David and the inhabitants of Jerusalem, to cleanse them from sin and impurity.'[8] This is understood as a Biblical prophecy of the atoning mission of Jesus Christ. Jesus redeems humanity from the curse of original sin through his sacrificial death on the Cross.

Human civilisation requires purification from original sin. This is a precondition for the people to experience God's spiritual presence, mercy, grace, and blessing. The divine message of purification in the Book of Zechariah points to the atonement of humanity's sin. This endeavour is secured through the crucifixion of Jesus Christ on the Cross. Just as the high priest Joshua was clothed in new garments, believers today are clothed in the righteousness of Jesus Christ. We receive our unmerited sanctification through the atoning sacrifice of our saviour—Jesus Christ.

Zechariah urges the people to repent and return to God. The people are encouraged to seek God's favour, mercy, blessing, and grace. God's word declares, 'return to me, and I will return to you.'[9] The Israelites' sin and disobedience led to their exile. Now the Israelites are being called to repent and secure their spiritual renewal. In addition to repentance, Zechariah emphasises the people must demonstrate justice, truth, mercy, courage, compassion, and love. The people must practice righteousness in their relationships with one another as part of their commitment to God. Repentance is not merely about turning away from sin. Repentance is about turning towards righteousness, mercy, love, goodness, peace, and justice. Repentance involves a transformation of our heart and mind. God desires people who live in holiness. Believers are to reflect God's character in their interactions with each other.

Zechariah envisions the future blessing and prosperity of Jerusalem. God's word informs the people, 'Do not be afraid, but let your hands be strong.'[10] God promises to restore the city, bring peace, abundance, prosperity, and joy. People from all nations shall come to Jerusalem and acknowledge God's sovereignty. God's providence for His chosen people is a world defined by peace, joy, love, justice, and prosperity. Zechariah's vision reminds us that God's providence incorporates a blessed future for humanity. A prosperous future in which God's kingdom is established and humanity realises His glory.

The Book of Zechariah offers humanity several invaluable lessons. Zechariah's prophetic messages emphasise repentance, holiness, empowerment, hope, love, and the future coming of the Messiah. The Book of Zechariah inspires humanity to live with the assurance that God's providence determines the destiny of humanity. God's Spirit empowers us to live with confidence, conviction, and certainty. God's providence is for the restoration, prosperity, and peace of humanity.

In the Book of Zechariah, we ascertain that prophet Zechariah's visions, messages, and prophecies do not follow a linear pattern. The Book of Zechariah emphasises the nuanced existential reality of life and the chequered history of nations. World history does not always conform to predictable and orderly patterns. World history is not confined to human-made sociological constructs. There is chaos, complexity, colour, and confusion in the production of world history. In this respect, the remarkable story of Jerusalem is no different.

[1] The Holy Bible (NIV). (2011). *The Book of Zechariah.* Chapter 1, Verse 16.

[2] The Holy Bible (NIV). (2011). *The Book of Zechariah.* Chapter 4, Verse 6.

[3] The Holy Bible (NIV). (2011). *The Book of Zechariah.* Chapter 6, Verse 12.

[4] The Holy Bible (NIV). (2011). *The Book of Zechariah.* Chapter 9, Verse 9.

[5] The Holy Bible (NIV). (2011). *The Book of Matthew.* Chapter 21, Verse 5.

[6] The Holy Bible (NIV). (2011). *The Book of Zechariah.* Chapter 14, Verse 1.

[7] The Holy Bible (NIV). (2011). *The Book of Zechariah.* Chapter 14, Verse 9.

[8] The Holy Bible (NIV). (2011). *The Book of Zechariah.* Chapter 13, Verse 1.

[9] The Holy Bible (NIV). (2011). *The Book of Zechariah.* Chapter 1, Verse 3.

[10] The Holy Bible (NIV). (2011). *The Book of Zechariah.* Chapter 8, Verse 13.

Chapter 39

The Book of Malachi

"Then all the nations will call you blessed,
for yours will be a delightful land,'
says the LORD Almighty.'

Malachi 3:12
The Holy Bible (NIV)

T he Book of Malachi is the final book in the Old
Testament. Malachi is characterised as the prophetic
book of rebuke and restoration. Prophet Malachi's
message is directed to the people of Judah in the post-exilic
period of Jewish history, particularly after the reconstruction of
God's temple. This was a time characterised by spiritual
complacency, corruption, and moral decadence. The prophet
Malachi examines several important issues, such as worship,
sacrifice, offerings, community life, and faithfulness. Despite
Malachi's reprimand of the people, he concludes with a glimmer
of hope for their future. Malachi points forward to the
predestined coming of the Messiah.

The opening chapter of Malachi emphasises God's perpetual
love for Israel, "I have loved you,' says the LORD.'[1] In spite of
the people's failure and disobedience, God reminds them of His
unconditional love. Even when we are unfaithful, God's love for
humanity remains ever-present. God's unconditional love
encourages us to return to Him. We must live in accordance with
God's will. Every person is able to experience God's love in their
life. Having said that, we ought not to receive God's love for
granted. We must live in accordance with God's word.

Malachi confronts the priests and the people that offer
blemished animal sacrifices to God—sacrifices they would not
offer to the governor. This abhorrent conduct of the Israelites is a
violation of their sacred covenant with God, "When you offer
blind animals for sacrifice, is that not wrong? When you sacrifice
lame or diseased animals, is that not wrong? Try offering them to
your governor! Would he be pleased with you? Would he accept
you?' says the LORD Almighty.'[2] God condemns this immoral
practice, it is disrespectful.

When the people present an offering to God that consists of
diseased animals, this demonstrates their spiritual demise. God

instructs the people to present offerings that honour and glorify Him. When we present offerings to God for atonement of our sin, we must remember that God deserves our best. This theological principle applies not only to our offerings, but also in the giving of our time, knowledge, expertise, wealth, and resources. In our worship and service, we must honour God with sincerity, integrity, reverence, and faithfulness.

Malachi condemns the people's violation of sacred covenants, in particular, unfaithfulness in marriage. Some of the Jewish men divorced their wives and married foreign women who worshipped idols. God condemns this immoral practice because it violates the sanctity of marriage. Such dishonourable conduct constitutes a flagrant violation of the covenant that God established with His chosen people. Marriage is a sacred covenant sanctioned by God. Our enduring faithfulness to our spouse reflects our commitment to God. In accordance with God's word, infidelity and divorce are significant transgressions, such immoral conduct undermines the integrity of relationships bound by covenant. Malachi encourages our faithfulness, not only in marriage, but in all relationships. Our faithfulness is a reflection of our loyalty and commitment to God.

The priests are reprimanded for their failure to guide the people towards righteousness. Not to mention, the priests also live in disobedience to God's word. God's word makes it categorically clear that priests are held to a higher standard, 'the lips of a priest ought to preserve knowledge, because he is the messenger of the LORD Almighty.'[3] Instead of guiding the people in worship, ethical conduct, and righteousness, the priests neglect their official religious duties. The priests mislead the people on their spiritual journey.

Worship is not merely characterised by rituals, customs, traditions, festivals, sacrifices, offerings, or ceremonies. Worship is about our obedience to God's commandments. Worship is defined by a life of prayer, humility, and love. To worship God means to live in accordance with God's word. Leaders, particularly spiritual leaders, assume responsibility to guide the community by example. Leaders have the duty to instruct members of the community to faithfully walk with God.

Malachi rebukes the people for their failure to honour their tithes to God. The people are withholding their obligatory tithes. In fact, God challenges the people to test Him on tithes, "Bring the whole tithe into the storehouse, that there may be food in my house. Test me in this,' says the LORD Almighty, 'and see if I will not throw open the floodgates of heaven and pour out so much blessing that there will not be room enough to store it."[4] Tithes are obligatory under the Law of Moses. Tithes serve a variety of objectives. In this day and age, tithes support the clergy and maintain the church building and infrastructure. Tithes also finance the church's educational, missionary, humanitarian, and welfare programs.

The requirement for tithes is specified in the Book of Leviticus, 'A tithe of everything from the land, whether grain from the soil or fruit from the trees, belongs to the LORD.'[5] Ultimately, everything within creation, including our life, is a sacred gift from God. We do not adequately recompense God when we give Him a tenth of our income, wealth, or produce. God is the creator of the universe. The purpose of tithing is to perfect our character and perception of reality. Fundamentally, everything that we possess in the world belongs to God.

When we donate a portion of our income, wealth, or produce to God, we effectuate the timeless principle to honour God and make a contribution to God's kingdom on earth. Through tithing, we consciously reflect upon the reality; everything we have is not absolutely ours. All real and personal property is merely in our temporary possession. We are stewards on earth. Philanthropy is an act of faith that acknowledges God's sovereignty over creation. When we tithe to God, we are only giving what always belonged to God. Tithing positions our life into perspective—creation is God's possession for eternity.

The people of Judah were disillusioned because they witnessed the wicked people prosper, while the righteous people suffered. Malachi observes, 'But now we call the arrogant blessed. Certainly, evildoers prosper, and even when they put God to the test, they get away with it.'[6] The people of Judah question God's justice and equity. They enquire: Why should we serve God, if it makes no difference to our circumstances? Spiritual complacency arises when we fail to perceive God's grace, blessing, love, peace, and providence in our life. The people of Judah were focused on their personal concerns, rather than to trust in God's providence. When we begin to grow weary in doing good or feel the inclination to question God's will, we must remember that God judges the wicked and rewards the faithful in His timing. The fullness of time is the primary determinant in all things.

Malachi foretells that God sends 'a messenger to prepare the way before Him.'[7] This is a reference to John the Baptist, who prepares humanity for the coming of the Messiah—Jesus Christ. The messenger refines and purifies the people. He prepares them for the coming of Christ—the Son of God. Herein we witness God fulfil His providence through messengers and prophets to prepare humanity for the coming of Jesus Christ. John the Baptist prepares the way for Jesus Christ. John encourages the people to repent and be redeemed. Similarly, God continues to employ messengers to encourage humanity to repent from their sinful conduct. Our spiritual awakening is essential, in order to complete the assignment that God has destined for us.

Malachi concludes with a vision of the day of the LORD. This is a future time when God judges the immoral people and He rewards the righteous people. The scripture informs us the 'sun of righteousness will rise with healing in its rays.'[8] Those people who fear the LORD will rejoice in Him. The immoral people are consumed by fire; however, the righteous are healed and exalted. The day of the LORD is a warning and promise to humanity. While it is a day of judgement for the unrepentant, it is also a day of restoration and victory for those who fear the LORD and are faithful to Him. This Biblical prophecy is a timely reminder, that we must live our life mindful of eternity. We must keep our body, mind, heart, and spirit aligned with God's word.

God's word informs us the 'sun of righteousness will rise.'[2] This symbolises the coming of the Messiah to earth. This event brings forth divine restoration to those who fear God. The righteous people are filled with joy. They experience freedom, peace, joy, love, and happiness in God's spiritual presence. Despite the challenges and difficulties along our journey, there is hope for our restoration through Jesus Christ. The Messiah's crucifixion secures redemption, not only for Israel, but for all people who trust in Him. Malachi's vision of the messenger— John the Baptist—reminds us that God's providence for humanity's redemption is an unfolding process. Believers anticipate their restoration in the future.

Malachi's prophetic messages constitute a warning and command to repent. They also contain hope for our future. Malachi's prophecies inspire us to live faithfully. We must honour God in all facets of our life. We live with the anticipation of the coming of the Messiah. The Messiah brings peace, justice, redemption, joy, and restoration to humanity. The Book of Malachi is a concise summary of the Israelites' moral and spiritual struggle in their fellowship with God. Malachi demonstrates how the Israelites failed to honour their covenant with God. The covenant that was established by God with their forefathers. Despite God utilising the twelve minor prophets to intercede between Him and the people, the Israelites fail to faithfully observe God's commandments.

While God constantly employs faithful remnants to preserve the Davidic line and honour the Davidic Covenant, it is evident that this Covenant shall be fulfilled by the coming of the Messiah. The divine revelation that God made to prophet Nathan, which concerns King David in the Second Book of Samuel, 'Your house and your kingdom shall endure for ever before me; your throne shall be established for ever,'[10] is fulfilled by the Messiah—Jesus Christ.

In the New Testament, we witness God's covenant to David fulfilled by the everlasting reign of the Messiah. The coming of Jesus Christ, as the son of David, is the saviour of humanity. Jesus Christ fulfils the Davidic Covenant for eternity. The Messiah—through his crucifixion, resurrection, and ascension—transcends death. Therefore, the Messiah's blessed reign on earth is without end. God's covenant to David has been fulfilled, period. Peace be with you.

[1] The Holy Bible (NIV). (2011). *The Book of Malachi.* Chapter 1, Verse 2.

[2] The Holy Bible (NIV). (2011). *The Book of Malachi.* Chapter 1, Verse 8.

[3] The Holy Bible (NIV). (2011). *The Book of Malachi.* Chapter 2, Verse 7.

[4] The Holy Bible (NIV). (2011). *The Book of Malachi.* Chapter 3, Verse 10.

[5] The Holy Bible (NIV). (2011). *The Book of Leviticus.* Chapter 27, Verse 30.

[6] The Holy Bible (NIV). (2011). *The Book of Malachi.* Chapter 3, Verse 15.

[7] The Holy Bible (NIV). (2011). *The Book of Malachi.* Chapter 3, Verse 1.

[8] The Holy Bible (NIV). (2011). *The Book of Malachi.* Chapter 4, Verse 2.

[9] The Holy Bible (NIV). (2011). *The Book of Malachi.* Chapter 4, Verse 2.

[10] The Holy Bible (NIV). (2011). *The Book of Second Samuel.* Chapter 7, Verse 16.

Chapter 40

The Book of Matthew

'But seek first His kingdom and His righteousness,
and all these things will be given to you as well.'

Matthew 6:33
The Holy Bible (NIV)

T he Book of Matthew is the first gospel in the New
Testament. Matthew focuses on Jesus Christ's ministry,
teaching, crucifixion, resurrection, and ascension.
Matthew characterises Jesus as the Messiah. Jesus is the fulfilment
of the Old Testament prophecies. Matthew emphasises the
establishment of God's kingdom on earth. Matthew highlights
the nature of discipleship, this includes the moral, religious,
social, and ethical teachings of Jesus Christ. Last but not least,
Matthew underscores the responsibility of Jesus Christ's disciples.

Matthew commences with a genealogy of Jesus Christ. The
gospel traces the origins of Jesus' lineage to 'the son of David, the
son of Abraham.'[1] The greater purpose to include this
genealogy is to demonstrate Jesus is the Messiah who fulfils God's
covenant to Israel. The preliminary chapters of Matthew
emphasise the miraculous nature of Jesus' nativity. The nativity
of Jesus demonstrates his divinity and humanity.

Jesus Christ is the fulfilment of God's providence. The
Messiah's nativity was not merely a historical event; however, it
was the realisation of God's covenant to the Israelites. Jesus is the
sacrificial lamb that assumes responsibility for the sins of
humanity. Through Jesus Christ, we are reconciled to God. As a
result, we are forgiven for our sins. Understanding Jesus' identity,
nativity, and assignment assists us to learn about God's
providence. Through Jesus, we witness the fulfilment of God's
providence.

A central theme in Matthew is the establishment of God's
kingdom on earth. Jesus teaches us that God's kingdom is not of
this world. God's kingdom is a spiritual realm that begins in the
heart of his disciples. Jesus guides the people to seek the kingdom
of God; 'But seek first His kingdom and His righteousness, and
all these things will be given to you as well.'[2] God's kingdom is a
priority for believers. To seek God's kingdom requires a

transformational reorientation of the believer's priorities. Believers must focus on moral values and eternal things, rather than temporal pursuits, secular endeavours, or material ambitions. Jesus' teachings challenge us to seek God in our life. Believers must live as righteous citizens of God's eternal kingdom.

John the Baptist and Jesus Christ preach the message of repentance. They call upon the people to repent of their sin and turn towards God. Jesus proclaims, 'Repent, for the kingdom of heaven has come near.'[3] We are reminded that repentance brings about our spiritual transformation. Repentance is not merely about the expression of remorse for our sinful conduct. Repentance is about turning towards God. Repentance is about a transformation of our heart, mind, and spirit. Jesus offers peace to those who are weary and burdened. Jesus demonstrates to humanity, that to follow him leads to redemption. In the scripture, Jesus affirms, 'my yoke is easy and my burden is light.'[4] Through Jesus, humanity secures their absolution from sin.

In the Sermon on the Mount, Jesus redefines what it means to be righteous. Jesus provides examples of people who are blessed. The Beatitudes constitute a series of blessings that, when effectuated, bring the believer their 'reward in heaven.'[5] Jesus teaches us that the Pharisees and scribes do not demonstrate righteousness. Jesus emphasises the importance of humility, mercy, love, goodness, and peace. Jesus encourages his disciples to exhibit righteousness that comes from the heart, not customary obedience to God's word.

Righteousness in the kingdom of heaven is not about the observation of rules, rituals, and religious rites. Righteousness is about the inner transformation of our heart. Jesus teaches us that the values of God's kingdom—humility, mercy, purity, love, justice, service, and peace—are the characteristics of a disciple.

We must demonstrate these values in our life. We are commanded to reflect the noble character of Jesus Christ in the world.

Matthew highlights Jesus' divine power and God-given authority through his many miracles. For example, consider Jesus walks on water. Jesus heals sick people. Jesus resurrects the dead. Jesus casts out demonic spirits that have possessed humans. Jesus pacifies violent storms. Jesus feeds the five thousand. Jesus turns water into wine. Last but not least, Jesus forgives sin. These miracles demonstrate Jesus' divinity and humanity. We learn about Jesus' ability to restore peace and harmony on earth. God has granted Jesus authority over creation, this includes the natural world, the spiritual realm, and the heavenly realm. God's word assures us that Jesus brings restoration and renewal to our life. As disciples of Jesus Christ, we trust in the Messiah's humanity, divinity, and authority, both in the natural world and spiritual realm.

Following Jesus' resurrection, he proclaims the Great Commission to his disciples. Jesus instructs his disciples to go and make disciples of all nations. The disciples are to baptise people and teach the nations of the world to obey all that God has commanded. This command is the foundation for the church's mission in the world. The mission of the church is to make disciples, not merely spread the teachings of Jesus Christ. Discipleship is to share the faith with humanity. Discipleship is to empower believers to live in accordance with the teachings of Jesus Christ. Believers must participate in the Great Commission by sharing the gospel and making disciples within their community, nation, kingdom, and throughout the world. The Messiah reminds us that he will be with us on our journey, 'And surely I am with you always, to the very end of the age.'[6]

Jesus teaches us that to follow him requires self-denial. We must take up our cross. We must demonstrate a willingness to sacrifice our desires and interests for Jesus' sake; 'whoever wants to be my disciple must deny themselves and take up their cross and follow me.'[7] Discipleship involves sacrifice. We must position Jesus' teachings above our worldly aspirations and material possessions. Discipleship is not a convenient endeavour. Discipleship requires a willingness to sacrifice our desires, aims, ambitions, and objectives, for the greater purpose to follow Jesus Christ. While the rewards of discipleship are great, it entails sacrifice. We are commanded to renounce the world and its pleasures, in the pursuit to serve God. Discipleship involves surrender, trust, belief, and commitment to God.

Matthew emphasises that Jesus consistently supports the marginalised people in society, such as sinners, tax collectors, the sick, destitute, and Gentiles. Jesus demonstrates compassion to those people who are rejected by conventional society. Jesus offers them love, peace, mercy, forgiveness, and hope. Jesus personifies that God's love is for all people, regardless of their social status, personal wealth, colour, sex, income, marital status, private property, gender, education, age, or vocation. As disciples of Jesus Christ, we are commanded to demonstrate compassion and empathy to humanity. We must reach out to the marginalised people and offer them the love of Jesus Christ.

Through the Biblical Parable of the Unmerciful Servant, Jesus teaches humanity the importance of forgiveness. Jesus narrates the tragic story of a servant who was forgiven a substantial amount of outstanding debt by his master. However, this servant, who was released from his debt, refused to forgive a small amount of debt owed to him by one of his personal servants. Jesus warns us, those who do not forgive, they will not receive forgiveness from God. Forgiveness is an important attribute of the Christian faith.

Just as God has forgiven us, we are commanded to forgive one another. When we harbour resentment and hold onto bitterness, we damage our relationships. Not to mention, this perspective also damages our fellowship with God. Discipleship involves the extension of grace, love, forgiveness, and mercy to every person, just as God has done for us. When it comes to forgiveness, we must not forget the Messiah's timeless principle, 'I desire mercy, not sacrifice.'[8]

In the Sermon on the Mount, Jesus encourages His disciples not to be concerned about their inconsequential personal needs. Jesus declares, 'do not worry about your life, what you will eat or drink; or about your body, what you will wear.'[9] We are commanded to trust in God. God provides for our personal needs. Jesus emphasises that God knows what we require along our journey. We must place our faith and confidence in God's providence. First and foremost, our objective is to seek God's kingdom. Faith in God's provision is instrumental to discipleship. Jesus instructs us to trust in God's providence. We are not to be consumed by worries, anxieties, concerns, and personal needs. We must remember that God is our loving Father who deeply cares for us. We must seek God's kingdom. We must trust that God provides everything we require along our journey.

Jesus is well-known for employing parables to convey his teachings to humanity. Jesus employs several parables to teach us about the nature of the kingdom of heaven. These include the Parable of the Sower, the Parable of the Weeds, the Parable of the Mustard Seed, the Parable of the Hidden Treasure and the Pearl, and the Parable of the Net. While these Biblical parables are straightforward Biblical stories, they convey symbolic and profound messages that are important. These parables reveal the mysteries of God's kingdom and the manner in which it develops on earth. God's kingdom develops gradually and sometimes in unexpected ways. God's kingdom does not appear powerful or influential by conventional standards. Nonetheless, it is a kingdom that develops from humble beginnings to the most profound institution on earth. Believers must remain confident and trust in God's kingdom.

Jesus Christ is the Messiah. Jesus is the saviour who came to serve and to 'give his life as a ransom for many.'[10] Jesus' transcendent purpose was to redeem humanity of their sin. Jesus offers forgiveness and eternal life to all those who believe in him; 'this is my blood of the covenant, which is poured out for many for the forgiveness of sins.'[11] Jesus' sacrificial death on the Cross is the foundation of the Christian faith. Jesus' crucifixion, resurrection, and ascension permitted humanity to be reconciled with God. Through Jesus, we receive eternal life in heaven. We are to honour Jesus' unconditional sacrifice. We must live our life defined by gratitude, community service, faithfulness, love, peace, mercy, justice, and integrity.

The Book of Matthew demonstrates how Jesus is the fulfilment of the covenant between God and Israel in the Old Testament. The Book of Matthew is foundational to understand Jesus' nativity, life, and ministry. Through Matthew, we learn about Jesus' teachings and God's providence. Matthew emphasises that faith, mercy, and obedience are essential attributes to discipleship. The Book of Matthew is an informative narrative on how to live a meaningful, blessed, and purposeful life.

[1] The Holy Bible (NIV). (2011). *The Book of Matthew.* Chapter 1, Verse 1.
[2] The Holy Bible (NIV). (2011). *The Book of Matthew.* Chapter 6, Verse 33.
[3] The Holy Bible (NIV). (2011). *The Book of Matthew.* Chapter 4, Verse 17.
[4] The Holy Bible (NIV). (2011). *The Book of Matthew.* Chapter 11, Verse 30.

[5] The Holy Bible (NIV). (2011). *The Book of Matthew.* Chapter 5, Verse 12.

[6] The Holy Bible (NIV). (2011). *The Book of Matthew.* Chapter 28, Verse 20.

[7] The Holy Bible (NIV). (2011). *The Book of Matthew.* Chapter 16, Verse 24.

[8] The Holy Bible (NIV). (2011). *The Book of Matthew.* Chapter 9, Verse 13.

[9] The Holy Bible (NIV). (2011). *The Book of Matthew.* Chapter 6, Verse 25.

[10] The Holy Bible (NIV). (2011). *The Book of Matthew.* Chapter 20, Verse 28.

[11] The Holy Bible (NIV). (2011). *The Book of Matthew.* Chapter 26, Verse 28.

Chapter 41

The Book of Mark

'Love the LORD your God
with all your heart and with all your soul
and with all your mind and with all your strength.'

Mark 12:30
The Holy Bible (NIV)

The Book of Mark is the shortest of the four gospels. The Book of Mark presents a vivid account of Jesus Christ's life, ministry, crucifixion, resurrection, and ascension. Amongst other things, Mark emphasises Jesus' destiny as the servant of God. The Book of Mark focuses on Jesus' actions more than his teachings. Mark characterises Jesus as compassionate, powerful, merciful, and loving. The Book of Mark reveals Jesus' identity and divine mission through his profound teachings, good works, and miracles. Mark emphasises Jesus' service, suffering, and sacrifice. In effect, Jesus is the archetype of a righteous, compassionate, forgiving, loving, and honourable steward.

The Book of Mark characterises Jesus as the suffering servant. Mark reiterates the revelation within the Book of Matthew, that Jesus came not to be served, but to serve and to 'give his life as a ransom for many.'[1] This Biblical verse reveals Jesus' assignment on earth—to serve and redeem humanity. Greatness in God's kingdom is found in humility and service, not in social status, authority, political power, wealth, personal income, private property, or secular knowledge. As disciples of Jesus Christ, we are commanded to selflessly serve humanity. The life of a disciple is one of unconditional love and service to humanity.

Throughout the Book of Mark, the importance of faith is repeatedly emphasised. Jesus heals and performs miracles in response to the people's faith. For example, consider Jesus healed the woman with the persistent bleeding issue. Simply by touching Jesus' robe, the woman was cured of her ailment. Jesus responded to the woman, 'Daughter, your faith has healed you. Go in peace and be freed from your suffering.'[2] Jesus challenges his disciples' lack of faith, especially during the storm on the Sea of Galilee. Jesus questions them, 'Why are you so afraid? Do you still have no faith?'[3] Last but not least, Jesus teaches us that faith is the power to move mountains, 'Truly I tell you, if anyone says to this mountain, "Go throw yourself into the sea," and does not doubt in their heart but believes that what they say will happen, it will be done for them.'[4]

Faith is the instrument by which we experience God's transformative power in our life. When we trust in God, even in difficult circumstances or unfavourable situations, we realise God's providence in our life. Jesus encourages us to demonstrate faith that is consistent and persistent. We must remember that God rewards those who believe in Him. Faith is crucial to live a purposeful and meaningful life. Faith is our belief in God and His providence for our life.

The Book of Mark emphasises Jesus' sovereignty and authority over the natural and spiritual world. For example, consider Jesus pacifies a violent storm on the Sea of Galilee. Jesus casts out demonic spirits in the world. Jesus heals countless sick people. These supernatural actions demonstrate Jesus' divine power and His ability to bring about restoration in a broken world. Jesus possesses God-given authority over creation, this includes nature and humanity. This theological fact reassures believers, that no matter what challenges they confront, Jesus possesses supernatural power to intervene. We trust in Jesus Christ as our saviour.

Jesus makes it clear that discipleship involves taking up one's cross and following Him. In the Book of Mark, Jesus invites every person who wants to follow Him to 'deny themselves, take up their cross, and to follow me.'[5] Jesus challenges a young wealthy man to donate his wealth to the poor and follow him. These Biblical teachings indicate how personal wealth, along with our material possessions in the world, become an impediment to our spiritual progress. Jesus informs his disciples, 'It is easier for a camel to go through the eye of a needle than for someone who is rich to enter the kingdom of God.'[6] Discipleship requires a willingness to sacrifice our personal comforts, material possessions, opulent lifestyle, and worldly desires to follow Jesus Christ. The path of discipleship with Jesus Christ involves privation and suffering; however, it leads to fulfilment with our being in the world, and thereafter, eternal life in heaven.

The Book of Mark portrays the disciples as unperceptive to understand Jesus Christ. The disciples struggle to comprehend: Who is Jesus? What is Jesus' assignment on earth? For example, consider Jesus rebukes his disciples for their lack of understanding after the 'breaking of the five loaves of bread for the five thousand.'[7] Similarly, Jesus rebukes the disciples in relation to who is the greatest. Jesus instructs his disciples, 'Anyone who wants to be first must be the very last, and the servant of all.'[8] We are called to accept the truth of who Jesus is and what he expects of us. Ignorance and error obstruct our spiritual progress. Jesus urges his disciples to demonstrate a humble, compassionate, and servant leadership attitude. We must understand Jesus' teachings and principles correctly, not through worldly ideologies, such as secularism, modernism, individualism, or rationalism.

Jesus teaches his disciples how greatness is measured in God's kingdom. We learn that greatness is not measured by social status, income, wealth, position, private property, education, knowledge, or power; however, through humility, love, mercy, compassion, forgiveness, and service. Jesus employs the example of an innocent child to demonstrate the desirable personal qualities of love and faith. Jesus teaches the importance of humility. Jesus rebukes James and John for seeking power, honour, and glory, 'they replied, 'Let one of us sit at your right and the other at your left in your glory.''[9] The secular world defines greatness through the inequality of power, private property, income, position, personal wealth, education, and social status. In

God's kingdom, every person is equal. Our being in heaven is predicated on humility, faith, love, mercy, peace, brotherhood, sisterhood, compassion, and service. Jesus commands his disciples to live as humble servants. They must provide for the needs of each other and serve humanity, rather than be served.

In the Parable of the Sower, Jesus teaches us how people have an incorrect, and often an ill-informed, understanding of the gospel's message. The seed represents God's word, and the various types of soil represent the different conditions of a person's heart. Some people's hearts are inconsiderate. Some people's hearts are superficial. Some people's hearts are preoccupied with worries, work, and wealth. However, those people who hear and accept God's word, with a good and receptive heart, they bear fruit, 'like seed sown on good soil, hear the word, accept it, and produce a crop—some thirty, some sixty, some a hundred times what was sown.'[10] The condition of our heart is crucial to how we respond to God's word. A considerate, compassionate, courageous, and courteous heart allows God's word to take root and bear fruit in our life. We must guard our heart against vanity, pleasure, ignorance, evil, sin, and deceit. We must remain receptive to God's word. In our fellowship with God, we must endeavour to develop and mature in our faith.

Jesus teaches humanity the power of prayer. Jesus emphasises that when we pray in faith, we can beseech God for anything. So long as what we request is within God's will, we shall receive it; 'therefore I tell you, whatever you ask for in prayer, believe that you have received it, and it will be yours.'[11] In the Garden of Gethsemane, Jesus demonstrates the importance of submission to God's will through prayer. Jesus was in the midst of considerable personal anguish; however, he affirmed, 'Yet not what I will, but what you will.'[12] Prayer is a powerful instrument to strengthen our fellowship with God. Through prayer, we align our heart, mind, and spirit with God's will. Through prayer, we invite God's spiritual presence into our life. Jesus encourages us to pray with conviction and persistence. We trust that God considers our prayers. God answers our prayers according to His will.

Mark accurately records the instances where Jesus Christ predicts his rejection. Mark highlights the significant events that lead to Jesus' crucifixion and resurrection. In fact, the Gospel of Mark records three instances where Jesus foretells his crucifixion and resurrection. In the first instance Mark records, 'He then began to teach them that the Son of Man must suffer many things and be rejected by the elders, the chief priests and the teachers of the law, and that he must be killed and after three days rise again.'[13] In the second instance Mark narrates, 'the Son of Man is going to be delivered into the hands of men. They will kill him, and after three days he will rise.'[14] In the third instance Mark affirms, 'the Son of Man will be delivered over to the chief priests and the teachers of the law. They will condemn him to death and will hand him over to the Gentiles, who will … kill him. Three days later he will rise.'[15]

The final chapters in the Book of Mark describe Jesus' arrest, trial, and crucifixion. These chapters reveal Christ's sacrificial death on the Cross as atonement for the sins of humanity. Jesus' suffering and crucifixion are pivotal to his destiny. Jesus is the Lamb of God. Through Jesus' crucifixion, he atoned humanity for original sin. Jesus Christ provided a mechanism for humanity to be reconciled with God. Jesus' willingness to suffer for humanity is the ultimate act of unconditional love and sacrifice. We are called to follow Jesus' example. We must live our life characterised by love, philanthropy, community service, peace, mercy, social justice, and obedience to God's will.

The Gospel of Mark concludes with the resurrection of Jesus Christ. Christ's resurrection affirms his decisive victory over sin, evil, and death. The empty tomb is unquestionable proof of Jesus' divinity and the fulfilment of his promise to rise again. The women who discover Jesus' empty tomb are instructed to inform the disciples 'He has risen!'[6] The resurrection of Jesus gives hope to believers. The resurrection of Jesus confirms death has been defeated. Eternal life is available to all those who repent and believe in Jesus Christ. As believers, we live in hope, faith, trust, and confidence in the resurrection of Jesus Christ. God's word reveals to us that salvation and eternal life are received through faith in Jesus Christ.

The Book of Mark is a call to follow Jesus Christ in humility, service, love, peace, and faith. Mark encourages humanity to embrace the profound challenges of discipleship. As believers, we live in the hope of eternal life in heaven. Mark encourages believers to strengthen God's kingdom on earth. Through Jesus' love, compassion, and victory over death, God's kingdom reigns sovereign on earth. The Gospel of Mark does not detract from the difficulties associated with being a disciple of Christ. Through the profound dialogue between Jesus Christ and his disciples, the gospel demonstrates how fear, anxiety, and doubt are conquered through trust, belief, faith, love, hope, peace, and confidence in God's word.

[1] The Holy Bible (NIV). (2011). *The Book of Mark.* Chapter 10, Verse 45.

[2] The Holy Bible (NIV). (2011). *The Book of Mark.* Chapter 5, Verse 34.

[3] The Holy Bible (NIV). (2011). *The Book of Mark.* Chapter 4, Verse 40.

[4] The Holy Bible (NIV). (2011). *The Book of Mark.* Chapter 11, Verse 23.

[5] The Holy Bible (NIV). (2011). *The Book of Mark.* Chapter 8, Verse 34.

[6] The Holy Bible (NIV). (2011). *The Book of Mark.* Chapter 10, Verse 25.

[7] The Holy Bible (NIV). (2011). *The Book of Mark*. Chapter 8, Verse 19.

[8] The Holy Bible (NIV). (2011). *The Book of Mark*. Chapter 9, Verse 35.

[9] The Holy Bible (NIV). (2011). *The Book of Mark*. Chapter 10, Verse 37.

[10] The Holy Bible (NIV). (2011). *The Book of Mark*. Chapter 4, Verse 20.

[11] The Holy Bible (NIV). (2011). *The Book of Mark*. Chapter 11, Verse 24.

[12] The Holy Bible (NIV). (2011). *The Book of Mark*. Chapter 14, Verse 36.

[13] The Holy Bible (NIV). (2011). *The Book of Mark*. Chapter 8, Verse 31.

[14] The Holy Bible (NIV). (2011). *The Book of Mark*. Chapter 9, Verse 31.

[15] The Holy Bible (NIV). (2011). *The Book of Mark*. Chapter 10, Verses 33-34.

[16] The Holy Bible (NIV). (2011). *The Book of Mark*. Chapter 16, Verse 6.

Chapter 42

The Book of Luke

'Do to others
as you would have them do to you.'

Luke 6:31
The Holy Bible (NIV)

The Book of Luke is the third gospel in the New Testament. The Book of Luke provides a comprehensive account of Jesus' life, ministry, crucifixion, resurrection, and ascension. Luke was a renowned physician and trusted companion of the Apostle Paul. Luke wrote the gospel with a focus on the universal scope of Jesus Christ's message of salvation. The Book of Luke emphasises Jesus' compassion for the marginalised people. Luke emphasises the Messiah's destiny as the saviour of humanity. Luke's gospel highlights the importance of prayer, the power of the Holy Spirit, and love for humanity.

The opening chapters of Luke's gospel proclaim Jesus' auspicious birth to the shepherds. This moment is a significant event in world history. The nativity of Jesus is filled with immense joy, peace, love, and happiness for humanity. The nativity of Jesus characterises the fulfilment of God's promise of redemption for humanity, 'Today in the town of David a saviour has been born to you; he is the Messiah, the Lord.'[1] Humanity's gift of redemption is a cause for immense joy, both in heaven and on earth. God's redeeming grace to humanity gives occasion to celebration and thanksgiving. As disciples of Jesus Christ, we rejoice in the unmerited grace that we have received. We must share the good news of salvation through Christ with humanity. Every person is invited to experience salvation in Jesus Christ.

Luke characterises Jesus as the saviour who came to 'seek and to save the lost.'[2] Whether we are spiritually lost, outcast, impoverished, or physically in need of assistance, Jesus redeems us from sin, temptation, immorality, death, and evil. Jesus gives humanity the gift of eternal life. The Biblical story of Zacchaeus, the tax collector, confirms Jesus' assignment—to redeem humanity from sin, greed, temptation, and evil. From Zacchaeus' story, we learn the mission of Jesus is to redeem those who are lost. Jesus Christ's assignment is to bring humanity redemption, salvation, and eternal life. As disciples of Jesus Christ, we must adopt the same mission of compassion, forgiveness, and love. We must proclaim the good message of salvation to the lost and marginalised people across the world.

Luke emphasises that Jesus reaches out to the poor, sick, sinful, tax collectors, and Gentiles. These are members of the community that are overlooked or rejected. Luke declares the Messiah's mission is to bring 'good news to the poor, freedom to prisoners, and sight for the blind.'[3] The Parable of the Good Samaritan highlights Jesus' boundless compassion for the marginalised members of society. Jesus instructs his disciples to love and serve everyone as their neighbour. Jesus' compassion challenges social norms, custom, cultural practices, secular values, and the notion of rational self-interest. Jesus encourages us to love and serve those whom society devalues or excludes. As Jesus' disciples, we are agents of mercy, compassion, peace, love, and justice. As disciples of Jesus Christ, we are commanded to reach out to people in need. We must share God's universal message of love with humanity, regardless of a person's social status, sex, age, gender, colour, income, nationality, citizenship, wealth, education, private property, or vocation.

In the Book of Luke, Jesus Christ narrates several Biblical parables. For example, consider the Parable of the Lost Sheep, the Parable of the Lost Coin, and the Parable of the Lost Son. These parables highlight God's joy to forgive the rejected, lost, or outcast members of society. These Biblical parables reveal God's compassion towards sinners who repent and turn to Him. God forgives humanity for their errors, sins, failings, and mistakes; however, we need to repent in order to be redeemed. Repentance is the path to reconciliation with God. Jesus demonstrates that no person is beyond the sovereign capacity of God to forgive. These parables emphasise, that when a sinful person repents and they return to God, they are redeemed and there is great rejoicing in heaven. As believers, we are called to repent and extend forgiveness to each other. We must reflect God's grace, love, peace, and mercy, so that God's kingdom reigns on earth.

From the especial moment of Jesus' nativity, which symbolised peace and good news for humanity, to Jesus' profound teachings on God's kingdom, Luke emphasises that God's kingdom is not exclusively for Israel. God's kingdom is for all nations and people. Jesus' mission, mandate, and message are universal. Jesus offers salvation and eternal life to the Jewish people and Gentiles, to the righteous and sinners alike. This unmerited blessing to inherit God's kingdom is available to every person. There are no foreigners in God's providence concerning humanity's atonement and redemption. Every person has the opportunity to secure eternal life through Jesus Christ. Jesus' ministry encourages us to deconstruct stereotypes and social paradigms. We must live in a manner that reflects God's desire to bring humanity into His kingdom, regardless of race, nationality, sex, wealth, colour, private property, gender, vocation, income, age, education, or social status.

The Book of Luke highlights the presence and function of the Holy Spirit throughout Jesus' blessed life. From Jesus' nativity to his baptism, and subsequent temptation by the devil in the wilderness, the Holy Spirit was with Jesus. In all respects, Jesus' ministry is characterised by the Holy Spirit. Luke emphasises the invaluable gift of the Holy Spirit is available to all believers, 'how much more will your Father in heaven give the Holy Spirit to those who ask Him!'[4] The Holy Spirit is integral to the disciple's life. Just as Jesus was empowered by the Holy Spirit, we too are commanded to rely upon the Holy Spirit for our guidance, strength, wisdom, and spiritual transformation. The Holy Spirit empowers believers to live a righteous life. The Holy Spirit assists us to fulfil our assignment in the furtherance of God's providence.

Luke emphasises Jesus' commitment and devotion to prayer. Jesus often prays to God, whether it is before important decisions, or in times of distress. Luke's gospel includes the LORD's Prayer, in which Jesus instructs his disciples how to pray to God: 'Father, hallowed be your name, your kingdom come. Give us each day our daily bread. Forgive us our sins, for we also forgive everyone who sins against us. And lead us not into temptation.'[5] Prayer is essential for our spiritual strength, moral guidance, fellowship, and communion with God. Through personal example, Jesus is the archetype for humanity on the importance of daily, faithful, and genuine dialogue with God through prayer. As believers, we must cultivate a life of prayer. We must seek God's will. We depend upon God for our salvation.

Jesus teaches us that the two greatest commandments are: '"Love the LORD your God with all your heart and with all your soul and with all your strength and with all your mind;" and, "Love your neighbour as yourself."'[6] Jesus further elaborates upon his universal message of love. Jesus teaches us to 'love your enemies, do good to those who hate you, bless those who curse you, pray for those who ill-treat you.'[7] Jesus' unconditional command to love humanity embodies the divinity of God. Jesus' life example and his teachings are the hallmark of discipleship. Love is at the heart of the gospel's message. We must love God with all our heart, mind, and soul. We must love our neighbour as ourselves, this includes those who oppose or persecute us. The command to love every person is universal, unconditional, and inclusive. It reflects the love Jesus Christ demonstrated towards humanity on the Cross.

In the Book of Luke, Jesus encourages his disciples to accept a life-changing commitment. Jesus teaches us that to follow him, one must 'deny themselves and take up their cross daily and follow me.'[8] Jesus speaks about the responsibility and duty of discipleship. Jesus emphasises that being his disciple requires commitment. Discipleship is not a convenient endeavour. Discipleship entails sacrifice and privation. To follow Jesus means to prioritise God's word in our life. We must put into practice the Biblical teachings into our life. Our reward is eternal life in heaven and fellowship with God.

The Book of Luke emphasises the immeasurable value of humility in God's kingdom. In the Parable of the Pharisee and the Tax Collector, Jesus teaches us that humility and repentance lead to justification, while pride and self-righteousness lead to condemnation. We are all sinners. We are all in need of God's redeeming grace, 'for all those who exalt themselves will be humbled, and those who humble themselves will be exalted.'[9] Jesus teaches his disciples that greatness in God's kingdom comes through service of humanity, not through social status, authority, wealth, private property, fame, glory, or power. Humility is a prerequisite to enter God's kingdom. We must be humble before God. We must acknowledge our need for God's mercy. Humility is the guiding principle to fulfilment in our relationships. The disciples of Jesus Christ seek to serve humanity, rather than to be served.

The Book of Luke emphasises the joy in heaven over one sinner who earnestly repents. The Parable of the Lost Son demonstrates the incredible joy God experiences to forgive and redeem sinners; '"My son," the father said, "you are always with me, and everything I have is yours. But we had to celebrate and be glad, because this brother of yours was dead and is alive again; he was lost and is found."'[10] We must not ruminate on the former negative experiences that create bitterness and resentment in our life. The present moment affords the invaluable opportunity for repentance, redemption, and restoration.

The Book of Luke teaches us the universality of God's word. Luke emphasises the importance of repentance, forgiveness, mercy, peace, grace, compassion, and love. We must follow the example of Jesus Christ, who came to seek and save the lost. Luke encourages believers to live their life defined by humility, prayer, and community service. Luke inspires us to be better, to come up higher, and to perform good deeds in the world. To benefit from the timeless wisdom in the Book of Luke, we must not merely read and listen to the passages of scripture; however, we must earnestly apply these Biblical principles in our life. We must personify these cosmopolitan and egalitarian values in our life. Peace be with you.

[1] The Holy Bible (NIV). (2011). *The Book of Luke.* Chapter 2, Verse 11.

[2] The Holy Bible (NIV). (2011). *The Book of Luke.* Chapter 19, Verse 10.

[3] The Holy Bible (NIV). (2011). *The Book of Luke.* Chapter 4, Verse 18.

[4] The Holy Bible (NIV). (2011). *The Book of Luke.* Chapter 11, Verse 13.

[5] The Holy Bible (NIV). (2011). *The Book of Luke.* Chapter 11, Verses 2-4.

[6] The Holy Bible (NIV). (2011). *The Book of Luke.* Chapter 10, Verse 27.

[7] The Holy Bible (NIV). (2011). *The Book of Luke.* Chapter 6, Verses 27-28.

[8] The Holy Bible (NIV). (2011). *The Book of Luke.* Chapter 9, Verse 23.

[9] The Holy Bible (NIV). (2011). *The Book of Luke.* Chapter 18, Verse 14.

[10] The Holy Bible (NIV). (2011). *The Book of Luke.* Chapter 15, Verses 31-32.

Chapter 43

The Book of John

'In the beginning was the Word,
and the Word was with God,
and the Word was God.'

John 1:1
The Holy Bible (NIV)

T he Book of John is the fourth and final gospel in the
New Testament. The Book of John is distinct from the
other three gospels (i.e., Luke, Mark, and Matthew) in
its focus on the divinity of Jesus Christ. John characterises Jesus
Christ as the personification of God's word; the logos embodied
in the flesh. John emphasises the profound spiritual truth about
the divinity of Jesus Christ, Christ's fellowship with the Father,
and Jesus Christ's crucifixion. Jesus fulfils God's providence for
humanity's redemption. The Book of John is characterised
by symbolism, signs, and scripture that reveal the timeless reality
of God's kingdom and what it means to secure eternal life
through Jesus Christ.

The Gospel of John introduces Jesus Christ as the 'word that
became flesh.'[1] Jesus was the 'one and only Son, who came from
the Father, full of grace and truth.'[2] This verse of scripture
establishes the divinity of Jesus Christ. It establishes Jesus'
assignment in the fulfilment of God's providence. Since the word
became flesh and dwelt amongst humanity in the person of Jesus
Christ, Jesus is not merely a prophet or authoritative religious
figure. Jesus is divine and the Son of God. Jesus' nativity in the
world is to fulfil God's providence to redeem humanity from
original sin. Without Jesus Christ, humanity's atonement for
original sin is not possible. We must understand Jesus' nativity,
identity, humanity, and divinity as the Son of God. This is
imperative to know Jesus Christ and secure our salvation.

One of the central themes in the Book of John is that eternal
life is a special gift from God. Eternal life is received by God's
grace to all those who believe in Jesus Christ. In the Book of
John, we find one of the most quoted verses in the Holy Bible,
'God so loved the world that He gave His one and only Son, that
whoever believes in him shall not perish but have eternal life.'[3]
Jesus offers humanity eternal life in heaven. Not to mention,

salvation is available to all those who believe in Jesus Christ. Eternal life is not merely a future hope, it is a foundational theological belief for those who trust in Jesus. Salvation through faith in Jesus Christ is at the heart of the gospel's message to humanity.

Jesus reveals to the world that he is the 'bread of life.'[4] This means that Jesus is the sustenance for our body, mind, and spirit. Just as bread sustains our body, Jesus provides the requisite nourishment for our spirit. Jesus is the security for our salvation. Jesus satisfies the spiritual poverty of our human condition. No material phenomenon, being, doctrine, partnership, entity, ideology, corporation, or person grants us peace and fulfilment like Jesus Christ. Believers must position their trust and confidence in Jesus Christ—the Messiah—for their spiritual sustenance, redemption, salvation, and eternal life in heaven.

Jesus is the light of the world. Jesus brings truth, hope, and guidance to human civilisation which is shrouded in spiritual darkness. In the Book of John, Jesus states, 'Whoever follows me will never walk in darkness, but will have the light of life.'[5] Jesus is the source of spiritual illumination. Jesus guides humanity out of the darkness of evil and into the light of truth. When we follow Jesus, we are led to God's kingdom. Through Jesus, we live with purpose, peace, prosperity, and passion. Believers are to radiate this light to the world and share the gospel with humanity.

Jesus Christ is the 'good shepherd.'[6] Jesus knows his disciples and he lays down his life for their welfare and protection. This theological reality contrasts with the false shepherds—the Pharisees—who seek to advance their personal interests and secure pecuniary gain at the expense of the people. Jesus cares deeply about his disciples. He protects and guides them to eternal life in heaven. The crucifixion of Jesus Christ is the ultimate act of atonement that liberates humanity from the curse of original sin. Jesus ensures humanity has the opportunity to secure eternal life in God's kingdom. As believers, we must put into practice Jesus Christ's teachings, trust in his leadership, and follow him with commitment.

In the Biblical story of Lazarus' resurrection, Jesus declares that he is the 'resurrection and the life.'[7] Jesus promises that those who believe in him do not perish, but secure eternal life in heaven. Jesus possesses divine power over life and death. Through Jesus Christ, believers secure an anchor of hope in their unavoidable encounter with death. Believers know that death in the world is not the end of their being. Jesus Christ offers resurrection to all people who believe in him. Beyond our transient life on earth, Jesus Christ gives believers eternal life in God's kingdom.

In the Book of John, Jesus Christ declares, 'I am the way and the truth and the life. No one comes to the Father except through me.'[8] Jesus possesses exclusive authority as the pathway to the Father. Jesus is the source of truth in the world. Jesus Christ is the legitimate path to God, our Father in Heaven. There are no other legitimate means of salvation, except through Jesus Christ. Believers must place their faith in Jesus for their salvation. Jesus is the intermediary who reconciles humanity to God through his sacrificial death on the Cross. Jesus provides humanity with the blessing of eternal life in heaven.

John's objective in writing the gospel is to encourage believers to accept Jesus Christ as their saviour. Jesus is the Messiah. Jesus is the Son of God. When we believe in Jesus Christ, we secure 'eternal life in his name.'[9] Our belief in Jesus Christ is an act of faith by which we are justified before God. Our belief in Jesus is pivotal to secure our redemption and eternal life in heaven. Our belief in Jesus is not an intellectual exercise. To position our trust and confidence in Jesus Christ, as our saviour, is an act of faith. Accepting this belief leads us to a transformed life in the world, and thereafter, eternal life in God's kingdom. Faith in Jesus Christ is the foundation to the good life. Belief in Jesus is a prerequisite to experience God's redeeming grace in our life. We are sinners; however, we are justified before God through faith in Jesus Christ. Our salvation is secured through—an act of faith—the acceptance of Jesus Christ as our saviour.

Jesus promises to send the Holy Spirit to his disciples after his ascension to heaven. The Holy Spirit is characterised as the 'Spirit of Truth.'[110] The Holy Spirit guides, instructs, and empowers believers to live a God-fearing life. The Holy Spirit assists believers to understand and apply the eternal truth of God's word in their life. The indescribable power of the Holy Spirit intercedes between believers and God. The Holy Spirit is essential to the Christian faith. The Holy Spirit empowers believers to understand God's will and live righteously in the world. The Holy Spirit enables believers to witness and testify about Jesus Christ. Jesus assures believers, that even though he is not physically present with them, the Holy Spirit is with them. The Holy Spirit provides believers with protection, wisdom, and guidance.

In the Book of John, Jesus demonstrates humility and servant leadership by 'washing his disciples' feet.'[111] This act is customarily reserved for the lowest servant. Nonetheless, it reveals Jesus' unconditional love towards his disciples. Jesus' actions demonstrate that he leads by personal example. Jesus effectuates the command he gives to his disciples—to serve humanity. Leadership in God's kingdom is characterised by service, humility, compassion, forgiveness, mercy, social justice, peace, and love. Jesus encourages his disciples to selflessly serve humanity. Disciples of Jesus Christ position the needs of humanity above their personal interest. As believers, we must personify servant leadership in our relationships and interactions with members of society.

In the Book of John, we witness the Passion of Christ. The Passion of Christ characterises the final period before the crucifixion of the Messiah. The Passion of Jesus Christ personifies his divinity and humanity. In the context of Christian theology, 'passion' means to endure or suffer. The Passion of Christ encapsulates Jesus' experience of pain, suffering, grief, betrayal, punishment, and injustice on earth. The Passion of Christ is beyond words. It symbolises Jesus' extreme suffering to redeem humanity of original sin. In the final analysis, it is through the Passion of Christ; the pain, suffering, and crucifixion of Christ, that our broken relationship with God is restored. As a result, human civilisation's atonement for original sin is wholly satisfied. God's grace, mercy, peace, and love, provide humanity with redemption through the sacrificial death of His beloved son, Jesus Christ. The redemption that humanity has long sought since the fall of man is attainable through Jesus Christ.

The Gospel of John focuses on Jesus Christ's crucifixion on the Cross as the fulfilment of God's providence. As a consequence of Christ's crucifixion, redemption has been secured for humanity. This historic event reconciles with the thematic symbolism of Jesus Christ as the sacrificial lamb of God. In Jesus' final words on the Cross, he declares, 'It is finished.'[12] This demonstrates Jesus' assignment to atone for humanity's original sin has been completed. Jesus' subsequent resurrection and ascension into heaven confirms his victory over death.

Through Jesus Christ, believers secure eternal life in heaven. Jesus' resurrection symbolises the victory of good over evil. Jesus Christ's crucifixion, resurrection, and ascension are foundational beliefs of the Christian faith. Jesus' crucifixion ensures forgiveness for humanity's sin. The crucifixion, resurrection, and ascension of Jesus Christ are pivotal events in world history. In fact, Jesus' life on earth, including his nativity, ministry, and crucifixion, is confirmation of God's providence for humanity's redemption. These significant events in the course of world history demonstrate God's love, mercy, sovereignty, forgiveness, and grace.

Jesus gives his disciples an important commandment; 'love one another. As I have loved you.'[13] Jesus further emphasises the profound importance of love. Jesus affirms there is no greater love, than to 'lay down one's life for one's friends.'[14] Love is the determinative characteristic of the Christian community. Believers are commanded to love one another unconditionally, just as Jesus demonstrated throughout his ministry. Jesus Christ's unconditional love is a testimony to the world of the remarkable wisdom in his teachings. Paul the Apostle subsequently confirms in the scripture, that love is the most important attribute in life, 'And now these three remain: faith, hope, and love. But the greatest of these is love.'[15]

The Book of John emphasises the divinity of Jesus Christ. Believers receive the blessing of eternal life in heaven through Jesus Christ. We trust in Jesus as the saviour of humanity. In John, the teachings and actions of Jesus reveal God's providence for humanity's redemption. We are enlightened to God's profound love for humanity. We learn about the transformative power of faith to live in fellowship with God. John provides humanity with unconditional hope, that despite our sin, transgressions, and trespasses, the penalty has been paid by the Messiah. As a result, humanity has secured its redemption through Jesus Christ. The priceless gift of salvation is not received by our righteousness, merit, good works, adherence to the Mosaic law, or pursuit of virtue. Our redemption is secured through faith in Jesus Christ. Peace be with you.

[1] The Holy Bible (NIV). (2011). *The Book of John.* Chapter 1, Verse 14.

[2] The Holy Bible (NIV). (2011). *The Book of John.* Chapter 1, Verse 14.

[3] The Holy Bible (NIV). (2011). *The Book of John.* Chapter 3, Verse 16.

[4] The Holy Bible (NIV). (2011). *The Book of John.* Chapter 6, Verse 35.

[5] The Holy Bible (NIV). (2011). *The Book of John.* Chapter 8, Verse 12.

[6] The Holy Bible (NIV). (2011). *The Book of John.* Chapter 10, Verse 14.

[7] The Holy Bible (NIV). (2011). *The Book of John.* Chapter 11, Verse 25.

[8] The Holy Bible (NIV). (2011). *The Book of John.* Chapter 14, Verse 6.

[9] The Holy Bible (NIV). (2011). *The Book of John.* Chapter 20, Verse 31.

[10] The Holy Bible (NIV). (2011). *The Book of John.* Chapter 14, Verse 17.

[11] The Holy Bible (NIV). (2011). *The Book of John.* Chapter 13, Verse 5.

[12] The Holy Bible (NIV). (2011). *The Book of John.* Chapter 19, Verse 30.

[13] The Holy Bible (NIV). (2011). *The Book of John.* Chapter 13, Verse 34.

[14] The Holy Bible (NIV). (2011). *The Book of John.* Chapter 15, Verse 13.

[15] The Holy Bible (NIV). (2011). *The Book of First Corinthians.* Chapter 13, Verse 13.

Chapter 44

The Book of Acts

'They devoted themselves to the apostles' teaching
and to fellowship, to the breaking of bread and to prayer.'

Acts 2:42
The Holy Bible (NIV)

The Book of Acts is the fifth book in the New Testament. The Book of Acts is the connection between the four gospels and the Epistles. The Book of Acts chronicles the history of the church's formative years and the proliferation of the gospel. Through Acts, we learn about the monumental assignment of the apostles—especially Paul and Peter—as they establish Christian communities across the Roman empire. Written by Luke, Acts emphasises the indispensable function of the Holy Spirit. Acts demonstrates the empowerment of the early believers. Acts narrates the tragedies and triumphs in spreading the message of Jesus Christ across the Roman world.

Acts enlightens us that the Holy Spirit is the source of the apostle's spiritual power. The Holy Spirit blesses and guides the church in its formative years. Jesus informs his disciples that they will receive divine power when the Holy Spirit comes upon them. The Holy Spirit empowers the disciples to be Jesus' witnesses 'to the ends of the earth.'[1] The presence of the Holy Spirit at Pentecost commemorates the beginning of the church's evangelical mission. The Holy Spirit empowers believers to practice their faith, to spread the message of the gospel, and to fulfil God's mission. As disciples of Jesus, we must seek the Holy Spirit's guidance, wisdom, and strength in our life and ministry.

In the early days of the church, the believers devoted themselves to four defining practices: 'apostolic teaching, fellowship, the breaking of bread, and prayer.'[2] Community life was defined by love, peace, generosity, and worship amongst the believers. The Christian community is essential to our spiritual growth. Fellowship with believers, consistency in prayer, reading the word of God, and participating in the LORD's Supper are foundational elements for a meaningful life. The early church's example encourages believers to prioritise these foundational practices in their communities.

Acts affirms that the gospel is for all people, regardless of nationality, sex, race, gender, colour, ethnicity, age, income, vocation, property, education, wealth, or social status. The scripture is categorically clear on this point, 'God does not show favouritism.'[3] This theological fact is self-evident in the Biblical story of Peter's vision, where God vis-à-vis the Holy Spirit reveals to Peter that the gospel is not only for the Jewish people; however, it is also for the Gentiles. In addition, the Council of Jerusalem confirms that Gentile believers do not need to be Jewish in order to follow Jesus Christ, 'that the rest of mankind may seek the LORD, even all the Gentiles who bear my name.'[4] Jesus Christ's teachings, doctrines, and principles are universal. God desires every person to secure their salvation in Jesus Christ. The church is a cosmopolitan and egalitarian institution. We must deconstruct ideological barriers that divide humanity. We are commanded to invite every person into God's kingdom.

Throughout the Book of Acts, we witness the apostles' remarkable courage to proclaim the gospel, even in the midst of opposition, persecution, and threats. For example, consider Peter and John stand before the Sanhedrin and declare that they cannot stop preaching about what they have seen and heard; 'Which is right in God's eyes: to listen to you, or to Him? You be the judges! As for us, we cannot help speaking about what we have seen and heard.'[5] Similarly, when Peter and his fellow apostles are commanded to stop preaching, they respond, 'We must obey God rather than human beings!'[6] Christians must be valiant in sharing their faith, regardless of the challenges or opposition they confront in the world. The apostles' example encourages believers to remain faithful to their assignment. Believers must trust in God for strength to proclaim His message of redemption with courage, clarity, compassion, certainty, confidence, coherence, and conviction.

In Acts, we witness the church flourish, not only through

preaching and conversion, but also through religious persecution. After Stephen's speech to the Sanhedrin, he was martyred for his religious beliefs. Thereafter, countless believers were persecuted throughout the Roman empire. The early believers continue their journey to faithfully disseminate Jesus' message and teachings. Furthermore, the church continues to grow in its members. Believers continue to preach the gospel in places such as Antioch. God utilises difficult circumstances, including religious persecution, to advance His kingdom on earth. Believers are encouraged to be faithful witnesses in the midst of trials, troubles, and tribulations. Persecution does not obstruct God's providence. Persecution is a powerful instrument to spread the gospel.

Throughout Acts, we witness the importance of discipleship to establish and strengthen the church. Paul mentors Timothy to become a godly leader who continues to spread the faith. In addition, Aquila and Priscilla assist Apollos to enhance his understanding of the faith. Discipleship means to educate and mentor the next generation of believers to develop their faith and guide members of the community. Believers are encouraged to invest their time, expertise, knowledge, wealth, talent, and skill in people to mentor, educate, and guide them to advance God's kingdom on earth.

Throughout Acts, we witness God's providence in the missionary journey of Paul and his companions. For example, consider the Holy Spirit guides Paul and his companions. The Holy Spirit directs them away from Bithynia and towards Macedonia, where they preach the gospel. God reassures Paul in a vision 'not to be afraid and to keep on speaking'[7] the word of God to the Corinthians. Through Paul's journey, we witness God's sovereignty over creation. God directs believers to preach the gospel. While believers have an invaluable function to proclaim the gospel to humanity, it is ultimately God who prepares the hearts and minds of individuals to receive Christ.

Christians trust that God's providence guides their journey, even during uncertain or difficult circumstances. God employs believers for the fulfilment of His providence.

The early church is committed to prayer. Prayer is an invaluable instrument which brings humanity together. Prayer brings out the best in humanity. In Acts, we witness believers unite to pray, as they await the presence of the Holy Spirit. Believers pray for strength, grace, peace, mercy, and love. In one instance, the meeting place where the believers are gathered is shaken as they are 'filled with the Holy Spirit.'[8] On another occasion, the church fervently prays for Peter's release from prison. Prayer is indispensable to the life of the church and the believer. Through prayer, Christians secure strength, guidance, peace, mercy, wisdom, and grace to fulfil their God-given assignment. The early church's example encourages believers to prioritise prayer in their life.

Paul and his companions confront numerous trials, these include torture, imprisonment, religious persecution, banishment, and martyrdom. Nonetheless, they remain determined in their mission to spread the gospel. Paul encourages the disciples to persevere in their faith, he acknowledges that 'we must go through many hardships to enter the kingdom of God.'[9] In addition, Paul declares that he considers his life worth nothing compared to the monumental 'task of testifying to the good news of God's grace.'[10] Paul's example demonstrates that ministry is a challenging endeavour. Ministry requires our dedication, commitment, and perseverance. Christians are to remain faithful, even when they are confronted with opposition, loss, grief, injustice, or privation. The advancement of God's kingdom on earth is the greatest cause, in the furtherance of which, we must transcend worldly challenges.

The early church is characterised by prayer, belief, and faith. The believers are united in body, mind, heart, and spirit. The believers demonstrate solidarity in their struggle against worldly forces. However, the early church also confronts significant opposition in relation to the inclusion of Gentiles. The Council of Jerusalem addresses this conflict between the Jewish people and Gentiles. The Council strengthens unity amongst the congregation. The Council emphasises that our salvation is secured by God's grace through faith in Jesus Christ, not by good works, merit, the law, or virtue. Unity is essential to the body of Christ. Unity amongst the congregation requires our conscious dedication, effort, and commitment, especially where there are differences of opinion. Believers must work together in the community, to support one another, and to strive for peace. Believers must uphold the truth of the gospel.

Throughout Acts, we witness how God employs ordinary people—fishermen, tentmakers, tax collectors, and even former persecutors of early believers, like Saul (now known as Paul the Apostle)—to accomplish His providence. Acts highlights how the learned religious leaders—the Pharisees—were astonished by the courage and faith of Peter and John. The Pharisees recognised Peter and John were unlearned and unsophisticated men. Peter and John were without the privilege of education, personal wealth, social status, or private property. Little did the Pharisees know that Peter and John possessed God's blessing. They believed in Jesus Christ as the Messiah.

From the example of Peter and John, we learn that God can employ any person for the fulfilment of His providence, regardless of citizenship, education, sex, colour, income, private property, wealth, or social status. Our faith, trust, and confidence in the Holy Spirit are more important than our ability, talent, expertise, knowledge, wealth, social status, income, authority, private property, or vocation. Every believer has an indispensable function to perform in the advancement of God's kingdom on earth.

The Book of Acts demonstrates how the early church, guided by the Holy Spirit, transcended significant worldly challenges. The early church disseminated the message of Jesus Christ. The early church established the foundation for modern-day Christianity. Acts encourages believers to live with courage, persevere in their faith, and rely upon the power of the Holy Spirit to fulfil their assignment on earth. Through the Book of Acts, we witness God's providence in action. We realise that God's providence cannot be undermined. Despite the Roman empire's power, prestige, prosperity, and privilege, the gospel and teachings of Christ continue to proliferate throughout the Roman world.

[1] The Holy Bible (NIV). (2011). *The Book of Acts.* Chapter 1, Verse 8.

[2] The Holy Bible (NIV). (2011). *The Book of Acts.* Chapter 2, Verse 42.

[3] The Holy Bible (NIV). (2011). *The Book of Acts.* Chapter 10, Verse 34.

[4] The Holy Bible (NIV). (2011). *The Book of Acts.* Chapter 15, Verse 17.

[5] The Holy Bible (NIV). (2011). *The Book of Acts.* Chapter 4, Verses 19-20.

[6] The Holy Bible (NIV). (2011). *The Book of Acts.* Chapter 5, Verse 29.

[7] The Holy Bible (NIV). (2011). *The Book of Acts.* Chapter 18, Verse 9.

[8] The Holy Bible (NIV). (2011). *The Book of Acts.* Chapter 4, Verse 31.

[9] The Holy Bible (NIV). (2011). *The Book of Acts.* Chapter 14, Verse 22.

[10] The Holy Bible (NIV). (2011). *The Book of Acts.* Chapter 20, Verse 24.

Chapter 45

The Book of Romans

'Love must be sincere.
Hate what is evil;
cling to what is good.'

Romans 12:9
The Holy Bible (NIV)

The Book of Romans is written by the Apostle Paul.
Romans is a theologically and doctrinally profound
book within the New Testament. The Book of Romans
provides a systematic explanation of the gospel. The Book of
Romans addresses consequential topics, such as sin, redemption,
grace, faith, prayer, and righteousness. Without a doubt, the
Roman world has made a profound contribution to the
development and promulgation of Christian theology. Roman
ideas, history, doctrines, culture, and thought have been
instrumental to our understanding of salvation and righteousness
through faith. History and context matter when we examine the
time and lived experience in which Paul the Apostle wrote the
Book of Romans.

Paul commences the Book of Romans with an emphasis on
humanity's need for humility. Both the Jewish people and
Gentiles are subject to the error of sin, and therefore, deserve
God's judgement. In Romans, Paul writes, 'For all have sinned
and fall short of the glory of God.'[1] The problem of sin is not
confined to a community, nation, empire, or kingdom. Sin is a
universal problem that concerns humanity. Sin affects every
person on earth. We must recognise the universality of sin, so
that we understand our need for salvation. Since the fall of man
and original sin, humanity has been in a precarious situation. Not
to   mention,   humanity   cannot   redeem   itself   through
righteousness, good works, or the Mosaic law. This reality
underscores the requirement for God's intervention to redeem
humanity through His beloved Son—Jesus Christ.

Romans informs us that we are justified before God through
our faith in Jesus Christ. In the Book of Romans, Paul declares 'a
person is justified by faith apart from the works of the law.'[2]
Justification is being declared righteous before God, not by good
works, merit, adherence to Mosaic law, or virtue; however, by

faith in Jesus Christ. To be declared righteous is a priceless blessing from God. This blessing is received through God's grace. Salvation is not earned by the performance of good deeds, nor by observation of the Mosaic law. Salvation is a special gift from God. Salvation is received through our faith in Jesus Christ. The Book of Romans teaches believers to rely upon God's redeeming grace, not on their abilities, virtue, merit, or accomplishments to attain salvation.

Through Jesus Christ, believers are reconciled to God. Believers secure an unsurpassable peace; this is the 'peace of God, which transcends all understanding.'[3] Paul explains that 'while we were still sinners, Christ died for us.'[4] Jesus Christ's crucifixion is the legitimate basis of reconciliation between God and humanity. Christ brings humanity hope and assurance of God's love. Jesus' crucifixion secures God's forgiveness of humanity. Through Jesus Christ there is atonement for humanity. Believers are no longer separated from God because of their sin, they are now reconciled to God. Through Jesus Christ, believers secure God's peace, love, mercy, blessing, and grace.

Paul explains the law is beneficial. The law reveals God's ideals and moral standards for humanity. Having said that, the law cannot justify or redeem humanity from the destructive consequences of original sin. Instead, the law highlights our inability to obey God's command perfectly. The law demonstrates humanity's inherent need for a saviour. Paul explains how the law affirms humanity's sin, by our inability to faithfully observe it. Nonetheless, the law does not possess the capacity to redeem humanity from the negative consequences of sin.

Logically, the law demonstrates humanity's inherent necessity for God's redeeming grace. The law establishes the standard of conduct required; however, the law is not the instrument by which humanity is redeemed from sin. Due to our fallen nature, we cannot perfectly observe the law. When we fail to observe the law, it lacks the inherent capacity to provide atonement for our sin, or secure our salvation. The law does not provide humanity with their justification. The law is important in regulating human conduct; however, it is through faith in Jesus Christ, and our empowerment by the Holy Spirit, that we are absolved of sin and secure our salvation.

In the Book of Romans, Paul declares, 'there is no condemnation for those who are in Christ Jesus.'[5] The Holy Spirit empowers believers to live a righteous and honourable life. The Holy Spirit transforms the believer's body, mind, heart, and spirit. The Holy Spirit assures believers of their acceptance as members of God's kingdom. The Christian faith is experienced through the blessing of the Holy Spirit. Through the Holy Spirit believers transcend sin, experience freedom from condemnation, and live in harmony with God's will.

Paul provides believers with assurance of God's unconditional love. Paul proclaims nothing in creation separates us from the love of God that is in Jesus Christ, 'neither death nor life, neither angels nor demons, neither the present nor the future, nor any powers, neither height nor depth, nor anything else in creation, will be able to separate us from the love of God that is in Christ Jesus our Lord.'[6] This includes trials, tribulations, pain, suffering, loss, religious persecution, trauma, and death. God's love is universal and unconditional. Believers possess confidence in God's love and faithfulness, regardless of their present circumstances. This theological assurance brings us immeasurable peace, faith, and hope, even in the midst of our troubles.

Paul addresses the mystery of God's sovereignty in salvation, particularly in relation to Israel. Paul explains that God's promises to Israel remain valid, even though a significant portion of humanity has rejected the gospel's message. God's providence includes the Gentiles, who have been incorporated into the promises of Israel through faith in Jesus Christ vis-à-vis the new covenant. God's providence in relation to humanity's redemption is sovereign and it includes the Jewish people and Gentiles. While God's providence is mysterious and beyond our understanding, we trust that God is faithful to His covenant. God's providence for humanity is realised.

Paul strongly urges believers to offer their bodies as a living sacrifice to God. This is a spiritual act of commitment to God. Paul teaches believers, 'do not conform to the pattern of this world, but be transformed by the renewing of your mind.'[7] Paul provides practical instructions to practice the Christian faith, these include to love one another, extend forgiveness, hope, mercy, peace, and live in harmony. The believer's life is characterised by spiritual transformation and renewal. Believers must live an honourable life. Believers must transcend the cultural norms, social expectations, secular values, and prevailing customs that condition us to live a mediocre life in the contemporary world. Believers must demonstrate unconditional love, mercy, peace, justice, and community service. Being a disciple of Jesus Christ means to live in a manner that reflects his exceptional character and advances God's kingdom on earth.

Paul emphasises the importance to maintain unity amongst the congregation. This is crucial, especially concerning theological matters, where there exist differences in opinion, ideas, and doctrine. The preservation of unity amongst members is imperative, even when consequential issues that concern the church are debated. In Romans, Paul teaches believers to prioritise love for humanity. Believers must not position 'any stumbling block or obstacle in the way of a brother or sister.'[8] Believers are commanded to pursue peace, love, and unity within the church, even if this means to sacrifice our freedom of opinion for the sake of fellow believers. Love for humanity supersedes the pursuit of personal ambitions, objectives, motives, or endeavours.

Paul expresses his desire to preach the gospel where Jesus Christ is unknown. Paul encourages believers to support his missionary journeys, as he continues to spread the gospel throughout the Roman world, making it known to numerous people. The mission of the church is to spread the gospel to all nations and people. Christians are Christ's ambassadors in their endeavour to promote evangelism. Believers support the church's missionary efforts. They disseminate Jesus Christ's message of redemption to those who have not yet heard it.

Paul strongly urges believers to become a resource that is 'holy and pleasing'[2] to the LORD. This divine act involves the believer's personal dedication and commitment—time, resources, wealth, knowledge, abilities, skill, and expertise—to further God's providence. Worship is not merely about the performance of rituals, periodical attendance at church services, or our participation in religious activities. Worship of God constitutes part of our meaningful contribution to the advancement of God's kingdom on earth. Christians must live in a manner that honours God in their life. This lifetime is an unprecedented opportunity to serve God. We must fulfil our destiny in the grand scheme of God's providence.

The Book of Romans teaches humanity the foundational doctrines of the Christian faith. Romans emphasises that our salvation is secured by God's grace, through faith in Jesus Christ. Romans encourages believers to live a transformed life empowered by the Holy Spirit. We must share the gospel with humanity. Romans encourages Christians to live in unity, prioritise love, and faithfully fulfil our ministry to spread God's message of salvation to the world. Romans is visionary, ambitious, and full of hope and encouragement. Romans provides us with practical wisdom and godly leadership on how to contribute to the advancement of God's kingdom on earth.

[1] The Holy Bible (NIV). (2011). *The Book of Romans.* Chapter 3, Verse 23.

[2] The Holy Bible (NIV). (2011). *The Book of Romans.* Chapter 3, Verse 28.

[3] The Holy Bible (NIV). (2011). *The Book of Philippians.* Chapter 4, Verse 7.

[4] The Holy Bible (NIV). (2011). *The Book of Romans.* Chapter 5, Verse 8.

[5] The Holy Bible (NIV). (2011). *The Book of Romans.* Chapter 8, Verse 1.

[6] The Holy Bible (NIV). (2011). *The Book of Romans.* Chapter 8, Verses 38-39.

[7] The Holy Bible (NIV). (2011). *The Book of Romans.* Chapter 12, Verse 2.

[8] The Holy Bible (NIV). (2011). *The Book of Romans.* Chapter 14, Verse 13.

[9] The Holy Bible (NIV). (2011). *The Book of Romans.* Chapter 12, Verse 1.

Chapter 46

The Book of First Corinthians

'Love is patient, love is kind.
It does not envy, it does not boast,
it is not proud.'

1 Corinthians 13:4
The Holy Bible (NIV)

T he Book of First Corinthians is written by the Apostle Paul to the Church in Corinth. First Corinthians addresses a number of important issues that confront the early Christian community. The Church in Corinth experiences difficulties with internal divisions and issues of immorality. The church must confront important questions that concern the Christian faith and correct fundamental misunderstandings concerning the gospel. Pauline theology provides clarity on Christian doctrines and Biblical principles. First Corinthians assists believers to practice the Christian faith in a tumultuous political and social environment.

One of the issues in the Corinthian Church is division amongst its members. Some of the church members align themselves with Paul, while other members prefer Apollos. Not to mention, a third group of members voice their support for Cephas. Paul urges believers to be united in their faith, and focus on their saviour, Jesus Christ, rather than on allegiances to individual leaders. The church must promote unity within the congregation, not entertain division. Our allegiance is to God and Jesus Christ. We must avoid the creation of religious factions in the church based on personal preferences, beliefs, ideologies, opinions, ideas, doctrines, or charismatic leaders. Unity in the body of Christ is attained when we recognise that we are part of God's family. We must work together for the advancement of God's kingdom on earth.

The Corinthians were influenced by Greco-Roman philosophy and the art of rhetoric. In response, Paul contrasts the wisdom of the world with the wisdom of God. Paul argues that God's timeless wisdom is of no value to those who do not understand it. Paul stresses that God's wisdom is evident in the transformative message of the Cross. To the unbeliever, the Cross symbolises weakness and defeat. Paul asserts, 'for the message of the Cross is foolishness to those who are perishing, but to us who are being saved it is the power of God.'[1]

According to Pauline theology, wisdom is obtained from God's word. Wisdom is not sourced from our inquiry into the natural world. We do not secure wisdom from the accumulation of empirical knowledge, through the study of philosophy, clinical science, rhetoric, logic, medicine, law, history, political science, nor the human-made construct of secular ideologies, doctrines, legal systems, social values, or cultural norms. The gospel's universal message, though it is incomprehensible to the atheist, is to provision humanity with their redemption from original sin. Christians live in accordance with God's wisdom. God's wisdom challenges the foundation of worldly doctrines and the secular authority of political systems. Paul describes God's wisdom as, 'what no eye has seen, what no ear has heard, and what no human mind has conceived.'[2]

Paul characterises the human body as a temple for the Holy Spirit. To receive the Holy Spirit, we must adhere to moral precepts. Pauline theology is categorically clear on morality, 'do you not know that wrongdoers will not inherit the kingdom of God?'[3] In First Corinthians, Paul addresses the issue of sexual immorality. He reminds believers that our body constitutes a temple for the Holy Spirit. Paul emphasises that Christians must abstain from adultery, greed, intoxication, idol worship, and theft. Christians must live a holy life. We must observe moral principles in our thought, speech, and conduct. To live a morally righteous life ensures that we receive the Holy Spirit. We are created in the image of God. Therefore, we ought to live in a manner that reflects God's vision for creation. When we engage in evil, we violate the sanctity of our body. The purpose of our being is to honour, praise, worship, and glorify God.

Paul instructs believers to exercise their freedom with discernment and wisdom. Paul writes "I have the right to do anything,' you say—but not everything is beneficial. 'I have the right to do anything'—but not everything is constructive.'[4] Pauline theology asserts that our freedom can be employed to commit acts of benevolence or malevolence. Our free will imposes a moral obligation upon us to employ our judgement, conscience, and morality, before we determine a course of action. Paul acknowledges that believers have secured their freedom through redemption in Jesus Christ. Nonetheless, Paul stresses that our newfound freedom must be exercised with love, goodness, and consideration of humanity. Christian freedom is not about the assertion of our opinions, rights, ideas, doctrines, and expectations, it is about love and service to members of the community. We ought to responsibly exercise our freedom, to support members of the community to strengthen their faith. The guiding principle of our freedom is not what we can do with it, but what actions strengthen the body of Christ.

Love is the greatest virtue that humanity is capable of expressing. In one of the most famous passages of scripture, Paul highlights the uncontested supremacy of love, when he declares, 'And now these three remain: faith, hope, and love. But the greatest of these is love.'[5] Pauline theology teaches us that if a person possesses remarkable spiritual gifts, natural ability, talent, willpower, intelligence, or knowledge, without love, they have not experienced the transcendent purpose of being. Love is tolerant, sincere, humble, forgiving, and selfless. Love is the foundation of the good life and ministry. Love is the highest virtue of humanity. Love defines the life of every believer. Love surpasses all other gifts, talents, victories, and achievements. Without acknowledging the primacy of love in the world, all our secondary actions and accomplishments are devoid of meaning. Believers are to love one another, with the same unconditional love that Jesus Christ demonstrates towards humanity.

In First Corinthians, Paul dedicates an entire chapter to

explain the importance of the resurrection of Jesus Christ. Through Jesus Christ, the future resurrection of believers is affirmed—death is not the end of our being. Paul emphasises that without the resurrection of Jesus Christ, the Christian faith is not realised, and believers are condemned for their sins. The resurrection and ascension of Jesus Christ are the cornerstone of the Christian faith. Jesus Christ's resurrection fulfils the believer's hope of eternal life in heaven. Through Jesus Christ, Christians are secure in their belief of eternal life. Christians believe that death has been defeated through Jesus Christ's crucifixion, resurrection, and ascension.

Paul explains the Holy Spirit provisions believers with spiritual gifts to contribute to the church and advance God's kingdom on earth. Every person in the world has a destiny to fulfil, 'there are different kinds of gifts, but the same Spirit distributes them. There are different kinds of service, but the same LORD. There are different kinds of working, but in all of them and in everyone it is the same God at work.'[6] Every believer possesses unique gifts; however, all believers are part of the universal body of Jesus Christ.

Paul addresses the proper application of spiritual gifts, especially the gift of tongues. Paul emphasises that love is the guiding principle that informs the employment of our spiritual gifts. Our spiritual gifts and talents must be employed to serve humanity and glorify God. They are not to be misappropriated to promote our pride, ego, or self-righteousness. Our spiritual gifts and talents must be employed to strengthen the community, advance our nation, and contribute to the progress of humanity. Love is the guiding force for the employment of our spiritual gifts. Our spiritual gifts must be employed to advance the faith and serve humanity. Every believer is an integral member of the body of Christ. No person's gift is more important than another person's gift. Every person's gift is not of equal measure or contribution; however, every person is of equal worth.

Paul juxtaposes unity and diversity in the body of Christ and the church. Paul employs the metaphor of the human body to illustrate the church's function, 'just as a body, though one, has many parts, but all its many parts form one body, so it is with Christ.'[7] Similarly, in the church, every person within the congregation serves a unique function. Thus, the church consists of countless members, each with their distinct abilities, skills, knowledge, and talents. Every member is indispensable, and all members are equally valuable in God's kingdom on earth. Diversity and inclusivity are valued and promoted in God's kingdom. The church is a community of diverse members, each with their unique gifts, talents, expertise, knowledge, and experience. Every member is imperative to the growth and development of the body of Christ. Christians are commanded to work together in unity, value every member, and employ their God-given gifts to serve humanity and fulfil their assignment.

In First Corinthians, Paul addresses procedural issues related to worship, this includes the proper use of head coverings, the LORD's Supper, and the employment of our spiritual gifts to further the church's mission on earth. Paul stresses the importance of orderly conduct and respect amongst the church's members when it comes to worship and prayer. Worship is an expression of our reverence for God. Worship must be performed in a 'fitting and orderly'[8] manner, one that is respectful and dignified to the body of Christ. Disorderly or inconsiderate behaviour in worship disrupts the unity and focus of the congregation.

Paul acknowledges the indispensable function of women in the church. Paul emphasises the importance of women's head coverings as a sign of modesty and respect. Paul affirms the participation of women in ministry is indispensable. Paul also teaches us about the important functions and responsibilities of men and women within the church and family. Women have an important function to perform in worship and ministry of the church. Pauline theology teaches us that both men and women must honour God and submit to His divine order. Both men and women are equally valued and called to serve in God's kingdom.

In this day and age, the theological discourse in relation to women's head coverings is misperceived as a controversial cultural, gender, and social issue. However, Paul's message must be understood in its historical context, with respect for the traditions, practices, and customs in the society and time in which he lived and wrote his letters. Nonetheless, the broader Biblical principle herein is to honour God's will for order and respect in worship.

The Book of First Corinthians offers profound insights into the challenges confronted by the early church and its members. First Corinthians provides invaluable counsel for believers to practice the Christian faith today. First Corinthians encourages believers to live in unity, love, holiness, peace, grace, and faith. First Corinthians affirms Jesus Christ is our saviour. We all possess unique talents, knowledge, experience, skills, abilities, and spiritual gifts. We have a moral obligation to employ them to further good in the world. The greatest satisfaction from the employment of our gifts is realised when we advance God's kingdom on earth. No matter how great or small our contribution to the world, every person has a consequential destiny to fulfil in the realisation of God's providence.

[1] The Holy Bible (NIV). (2011). *The Book of First Corinthians.* Chapter 1, Verse 18.
[2] The Holy Bible (NIV). (2011). *The Book of First Corinthians.* Chapter 2, Verse 9.

[3] The Holy Bible (NIV). (2011). *The Book of First Corinthians.* Chapter 6, Verse 9.

[4] The Holy Bible (NIV). (2011). *The Book of First Corinthians.* Chapter 10, Verse 23.

[5] The Holy Bible (NIV). (2011). *The Book of First Corinthians.* Chapter 13, Verse 13.

[6] The Holy Bible (NIV). (2011). *The Book of First Corinthians.* Chapter 12, Verses 4-6.

[7] The Holy Bible (NIV). (2011). *The Book of First Corinthians.* Chapter 12, Verse 12.

[8] The Holy Bible (NIV). (2011). *The Book of First Corinthians.* Chapter 14, Verse 40.

Chapter 47

The Book of Second Corinthians

'Grace and peace to you from God
our Father and the Lord Jesus Christ.'

2 Corinthians 1:2
The Holy Bible (NIV)

The Book of Second Corinthians is authored by the Apostle Paul. Second Corinthians is a profoundly personal letter in which Paul defends his apostleship. Paul reflects on the challenges and struggle he and the Corinthian Church have endured. Beyond the pain and suffering, Paul provides believers with encouragement in the midst of difficult times. The Book of Second Corinthians emphasises the themes of reconciliation, peace, integrity, and generosity. In Second Corinthians, we become acquainted with God's sovereignty. We realise that God's sovereignty is manifested through human frailty.

Paul begins his letter with an emphasis that God is the 'Father of compassion and the God of all comfort.'[1] Paul writes that God consoles us in our troubles, so that we console members of the community who experience challenges, privation, loss, grief, trauma, and suffering. Paul writes from personal experience. Paul has encountered numerous afflictions along his journey; however, he found strength and peace in God. Similarly, believers secure hope in the fact that God consoles and strengthens them in their pain and suffering. God's spiritual presence during our suffering equips us to assist members who are in the midst of grief. Our suffering is not devoid of meaning. Our suffering must be employed to bring consolation and restoration to humanity.

Paul narrates how God demonstrates His power through human weakness. In Second Corinthians, Paul writes, 'We have this treasure in jars of clay to show that this all-surpassing power is from God and not from us.'[2] Paul further explains that, despite his extraordinary trials, pain, suffering, grief, privation, and afflictions, God's sovereignty, mercy, and grace are always evident. Our weaknesses are an opportunity for God to demonstrate His infinite power. Christians are commanded to rely upon God's power, not on their strength. Christians trust that in the midst of their vulnerability, God's glory is revealed. God transforms our weaknesses, failures, pain, and traumatic experiences into an opportunity to further His providence. We must employ our lived experience to assist people to realise God's blessings and promises in their life.

One of the significant themes in Second Corinthians is reconciliation. Paul explains that through Jesus Christ, God forgives and reconciles sinners to Himself. As a result, God entrusts believers with the message of reconciliation; 'God was reconciling the world to Himself in Christ.'[3] Paul writes that 'if anyone is in Christ, the new creation has come: the old has gone, the new is here!'[4] Jesus Christ's crucifixion was the defining event in world history which made possible humanity's reconciliation with God. As believers, we represent 'Christ's ambassadors'[5] to the world. As Christ's ambassadors, we have a duty to share the gospel, promote reconciliation, and restore damaged relationships in the community.

In the midst of trials, tests, and tribulations, Paul encourages believers to 'live by faith, not by sight.'[6] Second Corinthians informs us that while our outer self (i.e., the body) diminishes daily, our inner self (i.e., the spirit) is constantly being renewed. Paul encourages the Corinthians to set their mind on the eternal glory of God, not on the secular endeavours of this world. Paul explains that long-term visionary thought is important because, 'what is seen is temporary, but what is unseen is eternal.'[7] Throughout the peaks and valleys of our life, we must 'not lose heart.'[8] Christians are commanded to live with an eternal perspective in mind. We trust in God's promises, even when our circumstances are difficult. Faith is the instrument to perceive beyond our challenges. We must run our race, knowing that we are forgiven in Christ, and with the hope of eternal life in God's kingdom.

Paul encourages the Corinthians to demonstrate generosity.

The Corinthians must assist the Church in Jerusalem, which experiences financial challenges. Paul characterises generosity as an act of grace that flows from God's boundless love for humanity. In Second Corinthians, Paul reminds believers, 'Each of you should give what you have decided in your heart to give, not reluctantly or under compulsion, for God loves a cheerful giver.'[9] Philanthropy is an expression of love, brotherhood, sisterhood, compassion, mercy, and grace. Christians are encouraged to be generous and considerate in their giving. Believers know that God provides everything they require. Generosity is not about the amount we give; it is about the donor's conscience. Philanthropy results in blessings for both the donor and donee.

Throughout Second Corinthians, Paul defends his apostleship against those who question his authority and criticise his ministry. Paul contrasts his ministry with the illegitimate 'super apostles'[10] who boast of their achievements. Paul emphasises that apostleship is characterised by humility, service, charity, suffering, and obedience to God's will, not by credentials, qualifications, power, position, fame, status, private property, or wealth. Christian leadership is not characterised by pride, honour, or self-aggrandisement. Paul's impassioned defence of his apostolic authority reminds believers that to preach the gospel is not about our accolades. To preach the gospel is to disseminate Jesus Christ's message of redemption for humanity.

Paul contrasts the old covenant of the Mosaic law, with the new covenant of God's grace through faith in Jesus Christ. The old covenant was temporary. The old covenant was unable to secure the believer eternal life, let alone forgiveness of sin. Observance of the Mosaic law could not ensure humanity's redemption from original sin. In contrast, the new covenant, established through faith in Jesus Christ, redeems believers from the consequences of original sin. Believers must reflect the glory of God, just as Moses reflected the glory of God. The new covenant, through Jesus Christ, is superior to the old covenant. The new covenant secures freedom, redemption, eternal life, and righteousness for believers. Christians experience and reflect God's glory through the presence of the Holy Spirit. The Holy Spirit transforms the believer's body, mind, heart, and spirit.

In Second Corinthians, Paul shares an unfortunate experience about a 'thorn in my flesh.'[111] Paul experiences a persistent problem and he is suffering. On three occasions, Paul pleads with God to remove this thorn from his flesh. God responds to Paul, 'My grace is sufficient for you, for my power is made perfect in weakness.'[112] As a result, Paul reasons that God has given him the requisite strength to conquer his challenges and surmount his problems, 'For when I am weak, then I am strong.'[113] Through Paul's experience, we learn that God does not promise believers a life without adversity, grief, privation, loss, trauma, pain, or suffering. Having said that, God gives us the grace to overcome our challenges. In our weakness, God's strength is made evident. Christians trust that God's grace is sufficient for any trial in their life. In addition, our circumstances, challenges, pain, trauma, and problems are employed by God to further His providence.

Paul encourages believers not to focus on their temporary troubles. Instead, believers are to focus on eternal life and the indescribable glory that awaits them in God's kingdom. Paul writes in Second Corinthians, 'For our light and momentary troubles are achieving for us an eternal glory that far outweighs them all.'[114] Christians are commanded to live with an eternal perspective. Christians recognise that their worldly struggles are short-lived. God employs challenges to test and perfect our character. God refines our conscience in this lifetime, so that we are prepared for eternal life in His kingdom. This divine perspective assists us to endure our difficulties, challenges, problems, trauma, pain, suffering, and losses with newfound hope, confidence, and purpose.

Paul candidly reflects on his experience in ministry. Paul and his companions have conducted themselves with integrity, despite the presence of privation and opposition in the world. Paul acknowledges the numerous trials he has personally endured, these include beatings, riots, false accusations, imprisonment, sleep deprivation, and exile. Nonetheless, Paul insists that he has not compromised his integrity. Paul affirms that he has been faithful to the truth of the gospel. Ministry is defined by compassion, righteousness, honesty, integrity, selflessness, faithfulness, mercy, compassion, and social justice. Even in the midst of privation, believers must live their life reflecting the truth of the gospel. The message of Jesus Christ is life-changing. Our life must be defined by integrity, love, good character, hope, mercy, and social justice.

The Book of Second Corinthians encourages believers to secure their peace and strength in God. We are called to live with humility, integrity, and authenticity. We are reminded of the hope, salvation, redemption, and forgiveness found in Jesus Christ. Second Corinthians highlights the paradox of the Christian faith—strength through weakness, victory through suffering, grace through mercy—and it commands Christians to be faithful ambassadors of reconciliation, peace, forgiveness, mercy, honour, social justice, and love in the world. The ephemeral nature of life presents us with an unprecedented opportunity to refine our state of being, so that we are prepared for eternal life in God's kingdom.

[1] The Holy Bible (NIV). (2011). *The Book of Second Corinthians.* Chapter 1, Verse 3.
[2] The Holy Bible (NIV). (2011). *The Book of Second Corinthians.* Chapter 4, Verse 7.

[3] The Holy Bible (NIV). (2011). *The Book of Second Corinthians.* Chapter 5, Verse 19.

[4] The Holy Bible (NIV). (2011). *The Book of Second Corinthians.* Chapter 5, Verse 17.

[5] The Holy Bible (NIV). (2011). *The Book of Second Corinthians.* Chapter 5, Verse 20.

[6] The Holy Bible (NIV). (2011). *The Book of Second Corinthians.* Chapter 5, Verse 7.

[7] The Holy Bible (NIV). (2011). *The Book of Second Corinthians.* Chapter 4, Verse 18.

[8] The Holy Bible (NIV). (2011). *The Book of Second Corinthians.* Chapter 4, Verse 16.

[9] The Holy Bible (NIV). (2011). *The Book of Second Corinthians.* Chapter 9, Verse 7.

[10] The Holy Bible (NIV). (2011). *The Book of Second Corinthians.* Chapter 11, Verse 5.

[11] The Holy Bible (NIV). (2011). *The Book of Second Corinthians.* Chapter 12, Verse 7.

[12] The Holy Bible (NIV). (2011). *The Book of Second Corinthians.* Chapter 12, Verse 9.

[13] The Holy Bible (NIV). (2011). *The Book of Second Corinthians.* Chapter 12, Verse 10.

[14] The Holy Bible (NIV). (2011). *The Book of Second Corinthians.* Chapter 4, Verse 17.

Chapter 48

The Book of Galatians

'But the fruit of the Spirit is love, joy, peace,
forbearance, kindness, goodness, faithfulness,
gentleness, and self-control.'

Galatians 5:22-23
The Holy Bible (NIV)

The Book of Galatians is authored by the Apostle Paul. Galatians is a passionate letter addressed to the churches in Galatia. Galatians addresses a substantive theological issue: the advocacy from orthodox religious groups to impose Mosaic law upon the Gentile Christians. Paul defends the doctrine of grace. Paul emphasises that our salvation is secured by faith in Jesus Christ. We do not secure our salvation through adherence to the Mosaic law. The Book of Galatians is Paul's spirited defence of salvation based on God's grace through faith in Jesus Christ. The Book of Galatians conclusively affirms that God's grace for humanity's redemption is secured through the Messiah, not through good works, the Mosaic law, virtue, merit, or righteous conduct.

Paul strongly condemns the Galatians for preaching a 'different gospel,'[1] one that requires adherence to the law for believers to secure their salvation. Paul categorically emphasises that the gospel he preaches is not inspired by knowledge or experience; however, it is the product of divine revelation. The gospel has been revealed to Paul by Jesus Christ through the Holy Spirit. Paul insists humanity receives their redemption by God's grace, it is through 'our faith in Christ Jesus that we may be justified.'[2] We are not justified by the performance of good works, virtue, merit, or the Mosaic law. The fundamental message of Pauline theology is that salvation is God's gift to humanity. Salvation is received by faith in Jesus Christ. We do not earn our salvation through good works, performance of rituals, or adherence to the Mosaic law. The doctrine of grace is foundational to the Christian faith. We must not amend the gospel's message.

Paul unequivocally condemns any teaching that modifies the gospel's message. The Galatians were influenced by Jewish Christians who insisted that Gentile believers must observe Jewish customs. For example, consider the requirement of circumcision imposed upon the male population in order for them to be redeemed. Paul is unequivocally clear, to add or remove anything from the gospel of grace undermines the universal truth of Jesus Christ's message. The gospel is complete as it is. We must be cautious of rules, customs, doctrines, or traditions that modify the message of salvation through Jesus Christ. Any distortion of the gospel is deceptive and it leads believers away from the truth.

One of the themes in Galatians is freedom. Paul declares in Galatians, 'It is for freedom that Christ has set us free. Stand firm, then, and do not let yourselves be burdened again by a yoke of slavery.'[3] Christ has emancipated believers from the burden of the law, the guilt of original sin, and the duty to make offerings as atonement for sin. However, our freedom must not be misappropriated to indulge in the pleasures of the flesh. Our freedom in Christ must be employed to serve humanity with love, peace, compassion, mercy, social justice, and grace. Freedom with responsibility and accountability empowers us to change the world for the better.

Christian freedom is not the freedom to sin. It is the freedom to live in accordance with God's will. We are liberated from the law's condemnation. We are liberated from the law's judgement. We are liberated from the requirement to make sin offerings to secure our atonement. We are liberated from the obligation to perform rituals to secure God's favour. Having said that, we are commanded to employ our newfound freedom—in Jesus Christ—to love God and serve humanity. We must spread the gospel across the world. Therefore, we must appropriate our free will for the pursuit of beneficial ends and constructive purposes. This is the moral litmus test of our lifetime—How do we employ our free will?

Paul contrasts the works of the flesh (i.e., sinful behaviour) with the desirable fruit of the Spirit. Paul characterises the fruit of the Holy Spirit to include 'love, joy, peace, forbearance, kindness, goodness, faithfulness, gentleness, and self-control.'[4] These admirable qualities are the result of the Holy Spirit's presence in the believer's life. The Holy Spirit's presence in our life is witnessed by the transformation in our thoughts, speech, beliefs, values, character, and conduct. To live by the Spirit means to produce good works that are characteristic of the Spirit. When we live by the Spirit, we reflect God's character, attributes, and divine nature. When we live by the Spirit, we become a living testimony to the strength of good over the weakness of evil. Believers are to cultivate the fruits of the Holy Spirit along their journey.

Paul explains that Abraham was justified by faith before the law was proclaimed. Righteousness comes by faith, not by works, or the law, 'so those who rely on faith are blessed along with Abraham, the man of faith.'[5] Therefore, we are justified by faith in Christ, not by the law. The law cannot justify any person before God. The law only reinforces our need for a saviour. Jesus Christ, through his sacrificial death on the Cross, redeemed humanity from the curse of original sin and the obligation of the law. Jesus Christ guides believers along the path of righteousness through faith in him.

Justification, that is being made right with God, is obtained through faith in Jesus Christ. We cannot secure our justification through our observance of the law. Through God, Abraham's faith was 'credited to him as righteousness.'[6] In the same manner, we are made righteous by placing our faith and belief in Jesus Christ. The law identifies our sin and error. Our inability to adhere to the law—due to our fallen nature inherited through the original sin of Adam and Eve—affirms our sinful nature. Having said that, it is our faith in Jesus Christ that secures us [unmerited] redemption.

Paul encourages believers to 'live by the Spirit.'[7] This means to receive the Holy Spirit's guidance, protection, wisdom, and strength, rather than to rely upon the flesh for willpower, discipline, self-determination, and resilience. This protracted conflict between the flesh and Spirit is real. The Holy Spirit empowers believers to overcome their sinful desires and evil temptations. Through the Holy Spirit, we live in accordance with God's will. The believer's life is not defined by a constant struggle to follow rules, rituals, and regulations. The believer's life is defined by fellowship with God in the presence of the Holy Spirit. We are empowered to live a godly life through the Holy Spirit. It is the unrivalled power of the Holy Spirit which assists us to overcome the powerful desires and temptations of the flesh.

Paul explains that the law was proclaimed as an instrument to demonstrate to humanity their sinful nature. The law is not the instrument by which people secure their justification and salvation before God. The law served as our 'guardian until Christ came that we might be justified by faith.'[8] The law confirms our need for a saviour to redeem us from the detrimental effects of original sin. The law serves a fundamental purpose, it reveals our inadequacy to observe God's command. The law points us towards Jesus Christ. Having said that, the law cannot redeem us from the consequences of original sin. Through faith, once we believe in Jesus Christ, we are no longer subject to the law's condemnation. It is the miraculous power of faith, that 'no one can say, 'Jesus is Lord,' except by the Holy Spirit.'[9] The law confirms our necessity for God's redeeming grace. Grace is received through faith in Jesus Christ.

Paul emphasises that the freedom believers secure in Christ is not a licence to engage in sin. Christian freedom is the opportunity to worship God and serve humanity in love. Paul reminds us, 'do not use your freedom to indulge the flesh; rather, serve one another humbly in love.'[10] Christian freedom is not about the pursuit of the desires of our flesh. Christian freedom is to faithfully walk with God in the presence of the Holy Spirit and to serve humanity. Freedom in Christ leads us to love and serve humanity. Freedom is to employ our free will to fulfil God's command to 'love your neighbour as yourself.'[11]

Paul encourages believers to demonstrate prudence in their life. We must appreciate that the choices we determine result in lifelong consequences. If we sow to the flesh (i.e., live according to our sinful desires), we reap destruction. On the contrary, if we sow to the Spirit (i.e., live according to God's will), we 'reap eternal life.'[12] The principle of sowing and reaping applies to our thought, speech, and conduct. We must self-determine to sow the Holy Spirit within us, by living in obedience to God's word. Thereafter, in the fullness of time, we will reap the blessed fruits of the Spirit. It is important to persevere in the performance of good deeds, especially towards fellow believers.

Paul concludes Galatians with a powerful declaration: 'May I never boast, except in the Cross of our Lord Jesus Christ.'[13] Paul affirms that to boast in the Mosaic law, good works, or personal achievements is meaningless, when compared to the eternal glory of the Cross. The Cross is the legitimate source of humanity's redemption from original sin. In accordance with Pauline theology, the only phenomenon worth boasting about is the Cross of Jesus Christ. Humanity's redemption is secured through Jesus Christ. Therefore, our identity is established in Jesus Christ, not in our victories, good works, virtue, character, merit, or accomplishments.

The Book of Galatians encourages believers to be sensible and responsible with the freedom that Jesus Christ has secured for them. Believers must live by the Spirit. Believers must reject any attempt to introduce legalistic practices or secular doctrines into the gospel. Amongst other things, Galatians emphasises that salvation is God's gift of grace to the believer. Believers, empowered by the Holy Spirit, are to live in love and service to humanity. In the final analysis, our thoughts, speech, and actions must align with the Holy Spirit. We must develop our character, morality, conscience, virtues, and attributes to become more like Jesus Christ. Peace be with you.

[1] The Holy Bible (NIV). (2011). *The Book of Galatians.* Chapter 1, Verse 6.

[2] The Holy Bible (NIV). (2011). *The Book of Galatians.* Chapter 2, Verse 16.

[3] The Holy Bible (NIV). (2011). *The Book of Galatians.* Chapter 5, Verse 1.

[4] The Holy Bible (NIV). (2011). *The Book of Galatians.* Chapter 5, Verses 22-23.

[5] The Holy Bible (NIV). (2011). *The Book of Galatians.* Chapter 3, Verses 9.

[6] The Holy Bible (NIV). (2011). *The Book of Galatians.* Chapter 3, Verse 6.

[7] The Holy Bible (NIV). (2011). *The Book of Galatians.* Chapter 5, Verse 16.

[8] The Holy Bible (NIV). (2011). *The Book of Galatians.* Chapter 3, Verse 24.

[9] The Holy Bible (NIV). (2011). *The Book of First Corinthians.* Chapter 12, Verse 3.

[10] The Holy Bible (NIV). (2011). *The Book of Galatians.* Chapter 5, Verse 13.

[11] The Holy Bible (NIV). (2011). *The Book of Galatians.* Chapter 5, Verse 14.

[12] The Holy Bible (NIV). (2011). *The Book of Galatians.* Chapter 6, Verse 8.

[13] The Holy Bible (NIV). (2011). *The Book of Galatians.* Chapter 6, Verse 14.

Chapter 49

The Book of Ephesians

'For it is by grace you have been saved,
through faith—and this is not from yourselves,
it is the gift of God—not by works.'

Ephesians 2:8-9
The Holy Bible (NIV)

T he Book of Ephesians is written by the Apostle Paul.
Ephesians is an elegant letter that contains several
theological truths, religious doctrines, and practical
instructions to practice the Christian faith. Ephesians focuses on
the believer's identity in Jesus Christ, the unity of the church, and
the instrumental function of God's grace in our salvation.
Ephesians provides guidance on how to live in a manner that
honours God, both individually and within the community. In
Ephesians, Pauline theology consists of two components: the
doctrinal and practical matters of faith.

Paul commences Ephesians with a reminder to believers of
their newfound identity in Jesus Christ. Through Christ, we have
been affirmed as God's chosen people, 'when you believed, you
were marked in Him with a seal, the promised Holy Spirit.'[1]
These spiritual blessings are not earned by us, they constitute a
special gift of God's redeeming grace. Our identity is established
in Jesus Christ, not in our achievements, good works, virtue,
character, merit, or fortune. We are God's beloved and chosen
people. We are redeemed through Jesus Christ, and sealed by the
Holy Spirit. When we understand our newfound identity in Jesus
Christ, it transforms the way we live, reason, and relate to each
other. Not to mention, our identity in Jesus Christ informs our
beliefs, values, priorities, and principles.

In Ephesians, Paul declares, 'For it is by grace you have been
saved, through faith—and this is not from yourselves, it is the gift
of God—not by works, so that no one can boast.'[2] Paul
reaffirms that salvation is a gift from God. We do not attain
salvation through good deeds. God's redeeming grace is the
foundation of our salvation. We do not secure God's grace
through good works or merit; however, through God's love and
mercy. It is not our pride, self-righteousness, virtue, good
character, deeds, or personal attributes that secure us God's

grace. It is a timeless truth that God's goodness towards humanity justifies our redemption from original sin. Salvation through Jesus Christ leads us to eternal life. When we personify gratitude, prayer, love, peace, forgiveness, mercy, and good works, we must not forget these positive attributes are obtained from the presence of the Holy Spirit.

Paul teaches us that through Jesus Christ, the Jewish people and Gentiles are united into one community. As a result, the 'dividing wall of hostility'[3] between equal members of humanity is deconstructed. In Jesus Christ, believers are reconciled to God and with each other. Believers constitute a diverse and inclusive community of people. The church is a united community, it transcends divisions, such as ethnicity, race, sex, wealth, political affiliation, colour, nationality, gender, vocation, age, knowledge, private property, ministry, income, and social status. Believers must advance reconciliation and unity amongst humanity. Believers must reflect the 'pact of peace' that Jesus Christ has made between humanity and God through his sacrificial death.

Paul urges believers to live their life worthy of the redemption they have received through Jesus Christ. Our life must be characterised by humility, gentleness, forbearance, mercy, peace, justice, and love. This perspective on life promotes unity and peace within the body of Jesus Christ. Christians must live in a manner that honours the ministry to which they are called. This means we are to live with humility, practice forbearance, and strive for peace and unity in the body of Jesus Christ. How we live as individuals affects the influence and impact of the church.

Paul teaches humanity that God bestows spiritual gifts upon believers. These spiritual gifts are for the advancement of the church and the body of Christ. Godly leaders must mentor believers to fulfil their destiny. Godly leaders must develop unity in the body of Christ and spiritual maturity amongst the believers. Every believer possesses unique spiritual gifts to serve humanity and strengthen the body of Christ. We are not meant to live in isolation. God did not create humankind to be defined by individualism. God created humanity to flourish within the institutions of marriage, family, community, church, and nationhood. We are members of a living and thriving community. We must employ our gifts for the common good of society. The church is an institution for hope, prayer, love, faith, worship, fellowship, pastoral care, forgiveness, mercy, and community service.

Paul urges believers to abandon their dishonourable way of life. A worldly life is characterised by sin, avarice, envy, concupiscence, temptation, jealousy, greed, and evil. Believers are commanded to embrace their newfound identity in Jesus Christ. We must embrace our new self, one that is envisaged to be 'like God in true righteousness and holiness.'[4] The believer's life is defined by spiritual transformation. We must eliminate our sinful behaviours, ideas, desires, thoughts, doctrines, and attitudes. We must assume the righteous character of Jesus Christ. To achieve this noble aspiration requires the psychological, spiritual, emotional, and physical transformation of our being. We must attain a total renewal of our body, mind, heart, and spirit.

Paul exhorts believers to 'live as children of light.'[5] Believers must embrace God's love and walk in the light of the Holy Spirit. Paul contrasts the behaviours of darkness (i.e., envy, avarice, greed, jealousy, and concupiscence), with the behaviours of light (i.e., goodness, righteousness, justice, honour, integrity, compassion, community service, mercy, and honesty). As believers, we must avoid negative worldly influences. Instead, we must live our life defined by holiness and community service. As disciples of Jesus Christ, we are called to reflect God's truth, holiness, and righteousness in our life. To realise this divine vision means to live with integrity and avoid sinful behaviour. We must walk in the light and truth of God's word. Our life must be a living testimony to the transformative power of the gospel.

Paul characterises the covenant between the husband and wife as a metaphor of Jesus Christ's relationship with the church. Husbands are commanded to love their wives, just as Christ loves the church. Both the husband and wife must respect each other. This mutual love and respect within marriage symbolises Christ's unconditional love for the church. Marriage is a sacred covenant that reflects the sacred relationship between Christ and the church. Marriage between husband and wife is defined by love, commitment, trust, intimacy, communication, forgiveness, equality, respect, loyalty, empathy, and responsibility. These desirable attributes are indispensable to a successful and enduring marriage. They reflect the authentic meaning of the gospel.

Paul concludes his letter with advice to believers to put on the 'full armour of God.'[6] We must categorically reject the schemes, stratagems, and swindle of the devil. God's armour includes the belt of truth, the breastplate of righteousness, the shoes of peace, the shield of faith, the helmet of salvation, and the sword of the Spirit. Believers are engaged in spiritual warfare. As a result, believers must be prepared to stand firm against the powerful forces of temptation, sin, and evil. The armour of God represents the spiritual resources that assist us to counteract temptation. With the armour of God, we remain faithful in our walk with God.

Paul emphasises the importance of prayer in the believer's life. Paul encourages believers to 'pray in the Spirit on all occasions.'[7] Prayer is essential for our personal growth, maturity, and self-development. Prayer assists us in the spiritual battle between good and evil. Prayer is the instrument for humanity to remain connected with God. Prayer is vital to the believer's life. Prayer empowers us to remain vigilant. Prayer strengthens our fellowship with God. It is through prayer that we obtain strength, wisdom, love, mercy, and peace. Through prayer, we consciously further the cause of good in the spiritual battle between good and evil. Prayer assists us to realise God's providence. Last but not least, prayer ensures our body, mind, heart, and spirit are aligned with God's will.

The Book of Ephesians offers a profound understanding of the believer's newfound identity in Jesus Christ. Ephesians provides us with practical guidance on how to apply the gospel in every facet of our life. Ephesians encourages us to embrace God's love, pursue unity in the church, live in holiness, and remain resilient in the good fight of faith. God's armour protects us along our journey. There is considerable practical wisdom within Pauline theology. A detailed examination of Ephesians provides believers with faith, truth, love, belief, hope, and encouragement in their walk with God. Above all, we are reminded that our salvation is an unmerited gift of God's grace. Salvation is obtained through our faith in Jesus Christ. Peace be with you.

[1] The Holy Bible (NIV). (2011). *The Book of Ephesians.* Chapter 1, Verse 13.

[2] The Holy Bible (NIV). (2011). *The Book of Ephesians.* Chapter 2, Verses 8-9.

[3] The Holy Bible (NIV). (2011). *The Book of Ephesians.* Chapter 2, Verse 14.

[4] The Holy Bible (NIV). (2011). *The Book of Ephesians.* Chapter 4, Verse 24.

[5] The Holy Bible (NIV). (2011). *The Book of Ephesians.* Chapter 5, Verse 8.

[6] The Holy Bible (NIV). (2011). *The Book of Ephesians.* Chapter 6, Verse 11.

[7] The Holy Bible (NIV). (2011). *The Book of Ephesians.* Chapter 6, Verse 18.

Chapter 50

The Book of Philippians

'For it is God who works in you to will and to act
in order to fulfil His good purpose.'

Philippians 2:13
The Holy Bible (NIV)

T he Book of Philippians is written by the Apostle Paul. Philippians is one of Paul's joyful letters, despite being written while he was imprisoned. In Philippians, Paul expresses his affection and gratitude to the Philippian Church. The Book of Philippians encourages believers to practice their faith with humility, joy, love, and perseverance. Philippians emphasises the sufficiency of Jesus Christ to transcend our challenges, crises, concerns, and circumstances. Philippians teaches humanity the importance of unity. We are acquainted with the everlasting joy found in the LORD. Philippians makes known to us the incomparable power of contentment. In addition, we learn about the Messiah—Jesus Christ.

Paul repeatedly encourages the Philippians to rejoice, regardless of their present circumstances. In the midst of our suffering, persecution, or trials, we are encouraged to seek joy in fellowship with Jesus Christ. Christian joy is not dependent upon our circumstances; however, it is founded on the everlasting and timeless reality of God. Regardless of our challenges, we experience joy in Jesus Christ. As we run our race, we trust God's love, mercy, peace, justice, blessing, and providence.

Philippians affirms the divinity and humanity of Jesus Christ. Paul encourages believers to embody the enlightened mindset of Jesus Christ. Jesus, the Son of God, 'humbled himself by becoming obedient to death.'[1] Jesus is the servant and saviour of humanity. Jesus accomplished his destiny to redeem humanity of their sin, through shedding his blood on the Cross. Through Jesus' crucifixion, we secure our salvation from sin and receive eternal life in heaven. Humility is not characterised by self-deprecation. Humility is considering the essential needs of humanity, above the egoistic pursuit of our endless and futile desires. Jesus' matchless example of humility, mercy, service, sacrifice, love, forgiveness, and compassion is the ideal model for how we ought to live and interact with members of the community. Humility and obedience to God's word leads us to exaltation. This is confirmed by God's exaltation of Jesus Christ following his crucifixion.

Paul expresses the noble aspiration of getting to know Jesus Christ intimately and imitating him. Paul utilises the well-known analogy of running a race; 'forgetting what is behind and straining towards what is ahead.'[2] Paul possesses a determined mind. His focus is on the heavenly prize that awaits him. The believer's life is a journey of spiritual growth and personal transformation. We are encouraged to remain fixated on Jesus Christ. We must continually strive to transform our thoughts, speech, and behaviour. We must establish our life on Jesus' teachings and principles. Paul encourages us to leave behind our past failures, transgressions, and mistakes. We are not to become burdened by anything that impedes our spiritual progress. The accolade of running a good race on earth is eternal life in heaven.

Paul strongly urges the Philippians to live their life in a manner that is consistent with the gospel of Jesus Christ. We must remain firm in our faith, without the fear of persecution, opposition, or criticism. Paul encourages believers to endure in their suffering for Jesus Christ. Our journey must reflect the gospel's message. We must conduct ourselves with integrity, faithfulness, sincerity, honesty, accountability, justice, mercy, and responsibility. We must demonstrate our willingness to endure privation for the sake of Jesus Christ.

Our life must be a living testimony to God's providence, prestige, peace, and power. Paul commands the Philippians to be united in their body, mind, heart, and spirit. Paul instructs the Philippians not to act out of selfish ambition, hubristic pride, or vain conceit. The Philippians must prioritise peace, love, justice, mercy, compassion, and harmony amongst the community. Paul stresses that unity is achieved through humility, hospitality, compassion, generosity, and love, not through self-righteousness, vanity, conceit, egoism, or pride. Unity amongst members is integral for the advancement of the church. Believers must prioritise the community's interest ahead of their self-interest. Humility, love, forgiveness, compassion, peace, justice, and mercy are the instruments to maintain unity within the body of Christ.

Paul narrates his experience of how he remained content, despite his changing fortunes and challenging circumstances. Whether in times of abundance or deprivation, we benefit from contentment. In Philippians, Paul affirms, 'I can do all this through Him who gives me strength.'[3] Paul's contentment comes from his reliance upon Jesus Christ's strength, support, and spirit. Paul demonstrates wisdom when he determines not to be defined by his external circumstances. Contentment is not secured through personal wealth, social status, knowledge, experience, income, authority, political power, or private property. We secure contentment through Jesus Christ. Jesus Christ redeemed humanity from sin by shedding his blood on the Cross. Jesus Christ's sacrificial death is the cause of our redemption from original sin. We confront every situation with trust, faith, and confidence in Jesus Christ. The Holy Spirit empowers us to endure our struggles through life and remain faithful to God's word.

Paul encourages believers not to be anxious about anything in life. Instead, believers must pray with thanksgiving to God for the fulfilment of their needs. Believers are encouraged to petition God with their requests. In doing so, believers experience God's profound and perpetual peace, which transcends understanding and shall 'guard your hearts and minds in Christ Jesus.'[4] Prayer is the antidote to anxiety. Instead of inviting fear and trepidation, we must share our concerns with God. We trust in God's sovereignty, providence, mercy, grace, favour, and goodness.

When we pray with thanksgiving, we experience God's peace. Prayer to God protects our body, mind, heart, and spirit, even in the most difficult of times.

Paul urges the Philippians to emulate his example, as he strives to live a Christ-centred life. Paul encourages the Philippians to effectuate the teachings and doctrines they have learned from him and other godly leaders. It is important to have honourable leaders in our life; believers who exemplify Jesus Christ in their thought, speech, and conduct. We must learn from disciples who follow Jesus Christ wholeheartedly. We must put into practice Jesus' timeless teachings. In our area of expertise, we too must become leaders in the community.

Paul expresses his heartfelt gratitude to the Philippians for their generous support of his ministry. Paul acknowledges the Philippians gifts please God. Paul reassures the Philippians, that 'God will meet all your needs according to the riches of His glory in Christ Jesus.'[5] Generosity is an important attribute of the Christian faith. To give joyfully and unconditionally reflects the heart of God. Philanthropy is one method to promote the profound message of the gospel throughout the world. When we give to others, we trust that God meets our needs. God is faithful to provide for humanity.

The Book of Philippians encourages us to live our life centred around Christ's teachings. The good life is characterised by joy, humility, unity, and contentment. Philippians encourages believers to share their faith with humanity. Believers secure strength through fellowship with Jesus Christ. Believers are encouraged to make their contribution to spread the gospel. Philippians reminds us, that no matter what challenges we confront, we can do all things through Jesus Christ. Like Paul, we too must seize the initiative and spread the teachings of Jesus Christ. We must share the gospel with humanity. In this respect, Paul has set a commendable example on how to become Christ-like and share the good news of our redemption with humanity.

[1] The Holy Bible (NIV). (2011). *The Book of Philippians.* Chapter 2, Verse 8.

[2] The Holy Bible (NIV). (2011). *The Book of Philippians.* Chapter 3, Verse 13.

[3] The Holy Bible (NIV). (2011). *The Book of Philippians.* Chapter 4, Verse 13.

[4] The Holy Bible (NIV). (2011). *The Book of Philippians.* Chapter 4, Verse 7.

[5] The Holy Bible (NIV). (2011). *The Book of Philippians.* Chapter 4, Verse 19.

Chapter 51

The Book of Colossians

'Whatever you do, work at it with all your heart,
as working for the LORD, not for human masters.'

Colossians 3:23
The Holy Bible (NIV)

T he Book of Colossians is authored by Paul the Apostle. Colossians emphasises the greatness of Jesus Christ. It is through Jesus Christ that humanity secures its redemption from sin and gains eternal life in heaven. The Book of Colossians invalidates the false teachings that threaten the Colossian Church. The Book of Colossians provides practical instructions to practice the Christian faith in accordance with the gospel. In Colossians, Pauline theology conveys the divine revelation that Jesus Christ is pre-eminent in all things. Believers are commanded to live in the everlasting light of Jesus Christ.

Paul commences Colossians with a declaration that Jesus Christ is the 'image of the invisible God.'[1] The Son of God reigns over God's creation. Jesus Christ is the head of the church. In Christ, the fullness of God dwells. Jesus Christ's sacrificial death reconciles humanity to God, through 'his blood, shed on the Cross.'[2] The presence of Jesus Christ is central to the believer's faith in God. Everything within creation reflects God's glory. Jesus Christ is not merely a prophet of the LORD. Jesus is the Son of God. Jesus' crucifixion is the foundation of humanity's redemption.

Paul reaffirms that believers are complete and secure in Jesus Christ. Christ's presence on earth represents the divinity and humanity of God. There is no requirement for additional knowledge, religious practices, doctrines, laws, customs, offerings, or rituals. We do not require anything beyond Jesus Christ for our salvation from original sin and eternal life in heaven. In the new covenant, we have secured our atonement through Jesus Christ. Christ's sacrificial death on the Cross constitutes sufficient recompense for humanity's sanctification and reconciliation with God. Believers are forgiven through Jesus Christ. No secular philosophy, economic ideology, socialist principle, political doctrine, scientific theory, theological inquiry, or legal discourse contributes to Jesus Christ's mission, ministry, or message.

Paul counsels the Colossians to remain vigilant about being taken 'captive through hollow and deceptive philosophy,'[3] ancient religious traditions, customs, and laws that are discordant with Jesus Christ's message. Paul cautions humanity against any attempt to seek spiritual fulfilment through traditions, customs, and rituals, such as religious festivals or idol worship. Paul informs us the one and true 'reality is found in Christ.'[4] The gospel of grace reflects the divinity and humanity of Jesus Christ. Jesus Christ is sufficient for our salvation. We must remain vigilant against false teachings. We must reject any endeavour which adds or detracts from the authenticity of the gospel, this includes traditions, rituals, customs, principles, doctrines, or ideologies. Our focus remains on Jesus Christ, not on secular ideas or worldly philosophy.

When we accept Jesus Christ, we reject our sinful way of life. Believers are born again and redeemed through Christ. Not only do we secure our unmerited salvation through Christ; however, we are assured of eternal life in heaven. Paul encourages believers to 'set your minds on things above, not on earthly things.'[5] In addition, Paul strongly urges humanity to cease their sinful behaviour, such as concupiscence, anger, idolatry, jealousy, envy, and greed. Believers are instructed to replace these undesirable behaviours with the noble virtues of compassion, mercy, forgiveness, peace, humility, gentleness, generosity, justice, and forbearance. Paul reiterates that love is the common denominator across humanity. Love perfects our relationships. Love creates harmony between members of the community.

The believer's life involves a radical transformation of being in the world. We are commanded to abstain from our former sinful behaviour. We are commanded to learn from Jesus Christ's example, this includes his character, integrity, principles, and teachings. This life-changing transformation is not merely about our moral refinement. We are encouraged to live in a manner that reflects our newfound identity in Jesus Christ. We must 'let the peace of Christ'[6] dwell in our heart. Our actions must reflect the eternal values of truth, duty, courage, integrity, love, mercy, compassion, faith, honour, forgiveness, peace, and justice. We must actively pursue holiness and love in our relationships.

One of the themes in Colossians is the divine revelation of the mystery that Christ is in believers. This revelation represents the hope of God's glory being revealed to humanity. Paul emphasises that the spiritual presence of Christ in the believer's life is a source of strength, peace, faith, love, and hope. The Christian faith is not an endeavour to live for Jesus Christ in our own strength, but rather about the acceptance of Jesus Christ to live in and through us. Christ's presence empowers us to live the Christian faith. Christ has provisioned humanity with [unmerited] redemption and eternal life in heaven. Our contentment with life is not secured through worldly accomplishments, political power, private wealth, pecuniary gain, social status, private property, or personal income. We attain contentment in the knowledge of the future glory that we share with Jesus Christ in heaven.

Paul instructs believers to be devoted to prayer and remain thankful to God. Paul requests fellow believers to pray for him. Paul hopes that God's providence provides countless opportunities for the gospel to be proclaimed throughout the world. Paul demonstrates that prayer is indispensable to the Christian faith. Prayer is the divine instrument by which we remain connected to God. Through prayer we express our gratitude towards God. Prayer empowers us to realise God's providence. Prayer is an effective method to intercede for members of the community. Prayer must be a consistent and integral part of our life. Prayer fosters our spiritual development.

Prayer is imperative to empower believers to share the gospel's message of salvation through faith in Jesus Christ.

In the final chapter of Colossians, Paul instructs believers to live wisely amongst unbelievers and to 'make the most of every opportunity'[7] to promote the gospel. Paul encourages believers to let their conversations be characterised by grace, so they bear witness to those who do not yet know Christ. As disciples of Jesus Christ, our faith is a living testimony to the world. Our words and deeds reflect Christ's love and truth in the world. Therefore, we are obliged to assist members of the community to accept Jesus Christ in faith. We must be authentic in how we interact with non-believers. We must seize every opportunity to share the gospel with humanity.

Paul provides practical wisdom on how to manage important relationships. For example, consider the husband-and-wife relationship, or the parent-and-child relationship. In each case, Paul emphasises the requirement for mutual respect, love, forgiveness, mercy, compassion, justice, and peace. In our relationships, the greatest endeavour is to reflect Jesus Christ's love and forgiveness. Good relationships are characterised by mutual respect, unconditional love, generosity, and forbearance. Whether we are at home, school, university, the workplace, or in the community at large, believers must live in a manner that honours God. We must promote harmony, peace, justice, love, mercy, joy, and faith in the world.

Paul concludes Colossians with greetings from his fellow companions, this include Aristarchus, Epaphras, Mark, Onesimus, and Tychicus. Paul encourages the Colossians to share his letter with the Laodiceans and to read the letter he had sent from Laodicea. We learn that the Christian faith is not meant to be practiced in isolation. Believers are encouraged to support one another in their journey as disciples of Jesus Christ. Fellowship with believers is instrumental to our spiritual growth, maturity, and sharing the gospel. Paul's greetings demonstrate the importance of working together as a community of believers, with each believer to contribute to the body of Christ.

The Book of Colossians teaches humanity that Jesus Christ is supreme, sovereign, and sufficient. Our life must reflect Christ's teachings. Colossians encourages believers to remain faithful to the message of the gospel and reject false doctrines. We must live a transformed life. A life that truly reflects the new covenant in Jesus Christ. Believers must live by personal example. Within the community, believers are responsible to educate their fellow members on Christ's goodness, grace, and glory. God's immeasurable gifts of love, peace, joy, mercy, grace, redemption, forgiveness, and eternal life in heaven must be shared with every member of humanity.

[1] The Holy Bible (NIV). (2011). *The Book of Colossians.* Chapter 1, Verse 15.

[2] The Holy Bible (NIV). (2011). *The Book of Colossians.* Chapter 1, Verse 20.

[3] The Holy Bible (NIV). (2011). *The Book of Colossians.* Chapter 2, Verse 8.

[4] The Holy Bible (NIV). (2011). *The Book of Colossians.* Chapter 2, Verse 17.

[5] The Holy Bible (NIV). (2011). *The Book of Colossians.* Chapter 3, Verse 2.

[6] The Holy Bible (NIV). (2011). *The Book of Colossians.* Chapter 3, Verse 15.

[7] The Holy Bible (NIV). (2011). *The Book of Colossians.* Chapter 4, Verse 5.

Chapter 52

The Book of First Thessalonians

'But since we belong to the day, let us be sober,
putting on faith and love as a breastplate,
and the hope of salvation as a helmet.'

1 Thessalonians 5:8
The Holy Bible (NIV)

T he Book of First Thessalonians is authored by Paul the Apostle. First Thessalonians reflects Paul's affection for the Thessalonian Church. Paul wrote to encourage and support believers in Thessalonica, particularly in light of their religious persecution. First Thessalonians provides us with guidance on how to live a righteous and honourable life. First Thessalonians contains messages of hope, grace, love, encouragement, and wisdom. First Thessalonians offers practical counsel to practice the Christian faith in a tumultuous world. Above all, First Thessalonians highlights the importance of love, hope, peace, and joy in our walk with God.

Paul urges the Thessalonians to live in a manner that pleases God. This means believers must live a holy, faithful, blessed, and sanctified life. Paul emphasises that abstinence from the sinful pleasures of the flesh, unconditional love for one another, and sincere diligence in one's assignment are the attributes of the good life that honours God. As Christians, our primary objective is to live in a manner that pleases God. The old adage, 'perfect is the enemy of good' is an important reminder that no person's journey is faultless. Therefore, while we are not perfect, we must strive for personal growth and spiritual development in our fellowship with God.

First Thessalonians is defined by the universal messages of love, hope, joy, and peace in the coming of Jesus Christ. Paul reassures the Thessalonians, that those who have been martyred are not left behind upon the coming of Jesus Christ. The scripture informs us 'the dead in Christ will rise first,'[1] and believers shall unite with them to be with the LORD in heaven. The coming of Christ is our source of hope, love, joy, and peace. Even in our inevitable confrontation with death, we possess the assurance that Jesus Christ returns to redeem believers. Through faith in Jesus Christ, we secure our salvation and eternal life in heaven. Hope in Jesus Christ encourages believers to live faithfully and navigate life's peaks and valleys with an eternal perspective in mind.

Paul emphasises the importance to encourage and support one another, especially in the midst of grief, pain, trauma, and suffering. During our journey, we have the hope of Jesus Christ's coming to sustain us through the peaks and valleys of life. Fellow believers are a source of mutual support and assistance. Believers ought to strengthen one another in their faith. Pauline theology is clear, we must 'encourage one another and build each other up.'[2] The Christian community is defined by encouragement and support of its members. Believers actively assist each other in times of privation. Believers offer members of the community unconditional love in times of adversity. Believers strengthen one another in their faith. Believers must encourage one another to promote hope, perseverance, and unity in the community.

Paul reminds Thessalonians the day of the LORD shall arrive unexpectedly. Therefore, it is incumbent upon believers to be prepared for that auspicious moment. Believers are encouraged to remain perceptive and attentive. Believers must persevere in their faith, love, promise of salvation, and belief in eternal life. We must remain attentive and prepared for the coming of Jesus Christ. Christians live with readiness for the coming of Christ. Christians are spiritually vigilant. Christians live in the light of God's truth. Christians hold on to faith, love, and hope. We must live each day in a manner that reflects the coming of Christ.

Paul encourages the Thessalonians to 'rejoice always, pray continually, and give thanks in all circumstances.'[3] These positive affirmations are part of God's will for believers. A heart replete with gratitude is foundational to the Christian faith. Regardless of our present circumstances, we must rejoice, pray, and give thanks to God. Gratitude assists us to cultivate a constructive perspective on life. Gratitude ensures our mind is focused on God's goodness, grace, mercy, sovereignty, and providence. Gratitude strengthens our faith. Gratitude enables us to witness Christ, so that a greater proportion of humanity affirms their belief in Christ.

Paul encourages the Thessalonians to 'live lives worthy of God.'[4] Paul reminds them, God has called the Thessalonians into His kingdom, presence, and glory. Therefore, Thessalonians must live in a manner that reflects God's will. In the Book of Luke, God's word is unequivocal, 'Your Father has been pleased to give you the kingdom.'[5] God blesses His chosen people. It is our responsibility to live our life consistent with God's word. Christians live with an awareness that they belong to God. Believers constitute an integral part of God's kingdom. Therefore, our conduct on earth must reflect the dignity of God's kingdom in heaven. We must live in a manner that honours God. We must advance God's kingdom on earth. Our conduct must be defined by love, faith, hope, forbearance, compassion, peace, integrity, honour, justice, mercy, and faithfulness.

Paul reminds believers to remain conscious of the spiritual battle between good and evil. We must not be spiritually ignorant. We must not live our life defined by sin, greed, concupiscence, and temptation. Instead, believers must put on 'faith and love as a breastplate, and the hope of salvation as a helmet.'[6] Believers must be spiritually vigilant as they await the coming of Jesus Christ. Christians must remain vigilant in the spiritual battle of good and evil that defines the world. We must live our life in the light of Christ's truth. Vigilance means to guard our heart and mind. We must live in a manner that reflects the hope we have in Christ. We must be prepared for the coming of Christ at any moment.

Paul counsels the Thessalonians to live in peace, love, joy, and harmony with one another. Thessalonians must demonstrate respect for their leaders and be compassionate with people who experience challenges in their life. Paul exhorts the Thessalonians to pursue what is good, both in their relationships and in their interactions with the wider community. The Christian community is characterised by peace, love, mercy, philanthropy, hope, justice, faith, joy, and respect. Believers must prioritise the well-being of community members, especially those who are frail, dependent, or vulnerable. The moral consideration of humanity includes being righteous, compassionate, and seeking to do 'what is good for each other and for everyone else.'[7] We must not forget that mercy has the power to transform humanity.

Paul instructs the Thessalonians to respect and honour their leaders, particularly those who preach the gospel. Paul encourages the Thessalonians to persevere in their pursuit of holiness and to avoid 'quenching the Spirit.'[8] Our spiritual growth incorporates respect for godly leaders. We must learn from their knowledge, experience, and wisdom. Our spiritual growth and development requires a conscious pursuit of holiness. We must avoid the temptation of sin, and allow the Holy Spirit to influence and transform our life. We must be receptive to the Holy Spirit's presence. We must permit the Holy Spirit to guide us towards a purposeful, meaningful, faithful, compassionate, and joyful life. Our walk with God is an evolving journey. No matter how far we have journeyed, we always have areas for improvement in our life. Progress in our walk with God is a never-ending endeavour.

Paul concludes his letter with a prayer for the Thessalonians. Paul prays that God 'sanctify you through and through.'[9] Just like the Thessalonians, we too must be 'kept blameless at the coming of our Lord Jesus Christ.'[10] Paul requests the Thessalonians to pray for him, while he sends them his greetings. Prayer is essential to the Christian faith. We must pray for our fellow believer's spiritual growth and transformation. Believers must trust that God strengthens them.

Christian relationships are founded upon hope, faith, forgiveness, compassion, love, peace, joy, and prayer. When believers exemplify these attributes, they strengthen the body of Christ. The Book of First Thessalonians teaches us how to live in anticipation of the coming of Christ. We are to live in a righteous manner that honours God. Believers must support one another in their journey. We must remain vigilant. First Thessalonians provides us with practical wisdom on how to live the good life. First Thessalonians grants us immeasurable peace in the promises of the gospel.

[1] The Holy Bible (NIV). (2011). *The Book of First Thessalonians.* Chapter 4, Verse 16.

[2] The Holy Bible (NIV). (2011). *The Book of First Thessalonians.* Chapter 5, Verse 11.

[3] The Holy Bible (NIV). (2011). *The Book of First Thessalonians.* Chapter 5, Verses 16-18.

[4] The Holy Bible (NIV). (2011). *The Book of First Thessalonians.* Chapter 2, Verse 12.

[5] The Holy Bible (NIV). (2011). *The Book of Luke.* Chapter 12, Verse 32.

[6] The Holy Bible (NIV). (2011). *The Book of First Thessalonians.* Chapter 5, Verse 8.

[7] The Holy Bible (NIV). (2011). *The Book of First Thessalonians.* Chapter 5, Verse 15.

[8] The Holy Bible (NIV). (2011). *The Book of First Thessalonians.* Chapter 5, Verse 19.

[9] The Holy Bible (NIV). (2011). *The Book of First Thessalonians.* Chapter 5, Verse 23.

[10] The Holy Bible (NIV). (2011). *The Book of First Thessalonians.* Chapter 5, Verse 23.

Chapter 53

The Book of Second Thessalonians

'Now may the LORD of peace Himself
give you peace at all times and in every way.
The LORD be with all of you.'

2 Thessalonians 3:16
The Holy Bible (NIV)

T he Book of Second Thessalonians is the second letter that Paul wrote to the Church in Thessalonica. Second Thessalonians examines several important issues that have arisen in the church since Paul wrote First Thessalonians. Some of these issues include uncertainty about the day of the LORD, idleness amongst believers, and the religious persecution of believers. Second Thessalonians contains messages of encouragement, hope, peace, mercy, grace, joy, and love. Second Thessalonians emphasises the importance to remain firm in our faith. We must live in hope of the coming of Christ. We must live our life defined by unconditional love and resolute faith in the midst of our tests, tribulations, troubles, and trials.

Paul commends the Thessalonians for their faith, love, joy, hope, and perseverance, despite the religious persecution they confront. Paul assures the Thessalonians that their suffering is a divine sign of God's impending judgement. The Thessalonians shall be rewarded upon the coming of Christ. Our suffering and persecution are not signs of God's abandonment, they are opportunities for believers to strengthen their faith, belief, and hope. In times of adversity, we must demonstrate fortitude. We must remain firm in the assurance that God is faithful. God administers justice and peace on earth. The trials we confront during our lifetime are temporary; however, the reward for our faithful endurance is eternal life in heaven.

Paul reminds the Thessalonians that when Christ returns, he administers justice to those who have persecuted believers. Jesus Christ grants peace to those who have suffered for his sake. The coming of Christ is characterised by love, peace, joy, mercy, grace, and glory. Unbelievers who do not adhere to the gospel endure eternal separation from God. Paul mentions in the scripture that 'God is just,'[1] therefore, we must trust in Him. The coming of Christ is a promise of justice, love, grace, mercy, joy, and hope on earth. For Jesus Christ's disciples, his coming is a time of redemption, revelation, and repentance. For unbelievers who reject Jesus, this is a time of divine judgement and eternal separation. We must live our life with the expectation of Christ's coming to earth. How we live in the present time has eternal significance.

Unfortunately, illegitimate doctrines have been disseminated amongst the Thessalonians. These doctrines falsely claim the day of the LORD has arrived. Paul reassures the Thessalonians this is not the case. Paul explains that before the coming of Christ, there shall be a great apostasy. That is to infer, humanity's rejection of the faith. Paul informs the Thessalonians about the revelation of the 'man of lawlessness'[2] (i.e., the Anti-Christ). The Anti-Christ endeavours to separate humanity from God. The coming of Christ is not premature. Believers have a duty to reject illegitimate doctrines and teachings about the end times. The inauspicious attributes that characterise the Anti-Christ include the proliferation of sin, immorality, and evil. Both the Anti-Christ and the coming of Christ are defined by God's sovereignty over creation. We must remain faithful to the eternal truth of God's word. We must not be deceived by knowledge that is contrary to God's word. God's providence determines the past, present, and future of creation.

Paul encourages the Thessalonians to remain faithful to the gospel's message. Believers must put into practice the teachings they have received from Paul, whether in person, or by letter. Furthermore, Paul prays for the Thessalonians, that God console 'your hearts and strengthen you in every good deed and word.'[3] In times of uncertainty or persecution, we must hold on to the eternal truth of the gospel. Our trust and confidence are firmly established in God's word, which is eternal and absolute. The truth of the gospel keeps us anchored in troublesome, tragic, and turbulent times.

Several members of the Thessalonian Church had become idle and were not engaged in productive work. Their undesirable attitude was due to the mistaken belief that the coming of Christ was imminent. Therefore, these members deliberately neglected their duties and responsibilities. Paul instructs the Thessalonians to engage in productive work with their own hands and to live amicably. The Thessalonians must not become a burden upon members of the community. The Thessalonians are instructed to 'keep away from every believer who is idle.'[4]

The Christian faith is one of responsibility and duty. Idleness does not honour God's grand design of creation. While we eagerly await the coming of Christ, we must diligently complete our assignment. In the process, we must provide for ourselves, sustain our family, and contribute to the good of the community at large. Employment is not merely a social and economic institution. Employment constitutes part of our witness to Christ and service to humanity. Every believer is responsible to live in a manner that promotes good order, peace, harmony, justice, equality, and witness to Christ.

Paul encourages the Thessalonians not to become weary in performing good deeds, even when it is difficult, or when they perceive members of society neglect their duties and responsibilities. The Thessalonians are commanded to perform good deeds and demonstrate forbearance. The Thessalonians must not permit the unproductive behaviour of a few members to discourage the greater community's efforts towards prosperity, love, harmony, peace, and justice. Through God's grace, Paul witnessed Christ upon his conversion on the Road to Damascus. Consequently, Paul became an ideal model for us through his exemplary speech and conduct; we must 'never tire of doing what is good.'[5]

Our persistence to perform honourable deeds is an integral part of the good life. At times, we become discouraged when fellow members do not make a meaningful contribution to society, or when we confront privation in our life. Nonetheless, we are called to continue our performance of honourable deeds in the community. We trust that God perceives our efforts. God rewards our work in His timing. Our actions must reflect Christ's love, even when our fellow members do not honour their commitments.

Paul concludes his letter with prayer. Paul prays the LORD of Peace give the Thessalonians 'peace at all times and in every way,'[6] and that the LORD be with them. In addition, Paul requests the Thessalonians to pray for him, so that he continues to spread the gospel. Prayer is a powerful mechanism to secure our invaluable peace in the midst of worldly troubles. Paul's counsel reminds us that peace is bestowed by the LORD. God's spiritual presence sustains us in every challenge and unfavourable circumstance that we confront. We must continually seek God's peace through prayer. We trust that God is with us in every trial, temptation, tragedy, tribulation, and test.

The Book of Second Thessalonians teaches humanity that Christians live with hope, joy, forbearance, love, peace, justice, and endurance. The Christian faith is established upon the truth of the gospel. Believers must remain vigilant against illegitimate prophets and their false teachings. Second Thessalonians emphasises the certainty of the coming of Christ. The coming of Christ occurs in God's timing. Second Thessalonians affirms the requirement for believers to maintain responsibility, discipline, duty, productivity, and diligence in their life. We must not become weary in the performance of honourable deeds. Second Thessalonians encourages believers to remain firm in their faith. We must pray to God for peace. We must live as faithful witnesses to Christ.

[1] The Holy Bible (NIV). (2011). *The Book of Second Thessalonians.* Chapter 1, Verse 6.

[2] The Holy Bible (NIV). (2011). *The Book of Second Thessalonians.* Chapter 2, Verse 3.

[3] The Holy Bible (NIV). (2011). *The Book of Second Thessalonians.* Chapter 2, Verse 17.

[4] The Holy Bible (NIV). (2011). *The Book of Second Thessalonians.* Chapter 3, Verse 6.

[5] The Holy Bible (NIV). (2011). *The Book of Second Thessalonians.* Chapter 3, Verse 13.

[6] The Holy Bible (NIV). (2011). *The Book of Second Thessalonians.* Chapter 3, Verse 16.

Chapter 54

The Book of First Timothy

'For we brought nothing into the world,
and we can take nothing out of it.'

1 Timothy 6:7
The Holy Bible (NIV)

The Book of First Timothy is a letter from the Apostle Paul to his protégé, Timothy. Timothy is the pastor of the Church in Ephesus. In the Book of First Timothy, Paul encourages Timothy to fulfil his God-given assignment to preach the gospel. Paul provides Timothy with specific instructions on how to lead the church, denounce false teachings, and demonstrate godly behaviour amongst the congregation. First Timothy examines a number of significant themes, such as godly leadership, theological doctrine, worship, prayer, discipleship, and holiness.

Paul urges Timothy to appoint trusted leaders in the church. This is to prevent the proliferation of false doctrine and protect the gospel's message from distortion. Paul reminds Timothy that the Mosaic law is good; however, the gospel's message is one of salvation, love, grace, faith, peace, hope, and mercy. Believers are encouraged to live the good life and exhibit a 'pure heart, good conscience, and sincere faith.'[1] The dissemination of truthful theological doctrine is foundational to the church's reputation and spiritual development of believers. As believers, we must remain vigilant of false teachings. We must guard the eternal truth of the gospel. False teachings and distortion of scripture guides believers astray from God's word. Leaders have a duty to spread the gospel's message with integrity, veracity, and authenticity. Leaders must ensure that the church promulgates accurate theological doctrine.

Paul reflects on his profound personal experience of conversion on the Road to Damascus. Paul expresses his gratitude for God's grace, blessing, mercy, and love in appointing him to spread the gospel. Despite Paul's chequered history as a persecutor of the church and its early believers, God has demonstrated mercy to him. Paul has been appointed to fulfil a great assignment that forever changes the course of human history. Paul emphasises that Christ came to the world to redeem humanity of original sin. Paul considers himself an example of God's boundless grace. God's redeeming grace is greater than our sins. In spite of our sinful conduct, God redeems and employs us to fulfil His providence. Leaders must be conscious of God's grace in their ministry. Leaders must remain humble in their service to the church and wider community. Leaders are instruments of God's providence, not their goodness, merit, or virtue.

Paul instructs Timothy to lead the church in prayer for the benefit of the congregation, this includes kings, queens, and leaders in positions of power. The wisdom in Paul's message is to promote harmony in society, so that believers live a peaceful and blessed life. In addition, Paul's theological writing directs our attention to the details of how we ought to pray and conduct ourselves in the church. For example, consider Paul emphasises the importance of men lifting their hands in prayer and women dressing modestly. Prayer is essential to the life of believers. Believers are to pray for all members of the community, this includes their leaders. Believers have a duty to spread the gospel throughout the world. Believers must actively support the church in its mission to spread the gospel. The church must reflect a cosmopolitan and egalitarian religious order. In addition, men and women shall fulfil their responsibilities with humility and devotion to God.

Paul details the requisite qualifications for church leaders, both for elders and deacons. Deacons must be beyond reproach, self-controlled, hospitable, proclaim the gospel, and possess a good reputation, both within the church and the wider community. Deacons must be respected, sincere, and faithfully discharge their religious duties. Leadership in the church requires an exceptional standard of holiness, integrity, righteousness, and godliness. Leaders must demonstrate an honourable example for the church's members through their noble character, righteous actions, and sound dissemination of doctrine. The church must appoint leaders on merit. Leaders within the church must demonstrate honourable qualities and desirable attributes.

Paul instructs the church to honour its leaders who faithfully guide the congregation. Having said that, Paul advises the church to investigate accusations against its leaders with prudence. The church must ensure the process of correcting its leaders is thorough and transparent. Paul counsels Timothy to be cautious in the ordination of new leaders. Timothy must maintain spiritual purity and moral integrity within his ministry. The church must honour and respect godly leadership, while it holds the leaders personally accountable for their words and deeds. Discipline and correction must be effectuated with wisdom, good judgement, and integrity. Leaders must be vigilant to maintain their credibility and the unity of the congregation.

Paul encourages Timothy to educate himself in godliness. Timothy must lead believers by example through his speech, conduct, love, faith, and compassion. Timothy is to devote himself to read scripture, learn, and teach. Paul candidly reminds Timothy, 'do not neglect your gift.'[2] Leaders must pursue godliness in their life. Leaders must establish the honourable precedent for believers to follow. A leader's integrity, accountability, and holiness are instrumental to ministry. We must commit ourselves to strengthen our faith. We must read, listen, and reflect on God's word. Comparable to distinguished leaders, we too must employ our spiritual gifts to serve humanity. In our walk with God, leaders and members must not cease to grow in their godliness.

Paul cautions believers against the dangers of an irrational desire for wealth, which leads people into temptation, moral decadence, and evil deeds. Paul informs us that 'godliness with contentment is great gain.'[3] Believers are encouraged to be abundant in good deeds and generosity, rather than to seek inordinate wealth for its own sake. Contentment is the means to live the good life. Paul characterises money as the 'root of all kinds of evil.'[4] The endless pursuit of wealth leads people to greed, self-aggrandisement, moral compromise, and sin. Believers are to prioritise contentment and be grateful for God's blessing in their life. We must employ our resources to serve humanity. We must prioritise philanthropy, generosity, service, equality, peace, justice, and charity over the extreme pursuit of pecuniary gain.

Paul encourages Timothy to distance himself from temptation and to pursue righteousness, godliness, love, honour, peace, and justice. Timothy is commanded to 'fight the good fight of faith.'[5] Timothy is to remain true to God's commandments. The Christian faith is a protracted spiritual battle between good and evil. We must actively pursue righteousness and godliness, while we resist temptation and sin. Believers must fight the good fight of faith and embrace the eternal truth of the gospel. We must live in a manner that reflects our hope in the coming of Christ. Faithfulness and perseverance in God's word are essential to our journey.

Paul provides specific instructions to the aristocratic members of the church. Paul urges them not to be arrogant, or position their trust and confidence in their personal wealth, but to 'be generous and willing to share.'[6] Paul exhorts Timothy to guard the faith and avoid worldly distractions along his journey. Private wealth is a gift from God. The accumulation of private wealth is not the primary objective of our life. Christians must utilise their affluence to assist humanity. For believers, it is of far greater importance to accumulate their treasure in heaven, through philanthropic acts of generosity, charity, compassion, service, and hospitality. We too must guard our faith from worldly distractions. It is our duty to remain faithful to the gospel's truth.

First Timothy provides guidance on leadership, godliness, and keeping the faith along the believer's journey. First Timothy encourages believers to be diligent in their journey. We must guard theological doctrine, exhibit godly behaviour, and lead with integrity, while we navigate complex challenges in the church and community. Our conduct in private life is equally as important as how we conduct ourselves in public life. First Timothy provides believers with the opportunity to engage in an open and honest introspection of their life. We ought to ask ourselves fundamental questions and carefully consider our answers. For example, how do we mature in our walk with God? What do we learn from Paul's message to Timothy? Where do we need to make transformative changes in our life? Why do we utilise our time, resources, wealth, and knowledge in the manner that we do? How do we maximise our influence for the betterment of humanity?

[1] The Holy Bible (NIV). (2011). *The Book of First Timothy.* Chapter 1, Verse 5.

[2] The Holy Bible (NIV). (2011). *The Book of First Timothy.* Chapter 4, Verse 14.

[3] The Holy Bible (NIV). (2011). *The Book of First Timothy.* Chapter 6, Verse 6.

[4] The Holy Bible (NIV). (2011). *The Book of First Timothy.* Chapter 6, Verse 10.

[5] The Holy Bible (NIV). (2011). *The Book of First Timothy.* Chapter 6, Verse 12.

[6] The Holy Bible (NIV). (2011). *The Book of First Timothy.* Chapter 6, Verse 18.

Chapter 55

The Book of Second Timothy

'For the Spirit God gave us does not make us timid,
but gives us power, love, and self-discipline.'

2 Timothy 1:7
The Holy Bible (NIV)

T he Book of Second Timothy is authored by Paul. Second Timothy was written by Paul while he was imprisoned in Rome. At this point in world history, Paul is confronted with his imminent execution by the Roman authorities. Paul's letter is deeply personal, spiritual, and emotional. In writing Second Timothy, Paul draws upon his lived experience combined with divine revelation. Paul's authorship of the Book of Second Timothy is guided by the power of the Holy Spirit. Paul employs reflective writing throughout this letter. Second Timothy is filled with exhortation, final prayers, and solemn warnings to humanity.

The Book of Second Timothy is addressed to Paul's beloved disciple, Timothy. Paul considers Timothy an invaluable companion in his mission to spread the gospel throughout the world. Paul's central message to Timothy is to remain faithful to the gospel. Timothy is encouraged to endure privation and guard the truth of God's word. Paul draws on the depth and breadth of his lived experience to impart considerable wisdom to Timothy. In the Book of Second Timothy, Paul discusses important issues that Timothy will undoubtedly confront along his journey, such as religious persecution, dissemination of false doctrines, illegitimate prophets, division within the church, and challenges associated with ministry.

Paul encourages Timothy to remain firm in his faith. Timothy must not hesitate to share the word of God with humanity, even though it may lead to religious persecution. Paul has been imprisoned for preaching the gospel, he is cognisant of the challenges associated with ministry and being a disciple of Christ. Nonetheless, Paul emphasises that God's grace sustains him. Timothy is urged to 'guard the good deposit'[1] of the gospel. The gospel's message of humanity's redemption from sin has been entrusted to Timothy. No matter the sacrifice, we must remain faithful to the gospel. We must not reject the gospel's truth, even in the midst of religious persecution. The gospel is the eternal truth as decreed by God. We must guard and share the gospel with humanity.

Paul reminds Timothy that to suffer for preaching the gospel to humanity cannot be avoided. To suffer for the sake of Christ is an undeniable reality that Timothy must accept. Not to mention, Paul is imprisoned and awaits his imminent execution for preaching the gospel. Paul is unapologetic of his predicament, because he wholeheartedly believes in Jesus Christ. Paul is confident in God's grace to redeem him. Paul encourages Timothy to accept God's will and preach the gospel throughout the Roman world. Being faithful to Jesus Christ involves grief, loss, sacrifice, persecution, and privation. In spite of worldly opposition, we must not hesitate to fulfil our destiny. God's grace enables us to endure the challenges along our journey. Our hope is in God's faithfulness, mercy, grace, and providence. The promise of eternal life in heaven sustains us through our many trials in the world.

Paul urges Timothy to 'fan into flame'[2] the spiritual gift that God has bestowed upon him when he was commissioned into ministry. Timothy's invaluable spiritual gift, accompanied by God's mercy, love, grace, favour, and blessing, must be utilised in service to the LORD. God has bestowed every person with spiritual gifts. As believers, we must employ our gifts and abilities to further God's providence. We must not neglect or permit our spiritual gifts to become ineffectual. We must actively cultivate and employ our talents, abilities, and gifts to strengthen the body of Christ and preach the gospel.

Paul instructs Timothy to remind believers to avoid inconsequential debates that are a distraction to preach the gospel. Timothy is commanded to preach the truth of the gospel, with gentleness, and where necessary, correct his fellow believers with compassion. Paul cautions Timothy against illegitimate prophets who distort the gospel's message. Paul reminds Timothy to remain strong in the grace of Jesus Christ. Timothy is advised to avoid debates that do not promote God's word.

In a world filled with distractions and false teachings, we must remain firm in the truth of God's word. We must avoid unproductive controversies that do not align with the gospel's message of salvation through Jesus Christ. We must sensibly deconstruct false doctrines with a heart of wisdom, compassion, mercy, and love. Our life must reflect sound theological doctrine and godly living. It is incumbent upon us to share God's word with the people that we meet along our journey.

Paul compares the Christian faith to that of a 'good soldier.'[3] We must run our race and fulfil our destiny with commitment, integrity, accountability, and excellence. The Christian faith is not a convenient endeavour. We must endure privation along our journey. We must remain disciplined in our thought, speech, and conduct. We must remain committed to our vocation. To convey divine revelation in practical terms, Paul employs the example that a 'hard-working farmer should be the first to receive a share of the crops.'[4] Likewise, Timothy must endure suffering, remain faithful, and maintain discipline in his ministry. Ministry and the Christian faith require discipline, commitment, integrity, courage, endurance, and accountability. Similar to a soldier, we must keep our focus on Jesus Christ and God's kingdom. We must not become distracted by worldly concerns. Faithfulness in ministry requires personal sacrifice. Having said that, our reward is eternal life in heaven.

Paul instructs Timothy to faithfully preach God's word. Timothy is to spread the gospel with compassion, mercy, forbearance, love, and wisdom. Paul counsels Timothy that in the last days, many people will turn away from the truth of the gospel and entertain sinful desires. Humanity shall demonstrate an inclination to accept false doctrines that satisfy their desires. But Timothy must remain faithful, maintain a good conscience, endure suffering, and 'discharge all the duties of ministry.'[5] We must be prepared to share the truth of God's word, both in favourable and unfavourable circumstances. In a secular world, where people often reject sound theological doctrine, the command to preach the gospel remains unchanged. We must be faithful when we teach, correct, and encourage people. We must share the gospel with compassion, mercy, peace, joy, and love.

In the final chapter of Second Timothy, Paul reflects on his life and speaks of being 'poured out like a drink offering.'[6] Paul indicates that his time on earth is nearing its end. Paul writes with confidence, conviction, and clarity that he has 'fought the good fight, finished the race, and kept the faith.'[7] Paul looks forward to receive the 'crown of righteousness'[8] in God's kingdom. Paul encourages Timothy to remain faithful in his ministry until the very end. The Christian faith is compared to a race that requires perseverance, commitment, love, peace, and faithfulness. Paul's commendable example encourages us to complete our race with accountability, dedication, honesty, and integrity. Throughout our race, we must remain focused on God's word. We must fight the good fight of faith. We must remain faithful to the spirit and letter of the gospel. We know that our reward of eternal life is secure in Jesus Christ.

Paul confides his predicament to Timothy. Paul remains with his trusted companion, Luke. Regrettably, Paul has been abandoned by many of his fellow companions. Nonetheless, Paul remains unwavering in his belief in Jesus Christ. Paul knows that the LORD is with him. Paul mentions a number of friends who were a source of immense support and encouragement in his journey. Paul also expresses his disappointment at those who abandoned him. In times of trouble, loss, grief, trauma, or loneliness, we secure strength from the LORD. Believers know that God will never abandon them. We must embrace fellowship with believers in the community. Having said that, our reliance must be upon God's spiritual presence, mercy, love, peace, and grace. God gives us strength when we are weak. God redeems us from temptation. God grants us favour to fulfil our destiny.

Paul instructs Timothy to continue to preach the word of God. Timothy is to preach the good message of salvation through faith in Jesus Christ to the world. All of scripture is inspired by God. Scripture is invaluable to educate, guide, and enlighten humanity on the path to righteousness. Believers deduce practical life lessons from Paul's enlightening message to Timothy. Believers must preach the gospel as faithful servants of God who are 'thoroughly equipped for every good work.'[2]

The word of God is essential for humanity's spiritual growth and transformation. God's word is the foundation for our journey. God's word empowers believers to transcend life's numerous challenges. We must immerse ourselves in the truth of scripture. We must allow the word of God to define our body, mind, heart, and spirit. Second Timothy is a powerful and personal letter by Paul. Second Timothy challenges us to remain faithful to Christ, endure suffering, and faithfully preach the gospel. Paul's heartfelt letter emphasises the importance of perseverance in our walk with God. Paul enlightens us to the remarkable power of scripture. In the final analysis, Paul's journey teaches us to diligently fulfil the destiny that God has entrusted to us.

[1] The Holy Bible (NIV). (2011). *The Book of Second Timothy.* Chapter 1, Verse 14.

[2] The Holy Bible (NIV). (2011). *The Book of Second Timothy.* Chapter 1, Verse 6.

[3] The Holy Bible (NIV). (2011). *The Book of Second Timothy.* Chapter 2, Verse 3.

[4] The Holy Bible (NIV). (2011). *The Book of Second Timothy.* Chapter 2, Verse 6.

[5] The Holy Bible (NIV). (2011). *The Book of Second Timothy.* Chapter 4, Verse 5.

[6] The Holy Bible (NIV). (2011). *The Book of Second Timothy.* Chapter 4, Verse 6.

[7] The Holy Bible (NIV). (2011). *The Book of Second Timothy.* Chapter 4, Verse 7.

[8] The Holy Bible (NIV). (2011). *The Book of Second Timothy.* Chapter 4, Verse 8.

[9] The Holy Bible (NIV). (2011). *The Book of Second Timothy.* Chapter 3, Verse 17.

Chapter 56

The Book of Titus

'For the grace of God has appeared
that offers salvation to all people.'

Titus 2:11
The Holy Bible (NIV)

T he Book of Titus is a letter from the Apostle Paul addressed to his trusted companion, Titus. Paul has entrusted Titus as a steward to govern the church on the island of Crete. Titus is responsible to administer the church's affairs, appoint elders, and ensure the church remains faithful to the gospel in the midst of a complicated cultural, social, religious, and political environment. In the Book of Titus, Paul provides practical instructions on leadership, godly living, and the importance to disseminate sound theological doctrine.

Paul instructs Titus to faithfully preach the message of Jesus Christ to the world. Titus is commanded not to deviate from the word of God contained within the gospel—our salvation is obtained through faith in Jesus Christ. Titus is entrusted to ensure leaders within the church remain committed to preach God's word, especially leaders who preach to a substantial audience. The elders must be 'self-controlled, upright, holy, and disciplined.'[1] Sound theological doctrine is essential for the growth and development of the body of Christ. Church leaders must be committed to teach the truth of God's word. Believers must live in accordance with the truth of God's word. Knowledge obtained through proper understanding of theological doctrine and experience informed by righteousness are inseparable elements to live the good life.

Paul provides specific instructions for various members of the church, these include elders, leaders, as well as disciples of Christ. In each case, Paul encourages believers to live in a manner that reflects the transformative power of the gospel. For example, consider men must be 'sound in faith'[2] and conduct themselves in a dignified and self-controlled manner. In addition, women assume important social, moral, and ethical responsibilities within society. Within the community and family, women 'love their husbands and children.'[3] Furthermore, women make meaningful contributions to ministry and strengthen the church. Women teach and mentor believers, they provide pastoral care, spiritual leadership, and theological education.

The gospel is God's revelation to humanity. Its message must be effectuated in our relationships. The gospel transforms all aspects of our life, this includes spiritual, emotional, cultural, ethical, moral, educational, psychological, and behavioural dimensions. In response to the transformative message of the gospel, believers must recondition their behaviour, relationships, and attitudes to become more like Jesus Christ.

Paul reminds Titus, the grace of God was revealed to humanity through Jesus Christ. God's grace 'offers salvation to all people.'[4] God's grace teaches us to renounce our futile desires and worldly passions. We must live a self-controlled, dignified, and spiritually enriched life. The coming of Christ motivates believers to live a holy and honourable life. God's grace not only redeems us from the consequences of sin; however, it also empowers us to live a godly life. The coming of Christ inspires us to live in a manner that honours God and reflects His holiness. God's redeeming grace is not a licence to sin. God's grace is a powerful instrument that empowers us to live with integrity, accountability, faith, peace, compassion, joy, and love.

Paul cautions Titus about the power and influence of 'rebellious people'[5] within the community. Paul is concerned about unbelievers that distort the gospel's message for pecuniary gain or disseminate false doctrines to believers. Paul instructs Titus to reprimand them, so they do not mislead believers. Paul provides counsel to members of the church to avoid unproductive conversations that cause division amongst the congregation. The church must be vigilant against false doctrines that direct believers away from the truth of the gospel. Church leaders must judiciously address the issue of heresy. Believers must avoid divisive debates that detract from the authentic message of Jesus Christ. Believers must focus their time and energy on endeavours that pertain to the advancement of faith, love, peace, harmony, and unity. Sound theological doctrine and unity of believers are indispensable to the church's growth and influence.

Throughout the Book of Titus, Paul reaffirms that good works constitute an integral part of the Christian faith. Paul encourages believers to live in a manner that reflects the truth of the gospel, 'in everything set them an example by doing what is good.'[6] The performance of good works is not the means by which we secure our salvation. Nonetheless, good works constitute a living testimony to the transformative power of the gospel. Faith in Jesus Christ produces good works through the incredible power of the Holy Spirit. Good works do not redeem us from sin. Nonetheless, good works demonstrate the formidable power of the Holy Spirit. Good works are confirmation to the world of God's transformative grace. Believers must demonstrate Christ's message of love, joy, peace, mercy, and grace in every facet of their life.

Paul instructs Titus to remind the Cretan Christians to obey worldly rulers and secular authorities. Christians must perform honourable work and live a productive life. Paul encourages the Cretan Christians to abstain from acts of evil, avoid quarrels, and demonstrate courtesy towards every person. Christians must be good citizens, live peacefully, and respect each other. We must avoid the pitfalls of conflict. We must speak in a courteous manner to one another. It is incumbent upon us to demonstrate the godly character of Jesus Christ in our interactions with members of the community. We must promote unity and peace within the church and nation.

Paul reminds believers that they were once foolish, disobedient, and enslaved by sin. Nonetheless, God redeems believers through the transformative power of the Holy Spirit,

'He saved us, not because of righteous things we had done, but because of His mercy.'[7] God's redeeming grace, received by His mercy, justifies believers and gives them hope of eternal life in heaven. Our salvation is secured through God's redeeming grace, not through good works, merit, reputation, character, or virtue. Humanity was condemned by original sin; however, God in His boundless mercy, redeemed humanity through His beloved son, Jesus Christ. God's redeeming grace leads humanity to gratitude, humility, peace, love, and joy. Our undeserved gift of salvation must be complemented by good works and godly living.

Paul informs Titus to 'warn a divisive person once, and then warn them a second time. After that, have nothing to do with them.'[8] A divisive person is self-condemned and they will not change, unless they repent. The church must address division and disunity amongst its members. While we are commanded to be compassionate and gracious, there comes a point in time, when a person's divisiveness must be confronted. If they refuse to repent, then they must be removed from the congregation, for the greater sake of harmony and unity amongst the body of Christ.

Paul proffers Titus practical advice on how to manage relationships in ministry; this includes how to support fellow believers to preach the gospel, such as Apollos and Zenas. Paul encourages believers to assist one another and continue to perform good works. The Christian faith is lived in community, not in isolation. We must proactively encourage one another, support one another in ministry, and work together for the advancement of the gospel. Fellowship, discipleship, and worship are essential to members of the church.

The Book of Titus provides practical instructions on how to live the Christian faith, govern the church, practice good leadership, and preach the truth of the gospel. Titus emphasises the importance of sound doctrine, good works, and godly living. Titus encourages believers to remain focused on the transformative power of God's grace. God's grace redeems and inspires people to live the good life. The Biblical teachings in Titus are indispensable to maintain a strong, unified, and faithful congregation.

[1] The Holy Bible (NIV). (2011). *The Book of Titus.* Chapter 1, Verse 8.

[2] The Holy Bible (NIV). (2011). *The Book of Titus.* Chapter 2, Verse 2.

[3] The Holy Bible (NIV). (2011). *The Book of Titus.* Chapter 2, Verse 4.

[4] The Holy Bible (NIV). (2011). *The Book of Titus.* Chapter 2, Verse 11.

[5] The Holy Bible (NIV). (2011). *The Book of Titus.* Chapter 1, Verse 10.

[6] The Holy Bible (NIV). (2011). *The Book of Titus.* Chapter 2, Verse 7.

[7] The Holy Bible (NIV). (2011). *The Book of Titus.* Chapter 3, Verse 5.

[8] The Holy Bible (NIV). (2011). *The Book of Titus.* Chapter 3, Verse 10.

Chapter 57

The Book of Philemon

'The grace of the LORD Jesus Christ
be with your spirit.'

Philemon 1:25
The Holy Bible (NIV)

The Book of Philemon is a personal letter from the Apostle Paul to Philemon. Philemon is a slave owner. Paul writes to Philemon in relation to his fugitive slave, Onesimus. Onesimus has become a believer of Jesus Christ within Paul's ministry. This letter addresses several important theological themes, such as forgiveness, reconciliation, social justice, Christian love, brotherhood, sisterhood, peace, and mercy. The Book of Philemon demonstrates the power of the gospel to transform our relationships, particularly those characterised by social, political, legal, and economic inequality.

Paul strongly urges Philemon to forgive Onesimus, who may have wronged him. Philemon is instructed to embrace Onesimus, not as a slave, but as an equal brother affirmed in the righteousness of Jesus Christ. Paul assumes personal responsibility for any outstanding debt or wrongful act committed by Onesimus against Philemon. Paul offers to repay Onesimus' debts, when he declares 'charge it to me.'[1] The gospel encourages believers to espouse forgiveness and reconciliation, even in situations where the offence appears unforgivable, or the wrongful act is irreparable. Just as God forgave humanity for our sins, through the crucifixion of his beloved son, Jesus Christ, we are to forgive one another and restore our damaged relationships.

Paul candidly points out that Onesimus was once of no utility to Philemon or himself, but through Onesimus' encounter with the gospel, 'he has become useful both to you and to me.'[2] Paul emphasises the transformative change in Onesimus' life—from slave to believer. Onesimus is now our beloved brother in Jesus Christ. The gospel possesses the unmatched power to transform a person's life, regardless of their experiences, errors, or mistakes. In the body of Jesus Christ, worldly distinctions, such as social status, race, sex, colour, gender, income, personal wealth, private property, vocation, and age are inconsequential. The gospel's message transforms people, not only spiritually, but also relationally. The gospel's truth creates opportunities for reconciliation, love, peace, forgiveness, faith, joy, and unity amongst believers.

Paul makes a direct appeal to Philemon's conscience. Philemon is encouraged to accept Onesimus, not as a slave, but as an equal brother and beloved believer in the LORD. The Book of Philemon underscores the formal equality that exists in the body of Jesus Christ. All believers, regardless of their social status, are equal in Christ. Through Jesus Christ, all believers are equal before the formidable spiritual presence of God. The countless desirable worldly attributes, such as social status, personal wealth, knowledge, authority, private property, income, and political power are non-existent in God's kingdom. Above all, our relationships must reflect the equality, inherent value, respect, and dignity of every person.

Paul appeals to Philemon to act out of love, rather than obligation or duty. Paul expresses his confidence that Philemon will do even more than what is requested of him. Paul appeals to Philemon's conscience to recognise that unconditional love goes beyond one's duty, obligation, or responsibility. There is a universality associated with love, that transcends all boundaries, distinctions, attributes, beliefs, opinions, and perceptions. Paul's appeal is grounded in faith in Jesus Christ. Christian love is voluntary, it is not compelled by the force of law, compulsion of obligation, moral necessity, or performance of duty. When we act out of compassion for our fellow brothers and sisters, it reflects the message of the gospel. The unmatched power of love transforms our life. The presence of love renews our body, mind, heart, and spirit.

Paul did not exercise his authority as an apostle of Jesus Christ to demand Philemon to forgive and accept Onesimus. Not to mention, Philemon was personally indebted to Paul. To consider a counterfactual perspective, Paul could have instructed Philemon to forgive Onesimus, as a formal release of Philemon's indebtedness to him. In any event, Paul did not demand Philemon to forgive Onesimus. Rather, Paul appealed to Philemon's conscience on the basis of love, mercy, faith, belief, peace, and hope in Christ.

Paul personifies the power of servant leadership. Paul did not exercise his authority in an autocratic manner. Instead, Paul appealed to Philemon's conscience, to respond with grace, justice, and humility. Christian leadership is characterised by benevolence, compassion, and love, rather than the employment of force, compulsion, duty, or authority to influence people to adopt a particular course of action. Godly leaders model Christlike humility. Godly leaders encourage believers to act out of love, not personal, moral, or legal obligation.

In Paul's letter, he acknowledges his fellow believers who are with him, this includes Aristarchus, Demas, Luke, and Mark. Paul emphasises the collective responsibility to preach the gospel and important duties of ministry. Paul's petition to Philemon in relation to Onesimus is not only personal, it reflects the broader context of Christian discipleship and fellowship. The Christian faith is lived in community. We are equal believers in Jesus Christ. The gospel's message informs the relationship amongst believers. Our relationships must reflect the cosmopolitan and egalitarian character of Jesus Christ. Believers must support and encourage each other in their personal, professional, and ministry endeavours.

Paul's letter to Philemon is established in God's redeeming grace. Paul does not instruct Philemon; however, Paul appeals to Philemon on 'the basis of love,'[3] peace, equality, brotherhood, sisterhood, and mercy. In return, Paul trusts that Philemon's response is inspired by the transformative power of God's grace, not by formal demands, legal requirements, or apostolic authority. The Christian faith is defined by love, mercy, hope, and grace, not by demands, traditions, customs, or rules. Our actions toward fellow members—whether in forgiveness, compassion, mercy, or reconciliation—ought to reflect God's redeeming grace.

Paul emphasises his heartfelt desire for restoration of the relationship between Philemon and Onesimus. Paul requests Philemon to embrace Onesimus as his brother. If Onesimus is indebted to Philemon, Paul personally assumes responsibility for such outstanding debts. The gospel offers us complete restoration in our relationships, no matter the significance of our former offence, sinful conduct, or past injustice. The gospel promotes reconciliation, restoration, and restitution. Through the power of forgiveness, we restore our damaged relationships.

Paul expresses his confidence that Philemon will do what is right in this situation. Paul is certain that Philemon will go above and beyond what is requested of him. Paul's appeal encourages Philemon to act out of the goodness of his heart. Philemon is requested to affirm the boundless power of love and mercy in the body of Jesus Christ. We must encourage other members in the body of Jesus Christ to initiate righteous actions, based on love, grace, peace, hope, faith, mercy, joy, and compassion. Positive reinforcement fosters unity and growth amongst the community of believers.

The Book of Philemon underscores the importance of the gospel in our relationships, in particular, when it comes to forgiveness, reconciliation, mercy, peace, joy, and love. The Book of Philemon demonstrates how the gospel transforms our perception of fellow believers. The Book of Philemon demands us to consciously deconstruct prevailing economic, legal, political, cultural, gender, and social inequalities within society. Philemon inspires us to embody Jesus Christ's unconditional love in a practical and meaningful manner. The Book of Philemon encourages believers to embrace the transformative power of God's grace in our relationships.

[1] The Holy Bible (NIV). (2011). *The Book of Philemon.* Chapter 1, Verse 18.

[2] The Holy Bible (NIV). (2011). *The Book of Philemon.* Chapter 1, Verse 11.

[3] The Holy Bible (NIV). (2011). *The Book of Philemon.* Chapter 1, Verse 9.

Chapter 58

The Book of Hebrews

'Now faith is confidence in what we hope for
and assurance about what we do not see.'

Hebrews 11:1
The Holy Bible (NIV)

The Book of Hebrews is a profound theological book within the New Testament. Hebrews contains immeasurable wisdom in relation to the new covenant with Jesus Christ. Hebrews enlightens believers to live in fellowship with Jesus Christ. The author of Hebrews is unknown. Hebrews is addressed to Jewish Christians whom confront religious persecution and the temptation to return to Judaism, or to renounce their faith altogether. Hebrews encourages Jewish Christians to persevere in their newfound faith in Jesus Christ. Jewish Christians are called to recognise the divine authority of Jesus Christ over the Old Testament rituals. The Jewish people are encouraged to practice their newfound faith with conviction, certainty, clarity, and confidence.

Hebrews commences with an emphasis that Jesus Christ is the realisation of God's covenant with His chosen people. Jesus Christ is the Messiah. Jesus fulfils the Old Testament covenant and prophecies. Jesus Christ surpasses all the prophets and angels that have preceded him. The author of Hebrews characterises Jesus Christ as the 'radiance of God's glory.'[1] The author compares Jesus Christ to angels and prophets, to demonstrate that Christ is superior to them in every way. Jesus' priesthood is of a greater order. Jesus Christ is the Lamb of God for the atonement of humanity's original sin.

God's providence destined his beloved son, Jesus Christ as the Lamb of God. Humanity must acknowledge and accept that Jesus Christ is not merely a prophet in world history. Believers possess trust and confidence in Jesus Christ. When the Messiah was crucified, he proclaimed 'It is finished.'[2] Jesus' sacrificial death constitutes the completion of his destiny—the atonement of humanity from original sin.

Hebrews explains that the new covenant, established by Jesus

Christ, is superior to the old covenant that was mediated by Moses. The crucifixion of Jesus offers 'eternal redemption'[3] for believers. In comparison, the old covenant requires constant sacrifices and offerings for the atonement of original sin. The new covenant brings salvation and eternal life to all those who believe in Jesus Christ. The Gospel of John enlightens humanity that Jesus is 'the bread of life.'[4]

The old covenant, with its recurrent sacrifices and rituals, points to the reality of Christ's crucifixion as the atonement for humanity's original sin. The new covenant in Christ is based on the realisation of God's providence. Christ offers humanity forgiveness and a transformed life. Believers are no longer required to rely upon the perfect observance of the Mosaic law, offerings, or sacrifices. Jesus Christ's crucifixion on the Cross is sufficient recompense to atone humanity for the guilt of original sin. Humanity has secured their redemption through Jesus Christ.

Hebrews encourages believers to endure privation and persecution with confidence in the new covenant with God. Believers are reminded of the 'great cloud of witnesses'[5] who persevered in their faith despite their suffering. Believers set their heart and mind on Jesus Christ, the 'pioneer and perfecter of faith.'[6] The Christian faith is one of perseverance. Believers are to run their race with endurance. Believers follow Jesus Christ as the ideal example of loyalty, faith, trust, love, mercy, compassion, and peace. Trials, tests, and tribulations are part of the believer's journey. Nonetheless, believers confront them with hope, belief, trust, and confidence in God's new covenant.

Hebrews contains the distinguished record of the Old Testament figures who lived by faith. These significant Biblical figures include Abel, Abraham, David, and Moses. These heroes of faith trusted in God; despite not witnessing the realisation of God's covenant in their lifetime. Faith is the divine instrument by which we honour God. Faith is to trust in God, even when His covenant is not wholly realised in our lifetime. Faith is to believe in God's goodness and providence. Faith is the foundation of the believer's life. Faith incorporates love, action, commitment, accountability, and discipline. Faith is anchored in our trust and confidence in God's word. The fruit of our faith is realised in God's timing. Amongst the towering Biblical figures who practiced the faith, the reality of faith is succinctly summarised in Abraham's lived experience, 'Against all hope, Abraham in hope believed and so became the father of many nations.'[7]

Jesus Christ is characterised as the 'great high priest'[8] who empathises with our errors, mistakes, and faults. Jesus intercedes for us. Unlike the Levitical priests, who repeatedly offered animal sacrifices for the sins of the people, Jesus Christ offered himself as the Lamb of God to atone humanity from original sin. Jesus is the High Priest who mediates between humanity and God. Through Jesus' crucifixion, humanity has secured their redemption and eternal life in God's kingdom. We approach God with confidence, in the knowledge that Jesus understands our struggles and intercedes on our behalf.

Hebrews informs us that God disciplines those whom He loves, just as parents discipline their children. While discipline is unwelcome, it produces correction and guidance. Discipline turns us away from error and positions us onto the path of righteousness. God's discipline is not a demonstration of His anger, but rather of His love and unwavering concern for humanity. God permits trials, tribulations, troubles, tragedies, and tests in our journey to refine our character, strengthen our faith, and enhance our integrity. Believers are encouraged to endure God's discipline, with the understanding that it is for their spiritual growth and development.

Hebrews encourages believers to pursue the just cause of peace in the world. In addition, believers are to cultivate holiness;

'without holiness no one will see the LORD.'[2] The pursuit of holiness is imperative to the believer's life. Holiness requires vigilance to avoid the pitfalls of sin, bitterness, temptation, concupiscence, evil, or worldly distractions. The Christian faith is a call to holiness, which incorporates our relationship with God and members of the community. We are called to live in peace and pursue godliness. Our holiness is witness of Jesus Christ to the world. Not to mention, our holiness is an essential attribute of our fellowship with God.

Hebrews contrasts the trembling mountain of the old covenant with the immovable kingdom of the new covenant in Jesus Christ. The trembling mountain represents fear and trepidation. In contrast, the immovable kingdom represents peace and joy. The author encourages believers to be grateful and live in reverence for God. We shall inherit a kingdom that cannot be shaken. In the Book of Hebrews, we are informed, 'what cannot be shaken may remain.'[10] The kingdom of God, established through Jesus Christ, is eternal, perfect, and secure. In a world defined by instability, unpredictability, brokenness, and perpetual change, believers must remain firm in the promise of God's kingdom. God's kingdom is perfect, complete, and everlasting.

The author encourages believers to motivate each other to demonstrate love, mercy, peace, compassion, social justice, joy, and forgiveness. Believers are not to neglect the art of fellowship. Believers must support each other in their walk with God. Fellowship creates opportunity for believers to provide mutual encouragement, accountability, love, and counsel. The Christian faith is not meant to be lived in isolation. Believers require one another to persevere, grow, and fulfil their destiny on earth. Fellowship and mutual encouragement are indispensable to practice the Christian faith and transcend our challenges.

Hebrews encourages believers to be content with their

possessions, accomplishments, gifts, and talents. Believers wholeheartedly trust in God's word; 'Never will I leave you; never will I forsake you.'[1] This trust and confidence in God's word strengthens believers to courageously confront their challenges, without fear, grief, concern, or intimidation. God's faithfulness empowers believers to live their life with favour, love, compassion, joy, and peace.

We are called to trust in God's promises. We know that God will never abandon us. In fact, God's providence is continually unfolding in our life. The Book of Hebrews commands believers to remain faithful to Jesus Christ. We must persevere through our difficulties. We are blessed to live in accordance with the new covenant in Jesus Christ. The Book of Hebrews emphasises that Jesus is the fulfilment of the Old Testament promises, parables, and prophecies. Last but not least, believers are to live in the light of Jesus Christ with trust, confidence, perseverance, and holiness.

[1] The Holy Bible (NIV). (2011). *The Book of Hebrews.* Chapter 1, Verse 3.

[2] The Holy Bible (NIV). (2011). *The Book of John.* Chapter 19, Verse 30.

[3] The Holy Bible (NIV). (2011). *The Book of Hebrews.* Chapter 9, Verse 12.

[4] The Holy Bible (NIV). (2011). *The Book of John.* Chapter 6, Verse 35.

[5] The Holy Bible (NIV). (2011). *The Book of Hebrews.* Chapter 12, Verse 1.

[6] The Holy Bible (NIV). (2011). *The Book of Hebrews.* Chapter 12, Verse 2.

[7] The Holy Bible (NIV). (2011). *The Book of Romans.* Chapter 4, Verse 18.

[8] The Holy Bible (NIV). (2011). *The Book of Hebrews.* Chapter 4, Verse 14.

[9] The Holy Bible (NIV). (2011). *The Book of Hebrews.* Chapter 12, Verse 14.

[10] The Holy Bible (NIV). (2011). *The Book of Hebrews.* Chapter 12, Verse 27.

[11] The Holy Bible (NIV). (2011). *The Book of Hebrews.* Chapter 13, Verse 5.

Chapter 59

The Book of James

'What good is it, my brothers and sisters,
if someone claims to have faith but has no deeds?
Can such faith save them?'

James 2:14
The Holy Bible (NIV)

The Book of James is a letter written by James, the brother of Jesus. James emphasises the practical dimensions of the believer's faith. James encourages us to put our faith into action. We are reminded of the importance of good works. The Book of James provides guidance on several practical issues, such as righteous conduct, the power of words, practical wisdom, and observance of humility. James encourages believers to practice their faith with accountability, honour, sincerity, and integrity. James commands believers to align their thoughts and actions with the teachings of Jesus Christ. Believers are to live a meaningful and authentic life.

James reveals that faith without good works is devoid of merit. Our faith is evidenced by our actions. James employs the Old Testament example of Abraham's willingness to sacrifice his son, Isaac to demonstrate that faith and good works complement one another. James teaches us 'the body without the spirit is dead, so faith without deeds is dead.'[1] Faith produces good works. It is not sufficient to merely believe in God's word. Our beliefs, thoughts, and ideals must be given effect by our actions. Believers are to demonstrate their faith through acts of love, compassion, peace, justice, forgiveness, mercy, philanthropy, hospitality, and generosity.

James highlights the potential of words to be employed for good or evil. The power of words must not be underestimated. Words can be employed to bless or curse a person. Speech reveals much about a person's character, morality, and conscience. James employs the metaphor of a rudder on a ship to illustrate the significance of his message. The rudder is a small mechanical component which determines the ship's trajectory at sea. In a comparable manner, 'the tongue is a small part of the body;'[2] however, through speech, the tongue 'sets the whole course of one's life'[3] into motion. The manner in which we communicate is an important reflection of our faith. We must carefully select our words to develop the faith of fellow believers, spread hope in the world, encourage members in their walk with God, and speak the truth of the gospel to humanity. We must avoid gossip, slander, and inappropriate language. Christians are commanded to demonstrate self-control over their speech and conduct.

In relation to our speech, our perception of reality is important. James teaches us that our worldly trials must be perceived as opportunities for our spiritual growth and development. James encourages believers to consider it 'pure joy'[4] when they confront trials. Worldly trials develop our perseverance, character, and judgement. Worldly trials augment our spiritual transformation. James reminds believers that God does not tempt any person. Rather, we are enlightened to learn that temptation comes from our 'own evil desire.'[5] Trials are an unavoidable part of our journey. Trials contribute to our personal growth and development. Without adversity, we will not be tested. Without tribulation, we will not have the opportunity to enhance our maturity, judgement, tenacity, discernment, character, integrity, gratitude, and willpower. Instead of engendering discouragement, believers must perceive their trials as an opportunity for spiritual growth. God does not tempt us. Having said that, God permits trials to strengthen our faith.

James provides counsel to believers. They must be 'quick to listen, slow to speak, and slow to become angry.'[6] When we permit anger to consume our thoughts and inform our actions, it prohibits us from living the righteous life that God desires for us. Emotional intelligence in relationships means to listen without judgement, empathise with how others feel, and demonstrate compassion. We must not react impulsively with irrational feelings, or ill-informed ideas. When we are quick-tempered or utilise inconsiderate words, we damage our relationships and obstruct the realisation of God's providence in our life. Much like other negative emotions, anger diminishes the cultivation of the Holy Spirit within us.

James instructs believers to faithfully accept the word of God. Through acceptance and application of God's word in our life, we secure our salvation. This means we abstain from the performance of immoral acts. We do not participate in evil that is prevalent throughout the world. We cast away the darkness of ignorance, prejudice, hate, injustice, and error. We effectuate into practice the wisdom of God's word, so that we perfect our body, mind, heart, and spirit. We are counselled to receive God's word, with gratitude, joy, love, and humility. The word of God is central to the believer's life. Believers must accept God's word with humility. We must allow God's word to transform our body, mind, heart, and spirit. A humble and receptive attitude toward God's word leads us to spiritual transformation.

James unequivocally condemns all forms of partiality, particularly when believers demonstrate favour towards the aristocrat over the plebeian. James teaches us that believers must not discriminate against [equal] members of humanity on the basis of wealth, power, social status, income, private property, sex, race, colour, or education. We are commanded to love all people equally, just as God loves humanity, 'For God so loved the world that He gave His one and only Son, that whoever believes in him shall not perish but have eternal life.'[7]

Christians are called to love humanity, regardless of their social status, personal wealth, sex, gender, nationality, colour, private property, income, vocation, education, or age. Partiality undermines the universal message of the gospel. God's word teaches us that all people are equal before God. Every person was created in the image of God. Every person is capable of redemption through Jesus Christ. We must treat every person with compassion, love, dignity, honour, and respect. We must demonstrate the love of Jesus Christ to every person.

James emphasises that to recite or listen to God's word is insufficient. Believers must effectuate the Biblical principles, doctrines, and teachings into practice. James compares a person who listens to the word of God, however, they do not apply it in their life, to a person who examines their appearance in a mirror, and thereafter, they cannot remember how they look. Obedience to God's word is an integral part of the believer's life. It is insufficient to merely know the word of God. We must put the word of God into practice in our life and realise its meaning.

James defines faith as 'looking after orphans and widows in their distress.'[8] This reflects the heart of God for the marginalised and vulnerable people in the world. Religion goes beyond discipleship, worship, fellowship, absolution, philanthropy, intercession, penance, confession, and prayer. To practice one's faith is to love humanity, especially those members who are in dire need of our assistance. We must live our life characterised by purity, spirituality, and holiness. Christians must be philanthropic members of society, in particular for the benefit of the vulnerable, marginalised, and destitute individuals. Our humanitarian activities possess the potential to transform humanity.

James teaches us to open our heart and mind to God's grace. We must not live for the fulfilment of endless temptations and the temporal satisfaction of our limitless desires. We must live for the advancement of God's kingdom on earth. James reminds us that 'God opposes the proud, but shows favour to the humble.'[9] Believers are to submit to God's will, resist the devil's malevolent influence, and approach God with humility. Humility and repentance are instrumental to experience God's redeeming grace and favour in our life. Humility is essential in our fellowship with God and other believers. We must recognise our dependence upon God and submit to His will. When we humble ourselves, we experience God's providence at work in our life.

James encourages believers to demonstrate forbearance in their suffering and to expect the coming of Jesus Christ. James employs the example of a farmer. Having completed their work of ploughing, harrowing, and sowing, they must now patiently wait for the opportune time to harvest their crop. In addition, James reflects on Job's endurance through his heartbreaking ordeal. James demonstrates the importance of forbearance and perseverance in the believer's journey. Forbearance is essential to the believer's life, especially when we experience trials and suffering along our journey. Believers are commanded to anticipate the coming of Christ. We trust that God administers justice and rewards those who faithfully endure challenges and privation. Our present struggles, which are real, painful, and difficult, are only temporary. Through our faith in Jesus Christ, we are assured of salvation.

James teaches us that prayer is a powerful and effective instrument to assist us in our walk with God. Believers are encouraged to pray in times of trouble, joy, happiness, loss, grief, celebration, or sickness. James emphasises the importance of confession. Confession is a powerful instrument to bring about our restoration. James highlights that the prayer of a righteous person is a 'powerful and effective'[10] antidote. Prayer is an effective spiritual instrument for believers. Prayer must be a consistent part of the believer's life. We are encouraged to pray in all circumstances. We trust that God listens to our prayers. Prayer brings restoration, peace, equanimity, and contentment to our being.

The Book of James concludes with a message to restore those who have deviated from the truth of the gospel. James reminds believers that to guide a fellow believer away from evil shall 'save them from death and cover over a multitude of sins.'[11]

Christians are responsible for each other's spiritual well-being. When a believer strays from the truth of the gospel, we must compassionately guide them back onto the path of righteousness. Through our fellowship with believers, we assist each other to strengthen our fellowship with God.

The Book of James teaches humanity that faith is not the mere acceptance of God's word. Faith is consciously demonstrated through our good behaviour, compassionate actions, mercy, love, forbearance, peace, forgiveness, and prayer. Faith assists us to navigate the highs and lows of life. Faith is to renew our mind and live a transformed spiritual life. The Book of James encourages us to put into practice the timeless teachings of Jesus Christ in our journey. We must demonstrate to the world the incredible impact of the gospel to transform humanity. Above all, faith is now. Faith is action. Faith is the decisive victory of good over evil. Peace be with you.

[1] The Holy Bible (NIV). (2011). *The Book of James.* Chapter 2, Verse 26.
[2] The Holy Bible (NIV). (2011). *The Book of James.* Chapter 3, Verse 5.
[3] The Holy Bible (NIV). (2011). *The Book of James.* Chapter 3, Verse 6.
[4] The Holy Bible (NIV). (2011). *The Book of James.* Chapter 1, Verse 2.
[5] The Holy Bible (NIV). (2011). *The Book of James.* Chapter 1, Verse 14.
[6] The Holy Bible (NIV). (2011). *The Book of James.* Chapter 1, Verse 19.
[7] The Holy Bible (NIV). (2011). *The Book of John.* Chapter 3, Verse 16.
[8] The Holy Bible (NIV). (2011). *The Book of James.* Chapter 1, Verse 27.

[9] The Holy Bible (NIV). (2011). *The Book of James.* Chapter 4, Verse 6.

[10] The Holy Bible (NIV). (2011). *The Book of James.* Chapter 5, Verse 16.

[11] The Holy Bible (NIV). (2011). *The Book of James.* Chapter 5, Verse 20.

Chapter 60

The Book of First Peter

'Be alert and of sober mind.
Your enemy the devil prowls around
like a roaring lion looking for someone to devour.'

1 Peter 5:8
The Holy Bible (NIV)

The Book of First Peter is written by the Apostle Peter to Christians in Asia Minor who experience religious persecution. Peter encourages believers to remain determined in their faith despite their suffering. Peter informs believers to place their trust and confidence in Jesus Christ—our saviour. The Book of First Peter offers profound theological insights into suffering, holiness, and the good life. The Book of First Peter provides counsel on how to live as exiles and foreigners in a secular world that is opposed to the gospel's message of salvation through faith in Jesus Christ.

Peter informs believers that to suffer is part and parcel of the believer's journey. Our suffering is not unexpected or unwarranted. Trials, tribulations, tragedies, troubles, and tests refine our character, they make it of 'greater worth than gold.'[1] Through our lived experience of pain and suffering, we attain spiritual growth. Suffering strengthens our faith in Jesus Christ. Christians acknowledge their suffering and religious persecution are part and parcel of practicing their faith. However, suffering is not without a greater purpose. Suffering refines our character, strengthens our faith, and draws us closer to God. We are to remain determined and courageous in the midst of our suffering. God employs humanity's suffering for the realisation of His providence.

Just as God is holy, Peter encourages believers to live a holy life. Peter reminds believers that they are 'a chosen people, a royal priesthood, a holy nation.'[2] As disciples of Christ, Christians must be distinct. Christians must live in a manner that reflects their newfound identity in Jesus Christ. As disciples of Christ, believers are encouraged to live their life in the holiness of God. This means believers set aside worldly desires. Believers prioritise the pursuit of a life that reflects God's character, providence, and love. Holiness is not merely concerned with our actions. Holiness involves a spiritual transformation that determines every aspect of our being.

Peter emphasises the 'living hope'[3] that believers have received through the resurrection of Jesus Christ. Our hope in Christ is imperishable, eternal, and resolute. For believers who trust in Jesus Christ as their saviour, their hope is actualised through eternal life in heaven. In the midst of pain and suffering, Christians are encouraged to fixate their heart and mind on Jesus Christ. The hope of salvation and eternal life in heaven is the foundation to endure grief, loss, pain, tragedy, and suffering in the world. Believers run their race with hope at the forefront of their mind. Believers are secure in the knowledge that their present trials are temporary, when compared to eternal life in God's kingdom.

Peter reminds believers they are 'God's elect exiles'[4] in the world. While we live in the world, our true 'citizenship is in heaven.'[5] Believers are instructed not to conform to the pattern of the world. Believers must live as witnesses of Christ's love, peace, joy, compassion, and truth. Christians are to live in the world, without being attached to it. As exiles on earth, our final destination is God's kingdom in heaven. Our life must reflect our newfound identity in Christ. This means we must avoid countless temptations, desires, evil, and sin of the world. Instead, we must be a guiding light to the world.

Peter teaches believers to 'submit yourselves to governing authorities'[6] and honour people in positions of power, such as emperors, dukes, princes, kings, and queens. This assertion includes when we are subject to the rule of unjust sovereigns. Christians are called to respect authority figures as part of their witness to Jesus Christ. Christians must live as honourable citizens in society. Christians ought to respect the laws of the land, unless those laws contravene God's word. Obedience to legitimate authority figures is part of our witness to Jesus Christ.

When we accept secular authority in the world, it demonstrates our trust in God's sovereignty and providence over worldly powers.

Peter points to Jesus Christ as the perfect example of how to live in peace, patience, and prudence. Jesus suffered unjustly. Jesus was not crucified for his sins; however, for the sins of humanity. Nonetheless, Jesus did not retaliate. Jesus entrusted himself completely to God's will. Jesus Christ is without sin. Jesus Christ's suffering was a predestined part of God's redemption of humanity. Jesus' example teaches believers how to comprehend their suffering in the world. Believers are encouraged to follow Christ's example on how to transcend suffering. This means to endure suffering without bitterness, hatred, or retaliation. We trust in God's justice. We remember that Jesus Christ's suffering secured redemption for humanity.

Peter stresses the importance of love, humility, and unity within the Christian community. Believers must 'love each other deeply, because love covers over a multitude of sins.'[7] Peter encourages believers to live in harmony and be compassionate towards one another. Believers must demonstrate forgiveness and love towards humanity. Christians are to live in harmony and unity with one another. Love is the foundation of our relationships, both within the church and across the world. Love unites humanity. Love promotes the just cause of peace. Love builds meaningful connections across distinct civilisations.

Peter encourages believers to give a defence of their faith in Jesus Christ when they are questioned. Believers must do this with gentleness, humility, and respect. Believers must demonstrate trust and confidence in God. Christians must be prepared to explain their faith and hope in Jesus Christ. This endeavour involves an intimate knowledge of the gospel and Jesus Christ's teachings. Believers must respectfully articulate their faith, especially when confronted with opposition or religious persecution. As believers, we have an important duty to witness Christ to humanity.

Peter encourages believers to express themselves with humility towards one another, because 'God opposes the proud but gives grace to the humble.'[8] Humility is a necessary virtue to submit to church leadership and perfect our walk with God. Humility is a defining virtue of the Christian faith. Christians must humble themselves before God and humanity. Believers must trust that God exalts them in due course. Humility promotes mercy, love, peace, compassion, and forgiveness. Through humility, we obtain an enlightened perspective on the finitude of our lifetime on earth.

Peter cautions believers to remain vigilant of the devil. The devil roams around the earth like a 'roaring lion.'[9] The devil is constantly scheming, strategising, and searching for his next victim on earth. Peter's remarkable spiritual insight is confirmed in the Book of Job. In discourse between God and the devil, the devil mentions he has been 'roaming throughout the earth.'[10] The devil's malignant spiritual influence across the world must not be underestimated. The devil is powerful and mighty. Nonetheless, God is all-powerful and almighty. Believers are to remain firm in their faith.

Christians around the world experience suffering. We are not alone in our suffering. We must utilise our pain and suffering to unite and strengthen the body of Jesus Christ. In fact, suffering is universal to the human experience of being in the world. Christians must remain vigilant in their spiritual walk with God. We must be conscious of the spiritual warfare between good and evil. The devil seeks to undermine our faith; however, we must remain firm in the eternal truth of God's word. We must resist temptation through God's armour, confession, prayer, worship, discipleship, and fellowship.

Peter concludes his letter with encouragement to believers.

When believers experience suffering in the world, God restores, confirms, strengthens, and establishes them in His goodness, favour, and mercy. God's grace is sufficient to guide believers through trials and to bring them into His eternal glory. Our direct and immediate experience of suffering is real; however, our worldly existence is transient. God's grace strengthens believers during turbulent times.

Ultimately, God's redeeming grace provides believers with eternal life in heaven through His beloved son—Jesus Christ. This theological assurance encourages perseverance and hope in the midst of our worldly trials. First Peter offers timeless wisdom for believers that experience opposition, persecution, injustice, or privation. First Peter emphasises the importance of holiness, love, integrity, discipline, and humility. Christians are encouraged to endure suffering, with hope in the gospel, trust in Jesus, and faith in God. Believers are reminded they are chosen, loved, and secure in God's providence. Peace be with you.

[1] The Holy Bible (NIV). (2011). *The Book of First Peter.* Chapter 1, Verse 7.

[2] The Holy Bible (NIV). (2011). *The Book of First Peter.* Chapter 2, Verse 9.

[3] The Holy Bible (NIV). (2011). *The Book of First Peter.* Chapter 1, Verse 3.

[4] The Holy Bible (NIV). (2011). *The Book of First Peter.* Chapter 1, Verse 1.

[5] The Holy Bible (NIV). (2011). *The Book of Philippians.* Chapter 3, Verse 20.

[6] The Holy Bible (NIV). (2011). *The Book of First Peter.* Chapter 2, Verse 13.

[7] The Holy Bible (NIV). (2011). *The Book of First Peter.* Chapter 4, Verse 8.

[8] The Holy Bible (NIV). (2011). *The Book of First Peter.* Chapter 5, Verse 5.

[9] The Holy Bible (NIV). (2011). *The Book of First Peter.* Chapter 5, Verse 8.

[10] The Holy Bible (NIV). (2011). *The Book of Job.* Chapter 2, Verse 2.

Chapter 61

The Book of Second Peter

'His divine power has given us everything we need
for a godly life through our knowledge of Him
who called us by His own glory and goodness.'

2 Peter 1:3
The Holy Bible (NIV)

The Book of Second Peter is written by the Apostle Peter. Second Peter is addressed to Christians that experience significant challenges to practice their faith. Some of these challenges include the presence of illegitimate prophets and increased moral decadence in society. In the Book of Second Peter, the Apostle Peter cautions believers about the dangers of false theological doctrines. Peter encourages believers to understand their faith in accordance with the eternal truth of the gospel. The Book of Second Peter reminds believers of the coming of Christ and the final judgement of God. Second Peter contains messages of vigilance, spiritual growth, and a command to live in agreement with God's covenant with humanity.

Peter instructs believers to strengthen their relationship with Jesus Christ through the pursuit of godliness. Believers are encouraged to develop positive qualities, such as mercy, forbearance, perseverance, godliness, compassion, hope, peace, social justice, forgiveness, and love. Our spiritual growth and development are essential to live a good and productive life. Christians are called to continually grow in their faith and knowledge of Jesus Christ. Spiritual maturity requires responsibility, integrity, commitment, dedication, accountability, and perseverance. We must endeavour to cultivate Christ-like character in our life. In our walk with God, we must strive to become like Christ.

Peter reminds believers of the promises that God has given to them. Promises such as eternal life in heaven and 'participation in the divine nature'[1] of being. Despite the passage of time in the coming of Christ, believers trust that God's covenant with them is fulfilled. God's covenant with humanity is fulfilled in God's timing. Christians confidently trust in God's covenant, even when its fulfilment is delayed in their life. We must remember our perception of time does not equate to God's perception of time.

In all respects, God's timing is perfect. God's covenant with humanity is always honoured by Him. This assurance encourages believers to live in the anticipation of Christ's return and the eternal reign of God's kingdom on earth.

Peter cautions us against illegitimate prophets who introduce unfounded doctrines, false principles, and mistaken ideas into the Christian faith. These erroneous ideologies lead humanity into the pitfall of sin. Illegitimate prophets exploit believers for pecuniary gain. They deny the divinity and humanity of Christ. Not to mention, illegitimate prophets alter the eternal truth of the gospel. Without a doubt, illegitimate prophets bring 'swift destruction on themselves.'[2]

Illegitimate prophets distort the truth of the gospel. They encourage immorality, idolatry, and guide believers astray from God's word. Believers must exercise vigilance and discernment in their journey of faith. Believers must avoid the influence of illegitimate prophets who distort the message of the gospel. It is important to remain grounded in the eternal truth of God's word. We must reject unfounded teachings that contradict God's word. If a teaching does not align with the truth of the gospel, then it is false.

Peter emphasises the certainty of Christ's return and God's judgement. We must not become impatient with our expectation for the day of the LORD to arrive. Everything comes to fruition in accordance with God's will. All events within creation are determined in accordance with God's providence, this includes the day of the LORD. Therefore, we are reminded, 'the LORD is not slow in keeping His promise, as some understand slowness. Instead, He is patient with you, not wanting anyone to perish, but everyone to come to repentance.'[3]

Despite pessimism amongst humanity in relation to the coming of Christ, believers live in the light of Christ's imminent return. The earth shall be consumed by fire, and all that is temporary will give way to a 'new heaven and new earth, where righteousness dwells.'[4] Christians live with an eternal perspective. We recognise the coming of Christ brings judgement and the fulfilment of God's covenant with humanity. This motivates believers to live a holy life in the anticipation of Christ's coming. Believers affirm the truth of the gospel.

In light of the certainty of Christ's return and God's impending judgement, the Apostle Peter encourages believers to live their life characterised by holiness and godliness. Believers look forward to the new heaven and new earth. Having said that, while we place our hope, trust, and faith in Jesus Christ, we must make every effort to live our life with integrity, honour, good character, love, peace, mercy, and social justice. Believers live in a godly and righteous manner, especially in light of the certainty of Christ's return. Our conduct must reflect the eternal truth of the gospel. We must be spiritually prepared for the coming of Christ.

The Apostle Peter affirms the word of God is 'completely reliable,'[5] as opposed to our lived experience, empirical knowledge, secular doctrines, transient emotions, partial perspectives, or subjective feelings. The Holy Bible is God's word. The word of God is revealed to humanity through prophets who are appointed by God and empowered by the Holy Spirit. Paul the Apostle is unequivocally clear on this theological point, 'all Scripture is God-breathed.'[6] The authenticity of scripture does not arise from the finite depth of human understanding. This theological reality affirms the supreme authority of scripture to educate, correct, and discipline the believer. The Holy Bible is the divinely inspired and authoritative word of God. Christians must establish their faith, customs, doctrines, traditions, and practices on the eternal truth of scripture. Believers recognise scripture's instrumental function to guide them in their journey.

Peter explains the delay in the coming of Christ is due to God's forbearance with humanity. God desires that no person perish, but that humanity repent of their sin and be redeemed through Jesus Christ. God's mercy is an opportunity for humanity to repent and return to Him. God's postponement of His judgement is an act of His mercy. This opportune delay provides humanity with invaluable time to repent. Christians must be compassionate towards each other. We must understand that God's delay in judgement is an opportunity for every person to become acquainted with the gospel and secure their salvation.

Peter cautions believers to remain vigilant against being misguided by unbelievers. Believers must not fall into the trap of temptation, which ultimately leads to sin—the root cause of evil. We must remain confident in our belief, faith, and hope in Jesus Christ. Christians must not be led astray by the false teachings and immoral practices of the secular world. To avoid being deceived or misled, believers must remain circumspect of falsehood in the world. The Christian faith requires diligence, discernment, discipline, and dedication. Believers must remain faithful and confident in Jesus Christ.

Peter concludes his letter with an important message. We must 'grow in the grace and knowledge'[7] of Jesus Christ. God's grace is pivotal to the Christian faith. Our spiritual growth and transformation are dependent upon God's grace. God's grace empowers believers to live a godly life and endure in faith until the end of their race. Our spiritual development is not characterised by our willpower or self-discipline, it is dependent upon God's redeeming grace. Christians must grow in their fellowship with Jesus Christ. Believers depend upon God's grace for their strength, wisdom, and spiritual transformation.

The Book of Second Peter encourages believers to remain committed to the faith. Christians must advance in godliness and remain grounded in the timeless truth of the scripture. We must remain vigilant against the dissemination of false teachings by illegitimate prophets. Second Peter emphasises the coming of

Christ and the fulfilment of God's covenant with humanity. Therefore, believers are to live a holy and godly life in anticipation of the new heaven and new earth.

[1] The Holy Bible (NIV). (2011). *The Book of Second Peter.* Chapter 1, Verse 4.

[2] The Holy Bible (NIV). (2011). *The Book of Second Peter.* Chapter 2, Verse 1.

[3] The Holy Bible (NIV). (2011). *The Book of Second Peter.* Chapter 3, Verse 9.

[4] The Holy Bible (NIV). (2011). *The Book of Second Peter.* Chapter 3, Verse 13.

[5] The Holy Bible (NIV). (2011). *The Book of Second Peter.* Chapter 1, Verse 19.

[6] The Holy Bible (NIV). (2011). *The Book of Second Timothy.* Chapter 3, Verse 16.

[7] The Holy Bible (NIV). (2011). *The Book of Second Peter.* Chapter 3, Verse 18.

Chapter 62

The Book of First John

'If we claim to be without sin,
we deceive ourselves
and the truth is not in us.'

1 John 1:8
The Holy Bible (NIV)

T he Book of First John is written by the Apostle John. First John focuses on specific theological themes, such as fellowship, love, truth, mercy, peace, justice, and salvation. First John addresses the proliferation of false teachings in the Christian community. In the Book of First John, believers are encouraged to live in accordance with the eternal truth of the gospel. Believers must demonstrate love for one another and obedience to God's word. First John emphasises God's attributes, particularly His love, grace, blessing, mercy, and peace. First John assures believers of their salvation in Jesus Christ.

The Book of First John informs us that 'God is light.'[1] This means that God is pure, holy, just, and compassionate. In addition, First John affirms that 'God is love.'[2] This demonstrates that love is the essence of God's being. God's word, light, and love define how believers relate to Him and members within the community. As God's chosen people, we are to reflect God's light in our life. We must love one another as God loves us. The most immediate and direct experience of God's love is that he sent His beloved Son—Jesus Christ—into the world as the sinless saviour of humanity.

John enlightens us about the importance of fellowship with God and believers of the faith. Our walk with God is what really matters in life. Fellowship is not merely about contact, communication, and community with believers. Fellowship means to practice the teachings of Jesus Christ and walk in God's light. Christians are to live in harmony with one another, support one another, and encourage one another. Fellowship provides us with the opportunity to hold each other accountable. Fellowship with God and believers is imperative to live the good life.

John emphasises believers who are in fellowship with God must 'walk in the light.'[3] This means to live in obedience to God's command. We must live a life that is devoid of sin. First

John refers to the matchless and distinguished example of how Jesus lived in the world. Fellowship with God requires obedience to God's word. Christians must avoid sinful conduct. When we engage in sin, we must confess and express remorse for our immoral conduct. Throughout our journey, we must strive to live in accordance with God's will. Believers must faithfully follow the matchless example of Jesus Christ in the world.

John assures believers that if they confess their sins, God forgives them. If we repent, God does not hold our iniquity against us. God provides us with the requisite grace, mercy, love, and blessing, to 'purify us from all unrighteousness.'[4] Believers must confess their sins. Believers are secure in the knowledge that God's forgiveness is available to them through Jesus Christ. God's mercy encourages believers to live faithfully, demonstrate integrity, and assume accountability. We must not deceive ourselves and contemplate that we are without sin—we are all sinners. No person is beyond the fallen nature of Adam and Eve which is a universal attribute of humanity. Acceptance of our errors, biases, mistakes, flaws, prejudices, infirmities, and failures creates the opportunity for forgiveness and reconciliation.

John emphasises the centrality of love in the Christian faith. John reminds believers that love is a virtue. The greatest commandment is to love God and humanity. Our love reflects God's love for humanity. We must demonstrate our love for humanity in meaningful ways, through forgiveness, empathy, compassion, philanthropy, community service, joy, mercy, and fellowship. Love is indispensable in our relationships, this includes the workplace, family, school, university, and community. Love is the hallmark of the Christian faith. Believers are called to love one another unconditionally, just as Jesus Christ loved us. Our capacity to love and be loved is unequivocal proof that humanity is made in God's image, 'For God so loved the world that He gave His one and only Son, that whoever believes in him shall not perish but have eternal life.'[5] Our fellowship with God and believers is predicated on love.

John acknowledges that believers struggle with sin. To transcend sin is not a convenient endeavour, it requires forbearance, courage, confession, love, prayer, forgiveness, reflection, grace, and fellowship. In spite of sin, temptation, and evil in the world, John enlightens us, that the person 'born of God'[6] abstains from acts of sin. Believers must confront the issue of sin in their life. While we are not without our flaws, we must not live our life characterised by sin. We must transcend the ignorance of sin, evil, and temptation, which lead us to error. It is through the Holy Spirit, that believers overcome sin and live in accordance with God's word.

John reassures believers they have certainty, clarity, and confidence of eternal life in heaven through Jesus Christ. This theological assurance is based on our faith in Jesus Christ. Following Jesus Christ's crucifixion, he was resurrected, and ascended to heaven. Christians are confident of their salvation in Jesus Christ. Assurance of eternal life comes through our faith in Jesus Christ. Nonetheless, we must adhere to God's covenant with humanity. We do not secure eternal life through our good works, observance of the Mosaic law, philanthropy, merit, or virtue. Believers secure a profound peace in God's love, grace, providence, sovereignty, and mercy.

John instructs believers to 'test the spirits,'[7] as many illegitimate prophets have claimed to possess divine revelation of the word of God. The truth about Jesus Christ, being the Son of God, is the litmus test of a prophet's authenticity. Christians must exercise discernment. Christians must ensure that a prophet's theological teachings align with the truth of Jesus Christ as the saviour of humanity. Believers must remain vigilant not to be misled by false teachings that deny the fundamental truth of the gospel.

John assures believers they can 'overcome the world'[8] through their faith in Jesus Christ. The world's temptations, pleasures, passions, desires, and deceptions command no power or influence over those individuals who believe in Jesus Christ. It is through the power of belief, that Christians secure their salvation by faith in the Son of God. Christians are victorious over secular values, contemporary ideologies, endless temptations, and popular culture. Faith in Jesus Christ grants believers the strength to transcend the desires of the world. Christians live for the greater purpose to advance God's kingdom on earth.

John affirms that believers receive the Holy Spirit as confirmation of their sacred fellowship with God. The Holy Spirit enables Christians to live in accordance with God's will. Christians realise that they are blessed with God's unconditional love. The Holy Spirit is imperative to the Christian faith. The Holy Spirit guides, strengthens, and empowers believers to live in obedience to God's word. The Holy Spirit strengthens believers to remain in fellowship with God. Our faith in God is expressed through our obedience to His commands and unconditional love for humanity. Christians do not merely affirm their faith. Christians practice their faith through acts of love, mercy, forgiveness, confession, philanthropy, compassion, and obedience to God's word. Christianity is defined by love and obedience to God. Faith is not merely a religious belief. We consciously demonstrate our faith through our actions that honour God and His commandments.

The Book of First John is a call to believers to live authentically as disciples of Jesus Christ. Believers must lead their life characterised by love, obedience, and fellowship with God and one another. First John assures believers of their salvation in Jesus Christ. First John cautions believers against the temptation to sin. We are to remain vigilant of illegitimate prophets and their false doctrines. Christians are commanded to live in the light of God's word. Christians must reflect God's character in their thoughts, speech, and conduct. The Book of First John underscores that love is the essence of the good life. Guided by the Holy Spirit, it is through love and obedience to God's word, that believers strengthen their fellowship with God.

[1] The Holy Bible (NIV). (2011). *The Book of First John.* Chapter 1, Verse 5.

[2] The Holy Bible (NIV). (2011). *The Book of First John.* Chapter 4, Verse 8.

[3] The Holy Bible (NIV). (2011). *The Book of First John.* Chapter 1, Verse 7.

[4] The Holy Bible (NIV). (2011). *The Book of First John.* Chapter 1, Verse 9.

[5] The Holy Bible (NIV). (2011). *The Book of John.* Chapter 3, Verse 16.

[6] The Holy Bible (NIV). (2011). *The Book of First John.* Chapter 3, Verse 9.

[7] The Holy Bible (NIV). (2011). *The Book of First John.* Chapter 4, Verse 1.

[8] The Holy Bible (NIV). (2011). *The Book of First John.* Chapter 5, Verse 4.

Chapter 63

The Book of Second John

'And this is love:
that we walk in obedience to His commands.
As you have heard from the beginning,
His command is that you walk in love.'

2 John 1:6
The Holy Bible (NIV)

The Book of Second John is a concise book in the New Testament. Second John is written by the Apostle John. Second John is addressed to the elect lady and her children. In Second John, the Apostle John warns humanity against the illegitimate prophet, referred to as 'the deceiver,'[1] also known as 'the antichrist.'[2] John's message urges believers to walk with God in truth, grace, peace, mercy, faith, and love. The themes in Second John include love, truth, and grace. Second John emphasises the importance to avoid illegitimate prophets in our fellowship with God.

John expresses immense joy when he learns that believers walk in God's truth, providence, grace, mercy, and love. John emphasises that when we walk in truth, we live in accordance with God's commandments and demonstrate love towards humanity. The believer's life incorporates truth (i.e., obedience to God's word) and love (i.e., to live in harmony with members of the community). The good life incorporates much more than mere knowledge of Biblical doctrines and prophecies. We must put our values, beliefs, and principles into practice through acts of love, generosity, philanthropy, mercy, peace, forgiveness, joy, social justice, and compassion. Biblical knowledge, the fear of God, practical wisdom, and righteous action characterise the good life.

The Apostle John reaffirms the command to love God and each other. Love is the expression of God's word in our life. Love is a commandment, not merely an emotion, thought, opinion, doctrine, or feeling. Believers must faithfully obey God's command. Believers must express unconditional love through their actions and attitude towards every person they meet along their journey. As we love humanity, we grow and mature in our fellowship with God. To walk with God means to express love across the wide array of our relationships. In the final analysis, our character must be perfected on earth, for eternal life in heaven.

The Apostle John cautions us against illegitimate prophets who do not acknowledge Jesus Christ's divinity. Jesus Christ—the Son of God—came to earth in the flesh to redeem humanity of original sin. This assertion constitutes a fundamental truth of the Christian faith. John cautions believers to avoid contact with illegitimate prophets. To associate with them is to participate in their evil deeds. Christians must be vigilant and exercise discernment. Christians must not confer recognition or extend legitimacy to false doctrines. When we empower illegitimate prophets to preach in the community, this leads believers away from the truth of God's word. We are commanded to remain firm in the eternal truth of the gospel. We must reject teachings that distort or deny the fundamental truths of the Christian faith, especially the truth of Jesus Christ—the Son of God.

John instructs believers that if a prophet approaches them with a theological doctrine that does not acknowledge the truth of Jesus Christ, they must not receive them into their house. To invite illegitimate prophets is to participate in their sinful conduct. Christians must remain circumspect in whom they associate with and support, especially in consequential matters that concern theological doctrine, fellowship, worship, discipleship, prayer, and ministry. If we admit illegitimate prophets into the church, or provide them with a platform to disseminate their false ideologies to the congregation, we inadvertently contribute to the proliferation of their falsehood. Our discernment and wisdom are necessary to preserve the truth of the gospel.

In his letter, John wishes the recipients 'grace, mercy, and peace,'[3] bestowed by God, the Father, and Jesus Christ, the Son, in truth and love. The foundation of fellowship is truth—the eternal truth of the gospel. Peace, love, and fellowship are realised when believers congregate in the eternal truth of God's word. The gospel of Jesus Christ, as revealed through scripture, is the legitimate basis for the good life. The eternal truth of the gospel informs us how to cultivate good relationships, promote civic engagement, flourish within the community, and fulfil our destiny.

John expresses his heartfelt desire to meet with the recipients of his letter. John hopes to converse with them in person, so that their mutual 'joy may be complete.'[4] The truth of the gospel and love for humanity are central to fellowship. While written and verbal communication are invaluable, nothing replaces the joy and happiness of in person fellowship with other believers. The eternal truth of God's word is best shared in person. In person fellowship strengthens our relationship with other believers and members of the community. When we are surrounded by fellow believers, we experience incredible joy and profound connection in each other's presence.

The Book of Second John teaches believers the importance to live in truth, peace, love, and harmony. Believers must preserve the Biblical truths of the faith. Believers must exercise discernment in their relationships. Second John cautions humanity against the dangers of illegitimate prophets. Second John urges Christians to reject any doctrine that distorts the truth of Jesus Christ's message of love, redemption, forgiveness, and eternal life. At the same time, Second John affirms love is the foundation of the Christian faith. We must express love in our fellowship, discipleship, and worship.

[4] The Holy Bible (NIV). (2011). *The Book of Second John.* Chapter 1, Verse 7.

[2] The Holy Bible (NIV). (2011). *The Book of Second John.* Chapter 1, Verse 7.

[3] The Holy Bible (NIV). (2011). *The Book of Second John.* Chapter 1, Verse 3.

[4] The Holy Bible (NIV). (2011). *The Book of Second John.* Chapter 1, Verse 12.

Chapter 64

The Book of Third John

'We ought therefore to show hospitality to such people
so that we may work together for the truth.'

3 John 1:8
The Holy Bible (NIV)

The Book of Third John is a concise book in the New Testament. The Book of Third John is written by John the Apostle to a fellow Christian named Gaius. Third John addresses several important matters, such as hospitality, generosity, philanthropy, financial support to preachers, and the exemplary conduct expected of leaders. Through the personal example of Gaius, Demetrius, and Diotrephes, the Apostle John teaches humanity important lessons on how to practice the Christian faith in the church and community. We learn how to cultivate our relationships, demonstrate godly leadership, strengthen brotherhood and sisterhood, and assist preachers in their missionary work.

John commends Gaius for his faithful support of the missionaries. The missionaries travel far and wide to preach the gospel to humanity. Gaius is praised for his hospitality and generosity. Notably, Gaius provides for the practical needs of the missionaries, without the expectation of personal benefit or pecuniary gain. The Apostle John encourages believers to support the invaluable work of preachers. Preachers perform an instrumental function in the proliferation of the gospel throughout the world. Believers must be generous, thoughtful, and charitable towards preachers engaged in the advancement of God's kingdom on earth. We must support missionaries to spread the gospel, whether through prayer, financial assistance, or hospitality. Missionaries engage in meaningful endeavours to further God's providence on earth.

John affirms that Demetrius has a good reputation in the community, this includes 'even by the truth itself.'[1] Demetrius is worthy of the community's continued support. A good reputation, predicated upon ethical principles that reflect the eternal truth of the gospel, is an integral part of the Christian faith. Believers must live in a manner that reflects their faith, beliefs, values, and God's word. Through Demetrius' example, we learn that a good reputation is important to influence, inspire, and invite humanity to accept the gospel. A good reputation is established upon our accountability, integrity, responsibility, honesty, and commitment. The eternal truth of the gospel must be evident in all facets of our life.

In contrast, John reprimands Diotrephes, a church leader who creates division in the congregation by 'refusing to welcome other believers.'[2] Diotrephes does not support members to preach the gospel. Diotrephes manipulates the church for his personal ambition, gain, wealth, fame, authority, and social status. Diotrephes not only rejects John's authority; however, he also speaks untruthfully about members. Not to mention, Diotrephes refuses to accept those members whom John has commended as honourable. Church leaders and members are cautioned against selfish ambition. The desire for power and influence, damages the unity and reputation of the church. Christians must avoid individuals like Diotrephes, who position fame, power, gain, ambition, glory, social status, wealth, and reputation above the eternal truth of the gospel. Diotrephes did little to spread the gospel, rather he promoted self-aggrandisement. Hospitality, generosity, forgiveness, philanthropy, love, compassion, social justice, mercy, and service to humanity, these values characterise the Christian faith.

On the other hand, Gaius is commended for his hospitality and generosity towards fellow believers, particularly those believers who preach the gospel. By supporting preachers, Gaius becomes a trusted partner in the evangelical mission to spread the gospel throughout the world. Generosity and hospitality are an integral part of the Christian faith. Generosity and hospitality are an important expression of our love and concern for humanity. Our generosity and hospitality must extend beyond our relationships. Our generosity must not be limited to fellow believers engaged in ministry. Generosity and hospitality are powerful instruments to spread the gospel. When we demonstrate these desirable values, we encourage others to accept Jesus Christ.

John has much more to share than the contents of his letter. As a result, John expresses his heartfelt desire to meet with Gaius. John appreciates that to meet Gaius in person brings great joy and satisfaction. John values the direct and immediate presence of fellowship amongst believers. John's message emphasises that the Christian community is not merely about doctrine, teaching, leadership, or ministry. A flourishing community thrives on the synergy of relationships. Fellowship, discipleship, and worship are vital attributes of the Christian faith. While communication through letters and other mechanisms is beneficial, the deepest fellowship is experienced through in person meetings with fellow believers. Therefore, believers are encouraged to prioritise their relationships within the church. We must foster mutual support and encouragement. We must develop strong faith-based relationships within society.

The Book of Third John teaches humanity the importance to support believers to preach the gospel, the development of good character, how to avoid division within the church, and how to lead by example in matters of faith. Third John emphasises that the Christian faith is not only defined by salvation; however, it is characterised by participation in community life and the church's mission. Believers are encouraged to promote the Christian message of truth, mercy, peace, joy, unity, love, and compassion. Demetrius, Diotrephes, and Gaius provide us with practical wisdom on how to live faithfully and avoid counterproductive behaviour.

We learn about leadership through our observation of Diotrephes and Demetrius. Most importantly, we learn how to become honourable and productive leaders within the community. Through Diotrephes, we learn what behaviours to avoid in our quest to further God's providence. In addition, Diotrephes' legacy informs us how our character and reputation are brought into disrepute by mistaken beliefs, intentions, motives, desires, thoughts, and actions. On the other hand, Demetrius' godly leadership secures him approval and commendation. Whereas, Diotrephes' self-centred leadership secures him condemnation and criticism. In both cases, Demetrius and Diotrephes' distinct leadership style defined their reputation and character. When it comes to faith, leadership is about the community and proliferation of the gospel, not our desires, pursuits, and ambitions. The Book of Third John encourages believers to advance the gospel and strengthen the community.

[1] The Holy Bible (NIV). (2011). *The Book of Third John.* Chapter 1, Verse 12.
[2] The Holy Bible (NIV). (2011). *The Book of Third John.* Chapter 1, Verse 10.

Chapter 65

The Book of Jude

'Mercy, peace, and love
be yours in abundance.'

Jude 1:2
The Holy Bible (NIV)

T he Book of Jude is a concise and powerful letter. Jude warns believers against illegitimate leaders and immoral forces within the community. The Book of Jude is attributed to Jude, the brother of James and a servant of Jesus Christ. The Book of Jude emphasises the importance for believers to persevere in their faith. Believers must remain true to the gospel's message. Believers must demonstrate vigilance in relation to the dangers of false doctrines, idol worship, and illegitimate leaders.

Jude encourages believers to 'contend for the faith'[1] that God has entrusted to humanity. This is an unequivocal command to remain firm in the gospel's message. Believers must guard the gospel against distortion or alteration. Jude's message addresses the issue of illegitimate leaders who have infiltrated the church with false doctrines that threaten the truth of the gospel. Believers must remain vigilant to defend the truth of the gospel. We must not add or detract from the truth of the gospel. The Christian faith is not based on subjective beliefs, desires, thoughts, opinions, ideas, philosophy, doctrines, or feelings. The Christian faith does not change to concur with popular culture, global fashion trends, political movements, personal tastes, or the preferences of prominent individuals. The Christian faith consists of objective theological truths that must be preserved and proclaimed with courage, conformity, conviction, continuity, cohesion, certainty, clarity, and confidence.

The Book of Jude acknowledges the problematic issue of illegitimate leaders throughout the Christian community. Illegitimate leaders are immoral people who 'pervert the grace of God.'[2] They engage in and promote acts of evil, injustice, and idolatry. Illegitimate leaders deny Jesus Christ's humanity and divinity. They live in disobedience to God's word. Jude compares illegitimate leaders to rebellious figures in the Old Testament, such as Balaam, Cain, and Korah. These characters warn us of the destructive power of sin, evil, temptation, greed, and hubris.

Illegitimate leaders distort the truth of the gospel to serve their desires, agendas, and endeavours. Illegitimate leaders employ half-truths to promote moral corruption in the community. They lead believers astray. Believers must exercise discernment and remain cautious about the teachings they accept. When believers receive a teaching, they must ensure its alignment with the gospel. The examples of Balaam, Cain, and Korah constitute admonitions against hubris, greed, envy, desire, temptation, and rebellion against God's sovereignty.

Jude reminds believers of specific instances where God judged disobedience. For example, consider the generation of Israelite slaves who were liberated from their Egyptian masters in ancient Egypt. This generation of Israelites, who were emancipated from Egyptian captivity, disobeyed God's word. They complained along their journey from slavery in ancient Egypt, through the wilderness, and towards freedom in the promised land. As a consequence, this generation of Israelites, who were emancipated from slavery, did not inherit the promised land flowing with milk and honey. Thereafter, God's covenant with Moses was fulfilled with the succeeding generation of Israelites.

In addition, there is the example of the fallen angels who abandoned their duty and remain imprisoned in chains within the bounds of darkness. Lastly, consider the example of the destruction of the ancient cities of Sodom and Gomorrah. The destruction of these two cities is an example of God's punishment for their immorality and injustice. These examples demonstrate that God does not tolerate sin. God's judgement effectuates on 'the great Day'[3] against those people who have committed evil deeds.

Jude's recollection of the history of God's judgement is a

solemn reminder of the dire consequences of sin. Believers learn about the repercussions of rejecting God's word. Believers are called to live in reverence and obedience to God. Believers must understand that God's judgement is final and inevitable for those who refuse to repent. We possess the unmerited opportunity in the present time to ensure that we repent for our sins. Through confession, we receive God's mercy, grace, favour, and forgiveness.

Jude exhorts believers to strengthen their faith. Believers are encouraged to pray in the presence of the Holy Spirit. The universal message of the gospel is love. Jude commands believers to 'keep yourselves in God's love.'[4] To remain in God's love is not an unconscious act. To remain in God's love requires our commitment, dedication, and perseverance. Jude emphasises the need for spiritual growth, prayer, and God's love to complete our race with victory, belief, trust, honour, and confidence. To run our race well, we must cultivate fellowship with God. Our fellowship is strengthened through prayer, Bible study, and obedience to God's word. We are responsible to keep the faith and avoid the influence of illegitimate prophets.

Jude instructs believers to 'be merciful to those who doubt'[5] the eternal truth of the gospel. Believers must exhibit compassion towards humanity. Through our witness to Jesus Christ, we encourage people to turn away from disbelief, denial, disillusionment, and discouragement. Believers are instructed to be merciful towards every person. We must condemn sin. Nevertheless, we must not judge any person. We are only to condemn the sin that is universal to humanity. This approach to resolving moral, ethical, and social issues demonstrates empathy towards the people who struggle with sin, without compromising on the truth of God's word.

Christians must be compassionate toward believers who waver in their faith. We must offer our assistance and encouragement to fellow believers who are in danger of being led astray by false teachings or sinful conduct. At the same time, believers must remain firm in their rejection of sin, false doctrine, and illegitimate leaders, even as they demonstrate mercy to the individual. Believers must make the important distinction between the sinner and their sinful conduct. Grace and mercy must be extended to every person. We only condemn the sinful conduct that is common to humanity, not the person.

Jude concludes his letter with the affirmation that God's mercy ensures believers do not lose hope along their journey. God's mercy is sufficient to complete our race. Through faith in Jesus Christ, we are presented as blameless before God's 'glorious presence.'[6] Jude's message is an important reminder for Christians to trust in God to keep their faith, be forgiven of their sin, and trust in their salvation through Jesus Christ. Our duty is to remain faithful to God. Believers are not rejected, nor are they abandoned in their spiritual journey. We must not lose heart in the challenges that come across our journey.

God employs remnants throughout world history to make a meaningful contribution to the realisation of His providence. For example, consider the Biblical story of Esther, Gideon, Noah, and Ruth. All four of these historical figures were remnants. They were employed by God to achieve an important objective in the grand scheme of God's providence. God's sovereignty, love, mercy, grace, and power are sufficient to strengthen believers. The Holy Spirit empowers believers. The Holy Spirit prevents believers from committing acts of evil. These theological truths provide trust, peace, and confidence to believers. In the final analysis, believers know their salvation is secure in Jesus Christ.

The Book of Jude is a call to believers to remain vigilant, faithful, honourable, righteous, and merciful. Jude is a timely reminder that God's grace is sufficient to ensure believers remain secure in their salvation through Jesus Christ. The Book of Jude inspires Christians to promote their faith, reject false teachings, and trust in the realisation of God's providence in their life. Our mission of ministry is never complete, it is a perpetual mission. Ministry requires the concentrated effort of believers to make a lasting and positive impact in the world. Above all, we must ensure that God's will is performed on earth.

[1] The Holy Bible (NIV). (2011). *The Book of Jude.* Chapter 1, Verse 3.

[2] The Holy Bible (NIV). (2011). *The Book of Jude.* Chapter 1, Verse 4.

[3] The Holy Bible (NIV). (2011). *The Book of Jude.* Chapter 1, Verse 6.

[4] The Holy Bible (NIV). (2011). *The Book of Jude.* Chapter 1, Verse 21.

[5] The Holy Bible (NIV). (2011). *The Book of Jude.* Chapter 1, Verse 22.

[6] The Holy Bible (NIV). (2011). *The Book of Jude.* Chapter 1, Verse 24.

Chapter 66

The Book of Revelation

"I am the Alpha and the Omega,'
says the LORD God.'

Revelation 1:8
The Holy Bible (NIV)

The Book of Revelation is the final book in the Holy Bible. Revelation is the most complex and symbolic book in the New Testament. The Book of Revelation is written by the Apostle John. Revelation consists of a series of visions that John experienced while he was exiled on the island of Patmos. Revelation examines the triumph of God over the devil, the victory of good over evil, the final judgement of humanity, and the new heaven and new earth. Revelation employs vivid imagery, this includes symbols, visions, and prophetic language, to portray the epic spiritual conflict between good and evil. The Book of Revelation provides believers with hope of victory, forgiveness, and salvation through Jesus Christ.

Revelation commences with a vision of God's majestic throne in heaven. Jesus Christ is revealed as the sacrificial lamb who is appointed to open the scroll. This signifies Jesus Christ's authority to effectuate God's providence in the world. Worship of God is a central theme in the Book of Revelation. Worship of God is essential to the believer's life. Our worship is directed towards God. The vision of God's glory and majesty in Revelation reminds believers to live in reverence of God's greatness. Through worship, we not only recognise, but we also reaffirm God's sovereignty over creation.

In accordance with John's vision of Jesus Christ, Revelation demonstrates that Jesus Christ is the 'King of Kings and Lord of Lords.'[1] Jesus Christ reigns on earth. Despite the challenges, tribulations, pain, trauma, privation, and suffering experienced by believers, Jesus Christ has secured victory over sin, evil, death, Hades, and Satan through his crucifixion, resurrection, and ascension. As a result, Jesus Christ possesses the 'keys of death and Hades.'[2] In the end, God administers His judgement upon the world. Thereafter, God establishes His kingdom on earth. No matter the trials, persecution, or evil that we confront throughout our lifetime on earth, believers are assured that Jesus Christ is their saviour. Jesus Christ has defeated Satan. The victory of Jesus Christ provides believers with hope, encouragement, trust, and confidence during difficult times.

The first part of Revelation consists of letters to the seven churches in Asia Minor. These seven churches are located in Ephesus, Laodicea, Pergamum, Philadelphia, Sardis, Smyrna, and Thyatira. These letters contain commendations and criticisms. These letters direct the aforementioned churches to remain faithful to the gospel's message. The churches in Asia Minor must condemn the teachings of illegitimate prophets that disseminate false doctrines. These churches must transcend internal division and leadership challenges. Some of the churches are encouraged to persevere through religious persecution, while other churches are warned against complacency, illegitimate doctrines, idolatry, and spiritual apathy. Most importantly, believers and churches are called to remain faithful to Jesus Christ. We must be vigilant in our walk with God. Believers have a moral duty to transcend temptation, sin, and evil. Through these letters to the seven churches, we learn invaluable lessons on integrity, love, holiness, righteousness, and perseverance.

Revelation portrays a sombre picture of the suffering and persecution that believers confront due to their adherence to the Christian faith. The martyrs' pleas for mercy and justice go unnoticed; however, God assures them that their sacrifice is not in vain. The faithful believers are rewarded with eternal life in heaven. In addition, God shall 'wipe away every tear from their eyes.'[3] Christians are called to remain faithful to God, even in their confrontation with grief, suffering, and persecution. God witnesses and honours the sacrifice of believers. The promise of salvation, eternal life in heaven, and peace in God's kingdom, gives hope to believers who endure privation during their lifetime on earth.

Revelation emphasises God's judgement against humanity's sin is administered with certainty and equity. The opening of the seals, the sounding of the trumpets, and the demonstration of God's wrath, these events collectively affirm God's judgement is progressively revealed to humanity. This culminates in the final judgement at the Great White Throne. Those who reject God's redeeming grace confront eternal separation from God. God is just and fair. God's judgement in relation to our sin is inevitable. God's final judgement encourages believers to live with integrity, faith, love, and accountability. In addition, as we run our race, we must go beyond the perfection of our character. We must share God's word with humanity. Revelation is the call to live righteously during our transient lifetime on earth. We know that God shall judge humanity.

Jesus Christ returns as the conquering king. Jesus defeats the Satanic forces of temptation, sin, evil, and death. Jesus Christ establishes his everlasting reign on earth. In the aftermath, a new heaven and new earth are revealed. Thereafter, God dwells with His chosen people forever. Through Jesus Christ there is reconciliation between God and humanity. This reconciliation between God and humanity is realised through Jesus Christ's sacrificial death on the Cross for our sins. The former things— sin, loss, grief, pain, suffering, and death—are no more. Evil is no longer an existential threat to humanity. The coming of Christ, and the establishment of God's kingdom on earth, provide hope, faith, and restoration to believers. The victory of good over evil encourages believers to persevere in their faith. Believers realise that God's providence is fulfilled in His timing.

Revelation concludes with a message to believers—remain vigilant and prepared for the coming of Jesus Christ. Jesus promises his return. Upon Jesus' return, believers are rewarded for their faithfulness. Each person's reward is 'according to what they have done.'[4] The church is commanded to keep the faith, endure institutional challenges, and remain true to God's word until the end of time. Christians are encouraged to live with preparedness for the coming of Jesus Christ. We must remain faithful in our walk with God. We must remain vigilant as we await the fulfilment of God's covenant with humanity.

In the Book of Revelation, the divine vision of a new Jerusalem is revealed. This is a place where God's spiritual presence is united with His chosen people. There is no more sorrow, death, evil, sin, temptation, greed, trauma, suffering, privation, or pain. The new Jerusalem is characterised by peace, joy, happiness, justice, love, grace, mercy, and eternal life. The vivid imagery of this beautiful city provides a glimpse of the restoration of God's creation. The hope of a new Jerusalem is fulfilled for those people whose name is inscribed in the 'Lamb's Book of Life.'[5]

In addition, Eden is restored to its former glory. As for humanity, we are informed that 'the LORD God will give them light.'[6] The future hope of eternal life with God in new Jerusalem encourages believers to persevere in their faith. Revelation offers a vision of the future, where God's chosen people experience fellowship with God. Believers are no longer subject to the negative effects of temptation, sin, evil, pain, suffering, injustice, grief, privation, loss, trauma, and death.

The Book of Revelation teaches us that God's providence is realised in the fullness of time. Believers must persevere in their faith. We must run our race with certainty, confidence, clarity, and conviction in God's word. Believers must complete their assignment to advance God's providence on earth. The coming of Jesus Christ brings social justice, righteousness, love, peace, mercy, and blessing to humanity. The vision of a new heaven, new earth, new Eden, new Jerusalem, and eternal fellowship with God, provision hope to believers who trust in Jesus Christ. Through Jesus Christ, we secure our salvation and eternal life in heaven. In the final analysis, not only in the Book of Revelation, however, throughout the Holy Bible, we are reminded that God is faithful to honour His covenant with humanity. Therefore, the responsibility is upon us, to make our contribution to the realisation of God's providence. Peace be with you.

[1] The Holy Bible (NIV). (2011). *The Book of Revelation.* Chapter 19, Verse 16.

[2] The Holy Bible (NIV). (2011). *The Book of Revelation.* Chapter 1, Verse 18.

[3] The Holy Bible (NIV). (2011). *The Book of Revelation.* Chapter 7, Verse 17.

[4] The Holy Bible (NIV). (2011). *The Book of Revelation.* Chapter 22, Verse 12.

[5] The Holy Bible (NIV). (2011). *The Book of Revelation.* Chapter 21, Verse 27.

[6] The Holy Bible (NIV). (2011). *The Book of Revelation.* Chapter 22, Verse 5.

Conclusion

The Holy Bible contains universal messages on redemption, sin, hope, love, grace, compassion, judgement, faith, social justice, repentance, salvation, good, evil, mercy, peace, and victory. From Genesis to Revelation, the Holy Bible narrates a unified story of God's covenant with His chosen people. Through Biblical narratives, we learn about God's character, love, peace, mercy, commandments, providence, grace, and sovereignty. Ultimately, God's providence is fulfilled with Jesus Christ's crucifixion, resurrection, and ascension. Through Jesus Christ, humanity has secured its redemption and eternal life in heaven. Jesus Christ has paid the penalty for humanity's original sin.

To understand the Holy Bible, we must reflect upon the entirety of God's word. Believers must anticipate the fulfilment of God's promises in their life. Throughout the Holy Bible, we witness God's providence in action. Through monumental historical events and towering personalities, God is at work within creation. God's providence is realised through the employment of remnants. For example, consider how God's providence is realised through Esther, Ezra, Gideon, Joseph, Noah, and Ruth.

The Holy Bible commences with Genesis, where God creates the heavens and the earth. Thereafter, God creates humanity in His image for fellowship with Him and stewardship of creation. However, the story of Adam and Eve in the Garden of Eden takes a tragic turn. The duo decides to disobey God's word. Adam and Eve consume the forbidden fruit. Consequently, original sin is introduced into the world. The fall of man creates the necessity for our redemption through a sinless saviour. Humanity's inability to redeem itself is constantly affirmed throughout the Holy Bible.

In the Old Testament, God's covenant with Israel is pivotal to the realisation of His providence. God's providence is witnessed through the remarkable lives of Abraham, David, Jacob, Joshua, Moses, and Solomon. Through God's laws, commandments, covenants, and decrees, He establishes the foundation for the coming of His beloved son—Jesus Christ—into the world. Jesus Christ is the sinless saviour who fulfils God's covenant to Israel. Jesus brings redemption to humanity. Hope of the Messiah is foretold in the prophetic books within the Old Testament. God's word proclaims humanity's redemption and the coming of a righteous king from the Davidic line.

Though the Israelites deviate from God's command, the Old Testament consistently testifies to God's faithfulness in relation to His covenant with them. Despite humanity's original sin, error, disobedience, and unfaithfulness, God demonstrates mercy and grace towards humanity. The Holy Bible's message is unequivocally clear: God is sovereign and just; however, He is also merciful and full of grace. God's providence is realised in accordance with His will and timing. Even though the Israelites experience several setbacks, lost opportunities, national crises, and personal failures, God's providence is not obstructed or frustrated. The peaks and valleys that we experience along our journey are a part of God's providence. God's blessed prophets, such as Abraham, Daniel, Elijah, Elisha, Jeremiah, John the Baptist, Moses, Nathan, and Samuel perform a pivotal function to reveal God's word to the Israelites. These prophets encourage the Israelites to remain faithful to God.

The New Testament reveals the fulfilment of God's covenant with humanity through Jesus Christ. Through Jesus' nativity, life, ministry, teachings, crucifixion, resurrection, and ascension, he is confirmed as the Messiah. Jesus is the saviour of humanity. The Gospel of John, Luke, Mark, and Matthew narrate Jesus' ministry and teachings. The four gospels are confirmation of Jesus Christ's authority over creation. Jesus possesses the power to forgive sin and redeem humanity from evil. Jesus' crucifixion is the atonement for humanity's original sin. Jesus Christ destroyed the dual curse of sin and death. Jesus Christ offers salvation and eternal life to all those who believe in him.

Jesus' resurrection signifies the beginning of a new chapter in world history—the inauguration of God's kingdom on earth. Jesus' ascension into heaven and the presence of the Holy Spirit at Pentecost empowers the early church to continue its mission. The Acts of the Apostles and Epistles provide important guidance to the Christian community. These books of the Holy Bible encourage believers to practice their faith, endure suffering, and spread the gospel to nations across the world. The teachings of James, John, Paul, and Peter reinforce the truth of the gospel. They collectively encourage Christians to live in accordance with God's will. Believers must remain faithful to Jesus Christ.

The Holy Bible concludes with the Book of Revelation. Revelation contains a series of visions given to the Apostle John. John's visions confirm the victory of Jesus Christ over the destructive forces of sin, evil, and death. Revelation portrays a dramatic picture of the spiritual warfare between good and evil, the ascension of the Anti-Christ, and the defeat of Satan. Through vivid imagery, John the Apostle characterises the end of the current age. We learn about God's judgement upon the nations of the world. The establishment of the new heaven, new earth, new Eden, and new Jerusalem is also revealed to us.

In the Book of Revelation, God's final promise to humanity is revealed. The establishment of a new world, where God and His chosen people reside in fellowship. There is no more suffering, pain, privation, injustice, grief, loss, heartache, trauma, or death. Everything is made anew. Everything is made right again. The new Jerusalem descends from heaven. God's spiritual presence pervades the earth. Believers secure eternal life. The promise of God's kingdom on earth is realised.

The central theme throughout the New Testament is the necessity of God's redeeming grace. Pauline theology reminds us that our salvation is secured through our faith in Jesus Christ. Salvation is not earned by good works, merit, virtue, or observance of the Mosaic law. Our salvation is God's unmerited gift to humanity. God's grace sustains our faith. God's grace provides us hope in the midst of our suffering. God's grace empowers us to live in accordance with His will. The coming of Jesus Christ is imminent. Believers must remain faithful to God's word. Believers must run their race with hope, love, mercy, and faith. Believers must share the gospel with all nations and people. Revelation represents a call to action. We must live in anticipation of the coming of Christ.

The Holy Bible concludes where it commenced. We learn about the fulfilment of God's will in all things, the establishment of God's kingdom, and the restoration of all things in God's image. While the Holy Bible concludes with the vision of a new heaven, new earth, new Eden, and new Jerusalem, the remarkable stories, God's covenants, and His promises continue to materialise in the lives of believers across the world. God's promises are not merely historical events or archaic assurances. God's promises are present-day realities, future hopes, grand endeavours, lofty aspirations, and big dreams that define the lives of believers in the contemporary world.

The Holy Bible is God's love story to humanity. We are encouraged to live in the light of God's providence. Believers must walk in accordance with God's will. Christians are to live as good citizens of God's kingdom, demonstrate love, social justice, mercy, peace, integrity, righteousness, and faithfulness. We must honour our commitment to love God and humanity. We must share the good news of Jesus Christ. Our actions must remain true to the gospel's message.

The Holy Bible reminds us to remain faithful to God's word. We are stewards of God's creation. We trust in God's providence and redeeming grace. We affirm our belief in salvation and eternal life in heaven through Jesus Christ. As for our lifetime on earth, we must run our race to the best of our ability. The answer to humanity's perennial question of life and death is: Jesus Christ is our saviour. The entirety of the Holy Bible points towards Jesus Christ as the fulfilment of God's covenant with humanity.

The endeavour of the believer is not merely a sophisticated understanding of the Holy Bible. The believer is to live a transformed life in fellowship with God. Our walk with God is the greatest journey of our lifetime. We experience God's blessing through our obedience to His word. Our faith in Jesus Christ, sustains us through the peaks and valleys along our journey. The guiding presence of the Holy Spirit illuminates our journey. God's grace be with you. Peace be with you.

Bibliography

Abraham, W. (1982). *Divine Revelation and the Limits of Historical Criticism*. New York: Oxford University Press.

Abraham, W. (2006). *Crossing the Threshold of Divine Revelation*. Grand Rapids, Michigan: Wm. B. Eerdmans Publishing Company.

Acklin, T. (2006). *The Unchanging Heart of the Priesthood: A Faith Perspective on the Reality and Mystery of the Priesthood in the Church*. Steubenville, Ohio: Emmaus Road Publishing.

Adam, K. (1933). *The Spirit of Catholicism*. New York: Macmillan Company.

Adams, N., and Elliott, C. (2000). 'Ethnography is Dogmatics: Making Description Central to Systematic Theology', *Scottish Journal of Theology* 53, 339–364.

Alston, W. P. (1986). 'Internalism and Externalism in Epistemology'. *Philosophical Topics* 14, 179–221.

Alston, W. P. (1991). *Perceiving God: The Epistemology of Religious Experience*. Ithaca, New York: Cornell University Press.

Alter, R. and Kermode, F. (Eds.) (1990). *The Literary Guide to the Bible*. Cambridge, Massachusetts: Harvard University Press.

Anderson, J. (2016). *Innovative Catholicism and the Human Condition*. London: Routledge.

Anderson, R. Dean, Jr. (1999). *Ancient Rhetorical Theory and Paul. Contributions to Biblical Exegesis and Theology*. Revised Edition. Leuven: Peeters Publishers.

Anselm. (1998). *The Major Works*. Oxford: Oxford University Press.

Augustine. (1961). *Confessions*. New York: Penguin Books.

Austin, N. (2018). *Aquinas on Virtue: A Causal Reading*. Washington, D.C.: Georgetown University Press.

Baillie, J. (1956). *The Idea of Revelation in Recent Thought*. New York: Columbia University Press.

Barger, L. C. (2018). *The World Come of Age: An Intellectual History of Liberation Theology*. Oxford: Oxford University Press.

Barker, M. (2003) *The Great High Priest: The Temple Roots of Christian Liturgy*. London: T & T Clark.

Barrett, C. K. (1965). 'Things Sacrificed to Idols.' *New Testament Studies* 11, 138-153.

Barth, K. (Hoskyns, E. C., Trans.) (1933). *The Epistle to the Romans*. New York: Oxford University Press.

Bauckham, R. (1998). *God Crucified: Monotheism and Christology in the New Testament*. Grand Rapids: Wm. B. Eerdmans Publishing Company.

Bauerschmidt, F. (2013). *Thomas Aquinas: Faith, Reason and Following Christ*. Oxford: Oxford University Press.

Beatrice, P. F. (2013). *The Transmission of Sin: Augustine and the Pre-Augustinian Sources*. New York: Oxford University Press.

Bell, M. (2023). *Catholic Social Teaching and Labour Law: An Ethical Perspective on Work*. Oxford: Oxford University Press.

Bettenson, H. (1963). *Documents of the Christian Church*. Second Edition. New York: Oxford University Press.

Beyer, G. J. (2021). *Just Universities: Catholic Social Teaching Confronts Corporatised Higher Education*. New York: Fordham University Press.

Boff, L. (1978). *Jesus Christ Liberator: A Critical Christology for Our Time*. Maryknoll, New York: Orbis Books.

Boff, L. (1987). *Passion of Christ, Passion of the World: The Facts, Their Interpretation, and Their Meaning Yesterday and Today*. Maryknoll, New York: Orbis Books.

Bohache, T. (2008). *Christology from the Margins*. London: SCM Press.

Bouyer, L. (Littledale, A. V., Trans.) (1956). *The Spirit and Forms of Protestantism*. London: Harvill Press.

Bouyer, L. (1961). *The Word, Church and Sacraments in Protestantism and Catholicism*. New York: Desclee Company.

Bouyer, L. (1969). *Orthodox Spirituality and Protestant and Anglican Spirituality*. London: Burns & Oates.

Buschcart, W. D. (2006). *Exploring Protestant Traditions*. Downers Grove, Illinois: InterVarsity Press.

Brown, R. E. (1981). *The Critical Meaning of the Bible*. New York: Paulist Press.

Brown, R. E. (1994). *An Introduction to New Testament Christology*. Mahwah, New Jersey: Paulist Press.

Bultmann, R. (1984). *New Testament and Mythology and Other Basic Writings*. Philadelphia: Fortress Press.

Calvin, J. (Beveridge, H., Trans.) (1989). *Institutes of the Christian Religion*. Grand Rapids, Michigan: Wm. B. Eerdmans Publishing Company.

Campbell, D. A. (2009). *The Deliverance of God: An Apocalyptic Rereading of Justification in Paul*. Grand Rapids, Michigan: Wm. B. Eerdmans Publishing Company.

Caputo, J. D. (2006). *Philosophy and Theology*. Nashville: Abingdon Press.

Cary, P. (2000). *Augustine's Invention of the Inner Self*. New York: Oxford University Press.

Cary, P. (2008). *Inner Grace: Augustine in the Traditions of Plato and Paul*. New York: Oxford University Press.

Cessario, R. (1991). *The Moral Virtues and Theological Ethics*. Notre Dame, Indiana: University of Notre Dame Press.

Cessario, R. (1996). *Christian Faith and the Theological Life*. Washington, D.C.: Catholic University of America Press.

Chadwick, H. (1993). *The Early Church*. Revised edition. New York: Penguin Books.

Chopp, R., and Taylor, M. (Eds.) 1994. *Reconstructing Christian Theology*. Minneapolis: Fortress Press.

Ciampa, R. E. and Rosner, B. S. (2010). *The First Letter to the Corinthians. Pillar New Testament Commentaries*. Grand Rapids, Michigan: Wm. B. Eerdmans Publishing Company.

Clarke, E. G. (1973). *The Wisdom of Solomon*. Cambridge: Cambridge University Press.

Cohen, N. G. (1993). 'The Greek Virtues and the Mosaic Laws in Philo: An Elucidation of De Specialibus Legibus IV 133-135.' *Studia Philonica* 5, 9-23.

Cohen, S. J. D. (1987). *From the Maccabees to the Mishnah*. Library of Early Christianity. Philadelphia: Westminster Press.

Collins, J. J. (2005). *The Bible after Babel: Historical Criticism in a Postmodern Age*. Grand Rapids, Michigan: Wm. B. Eerdmans Publishing Company.

Congar, Y. (1959). *After Nine Hundred Years: The Background of the Schism between the Eastern and Western Churches*. New York: Fordham University Press.

Congar, Y. (Philip, L., Trans.) (1966). *Dialogue between Christians: Catholic Contributions to Ecumenism*. London: Geoffrey Chapman.

Congar, Y. (1939). *Divided Christendom: A Catholic Study of the Problem of Reunion*. London: Geoffrey Bles.

Congar, Y. (Woodrow, A. N., Trans.) (2004). *The Meaning of Tradition*. San Francisco, California: Ignatius Press.

Connor, J. L. (1968). 'Original Sin: Contemporary Approaches,' *Theological Studies* 29, 215–240.

Cox, H. (2013). *The Secular City: Secularisation and Urbanisation in Theological Perspective*. Princeton, New Jersey: Princeton University Press.

Cremer, D. J. (2024). *Antiracist Leadership: A Spiritual Approach to Diversity, Equity, and Inclusion*. New York: Palgrave Macmillan.

Crossan, J. D. (1995). *Jesus: A Revolutionary Biography*. San Francisco: Harper San Francisco.

Crossley, J. G. (2012). 'An Immodest Proposal for Biblical Studies', *Relegere: Studies in Religion and Reception* 1, 153–77.

Crossley, J. G. (2012). *Jesus in an Age of Neoliberalism: Quests, Scholarship and Ideology*. Durham: Acumen Publishing Limited.

Crouzel, H. (1989). *Origen: The Life and Thought of the First Great Theologian*. San Francisco: Harper & Row Publishers.

Davies, B. (1992). *The Thought of Thomas Aquinas*. Oxford: Clarendon Press.

Davies, E. W. (2013). *Biblical Criticism: A Guide for the Perplexed*. London: Bloomsbury T&T Clark.

Davies, O. (2013). *Theology of Transformation: Faith, Freedom, and the Christian Act*. Oxford: Oxford University Press.

Dawkins, R. (2006). *The God Delusion*. New York: Houghton Mifflin Company.

Demacopoulos, G. E. (2016). *Christianity, Democracy, and the Shadow of Constantine.* New York: Fordham University Press.

Deneulin, S. (2021). *Human Development and the Catholic Social Tradition: Towards an Integral Ecology.* Oxford: Routledge.

Dubay, T. S.M. (1998). *Faith and certitude: Can we be sure of the things that matter most to us?* San Francisco: Ignatius Press.

Dulles, A. (2007). *Magisterium: Teacher and Guardian of the Faith.* Naples, Florida: Ave Maria University Press.

Dünzl, F. (2007). *A Brief History of the Doctrine of the Trinity in the Early Church.* Edinburgh: T & T Clark.

Emery, G. (2007). *The Trinitarian Theology of St Thomas Aquinas.* Oxford: Oxford University Press.

Erb, P. (1983). *The Pietists: Selected Writings.* Mahwah, New Jersey: Paulist Press.

Eusebius. (Williamson, G. A., Trans.) (1989). *The History of the Church from Christ to Constantine.* Revised edition. New York: Penguin Books.

Evans, C. (2006). *Fabricating Jesus: How Modern Scholars Distort the Gospels.* Downers Grove, Illinois: InterVarsity Press.

Farkasfalvy, D. (2010). *Inspiration and Interpretation: A Theological Introduction to Sacred Scripture.* Washington, D.C.: Catholic University of America Press.

Farrow, D. (2018). *Theological Negotiations: Proposals in Soteriology and Anthropology.* Ada, Michigan: Baker Academic.

Fiddes, P. (2009). 'Concept, Image and Story in Systematic Theology', *International Journal of Systematic Theology* 11, 3–23.

Fiddes, P., (2013). *Seeing the World and Knowing God: Hebrew Wisdom and Christian Doctrine in a Late-Modern Context.* Oxford: Oxford University Press.

Finney, C. G. (1989). *Lectures on Revival.* Minneapolis: Bethany House Publishers.

Fiorenza, F. S., and Livingston, J. C. (2006). *Modern Christian Thought.* Second Edition. Minneapolis: Fortress Press.

Fitzmyer, J. A. (2008). *The Interpretation of Scripture: In Defence of the Historical-Critical Method.* New York: Paulist Press.

Foster, R. J. (1998). *Streams of Living Water: Celebrating the Great Traditions of the Christian Faith.* San Francisco: Harper Collins Publishers.

Gardner, P. D. (1994). *The Gifts of God and the Authentication of a Christian.* New York: University Press of America.

Goodenough, E. R. (1933). 'Philo's Exposition of the Law and his De Vita Mosis.' *Harvard Theological Review* 26, 109-125.

Grabbe, L. L. (1997). *Wisdom of Solomon.* Sheffield: Sheffield Academic Press.

Hahn, S. (1998). *A father who keeps his promises: God's Covenant love in scripture.* Ann Arbor, Michigan: Servant Books.

Hahn, S. (1999). *The lamb's supper: The mass as heaven on earth.* New York: Doubleday.

Hahn, S. (2001). *Hail Holy Queen: The Mother of God in the Word of God.* New York: Doubleday.

Hahn, S. (2002). *First comes love: Finding your family in the Church and the Trinity.* New York: Doubleday.

Hahn, S. (2003). *Lord have mercy: The healing power of confession.* New York: Doubleday.

Hahn, S. (2004). *Swear to God: The promise and power of the Sacraments.* New York: Doubleday.

Hahn, S. (2005). *Letter and spirit: From written text to living word in the Liturgy.* New York: Doubleday.

Hardy, E. R. (1954). *Christology of the Later Fathers.* Philadelphia: Westminster John Knox Press.

Hays, R. B. (1997). *First Corinthians.* Louisville: John Knox Press.

Heppe, H. (Thomson, G. T., Trans.) (1978). *Reformed Dogmatics, Set Out and Illustrated from the Sources.* Grand Rapids: Baker Publishing Group.

Howard-Snyder, D. (Ed.) (1996). *The evidential argument from evil.* Bloomington, Indiana: Indiana University Press.

Hume, D. (2007). *A dissertation on the passions: The natural history of religion.* Oxford: Clarendon Press.

Hurtado, L. (2000). *At the Origins of Christian Worship.* Grand Rapids: Wm. B. Eerdmans Publishing Company.

Imbelli, R. (2014). *Rekindling the Christic imagination. Theological meditations for the new evangelisation.* Collegeville, Minnesota: Liturgical Press.

Jaspers, K. (Ashton, E. B., Trans.) (1967). *Philosophical faith and revelation.* New York: Harper & Row.

John of the Cross. (Kavanaugh, K., and Rodriguez, O., Trans.) (1991). *The Collected Works of Saint John of the Cross.* Washington, D.C.: ICS Publications.

Johnson, L. T., and Kurz, W. S. (2002). *The future of Catholic Biblical Scholarship: A constructive conversation.* Grand Rapids: Wm. B. Eerdmans Publishing Company.

Kaell, H. (2014). *Walking Where Jesus Walked: American Christians and Holy Land Pilgrimage.* New York: New York University Press.

Kelly, J. N. D. (2000). *Early Christian Doctrines.* Fifth Edition. New York: Continuum.

Legaspi, M. (2011). *The death of Scripture and the rise of Biblical Studies.* New York: Oxford University Press.

Leith, J. H. (1982). *Creeds of the Churches.* Third Edition. Louisville: John Knox Press.

Levenson, J. D. (2015). *The Love of God: Divine Gift, Human Gratitude, and Mutual Faithfulness in Judaism.* Princeton: Princeton University Press.

Lossky, V. (1976). *The Mystical Theology of the Eastern Church.* Crestwood, New York: St. Vladimir's Seminary Press.

Luther, M. (Dillenberger, J., Ed.) (1961). *Martin Luther: Selections from His Writings.* Garden City, New York: Anchor Books.

Machen, J. G. (1923). *Christianity and Liberalism.* Grand Rapids: Wm. B. Eerdmans Publishing Company.

Marshall, P. (1994). *The Catholic Priesthood and the English Reformation.* New York: Clarendon Press.

Martin, F. (2006). *Sacred Scripture: The Disclosure of the Word.* Naples, Florida: Sapientia Press.

McEwan, T. (2025). *Women and the Catholic Church: Negotiating Identity and Agency.* London: Bloomsbury Academic.

McGrath, A. E. (1990). *Luther's Theology of the Cross.* Oxford: Wiley-Blackwell.

McGrath, A. E. (1993). *A Life of John Calvin.* Oxford: Wiley-Blackwell.

McGrath, A. E. (1995). *The Blackwell Encyclopedia of Modern Christian Thought.* Oxford: Wiley-Blackwell.

McGrath, A. E. (1998). *Historical Theology: An Introduction to the History of Christian Thought.* Oxford: Wiley-Blackwell.

McGrath, A. E. (1999). *Christian Spirituality: An Introduction.* Oxford: Wiley-Blackwell.

McGrath, A. E. (2000). *Reformation Thought: An Introduction.* Third Edition. Oxford: Wiley-Blackwell.

McGrath, A. E. (2000). *Christian Literature: An Anthology.* Oxford: Wiley-Blackwell.

McGrath, A. E. (2002). *The Future of Christianity.* Oxford: Wiley-Blackwell.

McGrath, A. E. (2003). *The Intellectual Origins of the European Reformation.* Second Edition. Oxford: Wiley-Blackwell.

McGrath, A. E. (2008). *The Open Secret: A New Vision for Natural Theology.* Oxford: Wiley-Blackwell.

McGrath, A. E. (Ed.) (2011). *The Christian Theology Reader.* Fourth Edition. Oxford: Wiley-Blackwell.

McGuckin, J. (2004). *Saint Cyril of Alexandria and the Christological Controversy.* Crestwood, New York: St. Vladimir's Seminary Press.

McNeill, J. T. (1954). *The History and Character of Calvinism.* Oxford: Oxford University Press.

Milbank, J. (2005). *Theology and Social Theory: Beyond Secular Reason.* Second edition. Oxford: Wiley-Blackwell.

Miller, V. J. (2017). *The Theological and Ecological Vision of Laudato Si: Everything is Connected.* London: Bloomsbury Publishing.

Mulder, S. (2022). *The Turn to the Church in the Twentieth and Twenty-First Centuries: A Promising Ecclesiology.* Oxford: Taylor and Francis.

Najman, H. (1999). 'The Law of Nature and the Authority of the Mosaic Law.' *Studia Philonica* 11, 55-73.

Nichols, A. (1991). *The shape of Catholic Theology: An introduction to its sources, principles, and history.* Collegeville, Minnesota: Liturgical Press.

Noll, M., and Nystrom, C. (2008). *Is the Reformation Over? An Evangelical Assessment of Contemporary Roman Catholicism.* Grand Rapids: Baker Academic.

O'Collins, G. (2011). *Rethinking Fundamental Theology?* Oxford: Oxford University Press.

Olson, Roger E. (1999). *The Story of Christian Theology*. Downers Grove, Illinois: Intra Varsity Press.

O'Keefe, J., and Reno, R. R. (2005). *Sanctified Vision: An Introduction to Early Christian Interpretation of the Bible*. Baltimore: Johns Hopkins University Press.

Plantinga, A. (2000). *Warranted Christian Belief*. New York: Oxford University Press.

Pelikan, J. (1993). *Christianity and Classical Culture*. New Haven: Yale University Press.

Pieper, J. (1962). *Guide to Thomas Aquinas*. Notre Dame: University of Notre Dame Press.

Rahner, K. (1987). *Foundations of Christian Faith*. New York: Crossroad Publishers.

Ratzinger, J. (1983). *Daughter Zion*. San Francisco: Ignatius Press.

Ratzinger, J. (1986). *Behold the Pierced One: An approach to a spiritual Christology*. San Francisco: Ignatius Press.

Ratzinger, J. (1986). *Feast of Faith*. San Francisco: Ignatius Press.

Ratzinger, J. (1987). *Principles of Catholic Theology: Building stones for a fundamental theology*. San Francisco: Ignatius Press.

Ratzinger, J. (1988). *Eschatology*. Washington, D.C.: Catholic University of America Press.

Ratzinger, J. (1990). *Introduction to Christianity*. San Francisco: Ignatius Press.

Ratzinger, J. (1995). *The Meaning of Christian Brotherhood*. San Francisco: Ignatius Press.

Ratzinger, J. (1995). *The nature and mission of theology: Approaches to understanding its role in the light of present controversy*. San Francisco: Ignatius Press.

Ratzinger, J. (1997). *A new song for the Lord*. New York: Crossroad Publishers.

Ratzinger, J. (1999). *Many religions one covenant: Israel, the Church and the World*. San Francisco: Ignatius Press.

Ratzinger, J. (Horn, S. O., and Pfnür, V., Ed.) (Taylor, H., Trans.) (2003). *God is near us: The Eucharist, the heart of life*. San Francisco: Ignatius Press.

Ratzinger, J. (Miller, M., Trans.) (2005). *On the way to Jesus Christ*. San Francisco: Ignatius Press.

Reese, J. M. (1965). 'Plan and Structure of the Book of Wisdom.' *Catholic Biblical Quarterly* 27, 391-399.

Rist, J. (2008). *What Is Truth? From the Academy to the Vatican*. Cambridge: Cambridge University Press.

Ritchey, S. (2014). *Holy Matter: Changing Perceptions of the Material World in Late Medieval Christianity*. Ithaca, New York: Cornell University Press.

Rosenberg, R. S. (2017). *The Givenness of Desire: Concrete Subjectivity and the Natural Desire to See God*. Toronto: University of Toronto Press.

Sanders, E. P. (1983). *Paul, the Law, and the Jewish People*. Minneapolis: Fortress Press.

Shagan, E. H. (2019). *The Birth of Modern Belief: Faith and Judgment from the Middle Ages to the Enlightenment*. Princeton, New Jersey: Princeton University Press.

Sokolowski, R. (1995). *The God of Faith and Reason: Foundations of Christian Theology.* Washington, D.C.: Catholic University of America Press.

Spong, J. S. (1998). *Why Christianity Must Change or Die.* San Francisco: Harper San Francisco.

Stead, C. (1994). *Philosophy in Christian Antiquity.* Cambridge: Cambridge University Press.

Stump, E. (2010). *Wandering in Darkness: Narrative and the Problem of Suffering.* Oxford: Clarendon Press.

Sweeney, D. A., and Guelzo, A. C. (2006). *The New Haven Theology.* Grand Rapids: Baker Academic.

Swinburne, R. (1981). *Faith and Reason.* Oxford: Clarendon Press.

Tanner, K. (1988). *God and Creation in Christian Theology.* Oxford: Wiley-Blackwell.

Tillich, P. (2001). *Dynamics of Faith.* San Francisco: Harper San Francisco.

Tomson, P. J. (1990). *Paul and the Jewish Law: Halakha in the Letters of the Apostle to the Gentiles.* Minneapolis: Fortress Press.

Torrance, T. F. (1969). *Theological Science.* Oxford: Oxford University Press.

Torrell, J-P. (Guevin, B. M., Trans.) (2005). *Aquinas' Summa: Background, Structure, and Reception.* Washington, D.C.: Catholic University of America Press.

Tracy, D. (1981). *The Analogical Imagination: Christian Theology and the Culture of Pluralism.* New York: Crossroad Publishers.

Tull, J. E. (1984). *Shapers of Baptist Thought.* Macon, Georgia: Mercer University Press.

Vandervelde, G. (1975). *Original Sin: Two Major Trends in Contemporary Roman Catholic Reinterpretation.* Amsterdam: Rodopi Publishers.

Wahlberg, M. (2014). *Revelation as Testimony. A Philosophical-Theological Study.* Grand Rapids, Michigan: Wm. B. Eerdmans Publishing Company.

Walsh, D. (2008). *The Modern Philosophical Revolution.* Cambridge: Cambridge University Press.

Ward, K. (1995). *Religion and Revelation.* Oxford: Clarendon Press.

Westcott, B. F. (1892). *The Gospel of Life.* London: Macmillan Company.

White, T. J. (Ed.) (2010). *The Analogy of Being. Invention of the Antichrist or the Wisdom of God?* Grand Rapids, Michigan: Wm. B. Eerdmans Publishing Company.

White, T. J. (2015). *The Incarnate Lord: A Thomistic Study in Christology.* Washington, D.C.: Catholic University of America Press.

Williams, D. H. (1999). *Retrieving the Tradition and Renewing Evangelicalism: A Primer for Suspicious Protestants.* Grand Rapids: Wm. B. Eerdmans Publishing Company.

Williams, D. M. (2004). *Receiving the Bible in Faith: Historical and Theological Exegesis.* Washington, D.C.: Catholic University of America Press.

Williams, N. P. (1927). *The Ideas of the Fall and of Original Sin: A Historical and Critical Study.* New York: Longmans, Green & Company.

Williams, R. (2005). *Grace and Necessity: Reflections on Art and Love.* New York: Morehouse Publishing.

Wills, G. (2000). *Papal Sin: Structures of Deceit*. New York: Doubleday.

Winston, D. (1979). The *Wisdom of Solomon: A New Translation with Introduction and Commentary*. Garden City, New York: Doubleday.

Wright, A. (1965). 'The Structure of Wisdom 11-19.' *Catholic Biblical Quarterly* 27, 28-34.

Wright, A. (1967). 'The Structure of the Book of Wisdom.' *Biblica* 48, 165-84.

Wright, A. (1967). 'Numerical Patterns in the Book of Wisdom.' *The Catholic Biblical Quarterly* 29, 524-538.

Wright, C. J. H. (2006). *The Mission of God: Unlocking the Bible's Grand Narrative*. Downers Grove, Illinois: InterVarsity Press Academic.

Wright, N. T. (1991). *The Climax of the Covenant: Christ and the Law in Pauline Theology*. Minneapolis: Fortress Press.

Wright, N. T. (1997). *What Saint Paul Really Said*. Grand Rapids: Wm. B. Eerdmans Publishing Company.

Wright, N. T. (1999). *The Challenge of Jesus: Rediscovering Who Jesus Was and Is*. Downers Grove, Illinois: InterVarsity Press.

Wright, N. T. (2008). *Surprised by Hope: Rethinking Heaven, the Resurrection, and the Mission of the Church*. New York: HarperCollins Publishers.

Wykstra, S. (1984). 'The Humean Obstacle to Evidential Arguments from Suffering: On Avoiding the Evils of Appearance.' *International Journal for Philosophy of Religion* 16(2): 73–93.

Index

www.ingramcontent.com/pod-product-compliance
Lightning Source LLC
Chambersburg PA
CBHW040803150426
42811CB00082B/2381/J